INSIGHT GUIDE

Scandinavia

APA PUBLICATIONS

Part of the Langenscheidt Publishing Group

Editorial
Project Editor
Jane Hutchings
Managing Editor
Tom Le Bas
Editorial Director
Brian Bell

Distribution
UK & Ireland
GeoCenter International Ltd
The Viables Centre, Harrow Way
Basingstoke, Hants RG22 4BJ
Fax: (44) 1256-817988

United States
Langenscheidt Publishers, Inc.
46–35 54th Road, Maspeth, NY 11378
Fax: (1) 718 784-0640

Canada
Thomas Allen & Son Ltd
390 Steelcase Road East
Markham, Ontario L34 1G2
Fax: (1) 905 475 6747

Australia
Universal Press
1 Waterloo Road
Macquarie Park, NSW 2113
Fax: (61) 2 9888 9074

New Zealand
Hema Maps New Zealand Ltd (HNZ)
Unit D, 24 Ra ORA Drive
East Tamaki, Auckland
Fax: (64) 9 273 6479

Worldwide
**Apa Publications GmbH & Co.
Verlag KG (Singapore branch)**
38 Joo Koon Road, Singapore 628990
Tel: (65) 865-1600. Fax: (65) 861-6438

Printing

Insight Print Services (Pte) Ltd
38 Joo Koon Road, Singapore 628990
Tel: (65) 865-1600. Fax: (65) 861-6438

©2001 **Apa Publications GmbH & Co.
Verlag KG (Singapore branch)**
All Rights Reserved
First Edition 2001

CONTACTING THE EDITORS
We would appreciate it if readers
would alert us to errors or out-
dated information by writing to:
**Insight Guides, P.O. Box 7910,
London SE1 1WE, England.**
Fax: (44) 20 7403-0290.
insight@apaguide.demon.co.uk

NO part of this book may be reproduced,
stored in a retrieval system or transmitted
in any form or means electronic, mech-
anical, photocopying, recording or otherwise, without prior written permission of
Apa Publications. Brief text quotations
with use of photographs are exempted
for book review purposes only. Information has been obtained from sources
believed to be reliable, but its accuracy
and completeness, and the opinions
based thereon, are not guaranteed.

www.insightguides.com

This guidebook combines the
interests and enthusiasms of
two of the world's best known information providers: Insight Guides,
whose titles have set the standard
for visual travel guides since 1970,
and Discovery Channel, the world's
premier source of non-fiction television programming.

The editors of Insight Guides provide practical advice and general
understanding about a destination's
history, culture and
people. Discovery
Channel and its
popular web site,
www. discovery.com,
help millions of
viewers to explore
their world from the
comfort of their home
and encourage them to
explore it first hand.

How to use this book

This first edition of *Insight Guide:
Scandinavia* is carefully structured
to convey an understanding of the
countries of Denmark, Norway,
Sweden and Finland and their cultures as well as to guide readers
through their sights and activities:
◆ The **Features** section, indicated
by a yellow bar at the top of each
page, covers the history and culture
of the countries in a series of informative essays.
◆ The main **Places** section,
indicated by a blue bar, is a
complete guide to all the
sights and areas worth
visiting. Places of spe-
cial interest are coor-
dinated by number
with the maps.
◆ The **Travel Tips** section, with an orange bar,

EXPLORE YOUR WORLD
DISCOVERY CHANNEL

Map Legend

— ·· —	International Boundary
— — — —	Province/County Boundary
⊖	Border Crossing
_•_	National Park/Reserve
— — — —	Ferry Route
Ⓜ Ⓣ	Metro
Ⓢ	S-Tog (S-Train)
Ⓣ	Tunnelbanan
✈ ✈	Airport: International/Regional
🚌	Bus Station
Ⓟ	Parking
❶	Tourist Information
✉	Post Office
✝ ✝	Church/Ruins
✝	Monastery
☪	Mosque
✡	Synagogue
🏰	Castle/Ruins
∴	Archaeological Site
∩	Cave
🕴	Statue/Monument
★	Place of Interest

The main places of interest in the Places section are coordinated by number with a full-colour map (e.g. ❶), and a symbol at the top of every right-hand page tells you where to find the map.

provides a handy point of reference for information on travel, hotels, shops, restaurants and more.

The contributors

Insight Guide: Scandinavia was edited by **Jane Hutchings**, under the guidance of managing editor **Tom Le Bas**. The book builds on the solid foundations laid by the late **Doreen Taylor-Wilkie**, editor of the original Insight Guides to each of the four countries.

The history of Scandinavia was the work of **Rowlinson Carter**. Art historian **Kathryn Boyer** wrote about Scandinavia's culture and from her base in Trollhättan covered Sweden's West Coast and Great Lakes. Stockholm-based journalist **Amy Brown** contributed the feature on the Great Outdoors, and the chapters on Stockholm, Southern Swe-

den and Dalarna. The writer **Debra Williamson** provided her comments on The Swedes and the Insight on the Vikings. From Arjeplog in Lapland **Illona Fjellström** covered Northern Sweden. **Joanie Rafidi Oxhammar** compiled the Insight on the Stockholm Archipelago.

From Århus, Denmark, journalist **Jack Jackson** wrote about the Scandinavian passion for food and drink and contributed chapters on The Danes, Copenhagen and Jutland, and the Insight on Danish Design.

The chapters on Norway were compiled by the journalist and author **Michael Brady** with the assistance of **Samtext** in Oslo. Brady, a long-time resident of Norway, has written extensively about the country. **Yngve Kvistad**, a columnist with the Oslo daily newspaper *Verdens Gang*, has provided his comments on The Norwegians.

Joan Gannij, an Amsterdam-based American journalist and "Finnatic", contributed the chapters on Finland and The Finns. She also compiled the Insight on the Hurtigruten in Norway.

Writers whose text has been adapted from individual *Insight Guides* to the countries include: Denmark, **Fradley Garner**, **Bryan Wilder**; Norway, **Anita Peltonen**, **Robert Spark**, **John Harley**; Sweden, **Philip Ray**; Finland, **Anne Roston**, **Sylvie Nickels**, **Robert Spark**.

The Travel Tips section was compiled by **Anna Lia Bright** in Copenhagen, **Liv Bente T. Dybfest** in Oslo, **Elisabet Lim** in Stockholm and for Finland, **Joan Gannij**. The section was edited by **Sue Platt**.

Thanks also go to **Susannah Wight** for proofreading the book and to **Penny Phenix** for indexing it.

CONTENTS

Insight on ...

Information panels

Travel Tips

◆ **Full Travel Tips index
is on page 353**

MAIN PICTURE: Vibrant
colours in springtime,
southern Sweden.

Places

NORTHERLY NEIGHBOURS

At the top of the map, but no longer aloof, the
Scandinavian countries are Europe's best kept secret

To fly over Scandinavia is to discover a vast, sparsely inhabited, natural landscape of sparkling fjords and rocky mountains, glassy lakes and rushing rivers, dense forests and frozen tundra, extending from temperate Denmark far north to the land of the Sami and including Greenland and the Faroe Islands.

Norway, Denmark, Sweden and Finland are among Europe's most ancient civilisations. Theirs is an eventful shared history of prowess and intrigue. Early Norse traders ventured deep into Asia leaving graphic runic inscriptions on stones which provide clues as to their exploits. Later, the infamous Vikings who pillaged their way round the coasts of Ireland, Britain and France laid the foundations for kingdoms and Christianity across Scandinavia. They were followed by kings, queens and tsars who schemed and battled. Borders shifted, unions came and went, and by the start of the 20th century four distinct nations emerged which have grown into the modern, highly individualistic countries we know today.

The Danes are probably the most garrulous of the Scandinavians, though all will ensure the visitor receives a warm welcome. The Nordic reputation for cool reservedness has had its day, but not for cool design. Everything from beer bottle openers to the latest building has the stamp of chic understatement.

The Scandinavian capitals of Copenhagen, Oslo, Stockholm and Helsinki are vibrant cities housing some of the most inspirational museums and finest art collections in Europe, with concerts and festivals bringing music and life to the streets. In fact, at the slightest excuse Scandinavians will take to the outdoors, whether on a bicycle along the winding lanes of Denmark, skiing on floodlit trails around Oslo, escaping to little red-painted waterside cottages in Sweden, or plunging from sauna to ice pool in Finland. An inherent love of nature is deeply rooted within the national psyches. Perhaps this has to do with the long dark days of winter and the need to soak up the summer light. Arrive in any of the Scandinavian countries in mid to late June and you'll find the locals dancing and feasting around Midsummer maypoles and bonfires.

Transport and communications are excellent: roads join southerly Denmark with the North Cape, railways penetrate Lapland, ferries ply the fjords and link remote islands and lakeside villages, and planes cut the journey times. And now with the opening of the new Øresund bridge from Denmark to Sweden, Scandinavia is just a short step from its European neighbours.   ❑

PRECEDING PAGES: Danish football supporters in high spirits; a moment's contemplation, Hustad, Norway; winter festivities, northern Sweden; a Sami and his reindeer, Rovaniemi, Finnish Lapland.
LEFT: on the water – boating is a way of life in Scandinavia.

Decisive Dates

EARLY HISTORY: 10,000 BC–AD 800

From 10,000 BC Hunter-gatherer tribes follow the melting ice northwards, establishing settlements and farming communities in southern Scandinavia. Tribes from Eastern Europe settle the Arctic coast. They hunt deer and reindeer.

1500 BC Trade routes are forged through the rivers of Eastern Europe to the Danube.

c.500 BC–AD 800 Iron Age "Grauballe Man" and "Tollund Man" are buried in peat bogs in Denmark to be unearthed in the 1950s in remarkable condition.

c.AD 100 The historian Tacitus mentions the Fenni (the Sami of Finland) in his *Germania* and describes the Sveas who inhabit what is now central Sweden.

c.AD 400 Suomalaiset (Baltic Finns) cross the Baltic and settle in Finland. Sweden's influence over its "eastern province" begins. In Norway farmers push inland; forts have been found on Lake Mjøsa.

THE VIKING AGE

800–1060 The Scandinavian Vikings earn a reputation as sea warriors. In 862, at the invitation of the Slavs, Prince Rurik leads the Swedish Vikings (Varangians) east to bring order to the principality of Novgorod. They soon control the trade routes to Byzantium.

830 A Benedictine monk, Ansgar (801–865), lands on Björkö in Sweden and founds a church.

861 Vikings sack Paris.

866 After repeated raids along the English and French coasts and the plundering of monasteries, the Vikings control most of England and Normandy.

940–95 Harald Bluetooth brings Christianity to Denmark; Olav Tryggvason uses force in his attempts to convert the Norwegian Vikings.

1001 The sagas relate that it was Leiv Eriksson who discovered Vinland (America).

1030 Battle of Stiklestad in Norway and the death of King Olav Haraldson who later becomes St Olav.

1050 Harald Hardråde of Norway founds Oslo.

1066 Defeat in England at the Battle of Stamford Bridge brings the Viking Age to an end.

MIDDLE AGES C.1100–1500

1100 The first bishoprics appear, among them the see of Nidaros (Trondheim) in Norway.

1155 King Erik of Sweden launches a crusade into Finland; further Swedish invasions take place in 1239 and 1293 subjugating large areas of the country.

1319–43 Inter-Scandinavian royal marriages produce a joint Norwegian–Swedish monarchy.

1362 Finland becomes a province of Sweden.

1397 A union is forged by Queen Margarethe and signed at Kalmar which unites the kingdoms of Norway, Denmark and Sweden.

1417 Eric VII of Denmark makes Copenhagen his capital and builds a palace at Helsingør.

1460 Kristian I secures the duchies of Schleswig and Holstein for Denmark.

WARS AND REFORMATION

1520 Kristian II of Denmark invades Sweden and massacres the nobility in the "Stockholm Bloodbath". Gustav Vasa drives him out and the Kalmar Union is disbanded. Norway remains under Danish rule.

1523 In Sweden, Gustav Vasa (1523–60) ascends the throne, marking the start of the Vasa dynasty (1523–1720), which also holds power in Finland. He declares Stockholm his capital. Under Gustav II Adolf (1611–32) Sweden becomes a great European power, only to decline during the reign of Karl XII (1697–1718), the "warrior king". Fine arts flourish under Gustav III (1771–92).

1530 The Reformation passes through the Scandinavian countries and the Lutheran faith is introduced. In Finland Mikael Agricola's translation of the Bible forms the basis of Finnish literary language.

1536 Norway ceases to be an independent kingdom as the Danes take control.

1588–1648 Denmark flourishes under the long rule of Kristian IV (1577–1648). Attempts to regain territory lost to Sweden end in failure.

1625–57 The Thirty Years War launched by the Danish king, Kristian IV, to check Swedish expansion ends in defeat for Denmark.

1714–41 "Great Wrath" and "Lesser Wrath": Russia and Sweden battle over Finland. Under the Treaty of Turku (1743) Russia moves its border westwards.

NINETEENTH-CENTURY MANOEUVRES

1801–14 During the Napoleonic Wars English fleets twice bombard Copenhagen. Denmark sides with Napoleon and suffers further defeat. In 1814 the victorious powers dissolve the Denmark–Norway union and Norway is ceded to Sweden (1815–1905). A new Norwegian constitution is adopted at Eidsvoll.

1807–1905 Tsar Alexander I occupies Finland in 1807. The Treaty of Hamina cedes Finland to Russia. A programme of "Russification" is introduced in Finland; in 1899 the composer, Jean Sibelius, is forced to publish his *Finlandia* as *Opus 26, No 7*. Finnish resistance grows. In 1905 events in Russia lead to a degree of autonomy for Finland.

1812 Tsar Alexander makes Helsinki Finland's capital.

1815–1907 In Sweden, Jean Baptiste Bernadotte, French marshal of Napoleon, succeeds to the throne as Karl XIV Johan (1818–44). The 19th century is a period of reform and industrialisation in Sweden, Norway and Denmark. Railways are built. The great exodus to the United States takes place.

1864 Denmark and Prussia at war. Denmark loses Schleswig-Holstein.

MODERN TIMES

1905 Referendum in Norway leads to the end of the union with Sweden. The Danish prince Håkon VII is invited to be king of Norway.

1906 Finnish women become the first in Europe to be given the vote.

1917–19 Finland declares its independence from the new Soviet Union, but is plunged into civil war in 1918 over attempts by radicals to introduce a Russian-style revolution. The White Guard (government troops) under General Mannerheim, defeats the Red Guard.

1919 The Republic of Finland comes into being under its first president, K.J. Ståhlberg.

1919 Denmark recovers Schleswig, not Holstein.

1930s Sweden and Denmark establish welfare states.

PRECEDING PAGES: Sweden loses Finland at the battle of Poltava, 1709. **LEFT:** King Gustav Vasa of Sweden. **ABOVE:** Marti Ahtissari, Finland's president until 2000.

1939–48 Soviet territorial demands spark off the Winter War between Finland and the Soviet Union. The Continuation War follows. Finland is forced to cede land to the USSR. War reparations are severe. In 1948 Finland and the Soviet Union sign the Treaty of Friendship, Co-operation and Mutual Assistance, forming the basis for good neighbourliness. Sweden remains neutral in World Wars I and II. Norway proclaims neutrality in World War II, but is attacked by the Germans, who also occupy Denmark.

1949 Denmark becomes a founding member of NATO.

1951–86 In Sweden, Social Democrats hold office for several years at a time; the Riksdag (Parliament) is reduced from two chambers to one; the monarch's

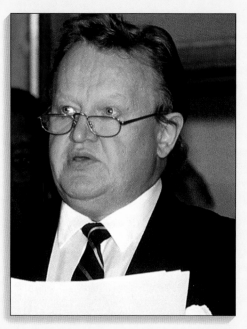

constitutional powers are removed. In 1986 Olof Palme, Swedish prime minister and international peacemaker, is assassinated.

1955 Finland is admitted to the United Nations. Helsinki becomes a centre for international peace and arms limitation talks in the late 20th century.

1960s Norway begins oil exploration in the North Sea and by the end of the 20th century is a major oil exporting nation. Later Denmark begins to exploit its North Sea oil reserves.

1972 Denmark joins the EEC (now European Union).

1995 Finland and Sweden join the European Union. Norway votes against membership (1972 and 1994).

2000 Øresund bridge opens between Denmark and Sweden, establishing new links across Scandinavia.❏

BEGINNINGS

As the ice floes retreated, so the hunter-gatherers moved north,
colonising the Nordic lands and giving rise to the Viking Age

For 1.6 million years, Scandinavia languished under an ice-sheet that oozed out of the Jostedalsbreen in Norway, stretched as far as the British Isles and Moscow, and was 3,000 metres (9,800 ft) thick. When eventually it melted, nomadic hunters and gatherers went after the plants and animals that surfaced in its wake. Some 12,000 years ago, the peninsula celebrated its final liberation from the crushing weight of the ice by rising like bread in an oven. Unleavened Denmark, however, remained barely above sea level, the land bridge with Norway and Sweden broken.

The first inhabitants

Some of the earliest arrivals in this re-sculptured land brought with them tame dogs, knew how to make leather boats, and kept a well-stocked armoury of bows, arrows, harpoons and spears. Not much else is known about them, so a case has been made for recognising the nomadic Lapps, also known as Sami, as Scandinavia's quasi-aboriginals. Other schools of thought put them down as comparatively recent arrivals from Siberia. In any case, Lapp women and children these days generally live in houses while their men in shrinking numbers drive reindeer herds over a territory which encompasses parts of Norway, Sweden, Finland and the Russian Kola Peninsula.

As for the Finns, the second group of somewhat exceptional Scandinavians, a 19th-century scholar, M. A. Castren, suggested that they and anyone else speaking a Finno-Ugric language, which included Hungarians, Estonians and indeed Lapps, hailed from Outer Mongolia and could therefore claim kinship with the likes of Genghis Khan. After searching self-examination, an increasing number of Finns see themselves as indigenous Baltic folk who drifted into their present location between the Bronze Age

LEFT: Viking raiding party sets out across the North Sea, 9th century.
RIGHT: latter-day Viking in traditional garb at one of Denmark's popular re-enactments.

and the start of the great European migration in the 5th century AD.

The real majority of Scandinavians are legendary types, like the 11th-century Norman crusader Bohemund who stopped in Constantinople on his way to the Holy Land. "Like no other man ever seen in the Byzantine Empire

whether barbarian or Greek," gushed the emperor's daughter, Anna Comnenus, "so tall in body that he exceeded even the tallest man by almost 50 centimetres... so narrow in the belly and flanks... so broad in the chest and shoulders... so strong in the arms. His whole stature could be described as neither constricted nor over-endowed with flesh, but blended as perfectly as possible."

Nevertheless, there were always significant numbers of shorter, darker people with more rounded skulls in the region, although more so in Denmark than in the northern forests and fjords. Lapps and Finns aside, they all spoke the same Primitive Nordic language, one of the

Germanic group, and had common notions of religion, law and culture. Bronze Age rock-carvings reveal a well-appointed world of horse-drawn carts, ships with curious beaks at either end, weapons and a religion devoted to the worship of the sun and fertility.

Travellers' tales

In 500 BC, however, a drastic turn in the weather killed off livestock which had previously spent the whole year outdoors, wrecked agriculture and forced men into trousers instead of belted cloaks. In the meantime, sun-drenched Athenians were building the Parthenon and,

healthy respect for wealth, recognised a king "with an unchallengeable right to obedience", and built powerful ships "unusual in that there is a prow at each end". Augustus and Nero sent expeditions to find out more, and it was through contact with Rome that the Scandinavians were inspired to produce their own alphabet.

Jordanes, the 6th-century historian of the Goths, was the first to identify "Dani" among the local tribes, all of whom were said to be taller than Germans and ferocious fighters. The Old English epic *Beowolf* planted the popular but erroneous idea that Scandinavians wore horned helmets, and Procopius, the Byzantine

like most Europeans, had no idea whatsoever of Scandinavia until the voyager Pytheas of Marseilles returned a little before 300 BC with tales of a land north of Britain where it was either dark for six months at a time or light enough, even at midnight, to pick lice out of a shirt. The local population were barbarians who lived on millet, herbs, roots and fruit because, he noticed, they had hardly any domestic animals, and threshing generally had to be done indoors. Nevertheless, grain fermented with honey produced a giddy drink they enjoyed.

Four centuries later, the Roman historian Tacitus reported significant improvements. The Suiones (Uppland Swedes) had developed a

historian, singled out the Lapps as people who had neither crops nor wine and wore animal skins held together with sinews. Lapp babies, he said, did not touch milk. Put into skin cradles and left dangling from trees while their mothers worked, they tucked into bone marrow. He also described hunters on skis and an excessive enthusiasm for human sacrifice.

Raiding parties

In 789, however, the Scandinavians spoke up for themselves. Three ships of an unfamiliar design appeared off the coast of Dorset in southwest England and the local magistrate ambled down to welcome them. Heavily armed warriors leapt ashore and subjected the hapless man to a fate known as "kissing the thin lips of the axe". As his head rolled, they stormed off to fill their ships with whatever caught their fancy, including a number of attractive natives, and were gone. The bemused *Anglo-Saxon Chronicle* could only say that they were apparently "Northmen from Horda-land" (Norwegians from the Bergen area). They returned four years later. As committed pagans, the raiders were unaffected by the sanctity of Chris-

RUNIC WRITING

To facilitate carving in wood or stone, the runic alphabet consisted of permutations of straight lines. It was used initially only for names and invocations against evil spirits.

navigable grid between the Gulf of Finland and the Caspian and Black Seas. At the far end lay Constantinople, the richest city on earth and an inexhaustible market for northern products like amber, furs, weapons and above all fresh-faced European slaves. The Arab traveller and diplomat Ibn Fadlan was impressed by the usual attributes of the Swedes – "perfect physical specimens, tall as date palms, blond and ruddy" – but had reservations about their insistence on exercising seignorial rites over the

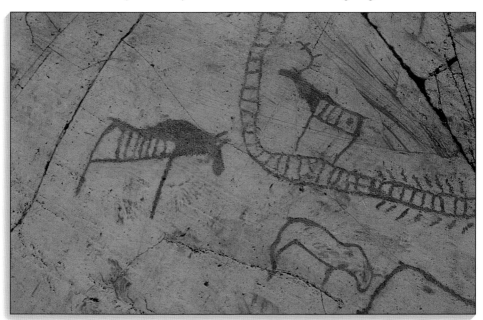

tian monasteries stuffed with valuables. Beginning with Lindisfarne in Northumbria, they murdered monks and ransacked coastal monasteries all around the British Isles, and repeated the performance every summer. Prayers went up everywhere for delivery from so-called Northmen. They, however, called themselves Vikings, meaning "pirates".

At more or less the same time, Swedish counterparts were capitalising on the fact that lakes and rivers formed an almost uninterrupted

LEFT: Bronze Age Sun Chariot, National Museum of Denmark, Copenhagen.
RIGHT: rock carvings at Hjemmeluft, Sweden.

merchandise in public and en masse. "A man will have sexual intercourse with slave girls while his companions look on," he said.

On a third contemporary front, Charlemagne's crusade against the heathen Saxons of northwest Germany brought him into contact with their Danish neighbours on the other side of the Eider, whose look he liked even less. As the Danes felt exactly the same way about him and his Franks, they built the Danevirke wall across the Jutland peninsula to keep them at bay and to secure the border town of Hedeby, the trade bridge between the North Sea and the Baltic. Thus were sown the seeds of the Schleswig-Holstein imbroglio, a territorial dispute of such complexity that anyone dragged into it even 1,000 years later, according to a 19th-century British prime minister himself involved, was in danger of going mad or dying.

Al-Tartushi, another Arab traveller, went to see Hedeby, "a large town at the farthest end of the world ocean". The carcasses of sacrificed animals swung from poles, but the main food was fish "as there is so much of it".

Both sexes used eye make-up, he said (not that anyone else ever noticed), and women could unilaterally divorce their husbands whenever they liked.

NO LOVE LOST

In Arthurian romances the Vikings were described as being "wild and savage and had not in them the love of God nor their neighbours".

Taken together, these developments across three fronts signalled the start of the "Viking Age" in which they went abroad to conquer most of the British Isles, carve a Norman province out of France, invade Germany, Spain and Italy, settle Iceland and Greenland, discover America, terrorise the Mediterranean, dominate the Baltic region, Poland, Russia and Ukraine, fight for and against Byzantium, attack the Muslim Caliphate in

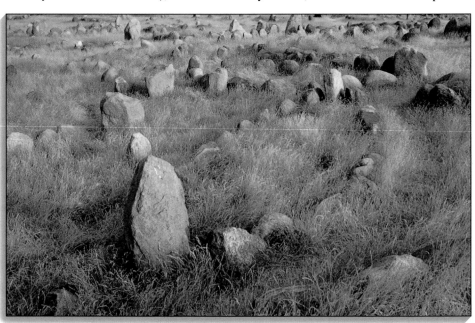

VIKING SHIP DESIGN

A Viking's ticket to foreign parts was the latest evolution of the ship design first shown in Bronze Age rock carvings. The prows at either end were the extremities of a keel made out of a single oak. It could twist like a tree in the wind, hence its immense strength. A fighting ship of the type found at Gokstad in Norway was 25 metres (82 ft) long, 6 metres (19 ft) wide, and carried a crew of 70. Clinker-built, caulked with tarred animal hair or wool, it had a hinged steering oar that swung out of the way so the ships could be aimed at a beach at full speed. An important innovation was the use of sail. Viking ships could cross the North Sea to England in 72 hours.

Baghdad, and contribute to the liberation of Jerusalem. Meanwhile, the pack of warring chieftainships and petty kingdoms at home was being shuffled and cut down to form the separate states as exist today.

Trade with Byzantium

Various factors combined to produce this explosive energy. The disruption of traditional trade by the 9th-century Muslim conquests in Europe, for one, encouraged the Swedes to open up the alternative routes through Russia. They put it about that the Slavs begged them to take over the running of the territory. "Our land is large and fruitful but it lacks order," the message allegedly read. "Come over and rule us." By 900, Swedish influence radiated throughout Eastern Europe from their strongholds at Novgorod and Kiev. The Swedes were soon assimilated under the weight of Slavic numbers, but they left an indelible mark in the name by which they were locally known, Rus.

Polygamy and primogeniture were also forces behind the Viking Age. Big as Scandinavia was, only a tiny proportion of the land was actually habitable, and the useful land in remote valleys or fjords could only be subdivided so many times. As the whole of a patrimony generally went to the eldest son, or

foray in 844 opened with a rebuff at La Coruna on Spain's Atlantic coast, improved with the sacking of Lisbon, Cadiz and Seville, and ended with the loss of two ships crammed with gold, silver and prisoners to the Moors.

Terrorising the Mediterranean

Back again in 859 with a fleet of 62 red-sailed ships, Hasting negotiated the Straits of Gibraltar, sacked Algeciras, spent a week in Morocco rounding up "blue men" for subsequent sale in Ireland and then wintered on La Camargue in the Rhone Delta, "causing great annoyance and detriment to the inhabitants". Come spring, he

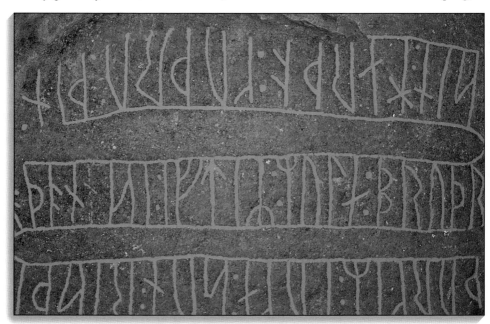

rather the eldest surviving son, Swedish kings with 40 women in their harem, or Norwegian earls with a dozen sons by various wives and concubines, were sure recipes for orgiastic fratricide. Harald Fairhair's ascendancy, c.890, went a long way towards defining Norway, but it necessarily involved stripping and disbanding numerous lessers dynasties, whose scions had no real choice but to try their luck abroad.

To begin with, Viking enterprise abroad was a matter of independent initiative, as epitomised by a certain Hasting. Born in Denmark, his first

LEFT: Viking burial ground, Jutland, Denmark.
ABOVE: runic script, National Museum, Copenhagen.

was ready for Italy. After looting Pisa, he turned south and came across a city of such marbled magnificence that it could only be Rome.

He despatched messengers with the story that their leader, a Christian of unparalled piety, was dying, and his last wish was to be given a Christian burial in such hallowed ground as now lay before them. Permission granted, the gates admitted a coffin followed by a long procession of mournful Vikings. As the local bishop was praying over the coffin it flew open and out leapt Hasting himself. The startled bishop was on his back, run through with Hasting's sword, as the mourners went off to reduce the city to ashes. Only then did Hasting learn that he had destroyed Luna, not Rome, and felt so cheated that he ordered the massacre of all male prisoners. His next port of call was Alexandria in Egypt. The campaign closed in 862 with an overland march to sack Pamplona.

England under attack

Three years later, in 865, Hasting appeared at the mouth of the Thames with a new fleet of 80 ships just as "a big heathen horde", according to the *Anglo-Saxon Chronicle*, arrived elsewhere in England under Ivar the Boneless. Their immediate mission was to avenge a private grievance, the cruel death of their father

Ragnar in a pit full of snakes, but with Hasting's fleet and other Danish private armies dotted around the country, the show took on the appearance of a concerted Danish conquest. The outcome was a Danish kingdom in England and the imposition of a stiff tax, Danegeld.

Ironically, Harald Bluetooth of Denmark (*c*.910–985) was in turn obliged to prostrate himself. His *bête noire* was the crusading Holy Roman Emperor Otto I, a German, who could be appeased only by Harald's submission to Christian baptism. Most of Europe had been Christian for five centuries or more, but Scandinavia was not inclined to abandon paganism. Harald's son and successor, Swein Forkbeard,

brushed aside his father's baptism as an aberration. The Norwegian king Olav Tryggvason (*c*.965–1000), a hell-raising pirate from the age of 12, was supposedly convinced by a wise hermit in the Scillies, but the methods he then employed to convert his subjects were pure Viking. Sweden remained true to paganism by turning Christian missionaries into martyrs. Sacrifices in the golden temple at Uppsala continued into the late 11th century.

Norman conquest

In France, Vikings who sailed up the Seine and attacked Paris were given 3,000 kg (3 tons) of silver by Charles the Bald of France to go away, while his successor Charles the Simple was ready to cede an entire province as protection money to Rolf (or "Rollo") the Ganger, a Viking too big to ride any horse. The province became the Duchy of Normandy, and within two centuries it was the springboard for the 1066 Norman conquest of Anglo-Danish England. But if the conquest was a great triumph for Norman arms, it also accelerated the end of the Viking Age.

Harald Hardrade of Norway (1015–66), the "Thunderbolt of the North", had tried to preempt William's seizure of England with an invasion of his own, and it was not long before Danish and Norwegian forces attempted to unseat William. But England under the Normans was a tough nut to crack; Normandy itself was no longer open to disgruntled Scandinavians, and Iceland was full. Greenland was the next possibility, and it was from here that Leif Erikson set sail to see if he could find something better in the unknown world to the west.

As it was Leif's own father who had coined the deceptive tease "Greenland", sceptics might have wondered about the son's tales of Vinland, a land of warm sunshine, trees, grass and, as the name implied, grapes. But his brother Thorvald believed him, followed his directions, and on landing in Vinland walked straight into an Indian arrow. The next assessment of the land's potential was by a fearsome woman, Freydid, who murdered most of her party en route. She was not over-impressed. The future America, she thought, was not more than "all right". ❏

LEFT: Lejre Iron Age village, Roskilde, Denmark.
RIGHT: Odin, the mythological Norse god of wisdom, war, culture and the dead.

MEDIEVAL THUGS OR MERCHANT TRADERS?

The Vikings plundered their way into the annals of Scandinavian history. But archaeology reveals there's more to these raiders than meets the eye

At first glance the Viking legacy appears to be little more than an impressive catalogue of violence and piracy. Archaeological finds have, however, shed light not only on the way the Vikings lived (everything from the food they ate to the clothing they wore) but also on their burial traditions.

Today, the Vikings are recognised for their skills as craftsmen, traders and of course as sailors.

The Viking longship, essential for both raiding and trading, was also used to bury kings and chieftains. Superb examples can be seen at the Viking ship museums in Roskilde, Denmark, and in Oslo, Norway, where textiles, household utensils and other artefacts excavated from the burial mounds around the Oslo Fjord are also on display. In Denmark, Funen's Ladby Ship Museum houses a magnificent burial ship with a dragon's head and tail.

Sites and open-air museums such as those at Birka outside Stockholm (see right), and Denmark's Fyrkat and Trelleborg, offer a unique look into the daily lives of the Vikings. Other places of interest include the burial ground at Lindholm Høje, Jutland and Jelling in Zealand, with its runes and burial mounds, often referred to as Denmark's "birth certificate". With a host of activities and re-enactments, these sites offer visitors a chance to relive the Viking experience first-hand.

▷ **CARVED IN STONE**
The Vikings would commemorate an event or a death on runestones like this one on Öland.

▷ **BURIAL SHIP**
The Oseberg ship in Oslo's Vikingskipshuset is thought to be the tomb of a queen buried in 834 with her maidservant and most valued possessions.

△ **ANCIENT LIFESTYLE**
Reliving life the Viking way Fyrkat in Denmark. Viking re-enactments are popular attractions in Jutland.

▽ **GRAVE OBJECTS**
Tools found in the graves at Birka, Sweden, are testimony to the society of skilled craftsmen who lived in the town.

THE VIKING SILK ROUTE

△ **DWELLING PLACE**
The reconstructed longhouse at Fyrkat, in Denmark, where four earth fortifications enclosed 16 large houses.

▽ **SAILING ONWARD**
Unlike other burial sites, graves at Lindholm Høje, Denmark, were marked by stones. This one is in the shape of a ship.

This bishop's crosier from Ireland, pictured above, was found at the site of Sweden's first Viking town, Birka. Situated 30 km (19 miles) west of Stockholm, Birka was founded towards the end of the 8th century.

Archaeological excavations have revealed trade networks stretching east to Byzantium and as far as China. The finds, which include silks from the Far East, Arabic coins and glass beads from Caliphate, have challenged the belief that the Viking age was all murder and mayhem. They point instead to a burgeoning, prosperous society made up of merchants, traders and farmers.

Birka was the first town in Sweden to come into contact with Christianity. But the town was never evangelised and in some graves Thor's hammer was found alongside a crucifix.

The museum at Birka is open between April and September. Boats leave from outside Stockholm City Hall, at Stadshusbron, three times a day.

△ **MONEY MATTERS**
Danish, Frankish and Arabic coins were found at Birka. This one depicts a trading vessel.

◁ **HAIR CARE**
Combs were popular items. Many fine examples were found in the graves excavated at Birka.

△ **SHIPSHAPE**
Manoeuvrability and speed were the key features of Viking ship design. A number of replicas have been built in Norway, like this one in Oslo harbour.

WAR AND PEACE

From the end of the Viking Age to the dawn of the 20th century, kings battled for supremacy, land changed hands and unions were made and broken

As the Viking Age drew to a close in the 11th century, the kings of Norway, Sweden and Denmark – "all handsome and big men, of noble looks and well-spoken" – met at Konghelle on the Göta River in 1098 to acknowledge one another's legitimacy and to adopt a common policy on robbery and theft, ever the crimes of greatest concern. To seal the pact, King Magnus of Norway – known as "Barelegs" since returning from Scotland sporting a kilt – married Inge of Sweden's daughter Margaret, hence "The Peace Maiden".

Five years later, however, Magnus fulfilled one of his own favourite sayings – "a king stands for his country's honour and glory, not for a long life" – by being killed in action in Ireland. Norway was then carved up among his three young sons, thereby undoing not only the single Norwegian kingdom hammered together by Harald Fairhair but also any real prospect of smooth Scandinavian co-existence.

Converting the heathens

Denmark's particular difficulty was not fragmentation but a succession of kings so ineffectual (e.g. "Harald the Hen") that several were simply taken out to sea and drowned. In Sweden, the throne bobbed between two dynasties who routinely murdered the opposing encumbent. Next to these goings-on, the princes of the new power in the land, the Church, looked purposeful. As comfortable in the saddle as the pulpit, Bishop Absalon of Roskilde (1128–1201) personally sorted out "the heathen Wend", a tribe of defiant Baltic pagans whose headquarters were on Rügen island. Smashing the four-headed god Svantevit, he offered everyone the choice of embracing Christ or dying immediately. The island then became part of his booming diocese. With bishops like Absalon around, ambitious kings were obliged to demonstrate their religious cre-

dentials by "taking the Cross" and joining a crusade. Sigurd of Norway, one of Barelegs' sons ("not good-looking but well-grown and manly; his few words were most often not friendly") went to the Holy Land. Valdemar I (1131–82), a more dashing king than Denmark had seen for some time, fought 28 battles

against heathens of one sort or another. His successor Valdemar II concentrated on Estonians, and in spite of a fleet of 1,000 ships was only rescued from one certain defeat by the miraculous apparition of a red-and-white banner in the heavens. It became Denmark's national flag.

Sweden annexes Finland

Erik I of Sweden did his crusader service among the Finns during the 12th century, marking the start of Sweden's 700-year annexation of Finland and Erik's climb to the status of his country's patron saint. But aggrandisement was all too easily reversed, as occurred in Denmark on Valdemar II's exit. "The crown fell off the

LEFT: Gustav Vasa (1523–60), first king of the Vasa dynasty, laid the foundations of the Swedish state.
RIGHT: Kristian II of Denmark (1513–23).

head of the Danes," a chronicle wailed, "and they became the laughing stock for all their neighbours through civil wars and mutual destruction."

In Sweden, the saintly Erik I was murdered by the son of the king he had removed, Sverker, leaving Erik's son in no doubt about what was expected of him. He did not disappoint.

Like the Church, German and Dutch Hansa traders recognised the chaotic absence of government as an excellent opportunity for themselves. The obvious fact

THE DANISH FLAG

The oldest national flag in the world is a source of pride among Danes. It must never touch the ground and only a pennant version may be flown at night.

Fishing vessels raced from all over Europe until some 40,000 were crammed into the Sound, temporarily loosening the Hansa's grip on the market. The 14th-century king, Valdemar IV of Denmark, launched a snap invasion of the Hansa's base at Visby in Gotland and, flushed with success, assumed the title of "King of the Goths". The Hansa were neither impressed nor amused. Throwing the resources of their 77 towns and cities into a military alliance with Sweden, they bounced Valdemar off his Danish throne and

of Scandinavian economic life was an abundance of fish versus a shortage of grain. By tying up the markets in both commodities, and the shipping in between, the Hansa had a goose of pure gold, and it gave them a network of strategic ports and market towns across the continent. But if Scandinavia was sapped by an extortionate exchange rate between fish and grain, it was then poleaxed by the Black Death in 1349. With the population of Norway, for example, cut by more than half, economics reverted to the Stone Age.

One interlude in the slow reconstruction process was the arrival of shoals of herring so dense that fish could be caught with bare hands.

invited applications. Margarethe, the young wife of King Håkon VI of Norway, proposed their son Oluf. He was five years old.

A scheming queen

Margarethe, who had married in 1363 at the age of 10 and given birth to Oluf at 17, knew what she was doing. With Denmark under Oluf's little belt and the Norwegian crown bound to follow in due course, she encouraged him to think of himself as "the true heir to Sweden" as well, a presumption that infuriated Albrecht, the reigning king of Sweden.

Nevertheless, Margarethe (described as "of dark complexion and somewhat masculine in appearance") had to think again when Oluf died at 17. While personally keeping the Danish throne warm, she persuaded the Norwegian nobility to recognise her grandnephew Erik of Pomerania as Oluf's successor. Erik, too, was five at this turning point in his career. Margarethe went behind Albrecht's back to offer the Swedish nobles perpetual rights to their property and privileges in exchange for their support against him. Albrecht could take no more. Raising an army of German mercenaries, he demanded satisfaction at Falkoping. A chronicler was surprised by the outcome: "God gave an unexpected victory into the hands of a woman."

of a war with Holstein when she collapsed. The Danish nobility were inclined to ask aloud whether their interests might be better served by Erik's nephew, Christopher of Bavaria, and the talk in Sweden was of a separate constitution and a fresh crowned head. Meanwhile, Erik retired to Visborg Castle in Gotland and applied himself, privately and very profitably, to the business of piracy.

Stockholm Bloodbath

After more than one trial separation Denmark and Sweden were together again under the Danish king, Kristian II (1481–1559). Anti-

Margarethe's grand scheme was at last realised at Kalmar in 1397 when Eric, now 14, donned the three crowns of Norway, Denmark and Sweden. "Rash, violent and obstinate," he faced the tall order of running an empire from the Arctic Circle (including Swedish Finland) to the Eider, and west to Greenland, with no money or support from the wary nobility. Margarethe had her hands full nursing the damage caused by Erik's railings against these constraints, and she was addressing the aftermath

LEFT: the Swedish army is defeated by Peter the Great of Russia at the battle of Poltava, 1709.
ABOVE: a depiction of medieval life at Turku Castle.

Danish feeling was growing apace in Sweden when the Swedish assembly voted to burn the fortress of the Archbishop of Sweden, a pro-Dane, Gustav Trolle. In the event Trolle was merely imprisoned, but in 1520 the Papal Court excommunicated the Swedish regent, Sten Sture the Younger, for this act. Kristian II had the justification he sought for invading Sweden. He invited Sweden's leading nobles to a feast in Stockholm at which he chopped off the heads of 82 of Sweden's finest. This "Stockholm Bloodbath" provoked a rebellion.

Kristian was driven out of Sweden and Gustav Vasa, a nobleman whose family had been victims in the massacre seized power.

Thus began a Swedish dynasty of exceptional distinction and durability.

Hounded out of Denmark, Kristian II sought refuge in the Netherlands. Norway's clergy, staunchly loyal to Rome, made him an offer of the Norwegian throne, which provoked violent intervention by Danish and Hanseatic forces with far-reaching consequences. Kristian spent the rest of his life in Sonderborg Castle, while the Norwegian church was purged of Roman Catholics to make it Lutheran, and the Norwegian monarchy was abolished. Norway was thereafter a mere province of Denmark. The tripartite Kalmar Union was dead.

squadrons crossed the ice and a resounding victory cost Denmark all its territory on the Swedish side of the Sound.

The warrior king

In Karl XII (1682–1718), Sweden seemed to acquire a reincarnation of the Vikings who fought and caroused their way across Russia. Taking over the mantle of the traditional Germanic *drang nach osten* (drive to the east), he collided with Peter the Great of Russia.

The Russians eventually got the better of a titanic struggle, putting Karl in the impossible position of trying to rule Sweden from his bolt-

Battle on ice

Kristian IV (1577–1648) was on the Danish throne for 52 years, building palaces and towns, trebling the size of the navy, and sending explorers to investigate the possibility of a northwest passage to Asia. He took an avuncular interest in Norway, renaming Oslo after himself ("Kristiania"), but never managed to achieve friendly relations with Sweden or his counterpart, Gustavus II Adolphus.

Inevitably they entered the Thirty Years War on opposite sides, but the Swedish king was quicker off the mark when the Sound (Øresund) between the two countries froze over during the winter of 1657. Two cavalry

hole in Turkey. Finally, he rode home with two companions, a journey of 1,300 miles, only to find that in his absence Sweden had been stripped of all his recent gains. His plan to put matters right began and ended with a siege of Frederiksten in southern Norway. The bullet through his head may have been fired by a genuine enemy sniper or a contracted assassin, but in any case Sweden decided to give absolutism a rest and explore constitutional government.

Denmark's first taste of quasi-constitutional government was deferred until the 1770s and even so only materialised in strange circumstances. Kristian VII's increasingly erratic behaviour clearly needed medical attention, a task entrusted to a German doctor, Johann Friederich Struensee. The patient was off his head, Struensee decided, so the best he could do was to run the country himself. And so he did.

In little more than a year, Struensee drew up 1,069 bills introducing freedom of speech and the press, a national budget, the decriminalisation of fornication and adultery, and the abolition of capital punishment for all but the most unspeakable crimes.

He could not have envisaged, as he extended his stately role to touch on the void in the lovely Queen Caroline Matilde's conjugal life, that he would be dragged out of bed at dawn and

Britain bombarded Copenhagen, Tsar Alexander I occupied Finland, bringing the ages-old Swedish rule initiated by St Erik to a close.

Russia wins Finland

Russia later changed sides and was sitting with the victors when reparations were decided after the Battle of Waterloo (1815). Russia was allowed to keep Finland; Norway was detached from Denmark and handed to Sweden, albeit not as a colony but as a supposed equal in a union under a common crown.

The king in question was a curious choice: Jean-Baptiste Bernadotte was French and not

charged with just such a crime, one that still carried the supreme penalty. Locked up in Kronborg Castle at Helsingor, his partner in crime was rescued from her fate by an English warship sent by George III, himself showing signs of instability but her brother nonetheless.

The same navy was again under the guns of Kronborg Castle at the outbreak of the Napoleonic War in the early 19th century, in this instance because Denmark had sided with Russia, at that stage Napoleon's ally. While

LEFT: the Swedish royal palace of Drottningholm, designed in the 17th century by Tessin the Elder.
ABOVE: *Conversation at Drottningholm*, 1779.

THE GREAT EXODUS

The 19th century witnessed a mass exodus of Scandinavians in search of a better life in the New World. "Potatoes, peace and vaccination" were blamed for a population explosion at home which contributed to an outflow of 750,000 Norwegian and one million Swedish emigrants – a quarter of the Swedish population.

The new settlers sent back glowing accounts of their lives in America, and money to support those left behind. These signs of prosperity and other factors such as The United States Homestead Act of 1862, which promised land almost free to settlers who dared to travel west, encouraged others to follow.

only a former general of the French Revolution but a key member of Napoleon's staff. If taking the name Karl Johan was meant to help him to blend into his new surroundings, this was offset by his refusal to speak anything but French.

Thus reorganised, the Scandinavian states stepped into the frenzy of romantic nationalism that swept across Europe and inspired phenomenal scientific progress and a flowering of the arts. In these respects Scandinavia did its bit and more. Sweden was especially strong in the sciences;

TROUBLED UNION

Sweden typically bribed North African pirates not to attack their ships, but to plunder those of the Norwegians who insisted on sailing under their own colours.

consider, for one, Linnaeus, the naturalist *(see box, below)*. Denmark's most notable contributions were the writer Hans Christian Andersen *(see page 127)* and the philosopher, Søren Kierkegaard. Norway offered Edvard Grieg (composer), Henrik Ibsen (dramatist) and Edvard Munch (painter), and Finland (pre-Sibelius) contributed the *Kalevala*, an epic which Elias Lönnrot compiled from old ballads and songs to reinvent his country's hitherto elusive past.

Language became a vexing issue in Finland and Norway. Mikael Agricola, the Bishop of Turku, had produced a Finnish translation of the Bible as early as 1642, and although Finnish had always been spoken by the majority of the population, it had no official status. The Russians even banned books written in Finnish.

In Norway, Old Norse had gone to Iceland with the Viking settlers, while the language in Norway itself had been affected by Danish connections. Pure Danish was used for official business, in literature and by the educated classes. In the 19th century Norwegian nationalists wanted to revert to untainted Norwegian. They concocted a cocktail from Norway's surviving rural dialects called "New Norwegian".

Friends and foes

One 19th-century development was that Swedish, Danish and Norwegian (but not yet Finnish) historians could at last get together for a chat without coming to blows, and in this spirit Swedish and Danish university students took advantage of the atrocious winter of 1838, when the Sound again froze over, to walk across the ice, meet in the middle, and improvise odes to Scandinavian solidarity.

If this was reminiscent of Magnus Barelegs and company at Konghelle, the dream was again upset by events in Norway, where the union with Sweden was in trouble. Norway strengthened its fortifications along the Swedish frontier, and Sweden had its army on alert before a compromise was worked out. The union dissolved and, as Norway went shopping for a new king, Scandinavia braced itself for the 20th century. ❑

LINNAEUS, THE PLANTSMAN

Carl von Linné, the Swedish naturalist who devised the modern classification system for plants and animals, was one of the great scientists of 18th-century Scandinavia. Born in 1707, Linnaeus studied medicine at the University of Lund and botany at Uppsala. He travelled widely and was a leading figure in the founding of the Swedish Academy of Science. As chair of botany, dietetics and *materia medica* at Uppsala, he pursued his research into nomenclature. His publications included *Systema Naturae* (1735), *Philosophia Botanica* (1750), and *Species Plantarum* (1753). Linnaeus died in 1778. His house and botanical garden can be visited at Uppsala.

LEFT: Alfred Nobel (1833–96), Swedish chemist, inventor of dynamite and founder of the Nobel Prizes.
RIGHT: Sami girls in traditional costume, 1898.

THE MODERN AGE

*Two world wars took their toll on the Nordic countries, but by the end of the
20th century they had emerged as sophisticated economic powers*

The 20th century dawned with not only the union of Sweden and Norway on the rocks but also the special relationship between Finland and Russia. A new tsar, the ill-fated Nicholas II, did not share his predecessors' fond view of Finland as a separate grand duchy and liked even less the privileges that went with it. So while breakaway Norway recruited Håkon VII, né Prince Carl of Denmark, as its first independent king for 600 years, Finland was delivered into the hands of Nikolai Ivanovich Bobrikov, a hard-boiled martinet whose previous assignment had been to knock some sense into Russia's wayward Baltic provinces.

King Håkon accepted the job only after a plebiscite indicated that three-quarters of the Norwegian population wanted him. Bobrikov did not bother with such trifles. Having abolished the Finns' exemption from service in the Russian imperial forces, he was systematically shredding the freedom of speech and other rights when he was met on the staircase to the Senate by Eugen Schauman, a civil servant. Schauman put three bullets into the brute before turning the revolver on himself.

The onset of World War I

Fortunately for Finland, the tsar was too involved in war with Japan and later in the St Petersburg uprising to avenge Bobrikov's murder. Every one of 40 previous wars with Russia had gone badly for the Finns, but they were always ready to try again. The first whiff of World War I saw volunteers flocking to Germany to join a special "Jagar battalion" which duly entered the field against Russia alongside Kaiser Wilhem's forces.

For their part, the three kings of Scandinavia met at Malmö in Sweden in December 1914 and declared their neutrality. However, putting the proclamation into practice was not so easy. After centuries of anguish over Schleswig-

LEFT: flag-waving during the annual National Day celebrations in Norway on 17 May.
RIGHT: evacuated Finnish family, 1939.

Holstein, Denmark was not Germany's greatest admirer, but it was in no position to defy the kaiser's orders to mine Danish sea-lanes against the British navy. Conversely, Norway received a warning from Britain that selling fish, iron pyrites or copper to Germany would not be tolerated, and Sweden was in fact blockaded,

eventually to suffer acute food shortages, for trading too eagerly with Wilhem. The worst blow, though, was Germany's declaration of unrestricted submarine warfare in 1916. Hundreds of Scandinavian ships and crews "on charter" to Britain had in fact been commandeered, but they went to the bottom all the same and with heavy losses.

On Russia's withdrawal from the war after the Bolshevik revolution in 1917, Lenin made a direct appeal to sympathisers in Scandinavia and Finland in particular. "Rise, rise instantly," he cried, "take over the government in the hands of organised labour." The Finnish Red Guard, about 30,000 strong, accordingly seized government offices in Helsinki and proclaimed a Socialist Workers' Republic. The government's response was to raise a White Guard, including the Jagar battalion, Swedish volunteers and 12,000 German troops, under the command of General Baron Gustaf Mannerheim, a former White Russian cavalry officer. The revolution lasted less than four months, but there were 24,000 casualties and a comparable number of Red sympathisers were subsequently executed or left to die in internment camps.

Consideration was then given to turning Finland into a kingdom with one of Kaiser Wilhem's sons on the throne, but Germany's

UNDERCOVER OPERATIONS

The Resistance movement in Denmark and Norway was crucial in undermining the German campaign during World War II. Anders Lassen epitomised the 20,000-strong Danish Resistance. By the time he died aged 24, he had fought in France, Greece, the Balkans and Italy. His commanding officer said, "Anders caused more discomfort to the enemy over five years of war than any other man of his rank and age." Other heroes included the Norwegians who knocked out the heavy water plant at Rjukan (*Heroes of Telemark, see page 180*). Two museums, Frihedsmuseet, Copenhagen, and Norges Hjemmefront-museum, Oslo, document the movement's history.

defeat in the war turned opinion in favour of a republic under the presidency of Kaarlo Juho Stahlberg, a local professor of law. The Soviet Union raised no objection to Finland's independence and signed the Treaty of Tartu to that effect, but Finland's fanatical Christian fundamentalists, the Lapua pietists, were determined to clear the nest of vipers. Suspected communists were kidnapped, beaten and dumped at the Soviet border. The pietists forced the government to ban communism completely and were arming themselves for a full-scale *coup d'état* when the army decided they had been around too long for any good they were doing.

Sweden sailed through the post-war years on a wave of international demand for Swedish steel and ball bearings, Ericsson telephones and Electrolux vacuum cleaners. While also doing well, Norway and Denmark clashed over Greenland and the Arctic islands of Svalbard (Spitzbergen) and Jan Mayen, which raised issues rooted in Viking times. Asked to arbitrate, the international court at the Hague gave Greenland to Denmark, the islands to Norway.

Scandinavia emerged from the second crisis of the inter-war years, the Great Depression, with improved political systems. The severity of the situation forced small parties with narrow interests – farmers' parties being a prime example – to remove their blinkers and join broader coalitions, the front runners generally calling themselves "Social Democrats".

World War II

With the Depression out of the way it was not long before the storm clouds of World War II gathered. Hitler's rise was especially worrying to Denmark because Germany had never formally agreed to the Schleswig-Holstein border as defined by plebiscite after World War I. Accepting his somewhat surprising offer of a non-aggression pact, Denmark nevertheless joined Sweden and Norway in another declaration of neutrality.

Finland was again a special case. When Hitler invaded Poland, Stalin assumed Russia would be next and seized a strip of Finnish territory to strengthen the defences around Leningrad. The 1939 Nazi-Soviet pact removed

LEFT: World War II poster published during the German occupation of Norway, 1941.
RIGHT: German aircraft on Finland's tundra, 1941.

this threat, but at the same time it allowed Stalin a free hand in Finland, and he ordered an invasion. Marshal Mannerheim, now in his seventies, came out of retirement to lead Finland in what came to be known as the Winter War.

Almost invisible in the white uniforms against driving snow, Finnish troops went into action on skis against Russian tanks. As Swedish volunteers arrived to help, Hitler had to restrain Mussolini ("that great man across the Alps") from sending in the Italian air force to give Stalin one in the eye. What really mattered, though, was the collapse of the Nazi-Soviet pact and Germany's invasion of Russia.

The Finns went in at the same time to recover their recent losses (the "War of Continuation") and were therefore stigmatised as Hitler's allies.

German aggression

The German invasion of Denmark and Norway began on 9 April 1940. Some troops crossed the Jutland border into Denmark, others emerged from hiding in German merchant ships in Copenhagen harbour, and paratroops landed at key points around the country. The Danish army was in barracks, the navy was too surprised to fire a single shot, and the air force was destroyed on the ground. If nothing else, the

THE DEMON DRINK

Stringent laws on the purchase of alcohol in Norway and Sweden have been somewhat at odds with the figure these countries have wanted to cut in the modern world. The time-honoured yearning for drink can be blamed on long winter nights, but ancient Scandinavians also drank like fish because their food was preserved with lashings of salt. King Sverre of Norway experimented with prohibition as early as the 12th century. In 1775, however, King Gustav III of Sweden turned the distillation and sale of spirits into a royal monopoly and encouraged his subjects to drink because he needed the money. Against this backdrop, 20th-century prohibitionists had problems. The conundrum in Norway was that France, Spain and Portugal, major consumers of Norwegian fish, had always bartered with wine or brandy. The issue of prohibition led to the downfall of three successive governments in the early 20th century.

Sweden, however, put its faith in the "Bratt Liquor Control System", a certain Dr Ivan Bratt having worked out exactly how much alcohol an individual could consume according to age, physique and other considerations, with the result that it was almost impossible for a married woman to qualify for a single drink in any circumstances. Today, as in Gustav III's time, the sale of wines and spirits in both countries is a state monopoly.

The Royal Line

I t used to be said, not so long ago, that there would soon be just five kings left in the world: of England, clubs, hearts, spades and diamonds. Come the turn of the millennium, however, there were still six monarchies alive in Europe, three of them in Scandinavia. Moreover, the royal families of Denmark, Sweden and Norway were probably as secure and popular as ever they had been.

Monarchy could hardly be more entrenched than in Denmark. Queen Margrethe II is the 52nd in an unbroken line of sovereigns spanning more than

1,000 years. Sweden, too, has had more than 50 kings since 980. The present King Carl Gustaf may be "XVI" but his direct line begins with Jean Baptiste Bernadotte, the French marshal who was installed on the throne in 1810. Norway's royal line ceased when Norway became a Danish province and the monarchy was only restored, after a referendum, following the dissolution in 1905 of the subsequent union with Sweden. The present king, Harald V, is the third of the modern line, the "V" notwithstanding. Finland also considered a monarchy on breaking away from Russia, but chose to become a republic instead.

Nevertheless, not a little craft has gone into keeping the Scandinavian monarchies in robust health. When Carl XVI Gustaf ascended the Swedish throne in 1973, the Constitution began with: "The King alone shall govern the realm..." Lest he got the wrong impression, this was hastily changed to: "All public power in Sweden emanates from the people..." The king decided his own official motto ought to be: "For Sweden – in Keeping with the Times". This was the cue for changing the rules of succession so that they no longer discriminated against daughters. Consequently, next in line is Crown Princess Victoria rather than her younger brother. Their mother, Queen Silvia, is the daughter of a German businessman.

Carl Gustaf is not averse to tearing around in a Ferrari and was reported to the police in Denmark for doing an alleged 250 kph (155 mph) on the Copenhagen expressway. Nonsense, the king retorted. He admitted having a lot to do on his way to Queen Margrethe's 60th birthday but had not exceeded 150. In contrast, King Harald loves boats – and has represented his country at the Olympic Games – but would not be seen dead in a Ferrari. He uses public transport. Harald works hard at being uninteresting, a quality Norwegians apparently like in their kings. Queen Sonja is the daughter of an Oslo shopkeeper and their children went to state schools. Fittingly, the Crown Prince found himself a bachelor flat in an unfashionable part of Oslo but let the side down, as it were, by sharing it with a waitress, and her three-year-old son by a man who was in prison for drug offences.

If conscientious exercises in non-charisma go down well in Norway, Queen Margrethe could not hope to do the same in Denmark. She has been showered with genuine academic honours from the likes of Cambridge, Oxford and the London School of Economics. While trying unsuccessfully to hide her distinguished output as a painter, writer and designer behind a string of aliases, she has at least persuaded her friends to call her Daisy. Crown Prince Frederik, her heir, is not much better at disguise. Dressing down for a night on the town, he turned out so scruffy that the bar refused to let him in. The situation was saved by an extremely attractive stranger, one Bettina Odum, stepping forward to say that he was with her. As a trained soldier, no mean dancer and the leader of a husky-drawn expedition across Greenland, Frederik looks set to retain his position with the voters as Denmark's "Man of the Year" for some time to come. ❑

LEFT: the ever-popular Queen Margarethe of Denmark celebrating her 60th birthday in 2000.

Royal Life Guards at Amalienborg Palace in Copenhagen prevented the Germans from capturing King Kristian X just long enough for him to order a surrender. Denmark remained in theory a sovereign state under German protection, but when the king ignored Hitler's effusive greetings on his birthday in 1942, the pretence was dropped. A new government was expected to jump at Hitler's whim, but it refused to sanction death sentences on members of the increasingly active Resistance movement and made arrangements to smuggle Denmark's endangered Jews to safety in Sweden.

Norway is overrun

In Norway's case, gunners in an old fortress on Oslo fjord had the satisfaction of sinking the German cruiser *Blucher* on the first day of the invasion, killing or at least drenching the bureaucrats earmarked to run the country with Hitler's local stooge, Vidkun Quisling, the leader of the National Socialist Party. King Håkon and most members of the government escaped to Tromsø in northern Norway and remained there while a combined force of British, French, Polish and Norwegian units recaptured the iron-ore port of Narvik. The sudden collapse of France, however, created a greater demand for the expeditionary force elsewhere, so as the Allies withdrew the king and his entourage were evacuated to England.

Neutral throughout the war, Sweden took in 300,000 refugees. The Swedish Red Cross, led by Count Folke Bernadotte, a nephew of the king, secured the release of 30,000 prisoners of various nationalities from German concentration camps, and the diplomat Raoul Wallenberg played "Schindler" to Jews in Hungary. But it was also the case that German troops and materials were given permission to cross Sweden on their way to Norway in 1940 and thereafter when they went on leave. Moreover, Sweden supplied iron ore critical to the German war machine. These are matters which Norwegians to this day cannot easily forget.

Peacetime recovery

The last stage of the war, with German forces scorching the earth in their retreat from the advancing Soviets, hurt northern Norway but

was utterly devastating in Finland. The latter, then, could hardly have been in a worse position to meet Soviet demands for US$600 million in reparations. These were to be paid within 10 years in goods other than what remained of the Finnish economy, namely trees. Barred by Moscow from accepting Marshall aid, Finland nevertheless beat the deadline by creating a diversified industrial economy from scratch.

Reparations out of the way, the bottomless Soviet market kept these new industries – shipbuilding, oil refineries, textiles – working flat out, with the extra bonus that the USSR paid for goods in dirt-cheap oil. So the even-

tual collapse of the Soviet Union was politically a pleasure but at the same time a threat to the Finnish economy – until, among numerous aspects of the country's second economic miracle, Nokia recognised the potential of the mobile phone and Porsche decided to build its new Boxster model in Finland. By the turn of the millennium, Finland was a member of the European Union.

A new way of life

Recovery from the war in Denmark and Norway was set in motion by the Marshall Plan, and within a decade or so they were able to join Sweden in presenting a seemingly united Scan-

RIGHT: the great long-distance runner Paavo Nurmi lights the Olympic flame at the 1952 Helsinki Games.

dinavian front to the outside world. In certain quarters, the image was a paradox, a combination of beautiful and talented people, an enviable standard of living, robust health, exceptional generosity to the Third World – and at the same time rather too much promiscuity, self-righteousness and suicide.

The Scandinavians themselves naturally saw things differently, although a newspaper in Norway might have gone over the top by interpreting the news that suicides had overtaken the number of deaths on the road as a clear indication of improved driving standards. At the heart of all this lay the desire to find a compromise

between capitalism and socialism, in Sweden's case "the Middle Way". While Denmark and Norway joined NATO after the war, Sweden remained nonaligned and spent a huge proportion of the national budget on its arms industry in the belief, or at least hope, that its products would therefore never be required.

To begin with, Scandinavians were willing to live with the punitive taxation needed to cover the cost of their vaunted "cradle-to-grave" social security if only because memories of bitterly hard times without it were still fresh. But if new generations were less susceptible to these fears and consequently concerned about the enormous cost of maintaining the

safety, in Norway and Denmark it suddenly didn't matter. They struck oil.

The new oil-rich nations

Denmark's agriculture was always on its toes. Characteristically quick to breed a pig that produced the streaky bacon popular on British breakfast tables, and companies like Lego, Bang & Olufsen and Carlsberg, which proved adept at exploiting particular market niches, it was the first time the country had enjoyed the luxury of natural resources since the herring shoals in the 14th century. Ironically, Denmark's North Sea windfall arrived in the middle of concerted efforts to start "wind farms", fields full of power-generating turbines.

Measured against population, the prize in Norway was much bigger and triggered fantastic expenditure on items such as long road tunnels through solid rock which served no indispensable purpose that anyone could think of. At one point it looked as if Norway might have blown more oil revenue than existed under the North Sea, but new discoveries, especially of gas, put such fears to rest.

Deprived of any share of the North Sea bonanza, Sweden's Middle Way showed signs of turning into a cul-de-sac. Industry had long been pampered with low taxes on profits while individual taxpayers were bled white. Companies like Volvo had a proud international profile but even they complained loudly of burdens like the costs attached to each employee in the form of national insurance, shorter working weeks, longer holidays and so on. Nevertheless, most Swedes were astonished and dismayed when Saab was swallowed by General Motors, Volvo by Ford, and a regiment of other prestigious companies decamped abroad.

Bridge to the future

While more than one proposed business merger along pan-Scandinavian lines tripped up on mutual misgivings as ancient as the Kalmar Union, the new millennium found a cure for the oldest schism of all. The Øresund road and rail bridge rejoined Denmark and Sweden in 2000, a connection broken by the cataclysmic convulsion at the end of the Ice Age. ❏

LEFT: Olof Palme, prime minister of Sweden and international peace campaigner, assassinated in 1986.
RIGHT: Øresund bridge linking Denmark and Sweden.

ART AND CULTURE

Rich in art, music and literature, and pioneers of modern design,
Scandinavians are justifiably proud of their cultural heritage

The history of Denmark, Norway, Sweden, and Finland has been so intertwined through the centuries that, while each country possesses a unique culture, there are strong similarities, perhaps best seen in design and an overall "feel" for visual expression. A bias towards simplicity pervades with clean lines, natural materials and a lack of pretence.

Although much of what is considered Scandinavian style is a product of the 20th century *(see page 54)* there is an underlying cultural heritage that complements the modern look. Exceptions exist, such as work commissioned by royalty with French design in mind, but the tastes of the people over the past 200 years make the strongest impression on the visitor.

DENMARK

The rich cultural history of Denmark finds expression in centuries-worth of art and artefacts, including Viking treasures, numerous castles and manor houses, churches (many from the Middle Ages), fortresses, stimulating museums, and some of the finest contemporary design in the world.

Denmark's strongest art tradition is literary, reaching back to sagas and medieval folk songs, to the most popular Danish playwright, Ludvig Holberg (1684–1754) in the Age of Enlightenment, the Romantic poet Adam Oehlenschläger (1779–1850) and, in the 19th century, to Hans Christian Andersen (1805–75) and Søren Kierkegaard (1813–55).

Thanks to stories such as *The Little Mermaid*, Andersen is probably the most widely read Danish writer today. His children's tales – including *The Ugly Duckling, The Emperor's New Clothes* and *The Princess and the Pea* – gained him world wide fame, and their popularity has not waned as a source for plays, ballets, films, visual arts and bedtime reading. In

the 20th century, Karen Blixen (1885–1962), working under the pseudonym Isak Dinesen, gained international recognition for her 1937 memoir of her years in Kenya, *Out of Africa*, which became a Hollywood movie in 1985.

The Danish philosopher Søren Kierkegaard, known as the father of existentialism, wrote in

the first half of the 19th century, but his work had the most impact in the mid-20th century, when in translation it became an important source for existentialists.

Masters of dance

More than a third of the state funds allocated for the theatre in Denmark finance the Det Kongelige Teater (Royal Theatre) in Copenhagen, founded in 1748. This building also houses the Royal Danish Opera, the Royal Danish Orchestra and the Royal Danish Ballet. The ballet company, formed 150 years ago, is one of the most influential worldwide. It has attracted great masters such as August Bournonville

PRECEDING PAGES: Norwegian composer Edvard Grieg; *Midnight* by Sweden's Anders Zorn, 1891.
LEFT: *The Girl in the Kitchen,* Anna Ancher, 1883–6.
RIGHT: Karen Blixen, Denmark, author of *Out of Africa.*

(1805–79), creator of today's "classical ballet" and choreographer of more than 50 productions, including the popular *La Sylphide*.

The big screen

Denmark's Nordisk Film Kompagni, founded in 1906, is the oldest film company still in operation. Carl Theodor Dreyer (1889–1968), a master of psychological realism who started his career here, produced classics such as *The Passion of Joan of Arc* (1928) and *The Word* (1955). Today the government-supported Danish Film Institute is the heart of a vibrant Danish film industry. *Babette's Feast* (1986), based

on a story by Karen Blixen, directed by Gabriel Axel, and *Pelle the Conqueror* (1987), directed by Bille August, both won Academy Awards for Best Foreign Film. In the 1990s Lars von Trier's *Breaking the Waves*, Thomas Vinterberg's *The Celebration* and Søren Kragh-Jacobsen's *Mifune's Last Song* have attracted international acclaim. These directors are signatories (along with Kristian Levring) of the Dogma 95 Manifesto. This set of "chastity" rules, which holds that films should be made on location without artificial lighting or sound, using hand-held cameras, was intended as a personal challenge to help to reinvigorate film.

LOUISIANA MUSEUM OF MODERN ART

Small museum treasures may be found throughout Denmark, but the most complete and satisfying of them all is the Louisiana Museum of Modern Art, situated in a sublime spot in Humlebæk, 35 km (22 miles) north of Copenhagen. Louisiana houses a splendid collection of 20th-century art, including pieces by Pablo Picasso, Andy Warhol, Alberto Giacometti and Asger Jorn. It lies on the water's edge, and the extensive sculpture garden, featuring work by Henry Moore and Alexander Calder, that surrounds the unassuming building (much of its space is underground) is backdropped by exquisite coastal scenery and landscaping (www.louisiana.dk).

The Skagen painters

In the visual arts, Denmark's most notable contributions were produced in the 19th and 20th centuries. C.W. Eckersberg (1783–1853), the father of Danish painting, and those who studied under him absorbed the artistic lessons offered from France, particularly a sense of classical nature. At the end of the 19th century, a group of artists – including P.S. Krøyer (1851–1909) and Michael and Anna Ancher (1859–1935) – based themselves in Skagen at the northernmost tip of Jutland. Known as the "Skagen painters", they turned away from Impressionism, the favoured French style of the day, while still being highly indebted to it. Their works captured the special northern light within images of the maritime landscape.

In the middle of the 20th century, Asger Jorn (1914–73), a member of the CoBrA art movement (including artists from Copenhagen, Brussels and Amsterdam), created large, bold, brightly coloured paintings. His expressionistic and experimental works on canvas and ceramics played a key role in the development and promotion of modern Danish art.

SWEDEN

Along with being the conqueror rather than the conquered throughout history, Sweden devel-

King", took many of his cues from the royal court of France and was a great patron of drama and the arts. In 1773, he built the Kungliga Teatern (Royal Theatre, known today as the Royal Opera), and Kunliga Dramatiska Teatern (Royal Dramatic Theatre or *Dramaten*) in 1788. In addition, he hired Swedish actors and singers, forming the basis for a tradition of opera and drama performed in Swedish instead of in the original French or Italian.

The most notable of Swedish dramatic venues is Drottningholms Slottsteater (Drottningholm Court Theatre), in the grounds of Drottningholm Palace outside Stockholm. Built

oped strong cultural traditions, particularly in theatre, music and dance.

Diplomatic as well as commercial ties with European cultural centres provided conduits for importing styles that left their mark on architecture and the performing arts. The prosperity of the Swedish monarchy resulted in the patronage of cultural venues, theatre troupes and court painters. Their private collections became the basis for national art museums.

King Gustav III (1771–92), the "Theatre

LEFT: Drottningholms Slottsteater, near Stockholm, built by "Theatre King" Gustav III in the 18th century.
ABOVE: interior at Sundborn, Sweden, by Carl Larsson.

in 1766 and rediscovered and restored in the mid-20th century, every summer this intimate stage draws spectators from all over the world eager to see Baroque and Rococo productions in an intact 18th-century theatre, complete with original backdrops and stage machinery.

Award-winning writers

One of the best known (at least among Swedes) and still popular writers of the past is Carl Bellman, a troubadour, whose lyrics and poems immortalised daily life in the 18th century.

Works such as *The Red Room* by August Strindberg (1849–1912) and *Gösta Berlings Saga* by Selma Lagerlöf (1858–1940), two of

Cool looks

Say "Scandinavian design"and most people visualise furniture, glass and domestic ware with pure forms and simple, clean lines. The aesthetic is immediately recognisable, especially since the Swedish home-furnishing giant IKEA invaded the world.

Elegant, light, sparse – these are all descriptive of the Scandinavian look – also, a respect for natural materials and superb craftsmanship. The key is not only to look good, it must also be utilitarian. This picture of Scandinavian design, while having

roots in traditional crafts, is very much a product of the 20th century and the age of Functionalism.

Taking off in the 1920s, led by architects and artists such as Le Corbusier in France and Walter Gropius in Germany, Functionalism applies to various movements such as the International Style and Bauhaus. In Scandinavia it has been a source of inspiration since the 1930s.

The move away from ornamentation in favour of clean shapes and lines, allowing for the pure expression of the essence of structures, was more than a mere change in taste. Adherents to this style, which manifested itself in new materials (tubular metal, steel and glass), also embraced a vision for a new world, one where architecture and

design could contribute to the levelling out of injustices in modern society. In Scandinavia, not only were the aesthetics of the modern, international style eagerly adopted, the social agenda behind the style was also very popular.

Earlier in the 1900s, Carl and Karin Larsson, taking their cue from the English Arts and Crafts movement, revived an interest in traditional Swedish crafts and craftsmanship. Their home at Sundborn, now a museum of Swedish country style *(see page 269)*, features textiles with simple checked and striped patterns, against a background of sparse wall designs, wooden floors, striped rag runners and furniture brightened with uncomplicated embellishments.

The influences of Art Nouveau were an important inspiration, but in the hands of Danish designers in the mid-20th century, the fluid lines that had served as mere decoration in southern countries became the impulse behind the quest for a satisfying form that fitted a function, as seen in the chairs of Hans Wegner and Arne Jacobsen from the 1940s and 1950s *(see page 110)*. Designers began to heed ergonomic research long at the service of industrial companies like the car-makers Saab and Volvo. Today, the adage "form follows function" is taken to a high science in Scandinavia. Aesthetics are fused with efficiency for everything from utensils to welding equipment, as seen in the products of Ergonomi Design Gruppen (Sweden). Numerous pieces from the early 20th century remain as popular as ever, for example, stools by the Finnish architect and designer, Alvar Aalto.

The success of Nordic design has made it a standard far beyond the boundaries of Northern Europe – from time-tested pieces, such as the Stokke Tripp Trapp chairs by the Norwegian, Peter Opsvik, to the works of the multitalented Stefan Lindfors, whose output includes designs for Finnish companies Arabia (porcelain) and Marimekko (textiles); from glass and crystal designed for Kosta and Orrefors (Sweden) by Ulrika Hydman-Vallien to Nokia telephones (Finland) by Frank Nuovo.

In a part of the world forsaken by the sun for half the year, Scandinavians exploit interiors to maximise light. Even national characteristics may be seen as a source of style. Just as their design is characterised as rather stark, cool, unadorned, the Scandinavian character is often reserved, sombre – hardly excessively embellished. ❏

LEFT: contemporary furniture design at the Kunstmuseet Trapholt, Kolding, Denmark.

the country's finest writers, set the foundation for modern Swedish literature. Strindberg, whose personal life was marked by a series of failed marriages, alcoholism and instability, produced books, stories and screenplays that often featured social criticism, satire and emotional angst.

The creative output of Lagerlöf, the first woman to win a Nobel prize for Literature (1909), is sharply distinct from Strindberg, depending more on legend, history and tradition, and childhood memories (*Jerusalem*, 1901–02, *The Wonderful Adventures of Nils*, 1906).

Other Swedes have been honoured with Nobel Literature prizes (Verner von Heidenstan, 1909; Erik Axel Karlfeldt, 1931; Pär Lagerkvist, 1951; Eyvind Johnson and Harry Martinson, 1974), and many other novelists have had their work translated for publication abroad, such as Vilhelm Moberg, whose four-volume novel, beginning with *The Emigrants*, is the inspiration for the hit musical *Kristina from Duvemåla*.

Undoubtedly the most widely read Swedish writer, both at home and abroad, is Astrid Lindgren, the indefatigable creative mind behind *Pippi Longstocking*, *Emil in Lönneberga*, and many other free-spirited child heroines and antiheroines.

Swedish design

The "Swedish look", as it is understood today, is greatly indebted to the graphic work and paintings of Carl Larsson (1853–1919) as well as to the design of his home at Sundborn *(see box, page 269)*. Larsson's images are marked by strong outline, subdued colours, and a gentle curvilinear quality.

Today, however, Swedish visual arts are extraordinarily multifaceted and bear little resemblance to preconceived notions of the Swedish look. Artists such as Ann-Sofi Sidén, Elin Wikström and Carl Michael von Hausswolff work in a variety of media, addressing complex contemporary issues. These trends can be seen at the Moderna Museet in Stockholm, which reopened in 1998 in a new building by Rafael Moneo. The museum has a fine collection of modern Swedish and international art.

RIGHT: Ingmar Bergman, internationally acclaimed Swedish playwright and film producer.

> ### THE SOUND OF YOIK
>
> *Yoik* is a form of singing traditional among the Sami. Composed in response to an event or emotion, it sounds like a yodelling chant.

NORWAY

After being a world power during the Viking Age, Norway went through various unions with and occupations by Denmark and Sweden until independence in 1905. Over the centuries the country's culture was suppressed rather than enhanced by those of Denmark and Sweden. Culture with a capital "C" was something the overlords brought with them from foreign capitals. And it was something they took away with them when they left. Under Danish rule Norwegian

> ### INGMAR BERGMAN
>
> Although Sweden was a cinematic powerhouse in the age of silent films, since the advent of sound it has been a relatively small player, with the exception of exports such as Greta Garbo and Ingrid Bergman, and one of the giants of film and theatre, Ingmar Bergman.
>
> Born in 1918, Bergman made his breakthrough with *Smiles of a Summer Night* in 1955. Among his most acclaimed films are *The Seventh Seal* (1956), *Wild Strawberries* (1957) and *Cries and Whispers* (1973). *Fanny and Alexander* (1982) was his final film, but he has remained active in the theatre. His work offers a very personal perspective on what is Swedish, yet universal.

"dialects" were forbidden for official documents and communications. As a result, the heritage of Norwegian culture is identified in the arts and crafts of rural populations.

The recreation of a national identity began in earnest in the 19th century. Not surprisingly, inspiration came from the sublime nature, ancient verbal traditions, and heroic sagas of a mighty Norway and Viking lords of long ago.

Henrik Ibsen (1828–1906), wrote many plays inspired by folklore. His best known works include *Peer Gynt* (1867), *A Doll's House* (1879) and *Hedda Gabler* (1890). Ibsen delved into the individual struggle for freedom and self-knowing. He commented on Norway's relationship with Denmark and Sweden as well on the individual's relationship with a society which would have him conform.

Rustic arts

The country's ancient stave churches represent some of the most distinctive examples of Norwegian artistic production. The rich ornamental carvings on door frames, around windows and on capitals in the interior owe more, stylistically, to the design motifs of the Viking period – dragons, tendrils, leaf patterns – than to Christian iconography found in carvings elsewhere in Europe. The most famous stave churches still standing can be seen in Borgund, Heddal and Urnes.

Another very "Norwegian" visual expression is found in the *rosemaling* or "rose painting" (more aptly called "rustic painting") of which there are as many styles as villages, since each isolated community developed its own interpretation. This decorative painting, used to adorn household utensils as well as interiors, features organic patterns and flowers, figurative representations and even geometric design. Most "genuine" *rosemaling* dates from the early 18th century to the late 19th century, but today many artisans continue the traditions of this very native art.

Golden age of music

Norwegian music flowered in the early 19th century, mainly as a result of the union with Sweden and the influence of the Royal Swedish Court. The violin virtuoso Ole Bull (1810–80), "The Nordic Paganini", proved a model for musicians and writers alike.

The 1870s and 1880s became known as the Golden Age of Norwegian music with such prominent composers as Halfdan Kjerulf (1815–68), Edvard Grieg and Johan Svendsen (1849–1911). Generally, they incorporated elements of folk music in their work, including Grieg (1843–1907), who fused folk music with Romanticism.

Today, Oslo, Trondheim and Bergen all have philharmonic orchestras, and the latter hosts the Bergen International Music Festival each May.

EDVARD MUNCH

Edvard Munch (1863–1944), perhaps Norway's most reproduced artist, is honoured with a museum in Oslo dedicated to his work, as well as an entire floor of the National Gallery.

A forerunner of Expressionism, his introspective, symbolist and angst-ridden paintings and prints, such as *The Scream* (1893), *The Kiss* and *The Vampire* (both 1895), verge on the dark side and are a product of Scandinavian themes, artistic developments in France and Germany where he studied, as well as personal idiosyncrasies and obsessions (Munchmuseet, Oslo; tel: 23 24 14 00; Nasjonalgalleriet, Oslo; tel: 22 20 04 04).

LEFT: *The Scream* by Edvard Munch, 1893.
RIGHT: the Alvar Aalto Museum, Jyväskylä, celebrates the work of Finland's renowned architect-designer.

FINLAND

What may properly be called "Finnish culture" has existed for only a little over a century. Until the late-19th century, the arts in Finland fell under the influence of the invading powers of Sweden and Russia. Prior to Finnish independence (from Russia) in 1917, talented artists and composers normally studied and worked in Stockholm or St Petersburg.

Today, Finnish architecture and design are the nation's most influential cultural exports

> ### TURNING POINT
>
> The 19th-century artist Akseli Gallén-Kallela was a seminal figure in Finnish culture whose contribution laid the foundations for contemporary Finnish design.

(see box, below). Purely modern and very Scandinavian, they combine a love of natural materials and purity of form and functionalism with an exquisite aesthetic.

As is true for all the Nordic countries, the innovations that emanated from France and Germany preoccupied Finland's artists, with Finnish nature and themes lending the art a special character. Albert Edelfelt (1854–1905) was one of the nation's greatest artists of the 19th century. Later the national style created by Akseli Gallén-Kallela

FINNISH ARCHITECTURE AND DESIGN

One of the more prominent architects of Helsinki is Carl Ludwig Engel (1778–1840) from Germany, who designed much of the capital, including Senate Square and the cathedral. But despite the neoclassical imprint of this import, his creations are not representative of what is considered Finnish architecture, which, by many definitions, is no more than a century old.

The National Romanticism of Armas Lindgren (1874–1929), Herman Gesellius (1874–1916) and Eliel Saarinen (1873–1950) defined Finnish architecture of the late 19th and early 20th century, gradually turning from a Gothic look to embrace Art Nouveau.

Alvar Aalto (1898–1976), Finland's most celebrated architect, designed the Finnish Pavilion at the New York World's Fair in 1939, gaining international recognition for himself and the unadorned Functionalist style. He designed many buildings around the world. In Finland he left his mark on housing, schools, governmental and industrial buildings, theatres, churches. His finest building, Helsinki's Finlandia Hall, was built in 1971 during his "white" period.

Possibly Aalto's most indelible imprint on the world is not from architecture but furniture design. His simple solutions for chairs and stools are classics (Alvar Aalto Museo, 7 Alvar Aallonkatu, Jyväskylä; tel: 14 624 809).

(1865–1931) became so popular that Finnish painters in the early 20th century tended to ignore foreign influences. The peasant and the landscape were considered to be representative of true Finnish qualities.

Musical notes

Although Jean Sibelius (1865–1957) still ranks as the most notable Finnish name in music, the contemporary scene is teeming with internationally acclaimed composers, conductors, opera singers and classical

OPERA FESTIVAL

Even the most recalcitrant sopranos come home for the annual Savonlinna Opera Festival. Held in a 500-year-old castle, it is one of the most delightful summer opera festivals in the world.

modern talent. Supporting this talent are numerous professional and semi-professional or chamber orchestras and ensembles. Finnish artists such as the principal conductor Esa-Pekka Salonen, the opera singers Peter Lindroos and Karita Mattila, and cellists Arto Noras and Erkki Rautio appear the world over. At home, musical festivals abound, of which the Savonlinna Opera Festival and the Pori Jazz Festival, both in late July, have become international attractions.

Literary heritage

Precious little writing in the Finnish language exists from prior to the early 19th century. Until Sweden ceded Finland to Russia in 1809, the Swedish language dominated Finnish culture.

In 1835, after many years of studying and collecting folk poetry and ballads, Elias Lönnrot (1802–84) published his remarkable poem, *Kalevala*. The work is a heroic epic on the scale of *The Odyssey* or *The Iliad* as well as a ragbag of narratives and light interludes, existing to preserve old customs and songs. The context – sea, farm, forest – is entirely Finnish.

The *Kalevala* has had an enormous impact on Finnish literature, art and music, not only in the 19th century where it inspired a nationalistic surge in writing in Finnish, but even today it continues to be a source of inspiration.

At the same time that Lönnrot was working, Aleksis Kivi (1834–72) wrote the first proper Finnish novel set in Finland, *Seven Brothers*, which celebrated rural life and contributed to a burgeoning national consciousness. The stage performance of Kivi's *Leah* in the late 19th century marked the beginning of Finnish drama. The Finns love theatre and even amateur groups perform to capacity audiences.

F.E. Sillanpää (1888–1964) took home the country's sole literary Nobel prize, in 1939.

Today, international audiences are probably most familiar with the books about the Moomintrolls by Tove Jansson. However, contemporary literature is vibrant and more introspective and critical than the roots of Finnish literature. ❏

musicians. Sibelius exemplified 19th-century Romanticism in his compositions, which drew inspiration from Finnish nature, folk music and poetry. His career began while Finland was still under Russian rule, and works such as *Finlandia* (1899; revised 1900), provoked such patriotic and nationalistic feelings that they were banned by the Russian authorities. His early symphonies, such as *Kullervo*, used material and motifs from Elias Lönnrot's classic poem *Kalevala*.

A generous policy of funding for musicians, musical institutes (of which there are nearly 130), conservatories and the celebrated Sibelius Academy has spawned a remarkable pool of

LEFT: the composer Jean Sibelius (1865–1957) set the scene for modern music in Finland.
RIGHT: Ingrid Bergman (1915–82), Swedish actress.

FOOD AND DRINK

Brace yourself for a gastronomic treat: fresh seafood, wild berries and succulent mountain meat washed down by fiery aquavit is the order of the day

Scandinavian food gets down to the basics of nature, finding deep flavour in simple and healthy ways. Meats and fish might be smoked, then served with little else than steaming new potatoes, fresh dill, rich butter and tart redcurrants. The general rule says "less is more", and Scandinavian cooks – from the fanciest restaurant to the basic home kitchen – make good use of native fruits and vegetables, grains, fish, meat and game.

Denmark, Sweden, Norway and Finland each have their own food cultures, but they share some gastronomic ground. Seafood is king, and this king spreads its rule into society. In Denmark, for example, model ships hang in every church, as if to remind parishioners to give thanks for the fruits of the sea. The North and Baltic seas have provided a solid economic base for strong fishing industries – and the societies that have revolved around them.

Herring delicacies

Herring might be the fish most associated with the region, and each country prepares it in variations on the same themes: marinated in sugar and vinegar with onions and herbs, or spiced with sandalwood (like *matjes*, which the Swedes frequently eat with boiled potatoes and sour cream); fried and then marinated; seasoned with mustard, curry, or sherry; smoked; salted; or baked. Usually, the dishes are eaten cold, and washed down with aquavit.

A Swedish summertime favourite is the smelly *surströmming*, fermented Baltic herring, eaten with raw onion, cheese and potatoes. Norwegians have a similar dish, *rakfisk*, a pungent cured trout. The uninitiated to these dishes run for cover in the opposite direction.

Other fish have their place on the dinner table or in the finest local restaurants, including plaice, cod, haddock, mackerel and eel. *Klippfisk*, a salty splitcod, is hung and dried in the open air in Norway's coastal villages. Salmon is king in Finland, where it is commonly made into a simple, tasty soup. *Fraavi lohi*, salmon marinated for a day in salt and herbs, is sometimes called the Finnish version of *sushi*. Danes, Swedes and Norwegians eat sweet, cured gravlax as a lunch-time delicacy.

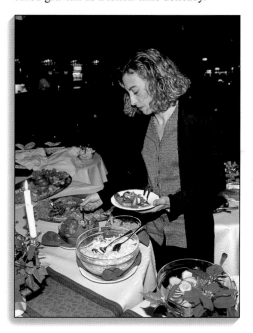

Feasting on open sandwiches

Fish is the focus of a Danish or Swedish lunchtime feast. In Denmark the *smørrebrød* (open sandwiches) start with rye bread. Extremely dense and packed with all kinds of seeds and grains, this bread could be used to build walls if one ran out of bricks. Sliced and spread with goose lard or butter, the Danish rye is topped with arty combinations of foods and eaten with knife and fork.

Some restaurants, most notably Ida Davidsen in Copenhagen, feature *smørrebrød* menus on scrolls several feet long. But certain unwritten rules apply to the feast, even at home: "You must have two or three kinds of herring,"

LEFT: an appetising spread of seafood and smoked meat toppings for Danish open sandwiches.
RIGHT: a Scandinavian buffet-style *smörgåsbord*.

explains Hanne Christensen from Funen. Her husband, Carl, adds that fiery shots of cold aquavit must "go down like hail stones".

"Then you need a little warm dish, like fried fish with lemon and remoulade," Hanne says.

"Sliced meats," adds Carl. "Small tenderloin steaks. Danish meatballs with red cabbage."

"And then cheese and fruit salad at the end," says Hanne.

The Swedish and Finnish *smörgåsbord* are equally artistic and elegant, with cold and hot dishes – similar to those eaten at a Danish lunch – laid out buffet-style on a table, to which guests visit five times. Special to these coun-tries are dishes such as roasted reindeer, Swedish meatballs and a baked anchovy-potato-cream casserole called "Jansson's Temp-tation". The Finnish dishes tend to be less sweet than those in Sweden, and Finns serve a greater variety of bread.

In Norway, a large selection of breads and toppings comes at breakfast, *frokost*, with copi-ous amounts of cold meats, crispbreads, cheeses, caviar from a tube and black coffee. *Myseost* is a food of national pride, a type of brown, sweet, goats' and cows' milk cheese flavoured lightly with caramel. At home and at celebrations Norwegians also enjoy *rømme*, a

SKÅL! TO THE SPIRIT OF LIFE

No herring dish in Scandinavia is complete without aquavit, literally "water of life". Distilled from potatoes or grain and flavoured with a variety of herbs and seasonings – such as caraway seed, cumin, fennel, dill or St Johnswort – ice cold aquavit warms the body (and mood). One of the best versions is Norway's Løiten Linie, which is matured partly by a sea voyage in oak casks across the equator and back (each bottle carries details of its "voyage" on the label). The Finns tend to pour bigger glasses of the drink, but they are also masters at distilling and drinking vodka.

To gain instant friends in Scandinavia, lift your drink and say the word for cheers: *"skål"* (pronounced *"skoal"*). The correct way to *skål* is to look at the person, say the word, lift the glass slightly, drink and look at the person again. There are some rules about when to *skål* at formal occasions. Never drink until the host has given a welcome toast. A gentleman must ensure that the woman on his right has something on her plate and in her glass. She must be the first he *skåls*, followed by the woman on his left. The host will *skål* each guest. The hostess may also *skål* her guests. It is not good form to *skål* a person who is older or of higher rank. Let them take the initiative and return the gesture within three minutes. A gentleman should *skål* the man sitting on the left of his partner, as well as her.

thick and extremely rich porridge made from cream, butter and milk. At Easter, the Finns eat *mämmi*, a whipped rye and malt porridge that takes up to a day to make.

Sausage fare

Sausage is common in all four countries, and its flavour and consistency depends upon the region where it is made. In Tampere in southwest Finland, *mustamakkara* (black sausage) is flavoured with spices, barley and blood. The Danes also make a blood sausage, *blødpølse*, which is seen commonly

CRAYFISH SEASON

Crayfish is eaten widely in Finland and Sweden in July and August, where it is boiled and peeled and served at outdoor parties.

ney and cooked for hours at a time, is another Finnish speciality.

Fruits of the forest

Along the same lines, nearly all Scandinavians do a hunting of a different sort in the summer and autumn – that is for mushrooms, which appear in several dishes, or berries (from raspberries to cloudberries and blueberries). Some restaurants have even gained fame for their use of foraged foods sold to them by local enthusiasts, fresh back from the woods or heath.

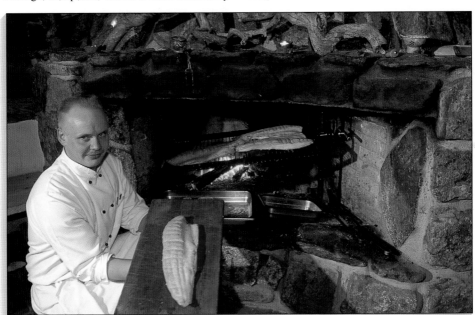

around Christmas; the south Jutland *ølpølse* (beer sausage) is a tasty snack found at the local butcher. Swedes eat little pork links (*prinskorv*) at a *smörgåsbord*.

Besides elk and venison, the Norwegians, Swedes and Finns eat reindeer, which can be found on the menus of fine restaurants – as well as stocked up in freezers across the area.

After a trek in the Finnish wilderness, try the hearty *poronkäristys* (reindeer casserole). Karelian stew, made of meats, liver and kid-

FAR LEFT: Norway's celebrated Løiten Linie aquavit.
LEFT: Danish open sandwiches *(smørrebrød)*.
ABOVE: baked salmon is popular in Finland.

Sweet treats

It nearly goes without saying that the Danish pastry, *weinerbrød*, became famous for a reason. When in Denmark, visit a bakery and try a rich, chewy "chocolate snail" pastry in the morning, or a layered cream cake in the afternoon. Danish waffle cones filled with ice cream, marshmallow topping and marmalade are also not to be missed.

The Finns eat *pulla* (wheat buns) with their coffee and indulge in cream cakes topped with strawberries. In Skåne in southern Sweden, *spettkaka* is a local speciality, a tower-shaped confectionery of sugar, eggs and potato flour baked over an open fire. ❏

THE GREAT OUTDOORS

Scandinavians are passionate about nature and the outdoor life.
Unfazed by the weather they hike, ski, skate, sail, fish and climb

The people of the Nordic countries are so at home in their natural surroundings that they seldom pause to consider how intertwined their daily lives are with the climate, the seasons, and the amazing and diverse beauty of the northern landscape. In winter, they take to their skis to traverse fields and forests, and pull on skates to blaze paths across icy lakes. They'll fish through the ice and even climb a frozen waterfall. Winter poses no obstacle to the hardy Scandinavian. In spring and summer, the mountains will beckon backpackers to scale their heights while the Swedish archipelago will be dotted with thousands of sailing boats, and the forests of the Nordic countries will be full of berry-pickers, picnickers, and hikers.

Danes will head for their magnificent beaches while Swedes, Norwegians, and Finns will celebrate the cool refreshing plunge of the thousands of lakes that dot the landscape. Come autumn, the people of the Nordic lands are combing the forests for mushrooms and admiring the gold- and red-hued foliage of the forest.

For Scandianvians, the great outdoors is a reflection of their national identity, an expression of their individuality and sporting spirit, and a valuable national asset that they will go to great lengths to protect. Some of the world's strongest green movements are to be found in Denmark, Sweden, Norway and Finland.

Country retreats

In a region where winter days are short and nasty weather can crop up any time of the year, comfort translates to secure shelter, often your own. A quarter of Norway's households own a holiday home, or *hytte*, a cottage or cabin.

In Sweden, many families save for years in order to buy a *stuga* (cottage) in the country or on the coast. Others are lucky enough to have inherited their little spot in a meadow. Most

LEFT: Norway, Sweden and Finland offer exciting opportunities for winter sports enthusiasts.
RIGHT: jet-boarding off Bornholm, Denmark.

Swedes are only a generation or two away from rural life and many have relatives who still live in their original home districts.

At the water's edge

Denmark and Sweden offer varied coastlines and a beach-life that is unique to each coun-

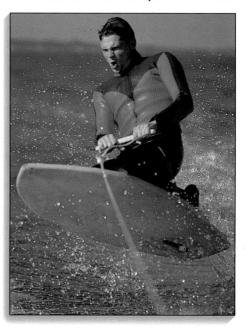

try's topography. There are 8,000 km (5,000 miles) of coastline in Sweden, offering clean, if often chilly, water to swim in, and rocks to sun on (but few sandy beaches). The most spectacular seascape is the Stockholm archipelago, with its 24,000 islands, but nearly as thrilling are the waves crashing on the rocks of Bohuslän's archipelago.

The Danes, on the other hand, are blessed with sandy beaches. With more than 7,400 km (4,600 miles) of coastline, the waters surrounding Denmark are a playground for outdoor activities. No point in the country is more than a 45-minute drive from the sea and many inland waterways or fjords are even closer.

Kayaks, canoes, rowing boats, smaller sailing or motor craft may be hired at resorts along the coasts or on the larger lakes. The air is hardly still in Denmark, and the windsurfing is excellent. Seasoned surfers may prefer the exhilaration of the North Sea, while beginners can try their hand in the lee of a fjord, bay or on a lake.

Norway has its fjords, which can be explored by steamers in summertime. In winter, when the fjords freeze over, families take Sunday "walks" on skates among the rocks and islets. Increased tourism along Finland's lake system is bringing the steamers back into business. There are now regular passenger routes on several of the lake systems, but the oldest and probably the most romantic are those across Saimaa's vast expanse.

Hitting the trails

The Nordic region is known for its great open landscapes and is a mecca for hikers and backpackers. The greatest proportion of Sweden is virgin country. You can stroll for miles along tracks without seeing another human being, or drive a car on serpentine gravel roads and never have to pass another vehicle, or cycle through untouched land on special bicycle trails.

Norwegians are quite at home in their wild,

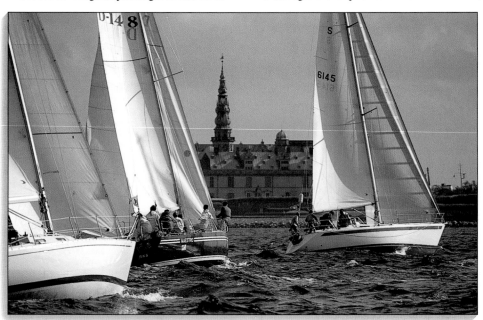

FREEDOM TO ROAM

The freedom to explore nature is considered a birth-right of most Scandinavians, and the politicians have seen fit to put that inheritance into law. Since 1957 Norway has had a *Lov om friluftslivet* (Outdoor Recreations Act), which states succinctly that: "At any time of the year, outlying property may be crossed on foot, with consideration and due caution."

In Sweden, it's called *Allemansrätten* (Everyman's Right), an old custom that permits you to camp any-where for a night, or to walk, ski or paddle a canoe anywhere, as long as the area is not fenced in or in close proximity to a private home.

unspoilt country, and have a great feeling for its mountains. Finland also offers pristine wilderness, quaint historical attractions, peace and quiet and free access to practically any-where – all forests are potentially yours for trekking, berry- and mushroom-picking or short-term camping.

The Danish countryside is a appealing patch-work of dense forests, coastal dunes, marshes, moors and meticulously manicured farmland. In every type of landscape walkers will find paths or trails that stretch for miles, and a labyrinth of winding country roads.

Throughout Sweden, there's an excellent network of waymarked footpaths. Close to

Stockholm is the 850-km (530-mile) Sörm-landsleden (Sörmland Route), starting at Björkhagen underground station. Carefully laid out, the trail offers hikers constantly changing vistas of deep forest, historic sites, lookout points and lakes. It passes several camps where you can eat, rest and buy supplies, with shelters at regular intervals. Sörm-landsleden is an easy hike, but it offers plenty of excitement. You rarely meet another soul, particularly in spring, autumn and winter, but you will spot deer, elk, capercaillie, hawks and grouse. The area is full of mushrooms and berries to pick. For the most exotic views, however, head for the Kungsleden (Royal Route) which runs for more than 500 km (300 miles) from Abisko to Hemavan.

Waymarked footpaths are found in the more scenically outstanding areas like the national parks. These areas are often well away from towns and villages, and as a result many of them have a chain of mountain stations set a day's walk from one another along the footpaths, providing shelter for walkers. Most of the mountain stations are equipped with cooking facilities, a shop and comfortable beds. Some even have a self-service restaurant and a sauna. They are not hotels, but simple accommodation designed to provide a haven at the end of the day for tired walkers.

In Norway, the bulk of the trails and lodges are conveniently in the middle of the triangle bounded by the cities of Oslo, Bergen and Trondheim. A central entry point is Finse, situated above the timber line at 1,200 metres (4,000 ft). Finse's main street is the station platform; there are no cars because there are no roads. When a train has gone and the last passengers have left, Finse returns to normal, a speck in a seemingly infinite expanse of rock, ice and snow.

Accessible mountaineering

To the north of Finse lie the Jotunheimen mountains, the range that took its name from Norse mythology, literally "Home of the Giants". The name is appropriate: peaks jut a

---

LEFT: the "Sjaelland Rundt" yacht race circumnavigates the Danish island of Zealand.
RIGHT: climbing in the mountains of Norway.

FOLLOW THE SIGNS

In Sweden and Norway, the extensive networks of walking and hiking trails are marked by a red "T". Lodges and cabins offer accommodation along the way.

kilometre and more skywards from lake-studded, moraine-strewn flats, all above the timber line. Nonetheless, even the loftiest of the Jotunheimen peaks, Galdhøpiggen and Glittertind, which are the highest in Northern Europe with summits rising more than 2,400 metres (7,900 ft), rank low on the international scale of noteworthy mountains where sheer altitude, not challenge, is the main criterion. Though this fact has led to relative anonymity – few Norwegian peaks appear in the classic mountaineering literature

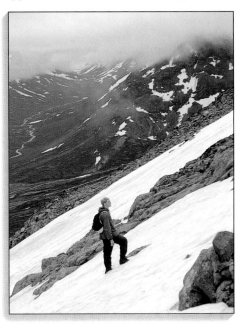

– it does mean that you can ascend the equivalent of the Matterhorn or Mont Blanc without having to cope with the problems of altitude. Most Jotunheimen trails meander from around 900–1,200 metres (3,000–4,000 ft) above sea level and there are no acclimatisation problems at that height.

Some of the glaciers that hewed the Norwegian landscape left offspring. One, Jostedalsbreen (Jostedal Glacier), is the largest on the mainland of Europe. Jostedalsbreen and its siblings throughout the country are the places to see crampon-shod parties wielding ice axes from spring until autumn.

Contact with the ice that shaped their land is

currently the Norwegians' fastest growing wilderness recreation and many centres now organise specialist courses.

Wilderness experience

In Finland, you can enjoy some of the region's best hiking along the Karelian Circle Trek, Finland's longest trekking route with approximately 1,000 km (620 miles) of marked trails. The Karelian Circle Trek offers genuine wilderness routes, variety in four different national parks, and the possibility to combine walking with mountain biking or canoeing. Fishing gear is common, and some even carry a hunting gun.

This is a friendly wilderness, with no fear of dangerous wild animals. Bed-and-breakfast accommodation is available, as are free wilderness huts (or ones that have to be reserved in advance). Pitching a tent is legal (and free) almost everywhere along this route.

On two wheels

Visitors to Denmark will notice within minutes of their arrival two signs of the country's greenness: windmills and bicycles. Windmills dot the landscape – including the area around Copenhagen's airport – churning out clean energy. The bicycle, meanwhile, is an important mode

NATIONAL PARKS

The Nordic region has many national parks, each with its own claim to unique native flora and fauna. Hiking trails are marked and it's often possible to engage a guide. Large areas of Norway have been designated as national parks to protect special habitats and support biodiversity.

In Sweden, strict laws protect the rarer mammals such as the bear, wolf, wolverine, lynx, musk-ox, Arctic fox and otter. Among the more common animals, roe deer live in the forest and only in Scandinavia will you see the traffic sign "Danger, Elk". National parks cover highland and lowland regions. To see herbaceous flora and listen to birdsong in Sweden, Dalby Söderskog near Lund in Skåne

is at its best in the spring, while Store Mosse in Småland is worth a detour for birdwatchers interested in whooper swans, marsh harriers and cranes.

Denmark's national parks include the heather-covered Svanninge Bakker on Funen and the beech and conifer woods of Rebild Bakker in North Jutland.

Finland's park network is mostly administered by the Forest and Park Service, which controls 29 national parks, including the rugged rift valley of Hiidenporrttin Kansallispuisto in Karelia and the Ramsholmen Nature Reserve on the Åland Islands. The organisation rents interesting accommodation in isolated wilderness cottages.

of transport for Danes and visitors alike. Bikes outnumber cars in some city areas, where the streets have bicycle lanes and traffic lights.

Denmark has thousands of miles of foot and bike paths and bikes may be taken on most trains and ferries. Tourist offices can provide detailed maps of routes. Hærvejen is a bicycle and walking trail that stretches from the German border to Viborg in north-central Jutland. Traders and travellers beat this path a few thousand years ago, and much of it still looks as it did during Viking times. All along the route there are inns, hotels or hostels, as well as shops for provisions.

there is the Sverigeleden (Sweden Bicycle Route), from Stockholm to Göteborg – a distance of 2,576 km (1,600 miles).

Cast your line

Anglers are beginning to appreciate the wealth of excellent fishing that Scandinavia provides.

One of the most remarkable and most accessible places to fish is right in the centre of Stockholm, in the fast-moving Strömmen channel which links the fresh water of Lake Mälaren with the Baltic Sea. A clean-up programme has brought salmon and sea trout back to the very heart of the capital. What is more, the fishing

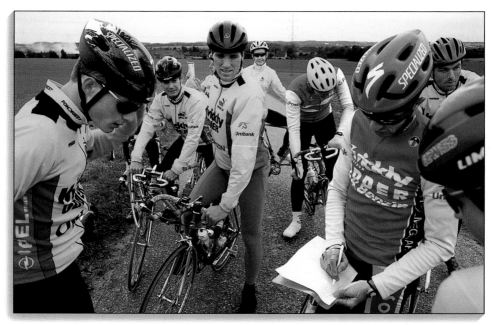

Cycling and, in recent years, mountain biking, are also popular outdoor sports for Swedes, and there are many well-designed and well-lit cycle routes all over the country. You could spend a week touring the island of Gotland on a bike. Keen cyclists also head for Östergötland, particularly along the banks of the Göta Kanal where the towpaths make ideal cycling tracks. Bikes can be hired at several places, and the most popular route for cyclists is between Berg and Borensberg. For the truly ambitious,

here is completely free of charge. Big salmon and sea trout can also be caught almost anywhere in Sweden – in world-famous waters like the Mörrum river in southern Sweden and, above all, in the large and wild rivers of northern Sweden, as well as along the coast when the fish are on their migration.

The salmon season varies between rivers, but it usually starts during the summer and continues well into the autumn. The sea trout tend to arrive a little later. Both spinning and fly-fishing can produce good salmon catches, but sturdy tackle is advised.

To Norwegians, fish is the standby staple. Even in modest markets, the variety of fish and

LEFT: the wide open spaces of northern Sweden and Finland offer superb wilderness trekking.
ABOVE: the Danes and Swedes are keen cyclists.

Life in Lapland

They call themselves "the people of the eight seasons". They are the Sami who live in Sweden, Norway, and Finland's most northerly provinces: vast wildernesses where nature and reindeer set the course of the year. Traces of their presence stretch back more than 8,000 years. They have their own language, religious traditions, and customs. While the life of the Sami has changed in modern times, the annual cycle of the reindeer – rutting, herding, separating, slaughtering, calving, marking – continues to shape the Lap-

land calendar. The winter round-ups are among Europe's most colourful events, resembling scenes from a Wild West film transposed to an Arctic setting. Visitors can enjoy this ancient culture at festivals and ceremonial occasions held throughout the year, where one can sample reindeer delicacies and marvel at Sami handicrafts.

A vivid way to experience the Sami lifestyle and landscape is to get outdoors. In spring and summer the mountains blossom with Sami heather, globe flowers, cloudberries and countless other species, inviting the visitor to take to the trails and woods of the many national parks in the Sami regions of Scandinavia. One not to miss is Padjelanta, the biggest national park in Europe. The name comes

from a Sami word that means "the higher mountain", and it is one of Sweden's most beautiful areas, with rolling plains, gently rounded mountain massifs, and huge lakes, such as Vastenjaure and Virihaure. Almost the entire park is above the tree line. There are many small streams, which the Lapps call *jok*, and it has always been an important pasture for their reindeer herds.

For golf enthusiasts, nothing can quite top the thrill of golfing under the Midnight Sun in the glorious days of summer, where (depending on latitude and cloud cover) the sun is visible for up to 70 summer days. Anglers will find a true paradise in the primeval wilderness of the north, laced by swift rivers and streams and punctuated by lakes and pools. Big salmon and sea trout can be caught almost anywhere in northern Scandinavia.

To enjoy the wintry wilderness in an entirely different way, try dog-sledging, which is offered by many firms in northern Scandinavia. Drive the dog-sledge yourself or sit back in the vast silence of the mountains and be driven by a team of huskies. Your guide will tell you how to take care of a sledge dog and share bits of trivia, like the fact that in the Inuit language there are 18 different words for snow. Dog-sledging, common in Greenland, is now well established in Sweden and is growing in popularity in Finland's northern wilderness.

The Sami winter vistas can also be enjoyed on reindeer sleigh rides and snowshoe treks. Ice climbing is popular, too. Fishing through the ice is common on most lakes and rivers.

To really soak up the hard life of the Sami, the visitor can stay in the world's largest igloo, the Jukkasjärvi Ice Hotel in Sweden. Each autumn, as the Arctic temperature plummets, Laplanders rebuild this celebrated igloo from 1,000 tons of ice and 2,000 tons of snow. Inside it houses a church, hotel, gallery, golf room, cinema and bar named appropriately Absolut Ice. Guests sleep in warm sleeping bags on mattresses of spruce bough and reindeer skins. Temperatures average –4°C (25°F). The hearty fare served from the kitchen and the activities waiting outdoors don't leave guests much time to feel cold. Next morning, the hotel will issue a certificate of survival. It's not quite the same as herding reindeer, but it brings you one step closer to understanding how climate, custom, and sheer human persistence have made the Sami what they are today. ❏

LEFT: a young Sami boy from northern Sweden dressed for winter in a traditional pom-pom hat.

fish products is amazing, and Norwegians look on a proper fresh fish shop as an asset to a community. It is not surprising, then, that Norway is a country of fishermen of all kinds, both commercial fishermen and anglers.

The long coastline is a mecca for saltwater angling, yet freshwater angling is the more popular pastime, and there are a quarter of a million fishable inland lakes and ponds. The most common of around 40 freshwater species are trout and char; in the northernmost parts, and in lakes and ponds at higher elevations, they are the only fish. Grayling and pike are more common in larger lakes and rivers in eastern and central areas.

Ice fishing is a prime winter-time hobby. It's a straightforward form of angling, which requires only a baited hand line or short pole and line, warm clothing, and lots of patience.

Sporting nations

Norway, Denmark and Finland consider sport both a pleasure and an athletic pursuit. Sweden is one of the world's most sporting nations, with nearly half the population engaged in some form of sport or outdoor recreation. One in four Norwegians competes in a sport.

From the broad base of people for whom sport is a major leisure activity come the élite, competitors who enter the many national championships and represent their countries in international sports meetings. In Sweden, great athletes like Björn Björg have made Swedish tennis prowess legendary.

The runner, Paavo Nurmi (1897–1973), put Finland on the map, breaking multiple world records and winning four gold medals, Nurmi first competed in the 1920 Olympics. Variously known as the Flying Finn, the Phantom Finn and the Phenomenal Finn, he is still remembered for his extraordinary running style, speed, and tough character. These days the Finns are better known for being world-class rally drivers. Tommi Mäkinen, Ari Vatanen and Hannu Mikkola may be known only to lovers of motor sports, but probably more non-Finns could

---

RIGHT: the Scandinavian countries are an angler's dream with numerous lakes, rivers and a varied coastline all offering a good catch.

> **TEEING OFF**
>
> Golf is the fastest-growing sport in Scandinavia, and its popularity has exploded in Denmark in recent years. In Scandinavia's far north enthusiasts like to play golf under the Midnight Sun.

name one of these sportsmen than could identify Finland's current prime minister.

Traditionally, Norwegian prowess has been in winter sports and in sailing, but Norwegians have also won international medals in a wide range of events, including marathon running, cycling, boxing, wrestling, handball, karate, canoeing, rowing, shooting, weight lifting and women's football.

All the Nordic countries share the European passion for football. Clubs are supported

through funds from the football pools and from the sale of players to major European leagues, in particular the English Premier League.

Winter sports

Not surprisingly, given the long winters and the beckoning snow-topped mountains, Swedes, Norwegians and Finns all excel at winter sports.

Downhill skiing in Sweden attracts a growing number of visitors thanks to the more reliable snowfall, the reduced risk of avalanches compared to Alpine resorts, and the variety of slopes. While slalom champion Ingemar Stenmark put Sweden on the international skiing map, it is Pernilla Wiberg, the World and

Olympic champion skier, who is keeping the country in the spotlight. As a result, Swedish downhill resorts such as Åre and Björkliden attract skiers from all over Europe. Sälen is the largest ski resort in Sweden with various Alpine and cross-country skiing facilities. World Cup Ski Championships are held in Åre, so there are hundreds of top-class, superbly groomed pistes served by high-speed lifts and cabins. Half-pipes and snow parks are available for snowboarding fanatics.

Norway has witnessed a reawakening of interest in the style of skiing called Telemark, which evolved in Morgedal, in the southern

county of Telemark. In the mid-1800s, Sondre Norheim, a young farmer, devised bindings (devices that hold ski boots to skis) that were firm and were the first to give the feet control over the skis. He also gave the skis what is known as "sidecut", the slight hourglass profile of a ski seen from above. Sidecut is what enables skis to run true and turn easily, even to this day.

Norheim and his fellow Morgedal skiers used the new designs to perfect new skiing manoeuvres, including landing from airborne flights off snow-covered rooftops and natural outcrops. Soon, they were ready to show off their new skills and this led to the first ski-

jumping contest in 1879. The bent-knee stance with one ski trailing soon became known as the "Telemark".

In modern Telemark skiing, the heel is free to lift up from the ski and turns are steered, with one ski trailing and at an angle to the other. Competitive Telemark ski races are now held on packed slopes, as are Alpine ski races, but true Telemark skiing has spawned the revival of skiathlons, in which competitors must ski jump, ski through a slalom course, and run a cross-country ski race, all on the same pair of skis.

The Vasaloppet

Another world-famous ski competition takes place in Mora, in the Dalarna region of Sweden. The Vasaloppet, a 53-mile (85-km) cross-country skiing race, is the most popular sporting event in the country. It is held every March to commemorate King Gustav Vasa's flight from his enemies in the 16th century. Each year the race includes more than 15,000 competitors, who in the past have included the present king, Carl XVI Gustaf. The first Vasaloppet was run on 19 March 1922. A victory in Vasaloppet is regarded by most of the world's best skiers as highly as a podium place in the Olympic games or the World Championships.

Skiing is also one of the top sports in Finland, and the sport most readily associated with this snow-covered nation. Along with its Scandinavian neighbours, Finland has produced champion cross-country and downhill skiers, who benefit from an extended winter season in which to perfect their sport.

Skiing is not the only winter sport in which the nation excels. Ice hockey is one of the most important team sports in Finland. Almost all males participate at school, and the élite are filtered through and chosen for the best teams. Ice hockey is highly commercialised: one of the leading teams, Jokerit (the Jokers, referring to a deck of cards rather than humour) is run like a large company. Teams in Helsinki, Tampere and Turku are usually the best and spectators can number up to 10,000 for a game. Many Finns play in the North American NHL and many foreigners play in Finnish teams. ❑

LEFT: skiing, both downhill and cross-country, is a national sport in Norway, Sweden and Finland.
RIGHT: hikers enjoy the solitude of the far north.

PLACES

A detailed guide to the Scandinavian countries, with principal sites cross-referenced by number to the maps

Whether you're in a car or coach, on a bicycle, boat or train, on foot or on skis, the Scandinavian countries of Denmark, Norway, Sweden and Finland have an enormous variety of sights and scenery to beguile the visitor.

Denmark is neatly beautiful rather than grand, with its white sand beaches, well-groomed farmland and gentle hills. Nurtured by the mild climate, the countryside in spring glows with fruit blossom and sharp yellow rape seed, and in late summer with the golden tinge of harvest fields. Brightly painted half-timbered buildings echo nature's colours and Renaissance castles dot the landscape. Copenhagen is one of Europe's most enjoyable cities, a relaxed place with pedestrianised streets, pavement cafés, superb shops and enterainment. This is the cultural as well as the political capital, but every Danish town has its museum and art gallery, every castle its collection.

Far out to sea, remote from the rest of Scandinavia but part of the Danish realm, lie the Faroe Islands – a paradise for bird-watchers – and Greenland, a fascinating destination for the adventurous.

As if to compensate for the flatter terrain of its neighbours, Norway is made up of mountains, not craggy like the Alps, but curved and etched with beautiful fjords and dramatic valleys. From the beaches and pastures of the south, the coastline stretches far north to the Arctic Circle and beyond, dotted with islands, fishing villages and historic towns such as Bergen. Inland, the rugged landscape beckons walkers and skiers. The capital, Oslo, offers all the attractions of a European city, but with a very Norwegian imprint.

A short journey from Copenhagen across the new Øresund bridge brings you to southern Sweden, the rolling landscape of Skåne and the sunny islands of Öland and Gotland. At the heart of Sweden lie two vast lakes, Vänern and Vättern linked by the Göta Kanal, a pleasure-boaters' mecca. Further north the folklore province of Dalarna gives way to lakes and forests, winter-sports centres and the rugged landscape of Lapland. Stockholm lies majestically on an archipelago of Baltic islands, the most sophisticated of the Scandinavian capitals.

For many centuries Finland came under Sweden's wing; later the Russians took control. Remnants of both cultures can be found, but with independence Finland's own identity has emerged. The south coast is a summer playground of islands and beaches, fortresses and painted towns. The capital, Helsinki, with its wealth of architecture, new and old, is known as the "Daughter of the Baltic". Lakes and forests cover central Finland, while easterly Karelia is a hiker's delight. Lapland, land of the Midnight Sun, attracts anglers, white-water enthusiasts and those in search of true peace and solitude. ❑

PRECEDING PAGES: modern reproductions of typical Norwegian boats at the Sunmore Boat Museum, Ålesund.
LEFT: the spectacular Dalsnibba panorama at Geirangerfjord, Norway.

Scandinavia

0   100 km

0   100 miles

N

NORWEGIAN
SEA

BARENTS SEA

Arctic Circle

Murmansk

Moncegorsk
Apatity

Pecenga
Kirkenes
Vardø

Umbs

Ozero
Imandra

Ozero
Ozero

Kandalaksa

Tikhozero

Ozero
Pyaozero

Ozero
Topozero

Ozero
Srednyeye
Kuyto

RUSSIA

Kostomuksha

Vadsø

Honningsvåg
Nordkapp

Inarijärvi

98

Ivalo

E75

Kemijoki

Kuusamo

Kuhmo

Nurmes
Pielinen

Lieksa

Teisozero

Hammerfest

Alta

E 6

Lokan
tekojärvi

Kittilä

Sodankylä

Kemijärvi

E 75

Muonio

Rovaniemi

81

FINLAND

Puolanka

Oulujärvi

20

Oulu

E 63

5

4

Kajaani

Iisalmi

E 75

Tromsø

E 8

E 6

Kautokeino

E 8

45

Karnträsk

Kiruna

E 10

Kebnekaise
▲
2117

NORWAY

Galllivare

E 10

E 8

Tornio

Kemi

Torneälven

Boden

Luleå

Piteå

Perämeri
Bottenviken

Kokkola

Harstad

Andenes

Vesterålen

Narvik

Svolvær

Lofoten

Vestfjorden

E 6

E 10

Fauske

Bodø

Stora
Lulevatten

Pileälven

97

Skellefteå

95

Umeå

E 4

Hornavan

Storuman

Uddjaure

45

Umeälven

Mo i Rana

Mosjøen

Sandnessjøen

E 6

Hornavan

Malgomaj

E 12

45

SWEDEN

E 6

Steinkjer

Levanger

Trondheim

Kristiansund

DENMARK

Small, but perfectly formed, Denmark is a country of
fun-loving, environmentally conscious people

Hamlet was wrong – there is nothing rotten in the State of Denmark. Yes, the winters can be dreary, but they're not biting cold and there is little snow – the Danes go to Sweden and Norway to ski – and summers can be sunny, with long hours of daylight. Yes, the tax rate is among the world's highest. But taxes are reinvested to help make this a country "where few have too much and fewer too little".

The world's oldest kingdom may be no empire as of yore, but the sons of those Vikings continue to pack plenty of clout. These days they're spreading their seed far and wide in canisters of frozen nitrogen: Denmark is the biggest supplier of meticulously screened and frozen human sperm on the planet – and a major purveyor of computer elements and electronic devices, windmills, agricultural products, arts and crafts and skilled professionals.

Denmark is also a nation of cyclists (two-wheelers outnumber bipeds) and recyclers – more than half the country's rubbish is turned into district steam heat for homes and other new things, nuclear plants excepted. Natural gas and windmills are the preferred energy sources of this windy country.

Nowhere is very far away, especially now that a network of motorways, railway lines and spectacular bridges link west to east from Germany, through Denmark to Copenhagen and across the Øresund to Sweden. Ferries still play their part, linking islands and crossing "fjords" as the Danes call their larger lakes, for this is a nation with a strong seafaring past.

Zealand, in the east, holds the capital, Copenhagen, Scandinavia's liveliest city, and Hamlet's castle, Kronborg at Helsingør (Elsinore). Jutland, in the west, is Denmark's link with mainland Europe. The North Jutland seascapes have captivated artists over the centuries; west-coast sands stretching as far as the eye can see draw summer holiday-makers. East Jutland has an intricate lake system, well-used for canoeing and water sports, and also Århus, Denmark's second city, with an international arts festival in the autumn. Funen, sandwiched between Jutland and Zealand, is the "garden of Denmark", with Odense, the birthplace of Denmark's most famous writer, Hans Christian Andersen. Out in the Baltic is the island of Bornholm, home to craftspeople and a popular holiday destination.

Far to the west and north lie the outposts of the Danish kingdom; the windswept Faroe Islands ("Sheep Islands"), a favourite haunt for birdwatchers; and Greenland, a true adventure travel destination offering stunning scenery and a pristine natural environment. ❏

PRECEDING PAGES: mustard field, Djursland; Den Gamle By, the historic old town of Århus, Jutland; Valdemars Slot (Castle) on the island of Tåsinge, Funen Archipelago.
LEFT: Amagertorv and the Stork Fountain in Copenhagen's main shopping area.

THE DANES

They're generally warm, witty and welcoming. But they can also be cool and reserved. It depends where you meet them

Danes have two reputations in the world; one at home and another abroad. Outside their homeland, Danes are known as warm, curious, friendly, funny, charming. In their modest way, Danish travellers bring on laughs and a sense of pure enjoyment for life. They try not to act too offended when, outside Europe, one too many people ask: "Is Denmark the capital of Sweden?" or "What language do you speak – Dutch?" A short, firm geography lesson is given on the spot, but modesty usually prevents the Dane to say that Denmark is the oldest monarchy in the world, dating from AD 935.

At home, Danes are seen by foreign visitors as distant, sombre, even cold. They keep to themselves. Danes blame this image on the wet, cool climate. "Not much of our social life happens on the pavements or out in front of the home," says Frans Kjær Nielsen, a teacher. "We spend much of our time indoors with our families and friends."

Cosiness prevails

Inside this thin barrier of social contact, Denmark is one of the warmest countries in the world. People are genuine. They speak their minds. They thrive on making life cosy, relaxing and enjoyable – from festive occasions to mundane coffee breaks. This is what Danish *hygge* is all about. *Hygge* (pronounced **whoo-guh**) stands for any and every sense of cosiness, and it is found everywhere in Denmark. A good meal has *hygge*, a house can have *hygge*, a story, a walk in the woods, a meeting at a café, even a person can have *hygge*.

Parties for weddings, birthdays, anniversaries and the like have *hygge* at their core. Tables are decorated with flowers and candles and creatively folded napkins. A three-course meal is usually interspersed with songs and speeches, which end in a collective "Hurrah!" Wine flows freely. As the Danish poet and troubadour

Benny Andersen wrote in a song well known among Danes: "One must keep the mood wet. I'm drunk and I'm feeling great."

Six hours into such a celebration and filled with spirits, a party-goer has a chance to get up from the table, dance a bit, then fetch some coffee and cookies and sit down again. Later, the

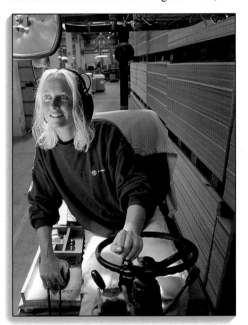

LEFT: a farmer practises the traditional art of canal-jumping in low-lying southwestern Denmark.
RIGHT: the modern face of Danish industry.

DENMARK: THE ESSENTIALS

Population 5.3 million.
Capital Copenhagen (pop. 1.3 million).
Notable towns Århus, Odense.
Climate Average maximum temperature in July: 22°C (71°F). In February: 2°C (36°F).
Top museums Nationalmuseet, Louisiana Museum of Modern Art, Vikingeskibshallen.
Famous home Hans Christian Andersen Hus, Odense.
Historic sights Christiansborg, Copenhagen; Kronborg, Helsingør; Roskilde Cathedral; Vikingeborgen, Trælleborg.
Natural wonders Råbjerg Mile sand dune; cliffs of Møn.
Tourist information www.dt.dk

hosts serve the final course, called "get out food", and guests gradually take the hint.

Hygge was born, no doubt, indoors during the grey winter months. From November to February, Danes go to work in darkness and return home in darkness. Warm candlelight fills flats, homes and offices in natural defence. During *Jul* (Christmas), live candles decorate Christmas trees indoors, around which families join hands and sing carols. Local ferries light up the black water with strings of white lights. On New Year's Eve, the Queen gives her annual talk to the nation on television, and fireworks spark and pop, lighting up the midnight sky.

A whiff of spring

By February, winter seems to drag on forever. In his essay, *Oh! To be Danish*, the author Klaus Rifbjerg writes of this time: "Sure, it can be grim, and now and then we might want to turn our collar up and jump in the river. But then the light suddenly changes and there's a melody in the air, a whiff of spring to come, the smell of the sea and a blackbird singing on a rooftop."

Fields of fluorescent yellow winter rape blossom in May, and the days turn long. In spring and summer, city Danes bike out to their garden houses on the edge of town, and country Danes collect dead branches and greenery

EQUALITY FOR ALL

Denmark is a society of non-extremes where, as Danes themselves say, "few have too much and fewer have too little". The welfare system gives everyone the same opportunities: free health service, education, support for the elderly and handicapped, unemployment benefits, pensions, and more.

The system carries a price: goods and services are taxed at 25 percent, and 50–70 percent of income is taxed. This equality carries through to social norms. Everyone is on first-name terms. The formal address, *De*, being reserved mainly for the Queen. Dress is casual and a tie in the workplace is rare.

into huge piles on the beaches and in the countryside. On the evening of 23 June, Midsummer's Eve, those piles of wood are topped with an effigy of a witch and set on fire to drive bad spirits from the land as Danes gather around the bonfires and sing. In July, nearly the whole country goes on holiday for three weeks. Barbecues are lit, clothes abandoned, bathing-suits donned.

By late summer, farmers' tractors haul grain and hay, holding up traffic. Towns hold harvest parties, children start school and families hunt for mushrooms and berries in the beech and oak forests. People start to complain about the diminishing light and increasing rain, and soon the frost hits and temperatures can drop so low the sea freezes solid. So, the Danes light a candle, make some *hygge* with hot cocoa and buns, and look forward to *Jul* again.

A sense of togetherness and looking out for each other can be felt not only in family *hygge*, but in society as well, starting with the generous welfare system. Workers unions are strong, and the co-operative spirit prevails. Only four out of 100 Danes do not belong to an association.

"We have a joke that if two Danes sit together for five minutes, they will start an association," says Frans Kjær Nielsen.

> **MANY VOICES**
>
> More than 100 dialects are spoken in Denmark. Some vary greatly. People in South Jutland are hardly understood by the residents of Copenhagen.

democracy, traditions, norms and welfare system were suddenly thrown into question by newcomers and Danes alike. Denmark found itself unprepared in how to deal with cultural misunderstandings, how to teach Danish effectively to thousands of immigrants, and how to help integrate them into the job market and society.

When Frans Kjær Nielsen began to teach Danish in Århus in 1985, the only option for foreigners was a local night school, which also offered hobby classes like painting and gardening. Only a couple of

The new Danes
In the 1960s and 1970s, Denmark experienced the first recent wave of immigrants – Turkish "guest workers". It was not until the early 1980s, however, that the effects of immigration on the Danish culture were felt, when refugees from the Far East, Middle East, the Balkans, Somalia, and elsewhere came to the country. The Danish social

Danish text books were available. Fortunately, things got better. The country passed immigrant education laws and improved teacher-training. Today, teaching materials fill entire school libraries. Yet unemployment remains high among immigrants, who have tended to congregate into their own neighbourhoods.

While politicians and public officials have tried to work things out on paper, the greater part of Danish society seems to be tolerant – it takes personal effort from both sides, many have pointed out. One letter in a national newspaper, addressed to the immigrants of the nation, said: "If you see a Dane on the street, smile. Many of us will smile back." ❑

LEFT: arts and music festivals are regular fixtures on the Danish cultural calendar.
ABOVE: looking to the future.

Denmark

92

Copenhagen

0   500 m
0   500 yds

HISONS
EGARD

Frihavnen
Langeliniebro
Lange-Liniekaj
Lystbådehavnen
Søfarts-Monument
Den Lille Havfrue
(Little Mermaid) **23**

Sydre
Refshalebassin

Refshalevej

Kristianiagade
Østbanegade
Oslo Plads
Folke Bernadottes Alle
Gustafs Kirke
Østerport
Kastellet **24**
Kastels-kirken

Forbindelsesvej
Langeliniebro
Langelinie-pavillonen

CHURCHILL-PARKEN

Gefionspringvandet
St Albans
Nordre Toldbod **22**
Toldbodens Bådehavn

SIXTUS

Krokodillegade
Nyboder **26**
Elsdyrsgade
Store Kongensgade
Grønningen
Smedelinien

Skt Pauls Plads
Skt Pauls Gade
Adelgade
Borgergade
Esplanaden
Vanførehjem
Frihedsmuseet **25**
(Resistance Mus.)
Amaliegade
Esplanade

Dir. for
Toldvæsenet

NYHOLM

Quintus
Bastion

Østre
Landsret
Bredgade
Kunstindustrimuseet **19**
(Museum of
Decorative Arts)

Toldbodgade

Margarethe
Holm

Alexander
Nevski Kirke
Frederiksgade
Medicinsk Historisk
Museum
Kirurg.
Akademi

Charlotte
Amalies
Bastion

Frederikskirken
(Marmorkirken)
(Marble Church) **20**
FREDERIKSSTADEN
Christian VIII's
Palæ
Frederik VIII's
Palæ

1. Redan

Amalienborg
Slot (Palace) **21**
Christian VII's
Palæ
Amalienborg
Plads

DOKØEN

Frederiks
Bastion

Odd Fellow
Palæ
Christian IX's
Palæ

AMALIEHAVEN
Kvæsthusgraven

HOLMEN

2. Redan

Sankt Annæ Plads
Garnis Kirke
Amaliegade
Bredgade
Store Kongensgade

FREDERIKSHOLM

Carls
Bastion

Kongens
Nytorv **16**
leterre
18 Nyhavn
Nyhavn
Charlottenborg **17**
Torden
Herluf Trolles Gade
Holbergsgade
Skildsgade
Niels Juels Gade

CHRISTIANSHOLM

Havforeningen
Strandhøj

3. Redan

Det Kongelige Teater
(Royal Theatre)

Grønlands
Handels Plads
Trangraven

ARSENALØEN

Havforen
Rosen

enskanal
National-banken
Inderhavn
Havne-
Krøyers
Plads
Islands
Plads

Vilhelms
Bastion

Haveforeningen
Kløvermarken

Imens
rke
Borgsgade
sen **34**
Dansk Arkitektur
Center **36**
Strandgade
Wilders
Plads

Havforeningen
Kløverblomsten

holmsgade
Asiatisk
Plads
Bådsmands-
gade
Refshalevej
Søkvæst-huset

Sofie Hedevigs
Bastion

4. Redan

Kløvermarksvej

isterial
ningerne
Brygge
Kongelige
otek
al Library)
Sorte Diamant
k Diamond
38
Christianskirke
Strandgade
Wilders
Torvegade
Ski Anna
Uderigsmin

CHRISTIANSHAVN
Christiania **37**

Havforen
Sommerly

Vor Frelsers Kirke
(Our Saviour's) **39**
Voldboligerne

Ulriks
Bastion

5. Redan

KLØVERMARKEN

Christians-
havns Torv
Ved Volden
Voldgade
Prinsesse Gade
stræde

Kanino

Løvens
Bastion

Overgaden oven Vandet
Dronningens-
Christianshavns
Anagergade
Torvegade
Ravelinen
6. Redan

Elefantens
Bastion

Havforeningen
Vennelyst

Uplandsgade

Rabeshave
Enhjorningens
Bastion
Panterens
Bastion
Stadsgraven

COPENHAGEN

Map on pages 94–95

*Denmark's capital city is the most exuberant in Scandinavia.
Pedestrians and cyclists rule, shopping is a pleasure,
cultural sights abound, and by night the city buzzes*

Copenhagen (København) is the "city of green spires". Copper plates, etched green by salt air, clad the spires of castles and churches in the old city, and tower over the medieval street network and newer houses. The Old Town you visit today would have looked different but for two devastating fires and a terrible bombardment. Blazes in 1728 and 1795 licked and leaped along the straw-roofed houses and turned most of the half-timbered medieval town to ashes. Only a few solidly built structures survived – among them, the Rundetårn (Round Tower). When Admiral Lord Nelson and the British fleet bombarded Copenhagen in 1807 the toll was also heavy. The old Copenhagen Cathedral was a victim.

Copenhagen is the liveliest – and many claim the most fetching – of the Scandinavian capitals, with things to see and do all the time. With Europe's longest pedestrian mall, this was the first capital to offer the pleasures of ambling through a network of streets free of motor vehicles and exhaust fumes.

A good way to get a first feel of Copenhagen is from the water. Take one of the 50-minute canal boat trips from Gammel Strand (Apr–Oct: every 30 minutes from 10am; tel: 33 13 31 05). If you're the adventuresome type you could explore the waterways in a kayak for two hours, starting at the same place. A

LEFT: the bright lights of Tivoli.
BELOW: dressed for the carnival.

FACT FILE

Situation Copenhagen is located on the east coast of Zealand facing the sound between Denmark and Sweden.
Population 1,379,413 in the Copenhagen area.
Climate Afternoon temperatures in February average 2°C (36°F); in July they are around 21 or 22°C (70–72°F).
Transport Bus and S-train network; bike hire.
Discount card Buy a Copenhagen Card for free entrance to museums, galleries, and free transport.
Best sightseeing tour Crosstown Walk *(see panel, page 103)*; canal boat trip from Gammel Strand.
Best shopping Strøget, Europe's longest pedestrian mall.
Top attraction Tivoli Gardens (open summer, Christmas).
Finest building Rosenborg Slot (Castle).
Best museums Nationalmuseet, Ny Carlsberg Glyptotek, Statens Museum for Kunst (National Museum for Fine Arts), the ruins of Absalon's castle beneath Christiansborg.
Best views of the city Rådhuset tower; Rundetårn (Round Tower); Vor Frelsers Kirke, Christianshavn.
Best *smørrebrød* Ida Davidsen, Store Kongensgade 70, tel: 33 91 36 55.
Tourist information office Bernstorffsgade 1, 1577 Copenhagen V (opposite the Central Railway Station); tel: 45 33 25 38 44; www.woco.dk; touristinfo@woco.dk

Bicycles are welcome on Copenhagen's suburban trains.

BELOW: the palace of Christiansborg, Denmark's seat of government.

guide paddles ahead of you (Copenhagen Adventure Tours; tel: 40 50 40 06).

Rådhuspladsen (**City Hall Square**) is the nexus of Copenhagen, grandly lit up at night with its coloured signs, digital news headlines and blinking neon, with the enormous **Rådhuset ❶** (City Hall; open 9.30am–3pm, free; tours in English, 3pm, for a fee; tel: 33 66 25 82) at its heart. Constructed in the National Romantic style, its inspiration was drawn from medieval Danish and Norwegian architecture with a touch of the Palazzo style of northern Italy. The façade and interior are trimmed with historic details from Nordic mythology. Looking for a bird's eye view of the city's spires and towers? The 106-metre (347-ft) tower (open daily; entrance fee) is for you.

Inside the foyer, look for the entrance to Jens Olsen's World Clock (open 10am–4pm; entrance fee). Its star dial mechanism shows the path of the pole star in re-settable periods, making it the "most accurate and complicated clock in the world", according to the *Guinness Book of World Records*.

Bordering the square to the east on Vester Voldgade are two of Copenhagen's fine traditional hotels. Closest to City Hall is the **Palace Hotel**, one of the few buildings in the Jugendstil (Art Nouveau style), and further north, past the square, **Hotel Kong Frederik** with the smart and pricey Queen's Pub restaurant.

To the west, on H.C. Andersens Boulevard, it's hard to miss a castle-like red-brick building nicknamed "Little Rosenborg". There's an entrance to **Tivoli Gardens ❷** (open late Apr–late Sept: Mon–Fri 11am–midnight, Sat–Sun 11am–1am; also at Christmas; entrance fee; tel: 33 15 10 01; www.tivoli.dk) and **Museet Louis Tussaud's** (open late Apr–mid-Sept: 10am–10pm; mid-Sept–late Apr: 10am–6pm; entrance fee; tel: 33 11 89 00).

Although smaller than Madame Tussaud's in London, the waxworks

HISTORIC TRADING POST

Before 1167, Copenhagen was just a trading post called Havn (Harbour), which gave easy access to Skåne (Scania) across the Sound. Skåne is now part of Sweden, but in those days southern Sweden was part of Denmark, and the village of Havn enjoyed a position in the middle of the kingdom. As wars and unrest changed the geography of Denmark, København (Merchant's Harbour) gradually moved to its point on the eastern shore of Zealand.

In 1167, King Valdemar I commanded the local bishop, Absalon of Roskilde, to fortify Havn in order to protect it against Wendic pirates. Absalon built a fortress on the spot where the Parliament building now looms across the canal from Højbro Plads (Square). Copenhagen was on the way to becoming Denmark's biggest and most important town. The fortress became Christiansborg, *borg* meaning castle. Centuries later, it remains the seat of Danish politics, housing the Folketing (Parliament).

During the long reign of Kristian IV (1588–1648), Copenhagen solidified its role as the country's seat of power. This visionary town planner built Børsen, said to be the oldest Stock Exchange in Europe, a Renaissance structure with a spire of four entwined dragons, steep copper roofs, tiny windows and gables galore.

museum offers a line-up including all the kings and queens of Denmark and many other notables, historic and contemporary.

Tivoli is a Scandinavian rainbow of gardens, open-air amusements, restaurants, cafés, theatres, an open-air stage and a major concert hall, home of Sjællands Symphony Orchestra. Tivoli is also the place to enjoy a good meal, coffee and cake, or a drink. The park has more than 20 restaurants.

For children, the greatest thrills come from the rides, roller coasters and merry-go-rounds. In recent years the lake has been machine-frozen for winter ice-skating, and the pleasure mecca's portals are thrown open for an old-fashioned market at Christmas time.

Danish design

A two-minute walk south of the City Hall on H.C. Andersens Boulevard is the **Danish Design Centre** ❸ (open Mon–Sat 10am–5pm, Sun 11am–4pm; entrance fee; tel: 33 69 33 69), with ongoing Danish and international exhibitions *(see Insight on Danish Design, page 110).*

Across the road and a block to the southeast is **Ny Carlsberg Glyptotek** ❹ (open Tues–Sun 10am–4pm, closed Mon; entrance fee, Sun and Wed free; tel: 33 41 81 41). This exquisite museum offers a grand art collection begun by the brewer Carl Jacobsen and maintained by the New Carlsberg Foundation. There are collections of ancient Egyptian, Greek, Roman and Etruscan sculptures, as well as some French masterpieces from Cézanne, Gauguin and Rodin. The lush, palm-lined indoor Winter Garden has a wonderful café.

On Bernstorffsgade, across from Tivoli's west entrance, is **Hovedbanegården** (Central Railway Station). Beyond it to the west lies **Vesterbro**, one of

---

Map
on pages
94–95

The tall tubes in front of the Moorish-style palace restaurant in Tivoli contain bubbling water. This unusual sculpture was designed by the Danish nuclear physicist Niels Bohr.

BELOW: City Hall dominates the bustling central square of Rådhuspladsen.

TIP

You'll find local news and listings in the weekly English-language tabloid newspaper, *The Copenhagen Post*, distributed free at some hotels and sold at Danish State Railway kiosks and 7-Eleven stores.

BELOW: a touch of the tropics in the indoor Winter Garden of Ny Carlsberg Glyptotek.

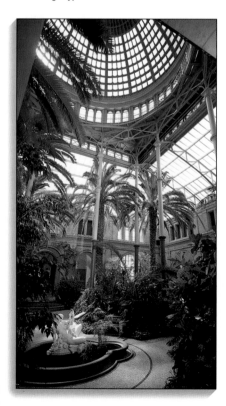

Copenhagen's old residential districts, today a multicultural community, vibrant with bizarre shops, exotic restaurants and its red light boulevard, **Istedgade**.

The **Copenhagen Tourist Office** ❺ lies across the street from Central Station on Bernstorffsgade, near the corner of Vesterbrogade. This travellers' ganglion has it all: information on sights, cultural activities, transport, eating places, events. A prime source is the free magazine *Copenhagen This Week* (www.ctw.dk).

The medieval city

If Rådhuspladsen is the heart of Copenhagen, then **Strøget** ❻, the 1.8-km (1-mile) pedestrian shopping street, is the spine. It has endless shops, street vendors and buskers and cellar galleries. Strøget ("*stroy-yet*") is where Copenhageners and visitors alike go to shop or just to promenade. The mainstream shops and eateries are on Strøget proper, while the more quirky boutiques, cafés and restaurants are situated on any of the quieter side streets.

Starting at Rådhuspladsen, Strøget meanders through five streets and four squares before it runs into Kongens Nytorv, the largest square in the old town. Good landmarks and meeting places are the squares at **Gammeltorv** (Old Square) and at Strøget's major crossroads, the crane fountain at **Amagertorv**. Here, another main pedestrian artery, **Købmagergade**, branches off to the north.

Near Gammeltorv, the area behind **Vestergade** is one of the few remaining residential areas in the inner city. Living in the picturesque neoclassical houses is a mixture of old-time Copenhageners, artists and students, and here you find some of the more exotic clothes shops and galleries – try Skt Pedersstræde for starters. **Sankt Petri Kirke** ❼ (St Peter's Church), on the corner of Nørregade and Skt Pedersstræde, is the oldest church in Copenhagen, its chancellery built in 1450. Hans Christian Andersen lived in No. 19 Vestergade when, as a young man, he first arrived in Copenhagen from Odense. Another famous Dane, the 19th-century philosopher Søren Kierkegaard, lived in the house on the corner of Nytorv and Frederiksberggade at Gammeltorv.

One block south and running parallel to Strøget, is **Kompagnistræde**, with shops specialising in antiques, china and pewter. At Rådhusstræde 13 you'll find **Use It** ❽ (tel: 33 73 06 20; www.useit.dk), an extremely helpful information centre for tourists on a low budget. Pick up its excellent guide, *Play Time*.

Two blocks south, across from the canal on Ny Vestergade, is Denmark's **Nationalmuseet** ❾ (National Museum; open 10am–5pm, Wed 10am–9pm, closed Mon; entrance fee, Wed free; tel: 33 13 44 11), highly recommended for its collections of ancient "bog" finds from the Stone, Bronze and Iron Ages. A fascinating and well-structured museum that takes days to cover, it has an interesting section on Danish cultural history.

From Nytorv, continue along Strøget towards Amagertorv. For a close encounter of the rich and sweet, stop at one of Copenhagen's premier confectioner's, **Konditori La Glace**, a few stops from Strøget at Skoubogade. Here, cream-layer cakes reign supreme. For tobacco aficionados, Amagertorv 9 is one of those rare places you find where you least expect it. W.Ø. Larsen is a smokers' emporium and houses the **Tobaksmuseet ⑩** (Tobacco Museum; open Mon–Thur 10am–6pm, Fri 10am–7pm, Sat 10am–5pm; free; tel: 33 12 20 50), with its display of ancient pipes, tobaccos and smoking history. The opposite side of Amagertorv is occupied by the shops most often visited by tourists: **Illums Bolighus ⑪**, showcase for superb Danish and international design; and the flagship stores of **Royal Copenhagen Porcelain** and **Georg Jensen** silver.

Map on pages 94–95

Latin Quarter

The streets to the north of Amagertorv form the old **Latin Quarter**, featuring the cosy **Gråbrødretorv** (Greyfriar's Square). The cobblestone square is a popular place to enjoy lunch (you can pour your own draught beers at Frimandskvarter) or dinner (Peder Oxe is a local favourite).

The streets just to the north hold **Københavns Domkirke ⑫** (Copenhagen's Cathedral) and the main building of the **University of Copenhagen**. The seat of the University Board, beside Nørregade, dates from 1420 and is the oldest building in Copenhagen. A fun stop for children is the sweets factory on Nørregade 36, **Sømod's Bolcher**, where confectioners make old-fashioned hard candy by hand (demonstrations Mon–Fri 9.15am–3pm; tel: 33 12 60 46). **Fiolstræde** is known for its antiquarian bookshops, and **Krystalgade** is the site of Copenhagen's synagogue. Try a sandwich from the busy, bowler-hatted organic butchers, **Slagteren ved Kultorvet** (Coal Square), on the open plaza near the Nørreport subway station, at the top of traffic-free Købmagergade.

On Købmagergade is one of Copenhagen's most fascinating buildings. The **Rundetårn ⑬** (Round Tower; open Sept–May: 10am–5pm; June–Aug:

A whiff of tobacco: W.Ø. Larsen's museum in Strøget.

BELOW: enjoying a break in Skt Anne's Passage.

TIP

For a taste of brewing, visit the famous Carlsberg Brewery and stables, Gamle Carlsberg Vej 11, Valby, and sample a glass of the best (open Mon–Fri 10am–4pm; free; tel: 33 27 13 14).

10am–8pm; observatory mid-Oct–mid-Mar: Tues, Wed, 7–10pm; entrance fee; tel: 33 73 03 73) was built in 1642 as an observatory for Denmark's renowned astronomer, Tycho Brahe. It still has a viewing platform on the top which offers a panorama on clear days and nights. The tower stands 36 metres (118 ft) high, and to reach the roof one walks up a 209-metre (685-ft) spiral ramp. In 1716 Tsar Peter the Great drove a horse and carriage to the top.

Around the corner off Landemærket is the **Det Danske Filminstitut** ⑭, home of Cinemateque, which celebrates Denmark's trailblazing successes in cinematography, and shows a programme of international and Danish films (performances: Tues–Sun 9.30am–10pm, closed Mon; tel: 33 74 34 12).

A few blocks south on Købmagergade is **Museum Erotica** ⑮ (open May–Sept: 10am–11pm; Oct–Apr: 11am–8pm; entrance fee; tel: 33 12 03 11), one of the best examples in town of the liberal-minded Danes. Here sex and sensuality are not an issue – they *are* the issue.

Haunts of the rich and famous

The last section of Strøget, from the Crane Fountain to Kongens Nytorv, is the home of the exclusive and expensive: fashion shops, furriers and jewellers. A fun historical photo gallery in the heart of the action, where you can get a coffee, is **Fogtdals FotoCafé**, Østergade 22.

At the end of Strøget, facing **Kongens Nytorv** (King's New Square), stands the grand old hotel of the city, **Hotel D'Angleterre** ⑯. The majestic buildings dominating Kongens Nytorv are **Det Kongelige Teater** ⑰ (Royal Theatre) – the national stage for ballet, opera, and drama – and, next door, **Charlottenborg**, the home of the **Royal Academy of Fine Arts**.

BELOW: time for a beer on the quayside at Nyhavn.

Nyhavn quayside

At the narrow waterway of **Nyhavn** ⑱, a famous landmark from 1673, colourful old wooden schooners line the quay, and the north side is a charming combination of sailors' bars and new restaurants. The south side was always "the nice side" but the north side used to be "the naughty side" where sailors on shore leave would spend their liberty drinking, whoring, and getting tattooed. Times have changed, and Nyhavn is now one of the most popular spots in town for a different type of visitor.

From Nyhavn, Bredgade and its parallel twin, Store Kongensgade, are the main shopping streets of the residential **Frederiksstaden** to the north. The area was planned and built in the 18th century for the well-to-do. No. 70 Store Kongensgade features **Ida Davidsen**, one of the best places in town to try *smørrebrød*, Danish open-faced sandwiches – open for lunch on weekdays only (reservations recommended, tel: 33 91 36 55). The Queen has been known to pop in for a bite to eat from her palace around the corner.

At Bredgade 68 is **Kunstindustrimuseet** ⑲ (Museum of Decorative and Applied Arts; open Tues–Fri 10am–4pm, Sat–Sun 12 noon–4pm; entrance fee; tel: 33 14 94 52) which features not only European and Oriental works, but classic Danish design as well. Opposite the museum, three domes tower over **Alexander Nevski Russian Orthodox Church**, which was built in 1881 by the Russian government and contains a number of fine icons.

Close by, there is almost no way one can miss the grand copper dome of **Frederikskirken** ⑳, popularly known as the **Marble Church**. The church was meant to be a majestic Rococo monument, but the king, Frederik V, ran out of money and the project was cancelled in 1770. The church was not completed

Map on pages 94–95

Nyhavn still retains some of the character of bygone days, when it was a haunt for sailors on leave.

BELOW: the Round Tower, built in 1642, offers good views of the city.

THE WALK OF THE TOWN

On your feet is the best way to discover this old town of narrow streets and cobbled courtyards. The "Crosstown Copenhagen Tour" starts outside the Tourist Information Office on Bernstorffsgade, across from Central Station (May–Sept: Tues and Fri 10.30am; tel: 32 97 14 40).

Led by the indefatigable Richard, the first stop is Rådhuspladsen, where the western wall came down in the 1850s to let the city expand. "Also," says Richard, "it was dirty and terribly crowded inside." He sets off along streets following the curve of the canal which once extended to Strøget – now Europe's longest pedestrian mall – pausing at the City Court House, profiled like a Greek temple. By the canal a buxom woman serves fishcakes. Over Amagertorv looms a Dutch Renaissance building from 1616, the mayor's residence taken over in 1911 by Royal Copenhagen Porcelain. Today, side by side, are Royal Copenhagen, Georg Jensen silver, Holmegaard glass, and Illums Bolighus with Danish gifts and furnishings. Then there's the Royal Theatre and the elegant Hotel D'Angleterre, where Victor Borge stays. And Nyhavn, where you can take a canal tour. What's this – Amalienborg Palace? Just in time for the noon-time changing of the guard. Have two hours really passed?

until the 1870s. When the project was resumed it was built not in marble but in limestone. From the dome, which is accessible to visitors (open Apr–May: Sat–Sun 12.45pm; June–Sept: daily 11am and 12.45pm; entrance fee), there is a splendid view across the Sound to Sweden. The statues outside the church represent important Danish churchmen and theologians.

Royal residence

Amalienborg Slot (Palace) ㉑, directly across Bredgade towards the harbour, is the residence of the Royal Family, one of Europe's less assuming royal domiciles, built in the 18th century. The Royal Guard are always on duty, and the changing of the guard at noon every day attracts both children and adults. If the flag is flying, then the Queen is in residence and the full ceremony will take place. The exquisite equestrian statue in the middle of the square represents Frederik V and was made by the French sculptor Jacques Saly.

Along the promenade

The other end of the east–west axis through the plaza ends in **Amaliehaven**, a modern park donated to the city by the A.P. Møller shipping company in 1983. Following the promenade to the north, you will find the dazzling fountain, **Gefionspringvandet** ㉒, dedicated to the Nordic goddess Gefion.

At the start of Langelinie is *the* symbol of Copenhagen, **Den Lille Havfrue (Little Mermaid)** ㉓. This bronze statue of the character from the Hans Christian Andersen fairy tale was created by Edvard Eriksen in 1917.

The quay of Langelinie follows, and Europe's busiest cruise ship pier is to the north of this at **Frihavnen (Free Harbour)**. Renovations have been taking

BELOW: royal guards on duty at Amalienborg Palace.
RIGHT: rococo splendour at the Marble Church.

place to rejuvenate the area. The most architecturally interesting of the new buildings is **Paustians Hus**, designed by Jørn Utzon, who also designed the Sydney Opera House. Paustian is one of Copenhagen's finest furniture stores and the building also houses a good restaurant.

Map on pages 94–95

War resistance

Return to the city centre via **Kastellet** ㉔ (The Citadel), a fortification that has kept its old ramparts intact. Part of the area is still military property.

Churchillparken, a tiny park just south of Kastellet, provides a home for **Frihedsmuseet** ㉕ (Danish Resistance Museum; open May–mid-Sept: 10am–4pm, Sun 10am–5pm, closed Mon; mid-Sept–Apr: 11am–3pm, Sun 11am–4pm, closed Mon; free; tel: 33 13 77 14), which commemorates the Danish underground fighters of World War II.

Continue past Store Kongensgade to visit Denmark's oldest housing development, **Nyboder** ㉖. The long rows of ochre houses were built in 1638 by Kristian IV as quarters for the Danish Royal Navy, and the 616 apartments are still used for staff and retired officers.

Lille Havfrue (the Little Mermaid), by Edvard Eriksen, was modelled on his wife.

Nearby, where Øster Voldgade and Sølvgade meet, is the superb **Statens Museum for Kunst** ㉗ (National Museum for Fine Arts; open 10am–5pm, Wed 10am–8pm, closed Mon; entrance fee; tel: 33 74 84 94). An extension was completed in 1999, housing four stories of modern art within stunning glass and whitewashed walls. Other Danish and European works are displayed permanently, along with changing international exhibitions. Behind the museum and across the park is **Den Hirschsprungske Samling** ㉘ (Hirschsprung Collection; open 11am–4pm, Wed 11am–9pm, closed Tues; entrance fee, Wed free;

BELOW: the Royal Library's shining "Black Diamond" extension.

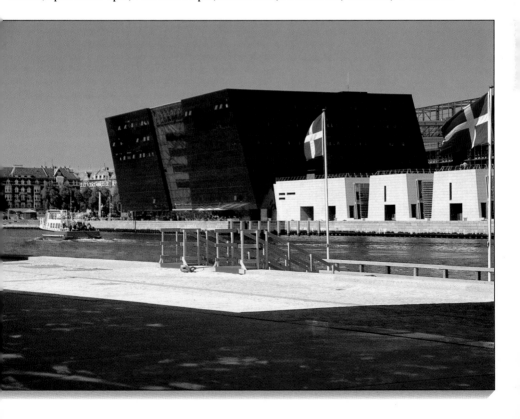

CHRISTIANIA – THE ALTERNATIVE STATE

In a beautiful position on Copenhagen's waterfront, Christiania offers a way of life far removed from the bustle of a city

I n 1971, a group of alternative thinkers founded Christiania, a 41-hectare (84-acre) "Free State" with woods, dirt roads, workshops, restaurants and funky houses. The hippie playground in the heart of the city – only 1 km from the Parliament buildings – retains the spirit of the Woodstock era.

You will find the area in Christianshavn in what was previously an abandoned 19th-century military barracks. The Christianites have converted barrack blocks, workshops and powder magazines into a place where they can live and work.

About 1,000 people of all ages, cultures and income levels live in this working

collective, but its existence is still a subject of controversy in the Danish Parliament. It was given official status as a social experiment in 1981.

There are only three rules here: no hard drugs, no cars, no weapons or violence. As part of their belief in their way of life, the Christianites refuse to condemn the open sale of hashish and marijuana, and they have successfully campaigned against hard drugs. The area's suggestively-named "Pusher Street" does, however, get visits from the city police.

From the entrance on, Christiania is a sensory overload. Buildings are painted with rainbows, spiritual figures and politically defiant graffiti. There are barefoot bicyclists, their baskets full of vegetables, earthy-smelling organic markets, recycling warehouses, workshops and stables. Resident children play in an "organic kindergarten", where modern equipment is replaced with nature. Houses along the leafy path have names such as "The Blue Banana" or "The Pyramid".

"The more secure people have felt to be here, the more money they have spent to restore the houses," says tour guide Nina Pontoppidan. "We take care of our own buildings, so the politicians look between their fingers. If they put the people in social housing, they would have to spend a lot of money."

Christiania has some of the best restaurants in the city, including SpiseLoppen (The Eating Flea), in the warehouse by the front entrance. In the same building is Loppen, a music club. Månefiskeren (The Moon Fisher), a café in the heart of the collective, serves excellent coffee in a "far out" atmosphere.

For an inexpensive walking tour, meet at the front entrance at 3pm – this is the best way to see the Free State and get a broader perspective. In addition, *Nitten*, Christiania's free tourist guide, provides a detailed history and self-guided walks. ❏

TOP LEFT: murals decorate many of Christiania's buildings. **LEFT:** relaxed lifestyle. **TOP:** child of the New Age. **ABOVE:** the streets are car-free.

tel: 35 42 03 36), a commendable private collection of 19th-century Danish art – including many of the originals from the Skagen painters.

Map
on pages
94–95

Gardens and jewels

The **Botanisk Have** (Botanical Gardens) is just across the street, along Sølvgade and Øster Voldgade (open summer: 8.30am–6pm; winter: 8.30am–4pm; free; tel: 35 32 22 40). Visit the rosarium, the perennials and a huge conservatory with tropical and subtropical plants.

One of Copenhagen's most attractive sights is **Rosenborg Slot** (open May–Sept: 10am–4pm; Oct: 11am–3pm; Nov–Apr: 11am–2pm, closed Mon; entrance fee; 33 15 32 86), the fairy-tale castle across from the Botanical Gardens. King Kristian IV's exquisite palace in Dutch Renaissance style is now a museum, and contains three centuries-worth of royal treasures, as well as the crown jewels. The garden surrounding it, **Kongens Have**, has been a favourite with Copenhageners for centuries.

For treasure and trash visit the city's antique and flea markets. Try Israels Plads on Saturday, 8am–2pm, and Gammel Strand, Friday and Saturday 9am–4pm.

Centre of government

To the southeast of Strøget and the main shopping area lies **Slotsholmen** (Castle Island). Surrounded by canals, the island is the seat of the Danish Parliament and government ministries. The imposing **Christiansborg**, built on the same spot as the original old castle of Copenhagen, contains Parliament, the Prime Minister's office, the Supreme Court and the Royal Reception Chambers. The public may join free conducted tours of the **Folketinget** (House of Parliament), and the **Royal Reception Chambers** (tel: 33 37 55 00).

Bishop Absalon built a fortress on this little islet in 1167, and from 1416 it was the home of the Danish king. Absalon's fortress was replaced by a new castle in 1367 and in the 1730s King Kristian VI ordered a new palace. This one, a magnificent Baroque building, burned in 1794 and was replaced yet again with a new palace which, ill-fated as it was, burned down in 1884. The present version of Christiansborg is less than 100 years old, built between 1907 and 1928. The granite façade was made from stones gathered in every parish in the country. The equestrian statue, erected on the Palace Square in 1876, depicts King Frederik VII (1843–63).

The **Ruins of Absalon's Old Fortress** (open 9.30am–3.30pm, closed Mon; entrance fee) and the medieval castle are now accessible to visitors and make an interesting "underground" visit.

The **Palace Chapel**, erected in 1826, is located to the north of Christiansborg. Behind the chapel is **Thorvaldsens Museum**, which contains the works of Denmark's great sculptor, Bertel Thorvaldsen (1770–1844), who lived and worked in Rome for 40 years (open 10am–5pm, closed Mon; entrance fee; tel: 33 32 15 32).

In front of Christiansborg is the **Ridebanen**, the royal riding grounds from the 1740s bordered by the only surviving buildings from the first Christiansborg. The royal horses are still exercised here today and their stables can be visited on the southeast side of the square – the **Kongelige Stalde & Kareter**

BELOW: exploring Copenhagen's waterways by boat.

Map on pages 94–95

The 17th-century Vor Frelsers Kirke on Christianshavn.

BELOW: the city's Botanical Gardens. **RIGHT:** Carlsberg Brewery drayman.

(Museum of Royal Stables and Coaches; open May–Sept: Fri–Sun 2–4pm; Oct–Apr: Sat–Sun 2–4pm; entrance fee; tel: 33 40 10 10). Adjacent to the stables, the **Teatermuseet** is one of the oldest court theatres in the world, designed in 1766 by the French architect Nicolas-Henri Jardin (open Wed 2–4pm, Sat–Sun 12 noon–4pm; entrance fee; tel: 33 11 51 76). The equestrian statue on the riding grounds depicts King Kristian IX, who died in 1906.

East of Christiansborg is another of Copenhagen's best-known buildings, **Børsen** ❸ (Stock Exchange), built in 1619 in Dutch Renaissance style by Kristian IV. Its prominent spire is formed by the entwined tails of dragons representing Denmark, Sweden and Norway. On the southeast side of the island is **Det Kongelige Bibliotek (Royal Library)** ❺ and its "Black Diamond" – an architectural wonder of old and new. Det Kongelige Bibliotek dates back to 1482 and is the largest library in Scandinavia, with more than 2½ million volumes. The Black Diamond, completed in 1999, is a modern extension in black polished granite perched on the water's edge.

Colourful Christianshavn

Cross the harbour via the Knippelsbro bridge to reach **Christianshavn**, one of Copenhagen's oldest and most colourful residential areas. Christianshavn was built on an island in 1617 by Kristian IV and is surrounded by the original star-shaped ramparts. Along the harbour wall, one of the meticulously restored warehouses is well worth a visit, the **Dansk Arkitektur Center** ❸ (Danish Architecture Centre; open 10am–5pm; entrance fee; tel: 32 57 19 30), which features various exhibitions, a bookshop and café.

Until recently a run-down, working-class neighbourhood and the site of Denmark's largest shipyard, Christianshavn has changed its appearance greatly and now features a quaint mixture of smartly renovated 18th-century city houses, big apartment blocks, old and new industry and commerce, and a good deal of the state's administration.

Take a stroll down the streets of Christianshavn and glance into the courtyards of some of the old houses on **Strandgade**. Amagergade 11, at the other end of Christianshavn, is said to have the finest courtyard in town, and is surrounded by old galleries.

Christianshavn is also the home of **Christiania** ❼, the hippie-style "free state" *(see Christiania, page 106)*. The main entrance is on Prinsessegade.

Two of Copenhagen's more notable churches are on Christianshavn. **Christianskirke** ❽ in Strandgade is a Rococo building from 1754. It was built as a theatre with boxes, including one for the royal family. **Vor Frelsers Kirke** ❾ (Church of Our Saviour; open Mon–Sat 11am–4.30pm, Sun 11am–4.30pm, closes 3.30pm Sept-Mar; tower closed in winter) in Prinsessegade attracts the most attention. Built in red brick in 1694, its tall copper-clad tower with a spiraling, external stairway can be seen from all over the city. For a magnificent view over Copenhagen, the tower is open to visitors who dare to climb through a maze of roof timbers and up the 150 gilded steps. It's the perfect place to get an overview of the city of spires, particularly when you're on one yourself. ❑

A FLAIR FOR DESIGN: FUNCTION WITH FORM

When a nation of craftsmen mixed with a late move towards industrialisation in the 1900s, an influential new school of design was born

A chair may be something to sit in, and a lamp may help to light up a room, but Danish designers have made these objects more than ordinary in the last 50 years. Behind glass in museums and in use in a wide range of places from conference rooms to homes, Danish design has brought a sense of elegance to everyday life.

"It always starts with a task," says designer Hans J. Wegner. "I never say to myself I'm going to make a piece of art. I tell myself I want to make a good chair" (Wegner's Round Chair, above). Danish designers "subtract and subtract" unnecessary elements from products and tools to find true function and form, says Jens Bernsen of the Danish Design Centre. "Sometimes these designs even turn out to be beautiful."

In Copenhagen, you should visit the Danish Museum of Decorative and Applied Arts, Bredgade (open Tues–Fri 10am–4pm, Sat–Sun 12–4pm, closed Mon; entrance fee; tel: 33 14 94 52), and the Danish Design Centre, H.C. Andersens Boulevard (open Mon–Fri 10am–5pm, Sat–Sun 11am–4pm; entrance fee; tel: 33 69 33 69). A good place for furniture is Illum's Bolighus.

▽ **CYLINDA LINE**
The architect Arne Jacobsen designed this stainless steel line of household objects for the company Stelton, and it is now one of the most recognised in Denmark.

△ **URSULA**
Ursula Munch-Petersen designed this well-loved table service for Royal Copenhagen.

▽ **PH LAMP**
Poul Henningsen saw a light fixture as more than just light, but something to create a sense of space.

DESIGN IN THE HOME

For all its elegance, Danish design is not something limited to galleries and museums. In Denmark, it is found everywhere – hotels, restaurants, cafés, offices, and most importantly, homes. Nearly every Dane, it seems, has some sort of sleek designer lamp hanging over the dinner or coffee table.

For special occasions, such as weddings, birthdays and office receptions, Danes give presents such as arty salad sets, candle holders, salt and pepper grinders, pot holders – even mixing bowls (*pictured above*).

"The kitchen drawer is good design's enemy number one," says Erik Bagger, whose wine serving tools are well known in Denmark. Danish-designed products are meant to be used, however, meaning that Denmark probably has the most stylish contents of kitchen drawers anywhere in the world.

The visually striking sound systems designed by Bang & Olufsen are praised worldwide, and are found in many a Danish home. Even such prosaic items as cupboard handles and other household fittings are given due attention by Danish designers.

◁ **EGG CHAIR**
Many of Arne Jacobsen's designs were intended for specific buildings or, in this case, hotel lobbies.

▽ **IC3 TRAIN**
Gone are the days of lumpish locomotives. Even Danish trains have a high quality of design.

ZEALAND

*Venture north from Copenhagen to Hamlet's castle at Helsingør,
or south to the white cliffs of Møn, and discover Zealand,
a colourful land rich in culture and tradition*

Map
on page
114

The island of Zealand is Denmark's largest, yet it is still compact and most of its many attractions make ideal day-trips from the capital. The area north of Copenhagen makes a classic tour for visitors, with its undulating countryside, beech forests, lakes and good beaches, as well as castles, manor houses, royal hunting lodges, art galleries and museums. The southern and western areas of Zealand have traditionally been the port of entry for new people and ideas coming from the Continent. This side of the island is an enchanting expanse of rolling hills, woodland and some wonderful seaside scenery.

Historically, Zealand played an important political role in the development of Denmark. The Viking influence was strong and the town of Roskilde, a trading post in Viking times, became the seat of kings and an important religious centre.

The Danish Riviera

The coast road from **Copenhagen ❶** to Helsingør is officially called Strandvejen, but is also known as the "Danish Riviera" for its stylish houses and fine views across the Øresund to Sweden. Small protected harbours shelter working fishing boats and millionaires' yachts alike, and converted marine buildings now house fresh fish restaurants.

While it's true that the essence of North Zealand can be glimpsed in a day, it really warrants more time, either by an overnight stop at a charming Danish *kro* (inn) or by taking several day tours from Copenhagen.

Starting from Copenhagen, drive north through fashionable Charlottenlund to **Klampenborg ❷** where just 15 minutes from the city centre you come to an ancient deer park, **Klampenborg Dyrhaven** (open daily), first mentioned in official documents in 1231. You can leave your car here and take a horse and carriage through the woods and parkland. Forest walks are indicated by yellow spots painted on trees.

In another part of the deer park lies what is claimed to be the world's oldest fun fair, **Bakken**. **Peter Lieps'** rustic restaurant in the forest is the place where the locals go to drink hot chocolate or beer after winter walks. Art lovers will enjoy the quiet elegance of the nearby **Ordrupgaard** (Vilvordevej 110; open 1–5pm daily, closed Mon; entrance fee; tel: 39 64 11 83). It has a permanent collection of Danish and French paintings, which include major works by Matisse, Corot, Manet, Renoir, Sisley and Gauguin.

Out of Africa

A further 12 km (7 miles) brings you to **Rungsted ❸**, site of **Rungstedlund** (open May–Sept: 10am–5pm; Oct–Apr: Wed–Fri 1–4pm, Sat–Sun 11am–4pm; entrance fee; tel: 45 57 10 57), the family home of

LEFT: the chalk face of Møns Klint.
BELOW: the chapel at Frederiksborg.

Zealand

```
0          10 km
0          10 miles
```

Karen Blixen, the Danish writer known as Isak Dinesen whose best-selling book, *Out of Africa*, became a film starring Meryl Streep and Robert Redford.

At **Humlebæk** ❹, art lovers could easily spend an entire day at the **Louisiana Museum for Moderne Kunst** (Louisiana Museum of Modern Art, Gl. Strandvej 13; open 10am–5pm, Wed 10am–10pm; entrance fee; tel: 49 19 07 91). A rich permanent collection is supplemented by frequent international exhibitions held in a breathtaking setting overlooking the Øresund to Sweden. Sculptures adorn the gardens and there is a children's wing *(see box, page 52)*.

Map on page 114

Hamlet's Helsingør

Helsingør ❺ is best known for its massive Renaissance-style **Kronborg**, Hamlet's "Castle of Elsinore" (open May–Sept: daily, 10.30am–5pm; Oct–Apr: 11am–3pm, closed Mon; entrance fee; tel: 49 21 30 78). Originally built by King Eric of Pomerania when he introduced the "Sound Dues" (fees paid to the Danish crown by all ships passing through to the Baltic), Kronborg has been rebuilt several times. It has provided a backdrop for many productions of Shakespeare's *Hamlet*. Inside, the richly decorated King's and Queen's chambers and the 62-metre (203-ft) long Great Hall are worth seeing.

Taking on the elements: a Zealand skipper.

Helsingør is one of Denmark's most historic towns, with entire streets of colour-washed buildings. The 15th-century **Skt Mariæ Kirke** and the **Carmelite Kloster** (Convent) are among the best preserved Gothic buildings in the world. Hans Christian Andersen described it as "one of the most beautiful spots in Denmark, close to the Sound, which is one mile wide and looks like a blue stream swelling between Denmark and Sweden".

The coast road leads on to **Gilleleje** ❻, the most northerly town of Zealand, a small working fishing port. **Hos Karen og Marie**, in an unpretentious green-painted wooden building, is one of the best fish restaurants.

BELOW: author Karen Blixen lived at Rungsted.

If the weather is good, you could stop at the sun-worshippers' beaches of **Tisvilde** ❼ or **Liseleje** ❽.

As one turns towards Copenhagen, Denmark's National History Museum is at **Frederiksborg** ❾ (open Apr–Oct: 10am–5pm; Nov–Mar: 11am–3pm; entrance fee; tel: 48 26 04 39), built between 1605 and 1621 on the outskirts of **Hillerød**. The most notable rooms are the Council Hall, Knights' Hall and the chapel with its original Compenius organ, built in 1610. North of the lake is one of the best Baroque gardens in Northern Europe.

Just 9 km (5 miles) from Hillerød is the royal palace of **Fredensborg** ❿. The palace was built in Italian style in 1722, and is now used as a residence for the Danish Royal Family in spring and autumn (guided tours; tel: 33 40 31 87).

Viking town

A major highlight of Zealand is the town of **Roskilde** ⓫, the island's second largest town, 20 minutes by train west of Copenhagen. The **Domkirke** (Cathedral), built in 1170, is the burial place of generations of Danish monarchs. The **Vikingeskibshallen** (Viking Ship Museum; open May–Sept: 9am–5pm; Oct–Apr: 10am–4pm; entrance fee; tel: 46 30 02 00)

Kronborg, Hamlet's "Castle of Elsinore" at Helsingør.

is one of the great delights of Denmark. Its five ships were found in 1962 at the mouth of the Roskildefjord. The vessels had lain there since the 11th-century defenders of Roskilde had sunk them to block the entrance of the fjord against enemy attack. The restored ships include an awe-inspiring longship, the dreaded Viking man o' war. To end the day with a truly Viking flavour, turn into the museum restaurant for a draught of *mjød* (mead).

On a Viking theme, **Vikingeborgen Trelleborg** ⓬ (open Apr–Sept: 10am–5pm; Oct–Mar: 1–3pm; entrance fee; tel: 58 54 95 06), near Slagelse in western Zealand, is an abandoned Viking fortress some 1,000 years old. It was once a huge fortified camp that housed 1,000 Vikings. One of the houses has been reconstructed and on a cold spring day it is easy to understand how tough the life here must have been, despite the Vikings' reputations as hardy souls.

Southern Zealand

The first stop for modern art enthusiasts south of Copenhagen is the sleek white **Arken Museet for Moderne Kunst** (open 10am–5pm, closed Mon; entrance fee; tel: 43 54 02 22) at **Ishøj** ⓭. For a summer holiday atmosphere, **Køge** ⓮ is popular for its bathing beaches, crowded with sun-loving Danes. Inhabitants claim that Køge has more half-timbered houses than any other town in Denmark. The oldest, dated 1527, stands at 20 Kirkestræde. **Skt Nikolai Kirke** has one of Denmark's most beautiful town church interiors. Not far from the market place is **Hugo's Vinkælder**, an historic inn serving good old-fashioned draught porter.

The cliffs of **Stevns Klint** ⓯ on the south headland of Køge Bay may not be quite as dramatic as those on the island of Møn, but they are impressive when the sun illuminates them in brilliant hues of white.

BELOW: Arken, the modern art museum at Ishoj.

Inland, 5 km (3 miles) south of the ancient town of **Haslev**, Hans Christian Andersen is said to have found inspiration for what is perhaps his most famous story, *The Ugly Duckling*, in **Gisselfeld Slot** ⓰ (grounds and stables open daily), a castle built in 1554. To the west of Gisselfeld at **Fensmark** ⓱ is the **Holmegård Danish Glassvæk** (Glassworks; tours Mon–Fri; entrance fee; tel: 55 54 50 00), a popular target for tours from Copenhagen. Here, visitors can watch fine pieces being formed. The **Glass Museum** has a notable collection, and at the shop, seconds often make superb bargains.

Næstved ⓲, 5 km (3 miles) southwest of Fensmark, has been an important trading town for most of its history and has an attractive city centre. About 6 km (4 miles) to the southwest is **Gavnø Slot** (open May–Aug: 10am–4pm; entrance fee; tel: 55 70 02 00), situated among magnificent gardens on a tiny island linked by road. In the 13th century it was used as a pirates' castle; today it has Scandinavia's largest privately owned picture collection.

Cliffs of Møn

The island of **Møn** ("The Maid") to the east is linked to Zealand by road bridges. According to legend, its spectacular stretches of luminous white chalk cliffs, topped with beech woods and studded with fossils, became a refuge for the most powerful of Nordic gods, Odin, when Christianity left him homeless. Over the past 200 years, most of the invaders of Møn have been writers and painters, lured there by the inspiration of its beauty and drama.

Liselund Slot ⓳ (open May–Oct; guided tours; entrance fee; tel: 55 81 21 78) is a thatched mini-château, built in 1796. Hans Christian Andersen wrote his tales *The Tinder Box* and *The Little Match Girl* in a summer house on the estate.

Møn's churches are noted for their frescoes, particularly those at **Keldby**, **Elmelund** and **Fanefjord** ⓴, the last standing on an isolated hill overlooking the narrows of Grønsund. Beside the church is the longest barrow grave in Denmark, **Grønjægers Høj**. The main town of **Stege** ㉑ has medieval ramparts.

Falster and Lolland

The Farø bridges connect Zealand to the island of **Falster**, and the ferry routes to Germany. The main town on the island is **Nykøbing** ㉒, noted for **Czarens Hus** (Tsar's House; open 11am–10pm, closed Sun; entrance fee; tel: 54 85 28 29), where Peter the Great stayed in 1716. The area around **Marielyst** ㉓, to the southeast, has miles of white sand dunes where families take beach holidays.

There is a choice of road bridges from Falster to **Lolland**, to reach one of the island's main attractions, **Ålholm Slot** ㉔ (open July–Aug: daily 11am–5pm; Sept–June: Sat, Sun 11am–5pm; entrance fee; tel: 54 87 10 17), near the old seaport of **Nysted**. The castle dates from the 12th century and was once known as the robber's castle. It has a fine collection of rare cars. From Ålholm, the road north and west runs past beautiful lakes to **Knuthenborg** ㉕ (open May–Oct; entrance fee; tel: 54 78 80 88), a safari park. In the far west, the **Tårs** ㉖ to **Spodsbjerg** crossing connects the island with Langeland and Funen. ❑

Map on page 114

TIP

On Midsummer's Eve along the coast north of Copenhagen, beach bonfires and fireworks light the skies and a procession of ships passes through the Øresund, blasting their horns to celebrate the peak of the short Danish summer.

BELOW: farmland landscape, North Zealand.

Map
below

Copenhagen

BORNHOLM

*Denmark's Baltic island of Bornholm is a haven for both
artists and holiday-makers, attracted by its climate,
peaceful lifestyle and natural beauty*

Bornholmers, and for that matter most Danes, will be happy to relate the tale of creation of Bornholm: when God had finished making Scandinavia, he had a few leftovers from the very best features of the regions, so he gathered them all up and tossed them into the Baltic Sea. The tale perfectly illustrates the island's nickname, "Scandinavian in a nutshell", since Bornholm features a variety of landscapes typical to different areas of Scandinavia.

The enchanting island stands in the middle of the Baltic Sea between Sweden and Poland, seven hours away from Copenhagen by ferry, and 30 minutes by plane. It is a peaceful place, home to about 48,000 Bornholmers. There are no large towns and almost no industry; visitors have a perfect opportunity to relax, although from early July until the end of August the population swells fourfold with holiday-makers.

Living history

BELOW: Olsker, one of Bornholm's medieval round churches.

Bornholm was a maritime centre in the Baltic Sea during the Iron Age. Jewellery, coins, and relics from as far away as Rome and the Near East have been discovered and two forts, both known as **Gamleborg**, found in **Paradisbakkerne** (The Hills of Paradise) and at **Almindingen Skov**, date from the

Viking period. It is generally believed that Bornholm became a part of the Kingdom of Denmark at around that time.

Hammershus ❶ (open Apr–May: 10am–4pm; June–Aug: 10am–5pm; Sept–Oct: 10am–5pm; free; tel: 56 48 24 31) was built around 1250 to defend the island against attack, and is today Scandinavia's largest fortified castle. Impressive ruins remain on a huge, rocky knoll on the northwest corner of the island. At the time the castle was built, Bornholm was owned by the Archbishop of Lund (in what is now southern Sweden, but then part of Denmark); he was openly at war with the kings of Denmark. Strong separatist feelings still exist among some Bornholmers. Their banner is a Danish flag with a green cross instead of the familiar white one.

Bornholm is a centre for Danish applied arts and handicrafts. Every village has its silversmiths, wood turners, jewellers, textile artists and more. Potteries and glass-blowing workshops are often open to the public.

The variety of plant life on Bornholm is almost overwhelming. The northern part of the island is extremely rocky and, by radiating heat picked up from the sun, the rocks keep the surface warm enough for figs, grapes, mulberry trees and other plants from southern Europe to grow well. Sweet cherry trees blossom in June and give a colourful show. Red orchids are common on the banks in the river valleys and thousands of woodland flowers, especially blue, yellow, and white anemones, cover large areas. About 20 percent of Bornholm is woodland: **Almindingen ❷**, in the centre of the island, is Denmark's third largest forest. **Paradisbakkerne ❸** is wilder in vegetation than Almindingen and is best enjoyed on foot. Small farms are scattered all over the island.

Around Bornholm

Rønne ❹, with 15,000 inhabitants, is the largest town on Bornholm, and its harbour is one of the largest provincial ports in Denmark. Some parts of the town

BELOW: Bornholm is a favourite with holidaymakers.

have been well preserved, especially in the area just east of **Skt Nikolai Kirke**. The beautiful **Kastellet** (Citadel) is on the east side of town; today it is a military museum, **Forsvarsmuseet** (open May–Oct: Tues–Sat 10am–4pm; entrance fee; tel: 56 95 65 83).

Bornholm has inspired many Danish painters, as well as having produced a few of its own: Oluf Høst is probably the best known. **Bornholms Museum** (Skt Mortensgade 29; open Tues–Sat 10am–5pm; entrance fee; tel: 56 95 07 35) and its collection of paintings, ceramics and exhibits from pre-history onwards relating to the island's past, is worth visiting .

Bornholm celebrates classical music with a festival from mid-July to September, which attracts music lovers from around the world.

Åkirkeby ❺ (pop. 1,400) is the main town in the southern part of Bornholm, and the only one of the larger towns situated inland. It was an ecclesiastical centre and its church, **Åkirke**, was built around 1150 as a chapter house in the Archbishopric of Lund. The large tower was extended around 1200, and at the same time it was fortified with walls even heavier than those of Hammershus. It is notable for its sandstone baptismal font depicting the life of Christ in 11 relief carvings; the figures are explained in runic script, and end with the signature of the stonecutter, "Sighraf, master".

The easternmost town in Denmark, **Svaneke ❻**, prospered with the success of its shipping captains. The largest buildings were originally merchants' houses. North of the town is an old Dutch mill, and nearby an untraditional water tower, built by the architect Jørn Utzon in 1951.

Bicycling downhill is forbidden in **Gudhjem ❼** ("good home"), a very pretty place, built on steep slopes down to the water. Windmills around the town once provided electricity. The former railway station has been converted into a model train museum, **Bornholms Model Jernbane Museum** (open May–Sept: 1–5pm, closed Sat; free; tel: 56 47 04 85), and provides an excellent way of exploring local history. There is an agricultural museum, **Landbrugsmuseet Melstedgård** (open May–Oct: 10am–5pm, closed Mon; entrance fee; tel: 56 48 55 98), just southeast of Gudhjem at **Melsted**, a settlement which first gained prominence as an important trading centre during the Middle Ages.

BELOW:
a great breakfast.

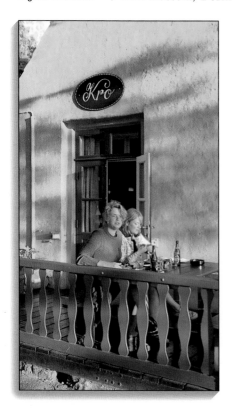

Fortress in the sea

From Gudhjem Harbour one can sail to the group of islands collectively known as **Ertholmene**. The largest of these are **Christiansø ❽** and **Frederiksø**. A naval base was constructed here in about 1864, but today only fishermen and their families live on this "fortress in the sea". It makes an interesting place to visit. The islands are rocky, with castle towers, batteries, and cannon serving as reminders of the past.

Round churches

Østerlars Kirke ❾ (consecrated to St Laurentius), just over 4 km (2½ miles) southwest from Gudhjem, is the largest of the four medieval "round churches" of Bornholm, which include **Nylars**, **Nyker** and **Olsker**. When the Slavic Wends ravaged the island they were occasionally used as places of refuge and in the 14th to 16th centuries Hanseatic merchants from northern Germany would move in during the herring season. At

Map
on page
118

Osterlars the enormous support pillars create the impression of a fortress, which was the second purpose of the structure. Inside the church (built around 1150), the vault is painted with fine frescoes of biblical scenes. On the north wall of the oval-shaped choir, stone steps lead to the second storey, where the hollow central pillar has two entrances. The outer wall has a watchman's gallery. The double altarpiece was painted by the local artist Poul Høm.

Edible delicacies

During the summer months, freshly landed herrings are delivered to the island's smokehouses. Here they are turned from their original silver colour into the "golden Bornholmers" dearly loved by Danes, which can often be seen drying on stands outside. Elderwood gives them their special taste. One can eat them warm from the oven or put them on black bread, sprinkle them with salt, and add chopped chives, radishes and an egg yolk on top.

Pickled herrings are a lunchtime speciality. The best spiced herrings are produced on Christiansø. Baltic salmon, said to be the finest edible fish in the world, is normally available, too.

A cheerful sign attracts diners. Try a delicious "golden Bornholmer", the island's smoked herring speciality.

Bornholm by bike

The best way to travel around Bornholm is by bicycle. An extensive network of cycle paths has been established and its easy to find houses, hotels, and campsites en route. Residents often rent rooms or houses to visitors. but remember to book accommodation in advance in summer, especially in the southeast part of the island where the wonderful beaches of **Dueodde** ❿ and **Balka** in particular attract crowds of holiday-makers in high season. ❏

BELOW:
Gudhjem village,
on the north coast.

FUNEN

Map
on page
124

*Bridging the water between Zealand and Jutland is the island of
Funen, the "Garden of Denmark", with the buzzing
cultural centre of Odense at its heart*

Copenhagen

Denmark's central island of **Funen** (*Fyn* in Danish) is known for its natural
beauty, flowered gardens, castles and manor houses. Danes call it "the
Garden of Denmark". Cycling tours take you along hundreds of kilometres of marked routes. Here, too, lies historic Odense, the birthplace of author
Hans Christian Andersen *(see page 127)*. South Funen and the island archipelago are a paradise for anglers and yachtsmen.

The Funen circle

When coming from Copenhagen, the usual way to reach Funen is by train or car
across the mighty Store Bælt bridge to Nyborg on Funen's east coast. The Lille
Bælt bridge links it to east central Jutland on the opposite side. Your choice
then is circling the islands from Nyborg or Middelfart, and basing yourself
either in Odense or Svendborg to make excursions. Driving is easy, but the
most satisfying way to see Funen is on a bicycle. You can lean your bike beside
one of the little whitewashed churches to take a look inside, and inhale the
scent of the wild flowers that lie beneath roadside rose hedges.

Before heading north out of **Nyborg ❶** for Kerteminde and the Hindsholm
Peninsula, take a look at **Nyborg Slot** (open Mar–Oct: 10am–3pm, closed Mon;
entrance fee; tel: 65 31 02 07), which dates from 1170.
It was built to defend the country from the Wends of
North Germany and, during the Middle Ages, was the
meeting place for the three ruling powers of monarchy, nobility, and clergy. But fashions change. In
1722, much of Nyborg Slot was demolished to provide building materials for Odense Castle. Part of the
original ramparts and moat remain, and the castle has
a fine interior of great echoing, empty rooms.

About 15 km (9 miles) north from Nyborg, near
Kerteminde, are the underground remains of a Viking
chieftain's burial ship at **Ladby ❷** (open Mar–Oct:
10am–4pm, closed Mon; Nov–Feb: 11am–3pm,
closed Mon, Tues; entrance fee). With him in his 22-
metre (72-ft) Viking ship, the chief took what he
prized most: his weapons, hunting dogs and 11 horses.

Kerteminde ❸ is Funen's foremost fishing village,
with old half-timbered houses. Most towns in Funen
have craftspeople of many different skills, and Kerteminde offers stoneware and pottery at local shops.

Odense

In the centre of Funen lies the quaint but lively capital of Funen, **Odense ❹**, Denmark's third-largest city
(pop. 200,000). Its name stems from Old Norse and
means "the sanctuary of Odin", the wise and mighty
chief god. So the place was important enough to be
worthy of Odin's protection before the Christian

LEFT: young visitor
at Hans Christian
Andersen's house
in Odense.
BELOW: decorative
doorway in
Ærøskøbing

The Kerteminde landscape has attracted some of Denmark's most renowned artists. Their work can be seen at the village's Johannes Larsen Museum in Møllebakken (tel: 65 32 37 27).

conversion of Denmark. The Gothic cathedral, **Skt Knuds Domkirke**, is one of the most beautiful landmarks of Odense. It was named after King Knud (Canute) II, who was murdered in the town in 1086 by his rebellious subjects and later canonised by the Pope. It's adorned with a gilded altarpiece made by Claus Berg in Germany in 1521. In the crypt lie the remains of Skt Knud.

Munkemøllestræde, west of the cathedral, is the cobblestone street with the tiny house where the storyteller Hans Christian Andersen grew up in the early 1800s (open Apr–Sept: 10am–5pm; Oct–Mar: noon–3pm; entrance fee). Northeast of the cathedral is the outstanding **Hans Christian Andersen Museum** (Hans Jensens Stræde; open Sept–June: 10am–4pm; June–Aug: 9am–7pm; closed Mon; entrance fee; tel: 66 13 13 72). The museum houses a collection devoted to the writer's life, with pictures, letters, manuscripts, and personal belongings.

Denmark's foremost composer, Carl Nielsen *(see page 127)*, spent his early years in the city and the **Carl Nielsen Museet** (Claus Bergs Garde 11; open 10am–4pm; entrance fee) is devoted both to his life and work and to that of his

Funen and its Archipelago

wife, Anne Marie Nielsen, a sculptor. His childhood home can be visited at **Nørre Lyndelse ❺** (open May–Sept: 11am–3pm; Oct–Apr: closed Mon; entrance fee; tel: 66 13 13 72), south of Odense.

Map on page 124

In few other cities will one find a river that is clean enough to offer amateur fishermen both sea trout and eel. This is an accomplishment for what was once a polluted industrial centre. Today, the quarter around the old factory buildings at Kongensgade and Vestergade has been revitalised and is a popular magnet for young people and the university crowd. The former textile mill, **Brandt's Klædefabrik**, off Vestergade, is now a spacious multipurpose building for concerts, complete with the **Museet for Fotokunst** (Museum of Photographic Art); the **Kunsthallen** art gallery, featuring a varied programme of exhibitions; **Dannmarks Grafiske Museum** (Danish Museum for Printing); and **Tidens Samling** (Time Collection) which follows daily life and fashion since 1900 (all open 10am–5pm, closed Mon except July–Aug; entrance fee).

Just south of Odense is a delightful spot, **Den Fynske Landsby** (Funen Village, Sejerskovvej 20; open Apr–Oct: 10am–5pm; Nov–Mar, 11am–3pm; closed Mon; entrance fee; tel: 66 13 13 72). It contains old farm buildings from different areas, with a vicarage, workshops, a windmill and water mill.

Gardeners admire De Syv Haver, the Seven Gardens southeast of Assens inspired by different countries.

Tuneful Fåborg

Fåborg ❻ on south Funen is a lovely little town where **Klokketårnet**, a carillon, chimes out a hymn four times a day. It's the largest carillon in Europe and the town's main landmark. If you could chose only one place to visit in Fåborg, it must be **Fåborg Museum for Fynsk Kunst** (Grønnegade 75; open Apr–Sept: 10am–4pm; Nov–Mar: 11am–3pm, closed Mon; entrance fee; tel: 62 61 06 45), an art gallery featuring the "Funen artists" (1880–1920), including Peter Hansen, Fritz Syberg and Johannes Larsen, with sculptures by Kai Nielsen.

BELOW: book sale on Funen.

The heather-covered **Svanninge Bakker ❼**, about 10 km (6 miles) north of Fåborg, is a national park. **Svendborg ❽** is a beautiful market town and a good centre for touring. Along with Fåborg, it is the gateway to the southern islands.

Egeskov Slot ❾ (open May–Sept: 10am–5pm, closes later in summer; entrance fee; tel: 62 27 10 16), 14 km (9 miles) north of Svendborg, is one of Denmark's most famous historic sights, set in magnificent Baroque and Renaissance gardens. Egeskov means oak forest, and the oaks were felled around 1540 to form the piles the castle stands on. The grounds also feature a re-creation of its 200-year-old **maze**. This "labyrinth", as it is called, has 1.6 km (1 mile) of paths screened by 2,200 bamboo shoots. There is a **Veteranmuseum** (Veteran Motor Museum; open 10am–4pm) with a fine collection of old cars, aircraft, motor cycles, and horse-drawn carriages.

Along the west coast

From Fåborg, turn northwest to explore Funen's west coast. At Ebberup, south of Assens, are **De Syv Haver ❿** (The Seven Gardens; open Mar–Oct: 10am–5pm; entrance fee; tel: 64 74 12 85), outstanding gardens created by Tove and Gunner

Map
on page
124

Map on page 124

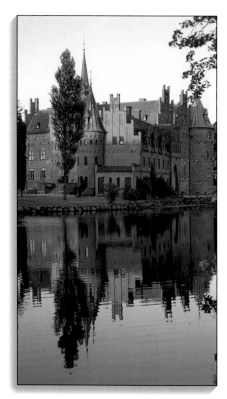

TIP

Whether driving, cycling or walking, follow the "Daisy Routes" marked by a flower sign. These guide you past some of the most beautiful scenery in Funen.

BELOW: Egeskov Slot, built in the 16th century.

Sylvest. Around 15 km (9 miles) north from Assens on the road to **Middelfart,** a broad west-facing bay at **Tybrind Vig** is a site for underwater archaeology. North of Middelfart dramatic steep cliffs line the shore.

About 3 km (2 miles) east of **Bogense** is the castle of **Gyldensteen,** a late-Renaissance building with an impressive gatehouse (closed to the public). Here, Karen Blixen (pen name Isak Dinesen), author of *Out of Africa,* wrote some of her books during the German Occupation of Denmark in World War II. From Bogense, you can complete the Funen circle by touring along the sparsely populated north coast to the Hindsholm Peninsula and Kerteminde. At low tide you can walk to the island of **Æbelø** ⓫, an unspoilt landscape rich in wildlife.

To the islands

You could spend a lifetime trying to visit all the islands of the Funen Archipelago and still miss a few. Only 19 are inhabited permanently. Even the largest islands hold no more than a few thousand people, and others just a couple of families. All summer long, the harbours are full of boats. You can take day trips aboard wooden sailing ships or longer cruises through the archipelago. This is also an angler's paradise.

From Fåborg, it is just a short trip to the most beautiful island of all, **Ærø.** Hire a bike for the short cycle run from Søby to **Ærøskøbing** ⓬, the main town, and on to the old naval port of **Marstal.** Cycling is easy and the roads wind past fertile fields and thatched farmhouses, medieval churches and windmills. The American author, Temple Fielding, said that Ærøskøbing was one of the five places in the world one should see. Certainly, the cobbled streets with their brightly coloured houses almost seem like a film set.

From Fåborg, ferries also run to the smaller islands of **Avernakø** and **Lyø** ⓭, both of which have good, inexpensive inns.

Svendborg is the ferry port for the southern islands. The first island, reached by a narrow bridge, is **Tåsinge,** with some 5,000 inhabitants. **Valdemars Slot** ⓮, is one of Denmark's oldest privately owned castles, with a wonderful view over Svendborgsund (open May–Sept: 10am–5pm; entrance fee). It was built in 1640 by King Kristian IV for one of his sons, Prince Valdemar Kristian. Most interesting is the castle church, with an excellent restaurant beneath. The Tea Pavilion, mirrored in its own lake overlooking **Lunkebugten Bay,** is now a café. The loveliest village on Tåsinge is **Troense** ⓯. Sitting on the veranda of the **Troense Inn** as the slim masts of the sailing boats gather in the harbour against a darkening sea, is one of the pleasures of a Funen summer.

Langeland, literally "long land", is connected to Tåsinge by a causeway-bridge. One of its famous sons was H.C. Ørsted, the discoverer of electromagnetism, who was born in the main town of **Rudkøbing** ⓰. Another famous resident was N.F.S. Grundtvig, a clergyman and founder of modern Danish education. To the south, **Ristinge** and **Bagenkop** both have excellent bathing beaches. In fact, nowhere along the coast of Funen and its islands are you far from good places to swim and sail. ❑

ANDERSEN AND NIELSEN: FUNEN'S FAMOUS SONS

In the 19th century, two Funen boys, the storyteller Hans Christian Andersen and the the composer Carl Nielsen, set off to make their fortunes in the world

Two of Denmark's most noted literary and musical figures, Hans Christian Andersen and Carl Nielsen respectively, were born on the island of Funen.

At the height of his fame, the composer Carl Nielsen (1865–1931) told an audience that his mother had always said to him: "Don't forget that Hans Christian Andersen was a poor boy like you." There may have been something in the Funen air that inspired poor boys to rise to fame, but it is more likely that Nielsen was inspired by Andersen, 60 years his senior. Both came from humble homes, both left Odense to seek their fortune in Copenhagen.

Andersen (1805–75) was born in Odense and spent his childhood in a small half-timbered house in Munkemøllestræde, now a museum. Quite apart from his skill as a writer, Andersen had a good singing voice and gifts as an artist. At the age of 14 he set off to Copenhagen to attend the Royal Theatre School. The Theatre Board recognised his skills and he was found a place at a grammar school in Helsingør.

After school, Andersen travelled widely; *Shadow Picture of a Journey to the Harz Mountains and Saxony* (1831) was the result of his early adventures. Through his life he continued to write poems, novels and plays. His autobiographical novel, *The Improvisatore*, described the rise to fortune of a poor Italian boy. His early fairy tales, including *The Tinder Box* and *The Princess and the Pea* (1835), brought him immortality. In 1840 he met and fell in love with the singer Jenny Lind, "The Swedish Nightingale", though she always called him "brother". His fairy tale, *The Nightingale*, was inspired by her.

When he was made an honorary citizen of Odense in 1867, Andersen said it was "an honour greater than I had ever dreamt of".

Carl Nielsen was born at Nørre Lyndelse, now a museum devoted to his life. His father was a folk musician and Carl played the violin. His earliest compositions, at the age of eight, were two dance tunes. Like Andersen, Nielsen wrote an autobiography, *My Childhood*.

At the Royal Theatre Orchestra in Copenhagen, where Nielsen became second violinist, the Norwegian conductor, Johan Svendsen, encouraged him to compose. At 25, Nielsen won a fellowship which allowed him to travel, and went to Dresden to steep himself in Wagner's ideas.

Nielsen composed two operas: the dark drama, *Saul og David*, and a comic opera, *Maskarade*, along with symphonies and choral works, such as *Hymnus Amoris*. ❑

TOP LEFT AND RIGHT: composer Carl Nielsen.
ABOVE LEFT: Hans Christian Andersen.
RIGHT: actor Ejnar Han Jensen plays Andersen.

JUTLAND

The dune-fringed shores of Jutland have captured the imagination of both painters and holiday-makers, while music lovers head for Århus, "the world's smallest big city"

Map on page 130

Jutland (*Jylland*) is the Danish peninsula that juts up above Germany, the "mainland" in this nation of islands. When Copenhageners talk about the provinces, they usually mean Jutland. With its rolling hills crisscrossed with rivers and creeks, patched with forests, crusted by sand dunes and scattered with palaces, Viking monuments and remains, Jutland is a land of contrasts.

Jutland's capital city is **Århus ❶**, a spunky college town known for its music, theatre, ballet, art and cafés, as well as its fun Festival Week every autumn. Denmark's second largest city – with a population of 280,000, only a fraction of Copenhagen's size – this harbour town is noted for its nearby forests, beaches and castles. The pointed spire of **Domkirken**, the Cathedral of St Clement (open summer: 9.30am–4pm; rest of year: 10am–3pm; free), is 93 metres (316 ft) high and offers one of the best views in the city from its belfry. Nearby are the winding, cobblestone streets of the Latin Quarter, with quirky boutiques and trendy cafés and restaurants. The **Århus Kunstmuseum** (Museum of Art; open 10am–5pm, Wed 10am–8pm, closed Mon; entrance fee; tel: 86 13 52 55) gives an overview of Danish art from the 18th, 19th and 20th centuries. The **Rådhus** (City Hall) was built in 1941 and designed by Arne Jacobsen, one of Denmark's most notable architects and designers.

Den Gamle By (The Old Town; open June–Aug: 9am–6pm; Sept–May: hours vary; entrance fee; tel: 86 12 31 88), is an open-air, national museum of urban culture and history, featuring reconstructions of 75 Danish urban buildings. From the front entrance onwards, the museum is a sensory overload in an environment that feels genuinely historic – with merchant and artisan houses and workshops, gardens, shops and stalls, streets and alleys.

One of the best museum exhibits in Denmark is the 2,000-year-old Grauballe Man at the **Forhistorisk Museum** (Museum of Prehistory; open Apr–Sept: 10am–5pm; Oct–Mar: 10am–4pm; closed Mon; entrance fee; tel: 89 42 11 00) at **Moesgård ❷**, 8 km (5 miles) south of Århus. To stand face to face with the grimacing man, who was found perfectly pre-served in a peat bog in 1952, is a chilling experience.

The ruins of the **Kalø Slot ❸**, built in 1313, are situated on a small island on the edge of a cove on the north side of Århus bay. The nearby hills of **Mols Bjerge ❹**, where Viking relics abound in beautiful nature, are well worth a visit. Several artists have set up shop on the pretty Djursland peninsula.

LEFT: dappled forest of East Jutland.
BELOW: beach life, West Jutland.

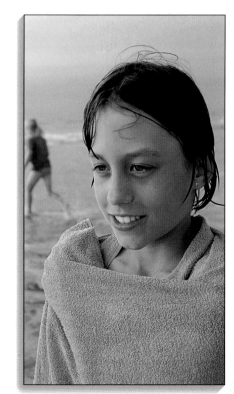

Island haven

Just south of Mols Bjerge is the immaculate town of **Ebeltoft ❺**, with its small, unaltered town hall from 1789. The island of **Samsø** can be seen from here, but

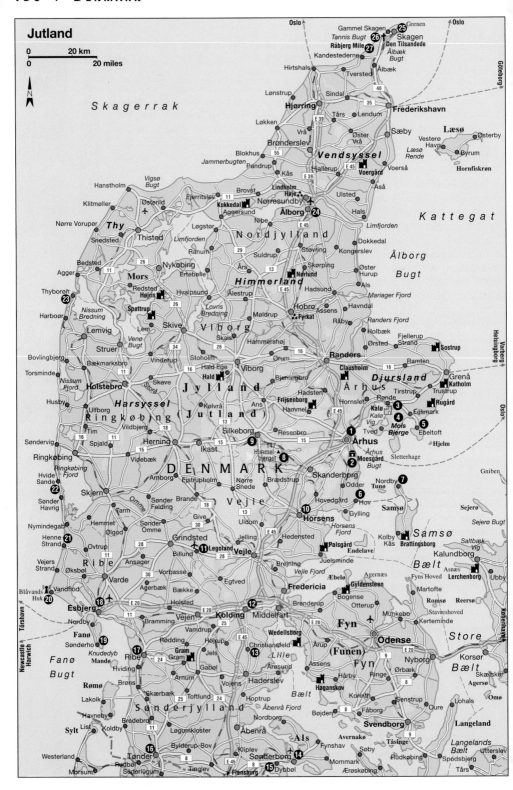

Jutland

0   20 km
0   20 miles

it must be reached by ferry from **Hov** , 25 km (15 miles) south of Århus. A haven for artists, farmers and nature lovers alike, Samsø is renowned for its new potatoes and cheese. **Nordby** ❼, on the northern tip, contains a wealth of colourful, crossbeam houses, as well as small art galleries. Also worth a visit in Nordby is **Samsø Labyrinten**, the world's largest maze (open June–Aug: daily; weekends only May, Sept–Oct; entrance fee; tel: 86 59 66 59 for times). Its 5 km (3 miles) of passages wind through a dense fir forest covering 6 hectares (15 acres). In the south of the island, **Brundby Rock Hotel**, owned by a group of Danish rock musicians, is a festive place to have dinner and hear live music.

Map on page 130

Lake District

A series of lakes snake through forested hills west of Århus, and a fun way to see them is from the paddle steamer *MS Hjejlen*, which has carried passengers from Ry to Silkeborg since 1861. For a bird's eye view, climb **Himmelbjerget** ❽ (Sky Mountain), at 147 metres (482 ft), one of Denmark's highest "mountains". The nearby town of **Silkeborg** ❾ features the **Silkeborg Kunstmuseum** (Museum of Art; open Apr–Oct: 10am–5pm, closed Mon; Nov–Apr: Tues–Fri noon–4pm, Sat–Sun 10am–5pm; entrance fee; tel: 86 82 53 88), which is built around the glorious, playful work of the painter Asger Jorn and others from the 20th-century CoBrA (Copenhagen, Brussels, Amsterdam) group.

Miniature world: Lego was developed by Ole Kirk Christiansen and his family in Billund in 1949.

Further south, historical **Horsens** ❿ hosts an annual Middle Ages Festival in the autumn, which is highly recommended. At **Billund**, 50 km (31 miles) southwest of Horsens, more than a million people a year visit **Legoland** ⓫ (open June–Aug: 10am–9pm; Sept–May: 10am–8pm; entrance fee; tel: 75 33 13 33), coming to marvel at the miniature world created from more than 35 million of the studded Lego plastic bricks.

BELOW: timber-framed cottages, Ebeltoft.

A good salami

South Jutland has some of the most patriotic Danes in the country, particularly the generations who remember the area when it was officially part of Germany's Schleswig duchy from 1864 to 1920. **Kolding** ⓬ was a border town on the Danish side at the time, and historical sights abound. Particularly of interest are the remains of **Koldinghus Slot** (open 10am–5pm; entrance fee; tel: 76 33 81 00), a castle built in 1208, and the **Kunstmuseet Trapholt** (Trapholt Museum of Art; open 10am–5pm; entrance fee; tel: 76 30 05 30) with a fine collection of modern art.

Driving south 15 km (9 miles), the Danish Moravian town of **Christiansfeld** ⓭ is famous for its scrumptious honey cakes. Further south, close to the German border, **Sønderborg** ⓮ is a striking town on **Als Island**, with a colourful harbour and the mighty **Sønderborg Slot** (open May–Sept: 10am–5pm; Oct–Apr:10am–4pm; Nov–Mar:1–4pm; tel: 74 42 25 39), a fortress built around 1100. Provincial Sønderborg happens to have one of the best cafés in Denmark, **Café Druen**, not far from the castle. South Jutland is known for its meats – particularly salamis. Stop at a local butcher to try a beer sausage.

Just to the west, **Dybbøl** ⓯ played a major role in the 1864 war with Germany. At a national historic

TIP

A good place to try South Jutland's local speciality of "marsh sausage" is the Rudbøl Grænsekro, an inn in the village of Rudbøl (southwest of Tønder) that has been serving this delicacy since 1791.

park, the **Dybbøl Mill**, restored and painted white, and its museum are open to the public (Apr–Oct: 10am–5pm; free; tel: 74 48 69 91).

On the western side of South Jutland is **Tønder** ⑯, a lace-making centre in the 17th century, documented in **Tønder Museum** (open 10am–5pm, closed Mon; entrance fee; tel: 74 72 26 57). Tønder has an attractive 17th- and 18th-century townscape, and many houses have distinctive painted doorways. At **Møgeltønder**, 3 km (2 miles) to the west, the village street is lined with lime trees – a beautiful sight. This is home to Prince Joachim (second in succession) and Princess Alexandra at **Schackenborg Slot**.

Night watchmen

Ribe ⑰, built around its 12th-century cathedral, ranks high on the list of historic centres in Scandinavia. Its brick and half-timbered houses, courtyards and *kroer* (inns) are much as they were hundreds of years ago.

Ribe Domkirke (Cathedral) stands on the site of one of Denmark's earliest wooden churches, built around AD 860. The "Cat Head Door" was said to be the entrance for the Devil. The choir has been stunningly decorated by CoBrA artist Carl-Henning Petersen. There are splendid views from the tower.

Ribe continues the Middle Ages tradition of night watchmen. On summer evenings at 10pm, the watchman walks around singing the traditional songs that once told the people that they could sleep soundly, all was well.

Western shores

BELOW: the Jelling Stones, *circa* 985.

West Jutland has a sense of space and time different from the rest of the region. In winter, the weather can be rugged, with storms blowing in off a

HARALD BLUETOOTH WAS HERE

Viking sights abound in Jutland. **Lindholm Høje** (open Apr–Oct: daily 10am–5pm; Oct–Mar: Tues–Sun 10am–4pm; entrance fee; tel: 98 17 55 22), just north of Ålborg, is a necropolis with 700 graves, a reconstructed village from the early Iron Age and Viking times, and a museum. Many of the graves are in the shape of Viking ships.

Elsewhere, near Hobro, is the Viking fort of **Fyrkat**. Four earth fortifications once enclosed 16 large houses on the site, and one of these longhouses has been re-constructed. Finds from Fyrkat are on display in **Hobro Museum** (open Apr–Oct: 11am–5pm, closed Mon; entrance fee; tel: 98 51 05 55). On the Mols peninsula near Århus is the **Poskjær Stenhus** barrow, which lies along the road from Agri to Grønfeld.

A memorial referred to as Denmark's "birth certificate" can be found in Jelling. The **Jellingstenene** (Jelling Stones) are covered with runic script carved by King Harald Bluetooth 1,000 years ago to proclaim his conversion to Christianity, and in honour of his parents, King Gorm the Old and Queen Thyra Danebrod, who were buried in the mounds beside Jelling town church. For a flavour of life in Viking times, re-enactments, including battles and blood oaths, can be experienced at Moesgård, and in Jels in July.

turbulent North Sea. In summer this part of Denmark, with its sandy beaches, is popular with holiday-makers.

Esbjerg ⓲ is the biggest port town on the coast, the main gateway for ferries from Britain. A 20-minute ferry ride away is the island of **Fanø**, a major ship building centre in the 18th and 19th centuries. **Sønderho** ⓳ village in the south of the island has colourful thatch-roofed cottages, an inn and Seamen's Church (1782). The island is characteristic for West Jutland: a superb stretch of white sandy beach, dunes, heath and forest.

Back on the Jutland coast, 30 km (19 miles) northwest, is **Blåvands Huk** ⓴ lighthouse, a popular holiday spot with a nature reserve nearby. At the beach during low tide if you see people standing in water up to their ankles staring down, don't be alarmed. They are hunting for nuggets of amber, a golden petrified tree resin that frequently washes ashore here.

To the north, 25 km (16 miles), at **Henne** ㉑, Denmark's television chef Hans Beck Thomsen runs the **Henne Kirkeby Kro** (tel: 75 25 54 00) in summer.

A narrow strip of land runs north from Nymindegab to Søndervig, separating the sea from **Ringkøbing Fjord**, a broad, shallow, saltwater "lake". Driving north towards the fishing village of **Hvide Sande** ㉒, the crashing waves from the North Sea can be heard but are hidden from view by tall sand dunes. No matter how many times one walks to the top of these dunes, the experience is breathtaking: an incredibly long, narrow beach stretches out of sight in each direction, a stiff, salty breeze slaps you in the face, and the churning ocean melts into the horizon.

From here to the northern tip at Skagen, the scenery is similar, broken by several attractive fishing villages and bathing resorts. At **Thyborøn** ㉓, a native

Map
on page
130

The night watchman of Ribe who recounts the town's history in song on his round.

BELOW: re-enacting the Middle Ages.

Map
on page
130

*Shell-covered house
at Thyborøn.*

BELOW: church in
the sands. **RIGHT:**
Hennes Strand.

has decorated a house with shells, covering all surfaces, inside and out. Take the 10-minute ferry from here across the Limfjorden to Vendsyssel, north Jutland.

At its advantageous location for trade on the Limfjorden, **Ålborg ㉔** – Denmark's fourth-largest city with a population of 155,000 – is full of historical buildings, castles and Viking monuments. The most well-known building in town is the opulent six-storey **Stenhus** (Stone House) on Østerågade, built in 1624 by a merchant, Jens Bang, to show off his wealth. Bang was annoyed that he had never become a town councillor; on the south façade of Stenhus is a carving of him sticking his tongue out at the town hall across the street. Also across the street lies the tourist information centre (tel: 98 12 60 22). The town's main entertainment artery is **Jomfru Ane Gade**, lined with restaurants and bars in courtyards and half-timbered buildings. This is the place to try Ålborg's most famous product: *aquavit*, the strong apéritif flavoured with caraway seeds that accompanies the traditional Danish *smørrebrød* (open-faced sandwiches).

Nordic light

Situated on a relatively narrow piece of land with the North Sea on one side and the Baltic on the other, **Skagen ㉕** has a magical quality to it. The air shimmers with a certain light that must be experienced in person to believe it. This was an irresistible lure to the Skagen painters, who made it their home in the second half of the 19th century, with Brøndums Hotel as their rallying ground. Artists such as Anna and Michael Ancher, P.S. Krøyer, and Viggo Johansen portrayed fisherfolk, local residents and each other with a true sense for light and colour. To see for yourself, visit **Skagens Museum** (open Apr, May, Sept: 11am–4pm, closed Mon; June–Aug: daily 10am–6pm; Nov–Mar: hours vary; entrance fee; tel: 98 44 64 44), and **Anchers Hus** (Ancher's House; open Apr: 11am–3pm; May–Sept: 10am–5pm; Nov– Mar: Sat–Sun only 11am–3pm; entrance fee; tel: 98 44 30 09), bought by the Anchers in 1884. The artists' colony still lives on in Skagen. A few kilometres southwest is **Gammel Skagen** (Old Skagen), a cosmopolitan resort known for its sun-yellow homes with red-tiled roofs and gourmet fish restaurants.

Just west of Gammel Skagen, **Den Tilsandede Kirke ㉖** (Sand-Covered Church; open June–Aug: 11am–5pm; entrance fee) peeps out of the dunes with only its steeple visible. (If your interest is piqued here, another church is on the way to a more dramatic end at **Lønstrup** on the west coast. Here, the powerful waves are eating away at the cliffs under Mårup Kirke, starting with its cemetery.) To see migrating dunes up close, you need go no further than **Råbjerg Mile ㉗**, 10 km (6 miles) south of Skagen. Pushed by the wind and sea, the dunes travel as much as 20 metres (65 ft) every year.

For the penultimate experience of nature moving at its own rhythms, go to **Grenen**, 5 km (3 miles) north of Skagen, continental Europe's northernmost point. At the tip, you can actually see the North and Baltic seas crash into each other in a symphony of splashes. The experience of standing here with one foot in each sea in a spot where the light is alive is one of the most exhilarating experiences in Denmark. ❑

GREENLAND

In spring and summer when the ice retreats and the temperature rises, Greenland's spectacular landscape becomes accessible for some of the most awesome adventure travel

Map on page 138

The world's largest island is a place of stunning natural beauty, dramatic weather and fascinating culture. Greenland, like the Faroe Islands, is a former Danish colony that has become a member of the kingdom, but with its own home-rule government.

Greenland is like no other place. Its vast Arctic solitude is profound and its silence almost consumes you. Here, where the North Atlantic meets the Arctic Ocean, is the cleanest environment in the world, and measurably the oldest. Where else can you sip a drink cooled by a 1,000-year-old ice cube?

Greenland is called Kalaallit Nunaat (Land of Man) by its own people. They number only about 45,000 (plus an additional 10,000 Danes) in an area of 2,175,600 sq km (840,000 sq miles). The distance north to south is 2,670 km (1,655 miles), and the widest part east to west is 1,000 km (620 miles). Its closest neighbour is Canada. The capital is **Nuuk** ❶ (Godthåb) on the west coast.

Greenlanders are Inuit and live in small towns around the coasts, mainly on the milder western side. Most of these people still earn their livelihoods by fishing and hunting. But thanks to its long association with Denmark, Greenland has a modern infrastructure and burgeoning tourist industry.

More than four-fifths of the country lies under 3 km (2 miles) of pack ice, but the southern coastal regions, especially to the west, are green and mild during late spring and summer. Daytime temperatures here can climb to a balmy 21°C (70°F) or more, but northerly winds in winter can make the mercury plunge to a bone-cracking –32°C (–25°F). Conditions in spring and summer make for excellent hiking and camping, not to mention some of the best fishing anywhere.

Adventure tours

The classic way of touring Greenland is by dog sled. You can hire a team and driver for a short sightseeing tour or for a longer journey. The season is usually from late February to May. In western Greenland it is possible to arrange trips from **Sisimiut** ❷, **Qeqertarsuaq (Disko Island)** ❸ and points further north. On the barely populated east coast, you can dog sled from **Tasiilaq** ❹ and **Ittoqqortoormiit** ❺.

A classic, though physically demanding, dog sled tour is the eight-day trip between Sisimiut and **Kangerlussuaq** ❻ at Søndre Strømfjord on the west coast, which is possible in March and April. The route takes you through the vast and beautiful landscapes of mid-Greenland, across frozen lakes and over hilly terrain. You sleep in hunting huts or tents.

Boat tours also offer breathtaking scenery and wildlife. Summer cruises to towns along the east and west coasts take you through sparkling seas alive with

LEFT: Greenland coastal settlement. **BELOW:** fisherman's hideaway.

Arctic foxes are common in Greenland's coastal areas; other species found in the harsh environment include polar bear, musk ox and caribou.

seals and other marine life, even whales. You can disembark at harbours and settlements for hiking trips, or dog sled tours in season. Between ports, you sail past icebergs and glaciers. On land you might see reindeer and musk oxen, and polar bears have been spotted. Bird life is not abundant in Greenland, but you can encounter Arctic terns, ravens, peregrine falcons and eagles.

Helicopter is an important, often essential, means of transportation here. Chopper tours are a breathtakingly beautiful way to travel around Greenland.

A novel way of exploring Greenland's nature is aboard a sturdy Icelandic pony. From Kangerlussuaq, you can join riding tours over gentle or demanding terrain, past lush flora and fauna, and inspiring scenery.

This vast, half-frozen island draws an increasing number of anglers each year. They come to fish for trout and Arctic char in the lowland lakes, rivers and streams. Off the coast and sometimes through ice, they reel in Greenland halibut, Norway haddock, catfish and cod. Fishing licences are required.

Among the spectacular natural phenomena in Greenland are the Northern Lights and the Midnight Sun. The *aurora borealis* occurs all year long but is only visible in a clear night sky in autumn and winter. These ethereal lights can appear as colourful curtains, veins of silk ribbon, or as ghostly souls flying to heaven. In summer, the midnight sun keeps the night sky blue.

Ruled by the weather

The only way to travel to Greenland is by air, either via Copenhagen; Keflavik, Iceland; or Ottawa, Canada. Once in Greenland, sailing is an option year-round, but schedules are highly dependent on the changing weather. The same applies to air services. In a climate which changes from hot sun and clear bright air to

BELOW: dressed in traditional costume.

a deluge of rain in a moment, the weather decides whether it's possible to keep to a plan made the day before. Many a visitor has been forced to "overnight" at **Narsarsuaq** in the south because aircraft couldn't land.

Most towns in Greenland have modern hotels in various categories of comfort. These and the local tourist offices are the best places to book excursions. The more footloose visitor may prefer a hostel, seaman's home, or a cabin. Camping sites are appearing and tent-roughing is permitted virtually everywhere, so long as campers observe the rules of nature and common politeness.

Fruits of the sea

Heart disease is a rarity for Greenlanders, thanks to a diet based heavily on the sea. Greenlandic specialities also include fowl, game and berries. The national dish is *suasaat*, seal meat cooked with rice and onions. A particular delicacy is *mattak*, pieces of whale skin with a thin layer of blubber. Slow chewing brings out its nutty flavour. If your taste buds are more "Western", try musk ox steak or Greenlandic lamb cutlets, considered to be some of the best in the world. The reindeer venison and honey-roasted eider duck breast aren't bad, either.

Then, of course, there is any kind of fresh Greenlandic seafood. This includes trout, salmon, Atlantic halibut, redfish, whale, bay scallops and the world-renowned large Greenlandic prawns. Smoked fish is a traditional lunch.

In the summer, families take to the highlands to cook in traditional Greenlandic style. This involves building a raised, flat stone base, gather heather and branches for a fire and place a pot or a piece of meat directly on the stone. Soon comes the delicious aroma of heather smoke and cooking fish or seal meat. ❑

Map on page 138

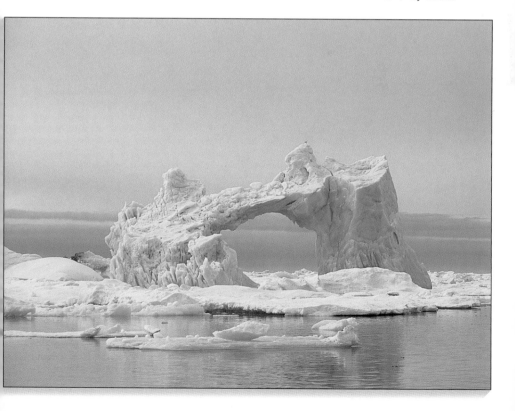

TIP

If you travel to Greenland in summer, it's wise to take shorts, gloves, and everything in between, plus waterproof clothing. Light waterproof hiking boots are the most appropriate footwear.

BELOW: Greenland's icy waters.

THE FAROE ISLANDS

The fruits of the sea have brought prosperity to the far-flung Faroe Islands. Visitors are attracted by the natural beauty and remarkable bird life

Map on page 142

The remote Faroe islands lie far to the north of mainland Europe, halfway between Iceland and the Shetland Islands. The sailing distance between this self-governing Danish outpost and Copenhagen is around 1,500 km (900 miles). The sea is serious business here, and nothing shows that more clearly than **Tórshavn's ❶** harbour. It is stuffed with boats of all kinds – visiting ships, inter-island ferries, sailing boats and other pleasure craft and, most numerous of all, the fishing boats which disgorge their cargoes at one of the big fish processors scattered around the islands' coasts.

The fishing fleet is one of the most modern in Europe. Fish products make up more than 95 percent of the country's export earnings and the not-to-be missed tang of fish permeating the harbour is also the smell of money.

Although the Faroe islanders are prosperous with a high standard of living – they claim to have more cars and more video recorders per head than anyone else in Europe – everything is relative. Only 43,700 live on the 18 inhabited islands – a dozen more are home only to the huge colonies of birds. Much of the surface area is virtually bare rock, and only a few areas are habitable. As though to contrast with the muted blues, greens and greys of rocks, sea and hills, modern Faroese favour brightly painted houses. Traditional, living, green turf roofs are becoming popular once more.

LEFT: the turf-roofed church at Saksun set against the green Faroese landscape.
BELOW: fishing boats at anchor in Tórshavn harbour.

Warm and wet

Far north as the islands are and feel, the Gulf Stream keeps the climate mild and moist. In the coldest month the average temperature is around 3°C (37°F), although wind chill makes it feel much colder. In the warmest, it reaches only 11°C (52°F). The weather is very changeable; one minute the sun is warm against the back, the next there is driving rain and mist.

No self-respecting tree could grow to a reasonable height against the islands' constant wind – though, as a joke, the Faroese call the small copse in the shelter of the park in the capital, Tórshavn, the islands' "forest".

The Faroe's other name is the Sheep Islands – even today, there are thousands more sheep than people, and lamb is a basic staple. The amount of arable land is extremely limited. Small kitchen gardens have robust plants, leeks, cabbages, carrots. Outside, people hang fish and lamb to dry in the wind.

On the trail

The inland trails cover a wonderland of stunning terrain. Footpaths crisscross all the islands and were originally the main routes between settlements. Most of the paths are marked by cairns, but some of them are not regularly maintained, and it's imperative to carry a map and compass. Campers may pitch tents

The puffin is a Faroese delicacy, caught during the open season in July. The meat has a distinctively tangy flavour.

virtually anywhere, but many a tent has been swept into the North Atlantic by powerful gusts, so remember to find a sheltered spot and weight the tent down.

Bird cliffs

Although Faroe has few mammals, the bird life is outstanding. The towering faces of the stacks and cliffs are home to thousands of sea birds and in the sheltered pools live phalaropes and red-throated divers. The stiff-winged flight of the fulmars follows the boats without ever tiring and clown-faced puffins gaze solemnly from cliff burrows. The Faroe's national bird, the black and white oyster catcher, calls worriedly from every hillock.

For the seafaring adventurer, boat operators sail from **Vestmanna** on an excursion of the islands to view the bird cliffs of **Vestmannabjørgini ❷**, or **Enniberg**. The restored sloop, *Norolysio*, takes visitors on an enchanting tour of the islands, sailing into fjords and grottoes when the seas permit. The island of **Mykines ❸** attracts birders from many lands.

Anglers may find great challenges in the brooks and lochs which hold trout and salmon. The season extends from 1 May to 31 August. Contact the tourist office in Tórshavn for permits and details (tel: 31 60 55).

Early settlers

The islands' first substantial settlers came from Norway in the 9th century. Even before that time, an early township, **Kirkjubøur ❹**, had been the centre of life for a group of Irish friars who colonised the islands around the 8th century. In 1380, as Norway came under Danish Rule, the islands, too, became part of Denmark and, when the union dissolved in 1814, the Faroes continued

BELOW: fish hanging up to dry – a common sight on the Faroe Islands.

Faroe Islands

as a Danish county. The present system of Home Rule dates from 1948 and the Faroe Islands also send two representatives to the Danish Parliament.

The islands' long seafaring history is traced in the **Fornminnisavn** (National Museum; open May–Sept: daily; Oct–Apr: Sun only; entrance fee) at Hoyvik, 2 km (1 mile) north of Tórshavn, and also in the **Nordoya Fornminnasavn** (North Islands Museum; open summer afternoons) at **Klaksvík ❺**, the second largest town, on **Bordoy** island.

Dancing with the Faroese

The Faroese are proud of the rich culture and traditions of their islands, where the language, costumes and customs are kept very much alive. On festive occasions all join in the Faroese chain dance, a slow, hypnotic dance accompanied by chanting. An older tradition that is still practised is the "door schnaps". Visitors are greeted at the door with a horn full of schnaps (*akvavit*) and everybody takes a sip before entering.

When visiting the **Smoke Room** (open June–Sept: daily) in Kirkjubøur, the first order of the day is a nip from the horn. The building is allegedly the oldest wooden structure in the world, built from logs that were towed from Norway.

Theatre and music abound. In the summer months a series of events including literature, music, theatre, traditional food and, of course, chain dancing – known as the **Faroese Cultural Evening** – is held on the island of **Eysturoy** and at Tórshavn. In late June and July the **Summartonar Music Festival** is staged at venues around the islands. The **Tórshavnar Jazz, Folk and Blues Festival** is a four-day event held in August, and the **Folk Music Festival** takes place in July in Tórshavn. ❑

Map on page 142

TIP

For the thirsty, Faroe is not the easiest place to find a drink. Alcoholic beverages are sold only at state-run monopoly stores. Hotels generally have fully stocked bars, as do restaurants.

BELOW: stacking hay Faroese-style.

NORWAY

Breathtaking scenery, historic sights and modern cities
are the big attractions for the traveller to Norway

The Norwegian landscape is both beautiful and brutal, hospitable and hostile; barren rock submits to soft fertile plains, majestic mountains tower above mysterious fjords; harsh winters are relieved by glorious summers; and long polar nights give way to the radiant Midnight Sun. One of the oldest civilisations in Europe has become one of its youngest nations. The Norwegians themselves have adapted rather quickly. The lusty Vikings have turned into global peacemakers. Norway has urban excitement and rural tranquillity; shopping malls and Mercedes rub shoulders with compass and rucksack; hi-technology parallels steadfast tradition.

A thriving offshore oil industry has brought prosperity, and as a consequence, social habits are changing rapidly, though, in a society where the divorce rate is high and cohabitation the norm, the home and family still remain important. Murray's *Handbook for Travellers in Norway* described the Norwegians in 1874 thus: "Great patriotism and hospitality are two of the leading characteristics of the Norwegians; they are often cold and reserved, and combine great simplicity of manner with firmness and kindness. 'Deeds, not words' is their motto." Today, little has changed.

Norway is a long narrow strip of a country, stretching north from mainland Europe far into the Arctic. The ancient capital of Trondheim is 500 km (350 miles) from the modern capital of Oslo, yet only a quarter of the way up the country's jagged coast. The southern coast is as far from Monaco as it is from the Nordkapp (North Cape), and Norway's northernmost outpost, the islands of Svalbard (Spitsbergen), are hundreds of kilometres further still. With a population of less than 4½ million, Norway has, above all else, space.

Yet travel is not difficult. From early times, the Norwegians were magnificent sailors, and this old way of travel continues today through the Hurtigrute coastal steamers and other ferries that link coastal communities. The Gulf Stream warms the western coastline so that the seas are ice-free all the year round. On land, the Norwegians have achieved the seemingly impossible, connecting even the most isolated settlements by building railways, roads and bridges across their fjords and by tunnelling deep into mountains and under the sea. Oslo, Stavanger, Bergen, Trondheim and Tromsø are small manageable cities that make good use of the surrounding countryside.

Norwegians are an outdoor people, and Norway a country where inhabitants and visitors alike can make the most of limitless space for walking, skiing, touring and just breathing in the clear air. ❑

PRECEDING PAGES: rocky outline of the Lofoten Islands; the reindeer reigns supreme in the far north; Art Nouveau architecture in the fishing town of Ålesund. **LEFT:** intrepid settlers built their homes in the most secluded spots.

THE NORWEGIANS

Forget the stereotypical image of a cool Scandinavian, visitors to Norway can be assured of a warm and friendly welcome

L eaving New York City recently, the author of this chapter was gallantly advised by a cab driver to go to Hell. Which he did. Hell is located in mid-Norway, its population is only a few hundred souls, and they have an annual blues festival in September where international stars get together to jam under the Midnight Sun. Expect the unexpected in Norway.

The myth about the Norwegians, as mirrored in a bumper sticker from Minnesota which reads, "You can always tell a Norwegian, but you can't tell him much," is of a selfish, stubborn, conceited peasant. Which, of course, is a big exaggeration. Peasantry was eradicated in 1968. That's when Norway struck oil. Today the country is nicknamed Little Kuwait, as if any piece of land could be smaller than Kuwait.

Too good to be true

"It's hard to be humble when you're Norwegian," another bumper sticker from Wisconsin, USA, reads. Originally an ironic remark. One New Year's Day in the early 1990s, however, the Prime Minister of Norway, Gro Harlem Brundtland, concluded her address to the nation with the words, "It's typical Norwegian to be good." Referring to Norwegian achievements in athletics (winter sports and soccer), international peace negotiations and a rare victory in the Eurovision Song Contest, Dr Brundtland's diagnosis of the national psyche was quite accurate, but not the way she intended. Her contribution to Norwegian comedy writers cannot be overestimated.

Dr Brundtland and her Labour Party government lost for the second time against the Norwegian people in a referendum in 1994 when the voters – as in 1972 – refused to join the Common Market, today's EU. The issue is still the hottest potato in Norwegian politics as the social democratic Labour and the two right parties, Høyre (conservative) and Fremskritts-partiet (right-wing protest party), form a majority coalition in favour of EU membership in the national parliament, the Storting.

Warming influence

Truly, Norway is a country of contradictions. It shouldn't have existed in the first place:

NORWAY: THE ESSENTIALS

Population 4.3 million, including 30,000 Sami.
Capital Oslo (pop. 502,867).
Notable towns Bergen, Stavanger, Trondheim, Tromsø.
Climate Afternoon temperatures in January are around −2°C (28°F), but lower in the north; July, 20°C (68°F).
Top museums Vikingskipshuset, Nasjonalgalleriet, Oslo.
Historic sights Gamle Bergen; Trondheim Cathedral; Røros; stave churches including Borgund and Heddal.
Natural wonders Fjord coastline; Preikestolen (Pulpit Rock); Lofoten Islands; North Cape.
Outdoor activities Water sports, hiking, skiing, fishing.
Tourist information www.visitnorway.com

LEFT: patriotism runs strong in Norway where national sport – whether football or skiing – is concerned.
RIGHT: young face of Norway.

according to the map and latitude, Norway should be the name of the world's largest glacier. But thanks to the Gulf Stream, visitors may get a warm welcome during summertime, when temperatures can be among the highest in Europe one day, the lowest the next. Oslo is said to be the only capital where you can experience four seasons within an hour and a half.

Although the climate can be rough in the north and on the coast, you'll never see a more beautiful summer's day − or night − as when you get above the Polar Circle. The landscape and the light are so special they have attracted visitors and painters for centuries.

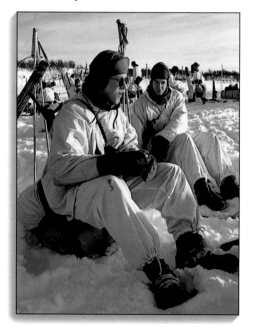

Land of many languages

Historically, Norway is one of the oldest nations in Europe, if not the oldest. Its people can trace an unbroken line of descent from those who inhabited the area in prehistoric times, a homogeneity the origins of which antedate the beginnings of Western civilisation in the Aegean.

During the era of the Vikings (*c*.800–1050 AD), Norway controlled an enormous territory from Russia to the British Isles, and the common European tongue was an Old Norse dialect. Yet today's Norway was reconstituted as late as 1905 when the union with Sweden was dissolved, and nobody speaks Norse dialects − except for the people of Iceland.

Modern Norwegians have English as their natural second language, and the increasing number of Asian immigrants have led to the development of a streetwise Pidgin Norwegian, especially among the youngsters, native Norwegians as well. While some look upon this as a problem for the pure Norwegian language, others tend to look at it as a part of any country's development of the spoken word.

Norwegians love language discussions. When Norwegians have nothing to talk about, they quarrel about languages − which they have plenty of. Every narrow valley and fjord has its own dialect, and the country is equipped with two official written languages − the Danish-derived *bokmål* ("book language") and the once radical construction *nynorsk* (new Norwegian), based upon a set of Norwegian dialects. Although the languages are quite similar, and hardly any foreigner understands why the Norwegians keep them both, the official debate is a never-ending story about national pride and culture − feelings, in other words. This has lead to the resignation of a prime minister, extra bureaucracy and wonderful Norwegian writing.

It's recognised that fine poets such as Halldis Moren Vesaas and Tor Jonsson as well as authors like Olav Duun (nominated for the Nobel Prize more than 12 times), the labour writer Kristofer Uppdal and the internationally acclaimed playwright Jon Fosse − a.k.a. Henrik Ibsen's heir − could not have expressed what they did in any other language than *nynorsk*.

Immigration is another hot, political issue in Norway. Being a country with great humanistic traditions (obviously some years after the Vikings raided England, raped the nuns at Lindisfarne and King Olav Haraldsson − later St Olav − chopped off the head of the Archbishop of Canterbury) Norway was named home of the Nobel Peace Prize.

Critics raise their voices from time to time to remind the politicians that Norway, the once humanistic pioneer nation, today has the strictest immigration rules and the most restrictive asylum policy in Europe. The country spends more per capita on foreign aid than any other in the west, but faces problems with the naturalisation and integration of "Our New Compatriots", as the immigrants are called.

Visitors often say that Norwegians are so open, so friendly. At least, that's what Norwegians like to think visitors say. But any visitor joining the 7.30am underground train at Oslo Central Station will have experienced the validity of the saying: "Show me a smiling, friendly commuter, and I'll show you a Moroccan", who probably isn't a passenger either, but the train-driver, holding a PhD in quantum physics.

The Great Norwegian Contradiction includes how visitors are treated. Norwegians, often mistakenly regarded as a bit reserved, are definitely not as outgoing as the Italians, not as lively as

HONOURED GUESTS

An American student visiting Norway for the first time summed up his stay – and his increased body mass – with the three words "coffee and cakes".

guest arrives, by habit, not by custom. It is a sign of welcome, probably a throwback to the days when, compounded by the long hours of winter darkness, houses shuttered against the cold were rather gloomy.

Norwegians have built their homes in the remotest places. Even though public transport is well developed in the rural districts as well as the cities, a car is a necessity in the countryside. Regarding the official political ambition to retain the rural population, one would think that motorised

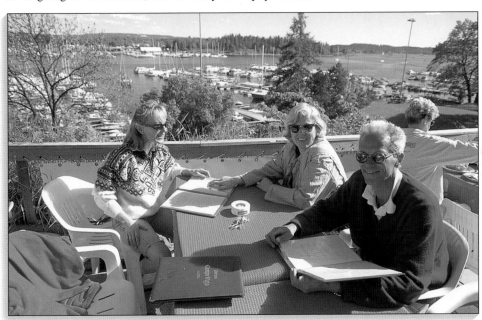

the Spaniards, not as open-hearted as the Greeks. But still the people of Norway and the people of Greece have a lot in common when it comes to welcoming guests. Both take the same kind of pride in opening their homes to visitors.

Norwegian hospitality is a chapter in itself, just be sure to have a strong stomach – there's a lot of coffee to be drunk. Entering a new home, there's always coffee – and cakes. Note the plural. The host will light a candle as the

LEFT: conscripts undergoing winter training in the far north of Norway.
ABOVE: enjoying the spring sunshine.

vehicles and fuel prices in this oil-nation would be subsidised. Right? Not at all. Norway has Europe's highest fuel prices and cars are heavily taxed. While Sweden has developed its famous Volvo and Saab cars, its oil-producing neighbour has only recently built its first serial-produced car – an electric vehicle called "Think". The patent was sold to the American Ford Motor Company and by now it has probably been nicknamed "Fjord".

Yet Norway wins the hearts of visitors. When the British actor Jeremy Irons visited the Haugesund International Film Festival he went into raptures, gasping: "Norway is Europe's best kept secret." ❑

Norway

100 miles
100 km

BARENTS SEA

RUSSIA

Lapland

Finnmark

Troms

Nordland

NORWEGIAN SEA

Arctic Circle

Norwegian Territory
- Svalbard (Norway)
- Bjørnøya (Norway)
- Jan Mayen (Norway)
- Greenland

ICELAND

UNITED KINGDOM

RUSSIA
FINLAND
SWEDEN
NORWAY

Svalbard

100 km
100 miles

ARCTIC OCEAN

Nordaustlandet

Spitsbergen

BARENTS SEA

NORWEGIAN SEA

Central Oslo

0 ———— 200 m
0 ———— 200 yds

OSLO AND ITS FJORD

Norway's capital offers a lively mix of galleries, museums, shops, restaurants and nightlife, with magnificent forests, ski trails and the beautiful Oslo Fjord close at hand

Maps:
City 158
Area 168

Oslo: the name has an English connection. According to the *Snorre Saga*, the city was founded by Harald III (1015–66), the half brother of Olaf II (later St Olaf). Crowned in 1045, Harald ruled so harshly as to earn the nickname Hardrade (Harsh Ruler). In 1066, he invaded England to claim its throne following the death of Edward the Confessor. The attempt failed; he was killed at Stamford Bridge on 25 September, barely three weeks before the Battle of Hastings that so changed English history.

Back home, Harald's subjects kept the name Oslo for six centuries, until 1624, when King Christian IV of Denmark and Norway immodestly renamed it Christiania. In 1877, at the height of the national romantic period following the dissolution of the union with Denmark in 1814, the government officially Norwegianised the spelling to Kristiania, and the city followed suit in 1897. State and municipal bureaucrats were obliged to use the new spelling, but the citizenry were divided and arguments raged. In 1924, the Storting (Parliament) settled the argument by reinstating the name Oslo. But the pronunciation has yet to settle down. The British say "Ozlo". The natives say "Osslo" or Oschlo, depending on whether they are East Siders or West Siders. Linguistic purists do it straight: "Os-lo", with two distinct syllables. Ask two Osloites to pronounce

LEFT: sculpture by Gustav Vigeland in Vigelandsparken.
BELOW: cafés spill out onto the street in summer.

FACT FILE

Situation Oslo lies in southeast Norway at 59°55'N.
Size 454 sq km (175 sq miles).
Population 502,867
Climate Average afternoon temperature in winter: –2°C (28°F); in summer: 21°C (70°F). Annual precipitation: 763 mm (30 inches).
Transport T-bane (underground), tram, bus, boat and commuter rail services. Trafikanten information, tel: 177.
Airports Gardermoen, 51 km (32 miles) north, and Torp at Sandefjord, 117 km (73 miles) south.
Biggest attraction Frogner Park, featuring works by the sculptor Gustav Vigeland in stone and bronze.
Newest attraction Aker Brygge (Aker Quay) gentrified former shipyard with trendy boutiques and eateries.
Finest building Akershus Slott og Festning (Castle), 1300.
Best view of the city Tryvannstårnet (Tryvann Tower).
Best museums Vikingskiphuset, Norsk Folkemuseum, Skimuseet, Barnekunstmuseet (Children's Art Museum).
Annual events Ski Festival (Mar); Jazz Festival (Aug).
Best ski resort Oslomarka, 2,500 km (1,553 miles) of cross-country ski trails. Snow report, tel: 82 05 20 20.
Tourist Information Vestbanen and Oslo S Railway Station, tel: 23 10 62 61; www.oslopro.no

*The classical façade
of Oslo's Det
Kongelige Slott
(Royal Palace).*

the city name and you trigger debate. Today the dialects of the city are declining, under the influence of television and an ever more mobile population.

The industrial complex that lined the banks of Akerselva (Aker River) from the 1840s is no more. The city's remnant heavy industry, the Aker Shipyards, where 550 ships were built, closed in 1982. In its place is Aker Brygge (Aker Docks), a gentrified complex of trendy boutiques, international eateries and luxury apartments overlooking the fjord.

Likewise, civil servants and service-sector professionals have displaced industrial workers as the stalwarts of the city. The myth of the blond, blue-eyed Viking weakens, as an influx of foreigners enriches the city. Oslo has the country's greatest percentage of immigrants. The East Side, in the city districts of Torshov, Grünerløkka, Dælen, Tøyen, Grønland and Gamlebyen, has become the international palette of the country, where daily life and business are conducted as much in Turkish, Vietnamese and Urdu as they are in Norwegian. Here are most of the city's ethnic eateries and shops, as well as mosques and Islamic organisations to serve the burgeoning Muslim population. Should you visit Oslo during traditional Norwegian holidays and find establishments closed, go east of the Aker River for shopping and sustenance.

The 19th century today

BELOW: more than 200 sculptures by Gustav Vigeland are on display in Vigelandsparken.

In many ways **Oslo** ❶ retains the features of the ideal city of the 19th century. Within easy walking distance, nestled around the northern tip of the fjord, are all the accoutrements of a capital: **Stortinget** Ⓐ (Parliament; tours in English July, Aug: 10am, 11.30am, 1pm; entrance free; tel: 23 31 35 96), **Det Kongelige Slott** Ⓑ (Royal Palace; park open all year; entrance free; changing of the guard daily 1.30pm), **Rådhuset** (City Hall; open May–Aug: Mon–Sat 9am–5pm, Sun noon–5pm; Sept–Apr: 9am–4pm; entrance fee; tel: 22 86 16 00), **Oslo Sentralstasjon** (Oslo Central Station), **Nasjonalgalleriet** (National Gallery; open Mon, Wed, Fri 10am–6pm; Thur 10am–8pm; Sat 10am–4pm; Sun 11am–4pm; closed Tues; entrance free; tel: 22 20 04 04), government ministries, courts, embassies, larger hotels and shops. The attractions not in this compact grid of streets are just a few stops away on the T-Bane (underground).

Maps:
City 158
Area 168

Munch-museet (Munch Museum; open Tues, Wed–Sat 10am–4pm; Thur, Sun 10am–6pm; closed Mon; entrance fee; tel: 23 24 14 00), near the Tøyen underground station to the east of the city centre, is dedicated to the works of Edvard Munch (1863–1944), the painter and graphic artist who fathered German expressionism. His most known work, *Skrik* (Scream), in the National Gallery, is probably Scandinavia's most famed work of art. The ever increasing popularity of Munch's works may be attributed to his violent, emotionally charged style and themes of fear and anxiety, that communicate as well today as they did a century ago *(see box, page 56)*.

One of Munch's contemporaries, sculptor Gustav Vigeland (1869–1943), also communicates through time. His works dominate **Vigelandsparken** (Vigeland Park; open year round; entrance free) at Frogner Park to the west of the city centre. Nowhere else is there so extensive a display of the scope of human life and emotion cast in stone and bronze. No matter that English novelist Evelyn Waugh called it a "subhuman zoo"; it remains one of Scandinavia's most visited attractions, drawing more than a million visitors each year.

At Frøen, a short stroll north from Frogner Park, is another one of its kind: **Det Internasjonale Barnekunstmuseet** (International Museum of Children's

TIP

Buy an Oslo Kortet (Oslo Card), for free admission to the city's museums, free public transport and parking, discounts at shops, restaurants and on car hire. Obtainable from tourist offices and hotels.

BELOW: youngsters are well catered for in Oslo with their own museum of art.

A CHILD'S-EYE VIEW OF ART

All too often, children's art – a subtle but essential trigger of the creative impulse – is overlooked or discarded. Yet were it not a tangible force, art could claim neither Chagall nor Picasso, nor other greats, who heeded its impetus. Indeed, Pablo Picasso once remarked that "when I was 18, I had Raphael's expertise. The rest of the time I spent learning to draw like a child."

In the world, there is one permanent walk-through monument to Picasso's mandate for artistic expression, Barnekunstmuseet (Museum of Children's Art) in Oslo. Founded in 1986 by Rafael Goldin (1920–94), an émigré Russian film director, it is dedicated to seeing the world from the eye of a child. The museum exhibits paintings, sculpture, ceramics, collages, tapestries and other items from its collection of the works of children from more than 150 countries. Moreover, it's a place of action where visiting children and adults can take part in artistic activities, from drawing to playing African drums.

Det Internasjonale Barnekunstmuseet, Lille Frøens vei 4, near the Frøen T-Bane station, is open July–mid-Aug: Tues–Thur, Sun 11am–4pm; late-Sept–June: Tues–Thur 9.30am–2pm, Sun 11am–4pm; closed Mon, Fri–Sat and mid-Aug–mid-Sept; entrance fee; tel: 22 46 85 73.

Art; *see box, page 163*). A few blocks uphill from Barnekunstmuseet near Slemdal T-Bane station is the **Emanuel Vigeland Museum** ❶ (Grimelundsveien 8; open Sun noon–4pm; entrance fee; tel: 22 14 57 88). Emanuel Vigeland (1875–1948), Gustav Vigeland's brother, made his living painting the great personages of his time. But like Edvard Munch, he was fascinated by themes of life and death, and used them in the alfresco decoration of a crypt, entitled *Vita* ("life"), the museum's major attraction.

Back to the city centre, on the south side of Drammensveien from Dronningsparken, **Ibsen-museet** ❶ (Ibsen Museum; open Tues–Sun noon–3pm, closed Mon; tours noon, 1pm, 2pm; entrance fee; tel: 22 55 20 09) is located partly in the flat once occupied by Henrik Ibsen (1828–1906), Norway's most noted playwright and one of the world's outstanding pioneers of social drama. A statue of Ibsen stands in front of the **Nationaltheatret** ❶ (National Theatre, Johanne Dybwads plass 1), a Rococo theatre built in 1899, with four stages, and the venue of the annual international Ibsen Festival in August.

History and the outdoors

The river that divides the city shares the root of its name with **Akershus Slott og Festning** ❶ (Akershus Castle and Fortress; bastions and ramparts open 6am–9pm; free entrance to grounds), a major complex begun in 1300, first finished in 1308 and extended through the 15th century. It was built principally to defend the city against attack from Sweden. The fort remains an imposing symbol of past military importance. **Norges Hjemmefrontmuseum** ❶ (Norway's Resistance Museum; open Mon–Sat 10am–4pm; June–Aug: 10am–5pm; Sun 11am–4pm; entrance fee; tel: 23 09 31 38) is located here, near the place where

Children will enjoy the old-fashioned candy store and horse and carriage rides at the Norsk Folkemuseum (Museumsveien 10; open daily; tel: 22 12 37 00), where more than 150 historic timber houses and a stave church are on display.

BELOW: off duty at the Royal Palace.

members of the Resistance were executed during World War II. It illustrates the intense story of occupied Norway.

Map on pages 158–159

Capital sports

For an Osloite, saying you ski is as exciting as saying you drive a car – unless, of course, you are a world-class competitor in the sport. And that many Norwegians are: Norway leads the world in the number of medals won in the Olympic Winter Games.

High on the hills overlooking the city is **Holmenkollbakken** (Holmenkollen Ski Jump; open all year; entrance free except during ski meets), venue of the annual Holmenkollen Ski Festival, among the world's oldest sporting events. Adjoining the ski jump is **Skimuseet** (Ski Museum; open May, Sept: 10am–5pm; June–Aug: 9am–8pm; Oct–Apr: 10am–4pm; entrance fee; tel: 22 92 32 00), featuring 4,000 years of skiing history. Alongside the arena there is a statue of King Olav V (1903–91) in a cross-country skiing pose, because here skiing is the sport of commoner and king alike. Indeed, Oslo is so much a "ski town" that an Olympic Winter Games (1952) and two World Nordic Ski Championships (1966 and 1982) have been held within the city limits.

Oslo's sporty profile is due in part to the closeness of outdoor recreation. On one side there's the fjord, a broad, sheltered expanse of water ideal for windsurfing and boating. On the other side is a huge woodland recreation area known as **Oslomarka** (Oslo's fields), covering some 1,700 sq km (656 sq miles). Here there are 2,500 km (1,550 miles) of ski trails marked with red painted slashes on trees and rings round sign-poles at trail intersections. The total length of the summer-time walking trails is even longer; they are marked in blue, the

Akershus Slott, built to defend against attacks from Sweden.

BELOW LEFT: high-tech façade.
BELOW RIGHT: the city's ski jump.

difference being that red-marked trails can cross lakes and marshes frozen in the winter, while blue-marked trails cannot.

Some 110 km (68 miles) of ski trails are illuminated with their trailheads at car parks or underground stations, for ease of after-dark access. All the illuminated trails, as well as some 500 km (300 miles) of other trails, are regularly maintained with tracks set by machine. Trail use is free, as cross-country skiing is regarded as part of public recreation. Along the trails, there are some 20 staffed lodges with lounges, cafeterias and toilets; most are open at weekends and during school holidays, and in the winter, some are open in the evening. There are also 16 Alpine ski lift hills and 48 ski jumps.

For details, contact Skiforeningen, tel: 22 92 32 00, or Skogvesen (Oslo Municipal Forestry Service; tel: 22 08 22 00), which maintains trails, operates the illuminated trails and 11 of the trailside lodges. In winter *føremelding* (snow conditions) for the Oslo area are recorded daily, tel: 82 05 20 20.

Although Norway gave the word "ski" (meaning "piece of split wood") to the world, the language has no verb equivalent to the act of skiing.

Great explorers

The pines and waters of Oslo were the training ground for Fridtjof Nansen (1861–1930) and Roald Amundsen (1872–1928), two of the greats of the heroic age of polar exploration. Their ships, *Fram* and *Gjøa*, are preserved in two museums on the **Bygdøy** peninsula, **Frammuseet ⊕** (Fram Museum; open May, Sept, Oct: 10am–4.45pm; June–Aug: 9am–6.45pm; Nov–Apr: 11am–2.45pm; entrance fee; tel: 22 43 83 70) and **Norsk Sjøfartsmuseum ⊕** (Norwegian Maritime Museum; open May–Sept: 10am–7pm; Oct–Apr: 10.30am–4pm; entrance fee; tel: 22 43 82 40). Nearby, the **Kon-Tiki Museum ⊕** (open Apr, May, Sept: 10.30am–5pm; June–Aug: 9.30am–5.45pm; Oct–Apr: 10.30am–4pm; entrance fee; tel: 23 08 67 67) has detailed displays including the preserved *Kon-Tiki* and *Ra II* craft used by ethnographic explorer Thor Heyerdahl (*b.*1914), and **Vikingskipshuset ⊕** (Viking Ship Museum; open May–Aug: 9am–6pm; Sept–Apr: hours vary; entrance fee; tel: 22 43 83 79) features the world's best-preserved collection of the elegant long ships of the Viking Age.

BELOW: old-style country store at the Norsk Folkemuseum on the Bygdøy peninsula.

Historic coat of arms

An event during the era of the city's founding is depicted in its coat of arms. One day, Hallvard Husaby (*d.*1053), came upon a young, pregnant girl being pursued by three men. He took her in his boat in an attempt to escape on the fjord. But the villains caught and slew them both, tied a millstone around his neck, and tossed the bodies into the fjord. A few days later, Hallvard's body was found floating on the fjord, millstone still securely tied to his neck. A saint was born. City coats of arms and seals depicting St Hallvard have been in use since the 14th century. The current version, designed in 1924, shows Hallvard on a lion throne, the three lethal arrows in his left hand, the millstone in his right, and the girl at his feet. Around the periphery is the Latin motto: *Unanimiter et Constanter* (Unanimous and Eternal).

Can an increasingly multicultural city be unanimous about anything? Perhaps. In the late 1980s, the public transport authorities decreed that trams were to be repainted red to promote visibility in traffic. The citizens were not pleased. Adamant that trams in Oslo are blue, preferably the cobalt blue of the city flag, they obliged the authorities to surrender. Cobalt blue now is the standard tram colour.

And the eternal? It also survives, subliminal in the soul of the city. Novelist Knut Hamsun (1859–1952), awarded the Nobel Prize for Literature in 1920, observed in his novel *Sult* (*Hunger*, 1888) that Oslo is "a strange city that nobody leaves without being marked by it". Translated to today's idiom, Oslo might be said to be memorable because it is a different sort of city.

Southward and outward

If you stand at a vantage point in Oslo and look south down the fjord, almost everything in view is in Akershus county. Further south, the fjord is flanked on the east by Østfold county and on the west by Vestfold county. Aside from being home to one in three residents of the country, the city and these counties play a key role in contemporary events and history.

In Akershus county, some 67 km (42 miles) north of Oslo lies **Eidsvoll ❷**, a town that grew around the iron works built in 1624. The works closed in 1825; Eidsvoll might be just another post-industrial town, save for the happenings of the spring of 1814. Following the dissolution of the union with Denmark, 112 representatives convened at the headquarters of the iron works, then the only convenient large building, to draw up the Norwegian Constitution. **Eidsvoll-byningen** (Memorial Building; open May–Sept: daily; Apr–Oct: weekends only; Nov–Mar: by appointment; entrance fee; tel: 63 92 22 10) is now a museum to the constitution and includes the room where the document was

Maps:
City 158
Area 168

The excellent Kon-Tiki Museum displays Thor Heyerdahl's Kon-Tiki and Ra II craft as well as artefacts from Easter Island.

BELOW: outdoor café, Aker Brygge.

Traditional architecture in Drøbak, south of the capital.

signed on 17 May 1814. The country's first railway, built in 1845, connected Oslo and Eidsvoll, and it's now on the E6 highway, the major north-south artery.

Historic provincial cities and towns are scattered throughout Østfold and Vestfold counties. The best way to explore the counties, whether you travel by bus, car or boat, is via **Drøbak ❸**. If you choose road, you will pass Vinterbro, at the junction of the E6 and E18 highways, the location of **TusenFryd ❹**, the country's major amusement park (open June–Aug: daily 10.30am–7pm; May and Sept: weekends only; entrance fee; tel: 64 97 66 99).

The village of Drøbak was once a fishermen's settlement. Fishing vessels still dock here to sell fresh prawns and fish on the quayside. Places of interest include the **Follo Museum** (Heritage Museum; open Tues–Fri 11am–4pm, Sat–Sun noon–5pm; entrance fee; tel: 64 93 26 01) and the **Oscarsborg Festning** (Fort) out in the fjord, whose cannons sunk the German heavy cruiser *Blücher* on the day the country was invaded in 1940 (guided boat trips from the harbour). Another point of pride is the cross-timbered **Drøbak Kirke** (church; built 1776; open all year; entrance free), with an elaborately carved model of a ship inside, a common church decoration in seafaring towns.

Farther south, **Fredrikstad ❺** is a gem among Østfold towns, and Scandinavia's only completely preserved fortress town, dating from 1567. History and prehistory figure largely hereabouts. The **Oldtidsveien** (Highway of the Ancients), the 18-km (11-mile) stretch of National Highway 110 between Fredrikstad and Skjeberg, has three **Helleristningsfelt** (literally "rock wall carving areas"; open all year; free access to grounds) with Bronze Age pictographs.

Halden ❻, south of Skjeberg and close by the Swedish border, is dominated by **Fredriksten Festning** (Fort), a largely intact ruin with many of its buildings

BELOW: musical serenade, Frogner Park.

serving as small theme museums. The streets below were laid out along the cannons' blast lines to give the fortress's defenders freedom to fire. In summer, passenger launches travel the **Haldenkanal** (canal) that runs east and then north, through several sets of massive locks. The **Kanalmuseum** (Canal Museum; open May–Aug 11am–5pm; Sept–Apr: times vary; entrance fee; tel: 69 81 10 21) at the locks at **Ørje 7** displays the implements of canal operations. It also arranges charter tours on the *Engebret Soot*, named after the designer of the canal and now the world's oldest propeller-driven steamship in service.

Throughout Østfold, *Olsok* (St Olav's day, 29 July) is celebrated with a great show of folk costume, music and dance. One of the best displays is at the **Borgarsyssel Museum** (open May–Aug: Tues–Fri 10am–7pm, Sat–Sun noon–5pm, closed Mon; entrance fee; tel: 69 15 50 11) in **Sarpsborg 8**, north of Skjeberg.

Viking Vestfold

The Moss-Horten car ferry connects Østfold and Vestfold in just under an hour. The **Marinemuseet** (Naval Museum; open May–Sept: noon–4pm; Oct–Apr: Sun only noon–4pm; free; tel: 33 03 33 97) at **Horten 9**, home port of Sjøforsvaret (Royal Norwegian Navy), bulges with maritime history. The are also museums of photography and veteran cars in Horten (both open all year; entrance fee).

To the south lies the heart of eastern Viking country, and **Borre Nasjonalpark 10** (open all year; free access to grounds), en route to Tønsberg, contains large turf-covered mounds concealing the graves of Viking kings. Keeping to the coastline along Road 311, **Munch's Lille Hus** (Munch's Little House, open June–Aug: 11am–7pm, closed Mon; Sept: Sat–Sun only 11am–7pm; entrance

Map
on page
168

TIP

A pleasant way to travel to fjord towns is by boat. Contact any travel agent or Trafikanten at Oslo S station for information on ferry and launch services (tel: 177).

BELOW:
Drøbak, a fishing port on Oslo Fjord.

Map
on page
168

TIP

Oslo has a wide
variety of restaurants,
both Norwegian and
international. Cafés
and *konditoris* offer
coffee and pastries.
For low-budget meals,
look for a *kafeteria*.

BELOW: stave
church at the Norsk
Folkemuseum.
RIGHT: Kragerø, the
summer home of
Edvard Munch.

fee; tel: 33 08 53 79) at **Åsgårdstrand** ⓫ is where the artist lived when he
returned to Norway from abroad. It was a setting for many of his paintings.

Between Åsgårdstrand and Tønsberg is a burial mound, **Oseberghaugen** ⓬,
the most important Viking site yet discovered (open all year; grounds free).
Oslo's Vikingskipshuset *(see page 166)* contains the finds, including the 20-
metre (65-ft) arch-ended wooden ship. Only the mound itself, near Slagen
church, remains, but as a symbol Oseberghaugen has a subtle, magnetic power.

Just south is historic **Tønsberg** ⓭, established in the 9th century. On the 65-
metre (200-ft) high **Slottsfjellet** are the fortress remains and tower. The main
street, **Storgata**, is flanked by Viking graves. These were excavated and incorporated, under glass, into the ground floor of the new library.

The most renowned king to hold court in Tønsberg was Håkon Håkonson IV
(1240–63). The ruins of his court can be seen on **Nordbyen**, a street with old
houses hunched along it. A more recent native son is Roald Amundsen, the
polar explorer. Less known outside Norway is Svend Foyn, the Tønsberg
whaling captain who invented the explosive-powered harpoon.

The steamship *Kysten I* (built 1909), moored on Byfjorden near the old
customs house, operates a three-hour islands tour.

Summer playground

To the south of Tønsberg, along the eastern side of the fjord, the islands of
Nøtterøy and **Tjøme**, and the skerries, are fantastic summer hangouts. **Verdens
Ende** ⓮ (World's End) is at the end – but for a few boulders – of the chain. The
old lighthouse here is a beautifully simple structure made of stone.

On the other side of Tønsbergfjorden lies **Sandefjord** ⓯, a whaling town.
The sea still dominates life here. One of the main
industries is marine paint production. The town
centre is compact, and near **Badeparken** are the
former spa and the old town. **Preståsen** is the hilly
park above it.

Just outside Sandefjord is another burial site,
Gokstadhaugen ⓰ (open all year; May–Sept: guided
tours; entrance free to grounds), in which the *Gokstad*
ship, now in Oslo's Vikingskipshuset, was discovered
in 1880. The **Vesterøy** peninsula is a supremely
peaceful place, ideal for walking, biking and boating.

Larvik ⓱ was home to two legendary boat lovers,
ethnographic explorer Thor Heyerdahl and master
boatbuilder Colin Archer (1832–1921), designer of
the polar ship *Fram*. Archer's first house was at
Tollerodden, on the fjord. At Larvik's back is Farris
lake and **Farriskilde** (Farris Spring), the country's
only natural mineral water spring.

People who live around Oslofjorden have a strange
modesty-pride complex. They are the first to point
out that the fjords of the west are more beautiful, the
central mountain ranges far higher. But once these are
out of the way, the superlatives begin to flow. The
birthplaces of the most intrepid explorers are here, as
are the best sailing races, the warmest summers, the
finest archaeological discoveries, the best drinking
water, summer resorts; for when it comes to this part
of Norway neither modesty nor pride is false. ❑

SOUTHERN NORWAY

Norway's southern beaches and picturesque seaside towns are a magnet for summer visitors. The west coast is blessed with glorious fjords and the oil-rich city of Stavanger

Map on pages 174–175

D raw an upward arc on the map from Oslo in the east to Bergen in the west, and south of it you see the part of Norway where the bulk of the natives take their home country holidays. Here is where much of the history of the country happened and where the myriad roots of the contemporary Norwegian character remain intact. In clockwise order starting at Oslo, Southern Norway can be divided into the principal regions of **Sørlandet** (Southern country) comprising Telemark, Aust-Agder and Vest-Agder counties and their coasts around to about 7 o'clock; **Rogaland** county centred at the city of Stavanger on the west coast; and **Hordaland** county around Bergen.

Sørlandet

Kristiansand ❶ is the unofficial capital of the southern coast, and rightfully so. In 1639, King Christian IV of Denmark and Norway selected the site of the city for a fort to control the approaches to the North Sea and the Baltic. Much survives of the first of many forts built there, such as **Christiansholm Festning** (fortress; open May–Sept: 9am–9pm; free; tel: 38 07 51 50). Present-day Kristiansand, a pleasant city laid out in a rectangular pattern by Christian IV's directive, invites strolling. The nearby **Kristiansand Dyrepark** (zoo and amusement park; open June–Aug: 10am–7pm; entrance fee; tel: 47 38 04 97 00), which includes the miniature town of Kardemomme By (Cardamom Town), is the most-visited theme park in Norway.

West of Kristiansand, the **Lindesnes Fyr ❷** (lighthouse; open all year; entrance fee to museum) marks the southernmost point of Norway. The last town before Vest Agder rises to meet Rogaland is the port of **Flekkefjord** and the idyllic island of **Hidra**. The terrain is mountainous, with many splendid waterfalls, especially around **Kvinesdal ❸**.

Coastal journey

The principal centres along the coast east from Kristiansand are, in order, Lillesand, Grimstad and Arendal. **Lillesand ❹** is a popular holiday town with a fine selection of cafés and restaurants around the harbour. **Grimstad ❺** is indelibly associated with Ibsen. It was here that he served his apprenticeship to a chemist. Ibsen and his works are commemorated in the **Grimstad Bymuseum** (Town Museum: open May–Sept: daily 9am–5pm; Oct–Apr: Mon–Fri 9am–2pm; entrance fee; tel: 37 04 46 53). **Arendal ❻** was struck by fire in 1863, and lost the houses on stilts that had earned it the nickname "Little Venice". Now overflowing onto a number of small islands, it retains its lovely setting. The **Arendal Bymuseum** (Town Museum; open: Tue–Fri 9am–3pm, Sat 10am–2pm;

LEFT: Preikestolen (the Pulpit Rock), one of Rogaland's best-known landmarks. **BELOW:** cascading waters of the southwest.

Southern and Central Norway

0 — 20 km

0 — 20 miles

TIP

New Signatur express
trains speed between
Oslo and Kristiansand
in 4 hours and 4
minutes, and between
Kristiansand and
Stavanger in 2 hours
and 25 minutes.

entrance fee; tel: 37 02 59 25) has extensive displays delineating local history, and the **Rådhus** (Town Hall), previously the home of a merchant, is said to be one of the largest wooden buildings ever constructed in Norway.

Telemark

Travelling northeast, the capital of Telemark is **Skien ❼**, which originally came into existence on the back of an industry producing stone projectiles for military slingshots. Norway's great playwright, Henrik Ibsen (1828–1906) spent his childhood here and his home, Venstøp, forms part of the **Telemark Museum** (Brekke Park; open May–Aug: 10am–6pm; entrance fee; tel: 35 52 35 94), where tulips bloom en masse in the gardens in summer.

Northwest of Skien lies **Ulefoss**, a village that until the end of the 19th century was a major exporter of ice, which was transported along waterways that became the **Telemarkskanal ❽**, which is still trafficked by passenger launches, such as the *MV Victoria* and *MV Henrik Ibsen* (May–Sept; tel: 35 90 00 30).

Although a finger of Telemark reaches the sea at **Kragerø**, not far from the mouth of Oslofjorden, the county is most associated with its inland terrain. Indeed, whenever a modern skier performs a Telemark turn, homage is done to the village of **Morgedal ❾**. It was there that Sondre Norheim (1825–97), the son of a sharecropper, first improved utilitarian skis and ski bindings for greater control in turns and consequently became regarded by history as the father of modern downhill skiing.

One of the major attractions west of **Notodden**, along Road 11, is at **Heddal ❿**, where the **Heddal Stavkirke (Stave Church)** is the country's largest (open Mon–Sat, May, June, Sept: 10am–5pm; July–Aug: 9am–7pm;

BELOW: southerly
Mandal's popular
bathing beach.

Sun 1–5pm; entrance fee; tel: 35 02 04 00). Its ornate carvings are rivalled only by the beautiful period rose paintings in the Ramberg room of the nearby **Heddal Bygdetun** (rural museum; open May–Sept; entrance fee).

About 10 km (6 miles) further on, Road 37 branches north past Tinnsjø lake towards **Rjukan** . The principal attraction of Rjukan is the hydroelectric plant where heavy water once was produced; see "Heroes of Telemark" *(page 180)* for an account of the daring sabotage that took place there in 1943. Today, the plant is the **Norsk Industriarbeidermuseum** (Norwegian Industrial Workers Museum; open May–Sept: daily 10am–4pm; entrance fee; tel: 35 09 51 53). Rjukan lies in the shade of the surrounding mountains and from **Gvepseborg**, 860 metres (2,800 ft), it is said that one can see about one-sixth of Norway.

Rogaland

Though Bergen is known as the capital of fjord country, Rogaland county, centred on the west coast port of Stavanger, has some of country's more spectacular fjord and mountain sights. It also has the country's highest average temperature, and in winter there is little snow and the fertile fields are green for most of the year. The Ryfylke area northeast of Stavanger is true fjord country. It starts with Lysefjorden and stretches north past long narrow lakes that once were open fjords, until it reaches Vindafjorden, Saudafjorden and Suldalsvatn. Every visitor should try to walk out through the heather moor to stand on the top of **Preikestolen** ⑫ (The Pulpit), a rock outcropping 597 metres (1,958 ft) above Lysefjorden, the country's most famous vantage point.

The sheltered bay north of Stavanger, and outer islands such as **Karmøy** ⑬, protect Ryfylke's inshore islands from the North Sea. Christianity flourished

The ornate altar at the Heddal Stavkirke, Norway's largest stave church.

BELOW: sheltered marinas dot the south coast.

COUNTRY AFLOAT

To the world, Norway and seafaring are synonymous. From the age of sail until after World War II, the Norwegian merchant fleet was one of the world's largest, and Norwegian could be heard in ports worldwide.

Norwegians seem happiest when they are in, on or around the sea. Each year, more than a third of the population spend their summer holidays partly or completely in craft that range from small dinghies to motor launches and ocean-going yachts. In all, there are more than 400,000 boats over 4.5 metres (15 ft) in length, and an untold number of smaller boats in the country. Most are motor boats, though sailing is popular on the fjords and as a competitive sport.

Geography and topography are the deciding factors. There are thousands of islands, and the fjords and coastal archipelagos are a paradise for competitive and recreational sailors, king and commoner alike. King Olav V (1903–91), the father of present King Harald V, won a Gold Medal in sailing in the 1928 Olympic Games, which made him the world's only Olympic medallist monarch.

Norway's first sailing club was founded in 1868 in Tøsnsberg, since when the nation has been a major force in championship sailing and regattas worldwide.

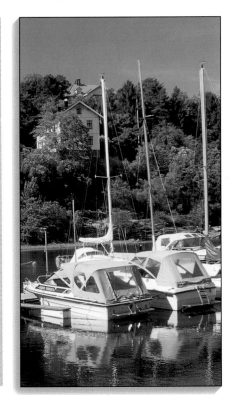

early here under the protection of the bishops of Stavanger and the islands have many churches. The 12th-century **Utstein Kloster** ⓮ on **Mosterøy** makes a beautiful setting for concerts (open May–Oct, closed Mon; entrance fee).

The many lighthouses are not only landmarks for islanders and seafarers but make excellent bird-watching sites. The waters around these peaceful islands are a sea kingdom for sailors with enough coastline to give every boat a bay to itself and many yacht harbours. Most of the island grocers also provide boat services, and it is easy to hire rowing boats and small craft with outboard engines.

In the northeast highlands of Rogaland the fjords, lakes and rivers are rich in fish and fine for sailing and canoeing. All these inland, eastern areas of Rogaland have good cross-country skiing tracks in winter and excellent Alpine slopes.

Among the best holiday areas is the Suldal district, stretching from Sand on the Sandsfjorden, along the Suldalslågen (river) – where the rushing waters have produced large salmon. At the Sand end of Suldalslågen is **Laksestudioet** ⓯ (open May–Sept: daily 12 noon–4pm; summer 10am–6pm; entrance fee; tel: 52 79 72 84), an observation studio built under a waterfall where visitors look through a large window at the salmon resting before their next leap up the fish ladder. Where river meets lake is **Kolbeinstveit Museum** (Rural Museum; open June–Aug: Tues–Sun 11am–5pm, closed Mon; entrance fee; tel: 52 79 72 84) with the 13th-century farm, Guggedalsloftet Bygdetun.

Back to the coast

The sea route to **Bergen** is a popular way to see the coast. By taking an express boat (a cross between a catamaran and a hydrofoil) you can drop off at any of the harbour stops and stay a night or a week according to your whim. Karmøy,

Following chemical analysis, it has been confirmed that the copper used to cover New York's Statue of Liberty came from one of the old Visnes mines on the island of Karmøy.

BELOW: Utstein Kloster (Cloister) on Mosterøy.

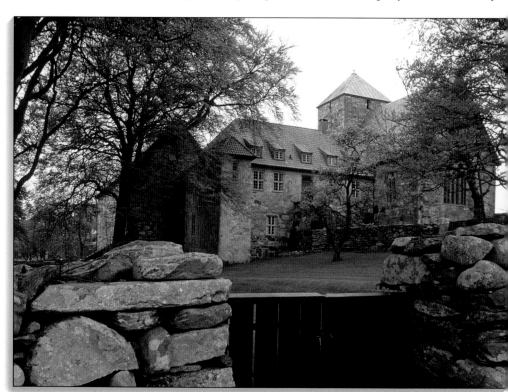

the island at the south of the outer islands chain, is big enough to merit its own boat service, which goes to Skudeneshavn in the south, an idyllic old port with white, wooden houses along narrow streets. The north of the island is linked to the mainland just south of **Haugesund ⑯**, the first sizeable coastal town north of Stavanger. Haugesund has long been a centre for fishing, shipping and farming. Today its harbour is filled with pleasure boats; the town has also become a festival and congress centre and host to the International Trad Jazz Festival and the Norwegian Film Festival (both in Aug; Tourist Office tel: 52 72 50 55).

Stavanger

The sea has blessed **Stavanger ⑰**, Norway's oil capital and fourth largest city; as one source of prosperity waned, another arose. It has taken the city's ships and citizens round the world and has in turn brought foreigners to Stavanger. Today, nearly one in ten of its 108,000 inhabitants was born abroad. This is a truly cosmopolitan city, international restaurants abound and in the fish market and the fruit and flower market nearby you will hear many many languages.

In the 19th and early 20th centuries, Stavanger was the principal port of embarkation for the great waves of Norwegian emigration to the United States, the history of which is documented at **Det Norske Utvandrersenteret** (Emigration Centre; open daily; free). In midsummer the centre stages the Emigration Festival with exhibitions, concerts, folk dancing and a crafts market. The highlight of the festival is the re-enactment of the 1825 sailing of the *Restauration*, the 38-ton sloop that carried the first 52 emigrants across the Atlantic.

The Stavanger *siddis* (colloquialism for a person from Stavanger, a contraction of "citizen" in English) claim to be the oldest true Norwegians, tracing

Map on pages 174–175

The Anglo-Norman cathedral at Stavanger dates from the 12th century.

BELOW: the harbour at Stavanger.

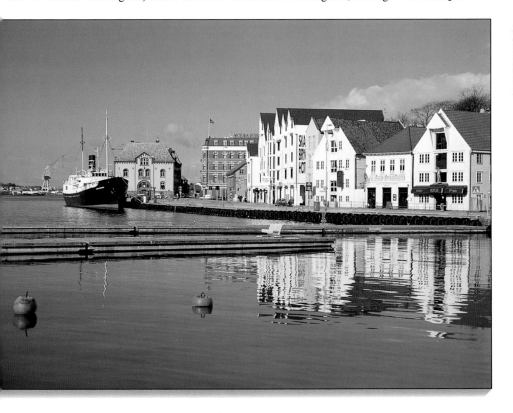

The Heroes of Telemark

The most celebrated act of resistance in Norway during World War II was the sabotage of the Vemork heavy water plant at Rjukan, in Telemark, in February 1943. No visitor to Rjukan, dwarfed and darkened by mountains all round, could fail to be awed by the audacity of the saboteurs. More importantly, the production of heavy water in the plant, if it had not been stopped, could conceivably have aided German development of an atomic bomb.

The operation was originally planned for a joint force of Norwegian volunteers and British commandos in two towed gliders. It ended disastrously when both gliders and one of the aircraft towing them crashed 160 km (100 miles) from Rjukan.

The next attempt was an all-Norwegian affair. "Gunnerside" was the code name for six men who had been trained in England.

They parachuted onto a frozen lake where they joined up with "Swallow", an advance party on the ground.

They skied to the ridge above Rjukan for the perilous descent on foot and slithered down, up to their waists in snow. Just after midnight, the covering party took up positions while the six-man demolition team cut a chain on the gates and crept forward to the basement of the concrete building where the most vital equipment and the heavy water storage tanks were located. All agreed that no lights would be carried; weapons would be unloaded and anyone captured would take his own life.

The best way in appeared to be a funnel carrying cables and piping. Two went through it. The solitary Norwegian guard was astonished but agreed to lead them to vital components. "I had placed half the charges in position when there was a crash of broken glass behind me," one of the pair wrote later. The other members of the team, not realising that their leaders had managed to get in, had decided to smash in through a window. With the rest of the charges laid, the six began a rapid withdrawal. The party had only gone a few yards when there was what members later variously described as "a cataclysmic explosion" and "a tiny, insignificant pop".

Five members of the parachute team reached Sweden after a 400-km (250-mile) journey on skis in indescribably difficult conditions; the sixth stayed on for another year. Of the Swallow party, Claus Helberg had the liveliest time. He was chased through the mountains by German soldiers, but escaped. Then he fell over a cliff and broke an arm. The next day he walked into a German patrol but had a good enough story to be taken to a hotel to await treatment. Most of the hotel guests (but not the injured Norwegian) were turned out of their rooms to make way for Reichskommissar Joseph Terboven (the Nazi who ruled Norway). Later, and through no fault of his own, he was bundled along with the remaining guests "into a bus and sent off to the Grini concentration camp". Helberg jumped from the bus. Later, he turned up in Britain, reporting for further duties. ❑

LEFT: Kirk Douglas played a saboteur in the 1965 film *The Heroes of Telemark*.

Map on pages 174–175

their lines to the Battle of Hafrsfjord. This decisive battle that first united the country under King Harald I Hårfagre, *c.*880, took place at a bay just southwest of the city. On the shore there is a monument to the event, **Sverd i fjell**, three larger-than-life Viking swords seemingly thrust into bedrock.

The heart of modern Stavanger is the area around **Breiavatnet**, the small lake in the middle of the city, near the **Domkirken** (Cathedral). Work began on the cathedral in 1125 in the Anglo-Norman style. Massive interior pillars give it a feeling of austere strength and contrast with the elegant arches of the chancel. One of the finest pieces is the ornate 16th-century pulpit by Andrew Smith.

Northwest of the cathedral are the winding cobbled streets and old timber houses of **Gamle Stavanger** (Old Stavanger), one of the most coveted places to live in the town.

Around 1870, as fishing and shipping were in decline, the fishermen turned their attention to *brisling* (small herring), which were cured and canned in the town and sent as Norwegian "sardines" all over the world. Stavanger thrived on sardines through the 1950s. Today, **Hermetikkmuseet** (Canning Museum; open daily 11am–4pm; entrance fee; tel: 51 84 27 00) is a reminder of the former smell of money.

In 1966, the city became the base for oil exploration in the North Sea. The black gold has brought prosperity to Stavanger – the city is second only to Saudi Arabia in oil exports. Visit the interactive **Norsk Oljemuseum** (Norwegian Petroleum Museum; open May–Aug: 10am–7pm; Sept–Apr: 10am–5pm; entrance fee; tel: 51 93 93 00) for an insight into this source of energy. Sadly, not all advances come without their disasters: in the suburb of **Kvernevik** the **Alexander Kielland Minnesmerke** (monument) commemorates the loss of 123 lives when the Alexander Kielland offshore oil platform capsized in 1980.

Hordaland

Hordaland county includes two of the country's prime natural attractions: **Hardangervidda**, the central mountain plateau at 1,300 metres (4,500 ft) above sea level and **Hardangerfjorden**, which gave its name to Norway's national musical instrument, the eight-stringed Hardanger fiddle, and provided inspiration for the composer Edvard Grieg (1843–1907), and the violinist Ole Bull (1810–80). Among these mountains and fjords, Grieg and Bull travelled on foot and horse, absorbing the old melodies of the land. Like the visitors of today, they came to Hardanger for its waterfalls, for the secret beauty of smaller fjords that lead almost to the plateau above, and for glaciers and mountains that rarely lose their snowcaps, contrasted with orchards lining the fjordside.

In days gone by, the fjords provided West Norway's main transport arteries, and **Utne** ⑱ was an important junction between east and west. Two establishments there that sum up Hardanger life over the past centuries are the **Hardanger Folkemuseum** (open daily; entrance fee), and the **Utne Hotel**, founded in 1722, the oldest hotel in Norway still in operation.

A ferry service connects Utne with **Kinsarvik** ⑲ on the east side of Sørfjorden, an arm of the

Violas growing wild by the roadside in southern Norway.

BELOW: sardines, once the lifeblood of Stavanger.

Map
on pages
174–175

*Edvard Grieg used to
visit a small "hytte"
poised on the edge of
Hardangerfjorden,
near the village of
Ullensvang, where
with piano and
writing desk at hand,
he would compose
surrounded by the
beauty of the
Norwegian fjords.*

BELOW: Heddal
Stave Church.
RIGHT: dramatic
Hordaland fjord.

Hardangerfjord. Heading northeast on National Highway 13, you'll find a beautiful stretch of water, Eidfjorden. It cuts far into the dramatic landscape that includes the **Skykkjedalsfossen ⑳**, Norway's highest waterfall.

Hang-gliding to skiing

If you loop back northwest, crossing Eidfjord by ferry and continuing on Highway 13, you come to **Voss ㉑**, which lies next to a lake, Vangsvatnet, in the middle of rich farmland. The Voss *kommune* (district) makes full use of its surroundings to attract visitors. In summer they come for touring, fjord excursions, mountain walking, parachuting, hang-gliding and paragliding from Hangurfjell, and fishing and watersports on Vangsvatnet. In winter, everything changes and Voss becomes one of the best centres for Alpine and cross-country skiing.

The top station of the cable car up Hangurfjell at 610 metres (2,000 ft) gives one of the best prospects of Voss in its bowl-shaped valley. The town has long been a centre for artists and musicians, and their monuments are scattered around. It is one of the best places to hear the Hardanger fiddle and see the old dances performed in beautiful costumes. On the main street is a shop where you can see, or even buy, the ornate silver belts and jewellery that go with the traditional Norwegian costume.

Around Bergen and north

From Voss the E16 highway or the train take you to **Bergen ㉒** *(see page 185).* Bergen's islands are linked so closely together that sometimes it is hard to realise that you have crossed water, but those such as **Askøy** and **Osterøy** to the north of the city have their own character, and the area round the Bjørnafjorden (Bear Fjord) to the south is particularly mild and green.

The long narrow island of **Sotra ㉓** shelters Bergen from the North Sea. It is a good base for sea canoeing in and out of the small offshore islands and rocks and, in good weather, as far as the open sea to combine canoeing with ocean fishing. In any case, shelter is never far away.

North of Bergen is **Nordhordland**, a district of islands that stretches as far north as Sognefjorden. Today, fish farming is the prime livelihood and the region exports salmon and trout all round the world. Fish farmers are now attempting to rear cod, halibut and other species. Some fish farms are open to the public. There is good sea fishing for cod and coalfish, and rosy-coloured trout inhabit many of the lakes. Diving and sub-aqua fishing, as well as treasure hunting, are easy in these transparent waters. Oil is a modern, though not conflicting, industry in this area with the night gleam of the light from Mongstad refinery.

To the north and most remote of all, is the island of **Fedje ㉔**, an important navigation point for many centuries with two 19th-century lighthouses still in use today. Norwegian maritime rules insist that all ships must carry a Norwegian pilot, which here is vital, as tankers serving the Mongstad refinery navigate through the ever-changing waters. ❏

BERGEN

Gateway to the fjords, mountains and islands, Norway's western seaport has a relaxed atmosphere, stunning setting and vibrant cultural life

Map on page 186

Should you tell a Bergenser that your spouse or a good friend hails from the city, the spontaneous response may be "how fortunate". Mirth is the currency of life in Bergen, humour among its better-known exports. A Bergenser wants you to laugh at a local joke, but seldom forewarns you that in laughing you might find yourself caught in a mental mousetrap.

During the city's official 900th anniversary celebrations in 1970, King Olav V visited an archaeological excavation and asked Councilman Knut Tjonneland: "How old is the city, really?" "That depends, your majesty," replied Tjonneland, "on the amounts appropriated for further excavation."

Although Bergen is said to have been founded in AD 1070 by the Viking king, Olav Kyrre, the city is probably older. Recent archaeological finds have dated the earliest settlements to 50 BC or earlier. The name Bergen derives from the old Norse *Bjørgvin*, still the name of the diocese.

International connections

Surrounded by seven mountains, Bergen is now a major port with 10 km (6 miles) of dockside. Until the railway eastwards over the high mountain plateau to Oslo was opened in November 1909, Bergen was isolated from the rest of Norway. Scotland by ship was closer than Oslo, England less distant than Copenhagen. As the westernmost city in Scandinavia, Bergen soon became a crossroads of the north and, in the 13th century, the capital of a united Norway. Its favourable location with respect to the other ports of Europe drew Hanseatic tradesmen, who established a commercial community at the harbour.

Fullriggers plied the port, with peak traffic in 1644, when more than 400 ships docked from Scotland alone. Many current everyday objects first came to Norway on ships docking here – not least wallpaper, which first appeared in the late 17th century in the homes of ships' captains who plied the oriental trade routes. With nine centuries of maritime tradition, it is hardly surprising that most "real" Bergensers have their roots elsewhere. Composer Edvard Grieg's family of diplomats, writers and musicians, for example, is an offspring of the Scottish McGregor clan.

Street and place names ring the register of central European origins. Even the crisp Bergen dialect bears the indelible stamp of international influence. To most Norwegians, an Englishman is an *engelskmann*, but to the Bergenser, an *englender*, from the German *Engländer*. A parade in Bergen is a *prosesjon*, from the English "procession"; the rest of Norway says *tog*.

Individuality prevails. Edvard Grieg was a Bergenser, a self-professed misfit at the 130-year-old Tanks

LEFT: shopfronts in Bryggen.
BELOW: selling fish in Bergen's famous fish market.

TIP

Buy a Bergen Kortet
(Bergen Card) from the
Tourist Information
Office near the Fish
Market. Benefits
include free admission
or discounts for
museums and free
public transport.

School, where he was known as Pupil No 139. Yet, today, annual summer concerts attract music lovers from all over the world to his home, **Troldhaugen**, 8 km (5 miles) south of the city (open May–Sept: daily 9am–5.30pm; Oct–Apr: times vary; entrance fee; tel: 55 91 07 10), and the **Grieghallen** Ⓐ music hall is renowned in Europe as the home of one of the world's oldest orchestras, Harmonien, founded in 1765, as well as of the annual Bergen Music Festival.

Most of the time, the city's backdrop is the glacial quiet of the mountains, but music, one is frequently reminded, is very much a part of its heritage. "Rat-a-tat-tat, rat-a-tat-tat." The sound pierces the mind. It's the **Buekorps**, an organisation for 10–20-year-old boys. They're easily recognised by their natty tunics and tasselled tam-o'-shanter caps dating from the 1850s, when the organisation was founded in emulation of the home guards, then the backbone of the country's defence. From mid-April until 17 May, when the boys march in formation in the annual Constitution Day parade, they practise before going to school, which makes early morning sleep a rarity.

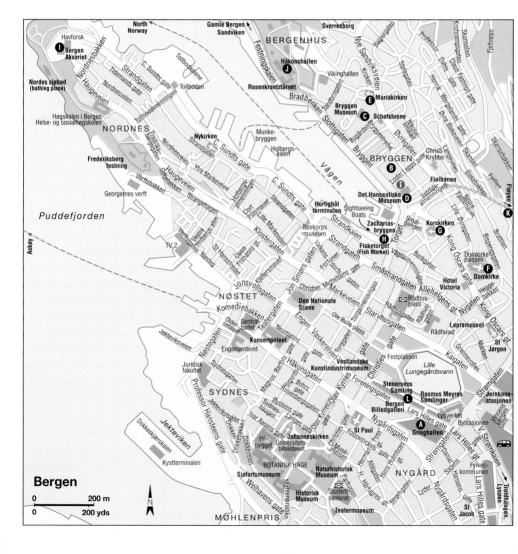

Bergen

0   200 m
0   200 yds

Water, water...

The Gulf Stream blesses Bergen with a benign climate and a harbour that is ice-free year round. But it also brings rain, some 2,250 mm (89 inches), making Bergen the country's wettest city. A local saying holds that "*I Bergen by, går alle med paraply*" ("In Bergen town, everyone carries an umbrella"). In other parts of the world, in other parts of Norway, teenagers refuse to carry umbrellas no matter how wet the weather. In Bergen, they are customary confirmation gifts.

Reminders of the city's seafaring tradition abound. The magnificently preserved full-rigged *Statsraad Lehmkuhl*, named after Christopher Lehmkuhl, a Bergenser and a man of the sea who ultimately became a cabinet minister, has her home port in the city. Today, Bergen is a port of call for cruise ships heading to and from the fjords. As the American movie producer Woody Allen said, "There is enough scenery for a dozen films." Quite rightly, the city calls itself the capital of fjord country.

Moreover, many of the Hanseatic **Bryggen** ❸ buildings remain – a film set in themselves, meticulously preserved and listed as a UNESCO World Heritage Site. A walk through Bryggen is a step back in time, to before the Reformation. Here are galleries, craft shops, fashion boutiques and eating places, interspersed with sailmakers, a freight company and a scrap metal dealer.

The earliest archaeological remains are in **Bryggen Museum** ❻ (open May–Aug: daily 10am–5pm; Sept–Apr: Mon–Fri 11am–3pm, Sat noon–3pm, Sun noon–4pm; entrance fee; tel: 55 58 80 10). Guides from the museum conduct tours through the row of Hansa houses and warehouses that line Bryggen. These were built after the great fire of 1702, which destroyed many buildings. One key to understanding the Hansa merchants' way of life is to visit the **Hanseatiske Museum** ❼ (open June–Aug: daily 9am–5pm; Sept–May: 11am–2pm; entrance fee).

Nearby is the oldest building still in use in the city, **Mariakirken** ❻ (St Mary's Church), built in the early 12th century and justly proud of its rich Baroque pulpit. The other medieval churches to survive the periodic fires are the present **Domkirke** ❼ (Cathedral) and **Korskirken** ❼, both of which merit a visit.

Fish for sale

To buy fish year-round in the open-air **Fisketorget (Fish Market)** ❼ on the nearby harbour is to walk in and out of a continuous conversation. Sturdy fishmongers ward their solid masonry tanks teeming with live cod or crawling with crustaceans. To the Bergenser, a fresh fish is one with the tail still flipping.

Bergen's shopping centre is situated south of the Fish Market around **Torgalmenningen**, a broad, traffic-free street where many of the best shops are to be found. Crowded in summer, these thoroughfares, known as *almenning*, were deliberately built wide to prevent flames from spreading to the opposite side of the street.

The view from the Nordnes peninsula over the town to the mountain of Fløyen is characterised by the contrast between the green woodland, blue sea and the mainly white-painted wooden houses. At the point of the peninsula is **Bergen Akvariet** ❶ (Aquarium;

Map on page 186

King Harald Harfegre sculpture at Bryggen Museum.

BELOW: statue of the violinist Ole Bull.

The summer home of Edvard Grieg (1843–1907) at Troldhaugen.

BELOW:
Bergen, seen from Fløyen mountain.

open May–Sept: daily 9am–8pm; Oct–Apr: 10am–6pm; entrance fee; tel: 55 55 71 71), one of the most extensive collections of sea life in Europe.

Historic highs

Håkonshallen ❶ (open May–Aug: daily 10am–4pm; Sept–Apr: noon–3pm; entrance fee; tel: 55 31 60 67), northwest of Bryggen, is an imposing Gothic festival hall built in 1261. It is arguably the best example of middle-age profane architecture remaining in Scandinavia. In it resides the fierce pride of the Bergenser. During World War II, Håkonshallen was nearly levelled to the ground when the *Voorbode*, a Dutch ship carrying German munitions, blew up in the harbour. The explosion flung parts of the ship 25 km (16 miles) from town and killed or injured its crew, dozens of Russian prisoner dock workers and more than 5,000 townspeople. One of the *Voorbode's* anchors still lies where it hit the ground, on **Fløyen mountain ❿**, some 300 metres (1,000 ft) higher than where the ship had been docked. A small park has been built around the anchor. Stand there, and you can tell the true Bergenser among the many elderly who pass by on their Sunday strolls: they're the ones who doff their hats.

A funicular, **Fløibanen** (open daily 7.30am–11pm, Sat from 8am, Sun from 9am; May–Aug closes at midnight) connects the city centre to Fløyen mountain and panoramic views of Bergen. At the top there is a restaurant and the start of eight marked walking routes. Concerts are held here on summer evenings.

Lakeside galleries

Bergen has several strong art collections, mostly centred on Lille Lungegårdsvann, an octagonal lake near Grieghallen. Here are the **Bergen**

Billedgalleri ❶ (Municipal Art Gallery) with a large collection of Norwegian painting; the **Rasmus Meyers Samlinger** (Rasmus Meyer Collection), which also specialises in Norwegian art, including Edvard Munch; and the **Stenersens Samling**, with work by Munch, Picasso and Klee among others (all open daily 11am–5pm; Sept–May: closed Mon; entrance fee; tel: 55 56 80 00).

The outgoing nature, taste for trade and concern for others typical of Bergensers are best reflected in Thoralf Rafto (1922–86). Before the fall of communism, Rafto dedicated his energies to awakening the West to the human rights abuses in the East, particularly of Soviet Jews. An annual Rafto Prize for Human Rights commemorates his work; fittingly it is administered at **Rafto-huset – Menneskerettighetenes Hus** (Rafto Human Rights House, Menneskerettighetenes Plass 1; open Mon–Fri 8.30am–4.30pm; tel: 55 21 09 30).

Excursions from Bergen

Not to be missed is the **Fantoft Stave Church,** 8 km (5 miles) south of the city in Paradis (open May–Sept: daily 10.30am–2pm, 2.30–6pm; entrance fee; tel: 55 28 07 10). It was built around 1150 and is one of the oldest wooden buildings in Europe. In 1992, it burned down, but has since been completely restored.

A short ferry ride across Lysefjorden brings you to the beautiful island of **Lysøen** (Island of Light) and the onion-domed summer residence of the violin virtuoso Ole Bull (1810–80). Bull called the villa, built in 1873, his "Little Alhambra" and often invited fellow musicians and artists. In summer, the old music room resounds to the music Bull played here with violin recitals and small ensembles (open May–Aug: Mon–Sat noon–4pm, Sun 11am–5pm; ferry from Buena quay; entrance fee; tel: 56 30 90 77). ❑

Map on page 186

TIP

The Hotel Terminus, across Kaaes Gate from Bergen's railway station, is known for putting on one of the country's most sumptuous breakfast tables.

BELOW: National Day celebrations.

THE HEART OF NORWAY

Central Norway encompasses a remarkable landscape from the shimmering fjords of the west across the peaks, plateaux and valleys that have inspired great writers and composers

Map
on pages
174–175

Oslo

he heartland of Norway is the upper part of the southern bulge of the country, extending from above Oslo and Bergen to below Trondheim. The area encompasses the highest mountains in Scandinavia, and freshwater lakes and watercourses abound. To the east there are two long valleys, **Østerdalen** (literally "Easterly Valley") and **Gudbrandsdalen**, orientated roughly parallel to the border with Sweden and knifing through the high interior cordillera to provide the major north–south land transport arteries. In the middle there are the lofty peaks and high plateau of the Rondane and Jotunheimen ranges, and to the west lies the coast with its fjords and archipelago islands in waters plied by boats since the land was first settled. Indeed, this part of the country embodies the *fjord og fjell* (fjord and mountain) landscape so deeply etched in Norwegian ethos.

Lake Mjøsa, a slender jewel

The glaciers that gouged the fjords also worked the inland and left **Mjøsa** ㉕, a jewel of a lake. Its southern end is at Minnesund just north of Eidsvoll, and its northern tip is at Lillehammer, 101 km (63 miles) to the northwest. It's slender, only 15 km (9 miles) at its broadest and like a fjord, deep, up to 449 metres (1,472 ft). Around Mjøsa lies some of the most arable land in the country, and its shores greet undulating countryside with large farms backed by densely forested hills. One of the best ways to enjoy the lake and its surroundings is a trip on the *Skibladner*, the world's oldest paddlewheel steamship still in service, named after a sailing ship of Nordic mythology. In summer, the *Skibladner* carries up to 230 passengers on excursions six days a week; contact any tourist information office in the region or her home port at **Hamar** ㉖ for schedules (tel: 62 52 70 85).

Hamar was a medieval centre of Roman Catholicism in Norway and the seat of a bishop. It is still a bishopric, but only ruins remain of its imposing cathedral, now protected under a glass canopy at **Hedemarksmuseet og Domkirkeodden** (Hedemark Museum and Cathedral Point; open May–Sept: 10am–4pm; entrance fee). In the 19th century Hamar became a railway junction with a locomotive works.

The works are gone, but there's a reminder, **Jernbanemuseet** (National Museum of Railway Transport; open May–Sept; entrance fee) with stations, railway buildings and vintage rolling stock. There are regular excursions on a narrow-gauge steam train.

Fertile local lands long ago led to cities and towns producing comestibles. Most stimulating, perhaps, is that seven of the country's eight distilleries are located hereabouts. One of them, **Løten Brænderi** (guided

LEFT: Ålesund abounds with Art Nouveau buildings.
BELOW: legendary Norwegian troll.

Lillehammer's coat of arms reflects a national pastime.

tours; entrance fee; tel: 62 59 49 10), at **Løten** ㉗, 18 km (11 miles) east of Hamar, is open to the public. A fascinating one-man show (Fri, Sat, Sun, 6pm, entrance fee) recounts the history of the distillery and the production of aquavit, the Norwegian liquor made from potato alcohol. Also worth visiting on the same site is **Løiten Lys** (open Mon–Fri 10am–8pm; Sat–Sun noon–6pm), a candle factory with a display of candles in every conceivable shape and size.

Two weeks of fame

Lillehammer ㉘ is best known in the world of winter sport as the venue of the 1994 Olympic Winter Games. Many of the Olympic facilities still stand, such as the ice event rinks at Hamar and Gjøvik. Other Olympic facilities include a new Alpine ski area at nearby **Hafjell**, and some 500 km (300 miles) of cross-country skiing tracks. The cross-country arena now is the finish for the annual trans-mountain Birkebeiner race, one of the world's oldest citizens' races.

For summer visitors, the biggest attraction is the open-air museum, **Maihaugen** (open June–Aug: 9am–6pm; May, Sept: 11am–5pm; entrance fee), with some 120 vintage buildings brought into the 40-hectare (100-acre) site from all over Gudbrandsdalen, including a stave church and two farms. The museum was the life work of Anders Sandvig. He came to Lillehammer in 1885 suffering from tuberculosis and with a life expectancy of just two years. Whether or not it was his interest in the museum he founded in 1887 which kept him alive, he lived another 65 years and died in 1950.

The **Norsk Vegmuseum (Road Transport Museum)** at **Fåberg**, to the north of Lillehammer on the E6 highway, has everything from horse-drawn sleighs to modern cars (open all year; entrance fee).

BELOW: the historic copper-mining town of Røros.

RØROS

Røros, a UNESCO World Heritage site on the E30 north of Alvdal, was until recently the archetypal company town, with life and society revolving around the mining business. Isolated, exposed, nearly 600 metres (2,000 ft) above sea level and surrounded by mountains, it owed its existence to copper, which was mined here from 1644 to 1972. Now the inhabitants make their living from sawmills, furniture making, wool processing and reindeer meat, as well as tourism. It is a harsh spot; the lowest temperatures in the whole of Norway are often recorded here.

By some miracle Røros escaped the fires that so often laid waste to the wooden buildings in Norwegian towns, and it has retained much of its mining town atmosphere. The wealthy folk lived to the east of the river in Bergmannsgate, while the miners had to make do with the area beneath the slagheaps and the smelter. Picturesque log houses remain, while the crooked houses in Slaggveien are particularly interesting. The most noticeable feature is the stone church, "the pride of the mining town", which was dedicated in 1784. Paintings of clergymen and mining officials decorate the interior. The smelter was the focal point of the town and has been restored as a museum.

Østerdalen

To the east of Mjøsa lake lies **Østerdalen**, cut through the mountains by the Glomma river, the country's longest river stretching 617 km (383 miles). The valley carries one of the north–south railway lines as well as National Highway 3. It starts at **Elverum** ㉙ in the south and continues northward for 250 km (150 miles) becoming broader and more open further north. Just south of **Aursunden**, one of the source lakes for the Glomma river, lies the old copper-mining town of **Røros** ㉚ *(see box, page 192)*, a UNESCO World Heritage site.

Gudbrandsdalen

To the west of Østerdalen lies **Gudbrandsdalen**, the country's second longest valley, cut by the River Lågen flowing south to Lillehammer. Perhaps because mountains surrounded it, the valley has a long tradition of folk dancing and folk music and is known for its wood carving and rose painting, sold by hand-icraft shops in the villages.

For Norwegians everywhere, as well as for curious visitors, Gudbrandsdalen is best remembered as the place where the indigenous Norwegian *geitost* (whey cheese made from goat's milk) was first made in the mid-19th century. The real variety, *ekte geitost*, made entirely of goat's milk, is still produced in the valley and elsewhere in the country. Tribute to the original cheese is paid in the name of *Gudbrandsdalost* (Gudbrandsdalen cheese), made from 10 percent goat's milk and 90 percent cow's milk, the cheese most likely to adorn all breakfast tables, from humble bed and breakfasts to the best of hotels.

About midway along the valley lies **Dombås** ㉛, a principal rail and road junction just southwest of the **Dovrefjell** (Dovre Mountains). The Dovre

The unsung hero of the Gudbrandsdalen valley is Anne Haav, the "budeia" (farm maiden) who first made the uniquely Norwegian "geitost" (goat's cheese) in the 19th century.

BELOW: canoeing is a popular pastime in summer.

A local hazard for drivers: elk on the road.

BELOW: carved ravens offer protection over this household in Stordalselva.

summits are lofty, but even the highest, **Snøhetta**, at 2,286 metres (7,498 ft), is lower than the peaks of the Jotunheimen. Yet the Dovre Mountains have a place in the national psyche like no other, embodied in the saying about the strength of the country, "*Enig og tro til Dovre Faller*" ("United we stand till Dovre falls"). Fittingly, the name Dombås derives from *Domba*, the name of a river, and *ås*, meaning "mountain ridge".

Home of the Giants

South of Dombås is an extensive area of peak and plateau. The Norwegian mountains are made for walking. As explorer Paul Belloni Du Chaillu observed in *Land of the Midnight Sun* (1881): "The difference between the mountains of Switzerland and Norway is this: those of the former are much higher, more bold and pointed, and sharp in the outlines of their thousand forms. On the other hand, the Norwegian mountains have a grave and sombre character, appearing like a gigantic stony wave, with a peak here and there, impressing more by their vastness than their height and ruggedness."

This "gigantic stony wave" has many hiking trails marked by red letter Ts painted on rocks and cairns. They meander between *hytta* (lodges), mostly above the timberline, between 950 and 1,600 metres (3,100–5,250 ft) above sea level, and the highest summits are around 2,400 metres (7,900 ft). Hence the lack of mention in mountaineering anthologies, where sheer elevation is the criterion. Therein lies part of the secret: you can enjoy the high-altitude experience without needing high-altitude lungs.

Moreover, in summer you can travel to the heart of the range in only a few steps, by boarding one of the passenger launches that ply the waters of lakes

Gjende and Bygdin. That joy has long been acknowledged by urban natives. In the late 19th century, the composer Edvard Grieg remarked that "when I contemplate the possibility of a future visit to the [Jotunheimen] mountains, I shudder with joy and expectation, as if it were a matter of hearing Beethoven's Tenth Symphony." That attraction was in part why Grieg wrote the incidental music for Henrik Ibsen's play *Peer Gynt*, based on a traditional legend of Gudbrandsdalen, in which braggart Peer leaps astride a reindeer, from a knife ridge into the lake below. The knife ridge and the lake are real: **Besseggen** and **Gjende** in the Jotunheimen, literally "Home of the Giants". The reindeer are equally real, as herds of them still graze here. One reminder of them is the reindeer pattern on the Gjende brand biscuits, sold throughout the country.

Map on pages 174–175

One of the best views in the region is from Besseggen in the Jotunheimen Mountains, the ridge immortalised by Henrik Ibsen in his play "Peer Gynt".

Out of this world

Accessibility is another allure of these wilderness areas. To the south of the Jotunheimen lies the hamlet of **Finse** 32 the highpoint at 1,225 metres (4,000 ft) on the Oslo–Bergen railway line. Its high street is the station platform; trains are the local traffic, as there are neither cars nor roads. It's a small speck in a seemingly boundless expanse of ice and snow. So remote yet accessible is this place that it was chosen for the filming of the initial sequences of *The Empire Strikes Back*, the *Star Wars* film depicting battles fought on the Ice Planet Holth.

Finse has the country's largest *hytta* for hikers and skiers, as well as a full-service hotel, as suits its location as the node between two giant trail networks, north to the **Jotunheimen** and south to **Hardangervidda** (Hardanger Plateau). As the crow flies, the trail networks stretch 225 km (140 miles) to the north and 100 km (60 miles) to the south, and in all have more than 5,000 km (3,000 miles)

BELOW:
finding warmth in
a cosy snow hole.

TIP

In summer, guides from the Jostedalsbreen National Park Centre, 20 km (12 miles) from Stryn lead tours and glacier explorations to the great Jostedal (details from the office in Oppstryn; tel: 91 58 00 78).

BELOW: the scenic Peer Gynt Way.

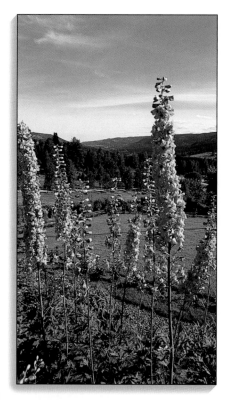

of T-marked hiking trails and at Easter-time, some 2,000 km (1,240 miles) of ski trails, marked by poles in the snow.

To the north and east of the Jotunheimen, on the other side of the Gudbrand-dalen valley, lies the **Rondane** range, which offers some of the country's finest hiking and cross-country skiing. Here the trails are not steep, the peaks not as high, the walks not as long and the *hytta* not as numerous in the Jotunheimen. But the connection to the Gudbrandsdalen legend remains, as there is a Peer Gynt Hytta here. Moreover, to the south and on the west flank of the valley there is a **Peer Gyntveien** (Peer Gynt Way) which leads from Gausdal north of Lillehammer to Golå south of Vinstra. A hike or drive along it affords views of much of the central cordillera.

Easy hiking

The trails and the *hytta* reflect the Norwegian view of wilderness; it is for all. Pristine perhaps is the best word; only the red Ts and an occasional electric power line belie modern times. Little has changed since three English adventurers, with the pseudonyms Skipper, Essau and John, came to the Jotunheimen in the 1880s. Their subsequent book, *Three in Norway by Two of Them*, became one of the classic travelogues of the Victorian age. The remnants of their camp are carefully preserved near **Memurubu** ❸ on lake Gjende in the Jotunheimen, one of the *hytta* that dot these wilderness areas.

The *hytta* are one of the secrets of Norwegian mountain hiking and skiing. The word has the same root as "hut" in English, but there the similarity ends. One need carry only a light sleeping bag for overnighting, because there are comfortable bunk beds in the *hytta* and meals are provided in most of them. Indeed, "full-service lodge" would be the best translation.

You need not stay at the *hytta*; trail use is free, and many carry packs with a full array of gear to be self-sufficient. But after a few days on the trail, or even on their first night, they camp near one of the *hytta* for a good meal and the conviviality of evenings there.

Most of the *hytta* are owned and operated by Den Norske Turistforening (DNT) and its affiliated local organisations; hence the red Ts on rocks and cairns. You need not be a DNT member to stay in a DNT *hytta*, but membership is a good investment, as the price is soon offset by the accumulated discounts on accommodation. You can join DNT at any of the *hytta* or at the head office in Oslo (tel: 22 82 28 00).

From Sogn to Nordfjord

The county of **Sogn og Fjordane** lies between the coast and the Jotunheimen mountains. Narrow fingers of water push inland from the main fjords to reach far into the mountains, and waterfalls tumble hundreds of metres into the fjords below. In the past, the terrain was impassable in winter. Today travel is easier thanks to the network of ferries, tunnels and bridges. The county is easily accessible from Bergen. Indeed, until 1918, it was named Nordre Bergenhus (Northern Bergen Province).

The **Sognefjorden** is unmatched. On both sides of it small villages cling to the land, each with its own atmosphere. **Balestrand** ❸ has been a favourite since the 19th century and has an English church, St Olav's. A narrow side-fjord leads to **Fjærland** ❸ near the two southernmost tongues of the **Jostedalsbreen Glacier**. Nestling at its base is the **Norsk Bremuseum** (Norwegian Glacier Museum; open Apr–Nov 9am–7pm; entrance fee; tel: 57 69 32 88, where interactive models, displays and films provide an insight into Europe's largest glacier.

Going east from Balestrand, a short crossing takes you to **Hella** and past the glistening arc of **Kvinnfoss** (Lady's Waterfall) close to the main road. At the head of the fjord, **Sogndal** ❸ is the centre for trade and administration. It swells considerably during term-time because it is also a centre for education, with university colleges and Norway's oldest folk high school.

Cool, green waters

In **Luster** ❸, 25 km (15 miles) to the northeast of Sogndal, is another of Sogn's many stave churches, **Urnes Stavkirke**. Built around 1130 and believed to be the oldest stave church in Norway, it is now a UNESCO World Heritage site (open June–Aug: daily 10.30am–4pm; entrance fee).

Aurlandsvangen, Flåm and Gudvangen lie along the innermost recesses of the fjord, which stretches south from the main fjord like an upside-down "Y". Not to be missed is the mountain railway from **Flåm** ❸ which spirals up the steep mountain gorge to meet the Bergen Line at **Myrdal**.

If from Balestrand you head northwest toward **Førde** ❸ and the coast, you cross a region of many lakes – Jølstravatnet – that penetrate the foothills of the high tops in the east and feed into the fjords in the west. One of the rivers, the Jølstra, said to be one of the best salmon rivers in the area, drops precipitously

Map on pages 174–175

The railway from Flåm to Myrdal winds through spectacular mountain scenery.

BELOW: fjords punctuate the landscape in Sogn og Fjordane.

before reaching Førde on **Førdefjord**. Here is **Sunnfjord Museum** (open June–Aug; entrance fee; tel: 57 72 54 11), a collection of 24 historic buildings.

Oddly, **Florø ⓐ**, the only community in this large county big enough to be called a town, lies on the remote edge of the sea, but not so odd considering that Norway has always depended on the sea for food, trade and transport. The **Sogn og Fjordane Kystmuseet** (Coastal Museum; open all year; entrance fee; tel: 57 74 22 33) in Florø has a fine collection of old boats.

Inland along Nordfjorden

Nordfjorden is 100 km (60 miles) shorter than the Sognefjorden. With so many side-fjords, lakes and valleys it is easy to get into the mountains or make the journey up **Briksdalsbreen**, one of the most beautiful glaciers in the fjord country. Even better is that you can climb up to the base of the glacier in the two-wheeled farm carriages, *stolkjaerrer*, pulled by small sturdy, cream-coloured *fjording* (fjord horses) native to Nordfjord.

The traditional home of the *fjording* is the Eid district, centred around Nordfjordeid, where Nordfjorden proper has already divided itself into Eidsfjorden and Isefjorden. **Eid ⓐ**, which is also connected to the coast by Road 15, is known for Firdariket, the seat of the last Viking chief. The town has traditional white-painted buildings, and the church, which dates from 1849, is decorated with beautiful rose painting.

Further along you reach the Inner Nordfjorden, where the fjord system ends at Stryn, Loen and Olden, the start of three spectacular valleys stretching up to the northwest edges of the Jostedalsbreen. Nowadays, three tunnels out of the Stryn valley cut right through the mountain to the renowned **Geirangerfjorden**

BELOW: remote farmstead in the mountainous hinterland.

FJORD FORMATION

Fjords are found in Alaska, Canada, Chile, Greenland, New Zealand, Norway and Scotland. But nowhere are they more prominent than in Norway. A direct line along the coast measures 2,650 km (1,568 miles), but the stretch of the entire coastline, including the archipelago islands, is 57,260 km (33,880 miles), a third more than the distance around the earth at the equator. The coast of Norway is more jagged than any other, and Norwegian gave the word fjord to the languages of the world.

The fjords were formed about 100,000 years ago, during the last ice age. Glaciers gouged valleys from the land, to depths that lessened at the coast, where the ice was thinner. When the ice retreated, the sea inundated. So a typical fjord is deepest at its midpoint and far less deep at its mouth: the Sognefjord, for instance, reaches a depth of 1,244 metres (4,080 ft), but is only 158 metres (518 ft) deep at its mouth.

The fame of these fjords has made them part of the myth of science fiction. In *The Hitch-Hikers Guide to the Galaxy*, the venerable planet-builder Slartibartfast recalls "…doing the coastlines was always my favourite, used to have endless fun doing all the little fiddly bits in fjords…did you ever go to a place…I think it's called Norway?"

to the north. **Stryn** ⓮ is known for summer skiing on the northeast of Strynsvatn, where the ground rises to Tystigbreen. Until you watch, it is hard to imagine skiers in swimsuits or shorts and T-shirts with deep tans, but there they are enjoying every moment.

Møre og Romsdal

Coastal vessels have long called at Ålesund, Molde and Kristiansund on their way to Trondheim and the north. Looking at the jumble of coastline, islands and fjord mouths on a map, it is difficult to distinguish where sea and islands end and fjords and mainland begin. Yet move inland and half the area lies above 600 metres (1,800 ft).

Ålesund ⓭ is Norway's largest fishing town. Yet it is best known for its Art Nouveau architecture, built in 1904 after fire destroyed its centre. First to the rescue came Kaiser Wilhelm II of Germany, who sent four ships laden with supplies and building materials. With help and donations from all over Europe, the people of Ålesund completed the rebuilding of their town.

Until the 1950s, fishing supported Ålesund, and *klippfisk* (traditional Norwegian split dried cod) was its principal export. But as fishing changed so did Ålesund, which added fish processing and aquaculture. Many former warehouses are now offices and restaurants, where you can try one of the more unlikely local specialities such as *bacalao*, made from boned *klippfisk*.

Bird island

To the southwest of Ålesund is **Runde** ⓮, the island that draws naturalists from around the world, as more than 200 bird species have been recorded there. One

Map on pages 174–175

TIP

Explore the colourful Art Nouveau town of Ålesund: guided walks depart daily from the Tourist Information Office (Rådhuset; June–Aug; tel: 70 15 76 00).

BELOW: the magnificent setting of Geirangerfjorden.

Map on pages 174–175

of the best ways of seeing the island is by taking a four-hour tour on boats departing from **Ulsteinvik** daily from June to August. As a bonus, the waters round the island close over myriad wrecks; in 1972, divers found a hoard of gold and silver coins on board the *Akerendam*, a Dutch vessel that sank in 1725; it was one of the largest finds of sunken treasure ever.

Roses, jazz and ocean driving

Molde ⓸, halfway along the coast from Ålesund north to Kristiansund, is part of an archipelago sheltered from the Norwegian Sea; its mild climate, lush vegetation and rose gardens earn it the title "Town of Roses". It is known at home for the might of its football team and for the annual Molde International Jazz Festival (mid-July; many free concerts; tel: 71 21 60 00).

From **Bud** on the coast west of Molde, a road leads to the **Atlanterhavsveien** (Atlantic Road) to Kristiansund, over **Averøya** ⓴, the biggest island in the area. It heads north across the rim of the ocean, so driving seems like a voyage. Averøya deserves more than the view from a car window. Archaeologists believe that this was one of the first places to be settled after the last Ice Age, and their finds include remnants of the early Fosna Culture that existed around 7000 BC.

Detail from the marble church on the island of Giske, near Ålesund.

The klippfisk capital

BELOW: Molde is the "Town of Roses". **RIGHT:** at the foot of the Jostedalsbreen Glacier.

Unlike Ålesund and Molde, **Kristiansund** ⓸ has little protection from the worst the North Atlantic can do. It is right on the coast, with weather-beaten rocks pounded by the sea, yet not far inland are grassy areas and small woods. This is the *klippfisk* town, for long the biggest exporter of Norwegian dried cod. A recent census counted only 17,000 inhabitants but, because of the centuries-old links with other countries through its sailors and fishermen, and the foreign merchants who settled here, the atmosphere is cosmopolitan. Like most Norwegian towns with "Kristian" in their title, Kristiansund was named after King Christian VI. A good introduction is by *sundbåtene*, the harbour boats that for more than 100 years have linked the town's three islands.

Mellemverftet, once one of four shipyards in Vågen, is working again as a centre for preserving the craft of shipbuilding, carefully restoring the beautiful lines of traditional Norwegian boats.

Land of the trolls

Inland, the northern part of Møre og Romsdal ends in a crisscross of fjords eating into the islands and peninsulas which lead to **Trollheimen**, the "Home of the Trolls", where the mountains reach nearly 1,600 metres (5,000 ft).

This haunt of climbers and skiers is bounded by two important valleys, Surnadalen and Sunndalen, with between them the tiny Todalfjorden. Beside the last is the surprise of the **Svinvik Arboret** ⓸ (Arboretum), beautiful gardens with thousands of rhododendrons, conifers and other plants (open May–Sept; entrance fee). Despite the northern latitude, plants from all over the world grow at Svinvik, owned and run today by the University at Trondheim. ❑

NORWAY'S MOST BEAUTIFUL VOYAGE

The splendid coastal voyage from Bergen to the North Cape and beyond has long been regarded as one of the great sea journeys of the world

Travelling on board the Hurtigruten (literally "swift route") steamships is to partake in what has been described as one of the world's most beautiful voyages. What began in 1891 as an idea to provide an express shipping service along the rugged Norwegian coast between Trondheim and Hammerfest has evolved into a lucrative form of tourism. Yet part of the charm is watching a working ship going about its business. Out of season, it reverts to its traditional role of carrying west-coast Norwegians, who treat it as a bus, for business and pleasure.

PORTS OF CALL

In spring and autumn, the 12-day round trip from Bergen across the Arctic Circle to the Nordkapp (North Cape) and Kirkenes lets you feast on the dramatic seasonal changes. In May, the fjord valleys are brilliantly in bloom, and the hills and the mountains of the north are still covered with snow. Returning south one meets the swift Norwegian summer marching north.

The Hurtigrute makes 34 ports of call along this ever-changing coast, some at places no bigger than a handful of houses round a harbour, others at cities such as Trondheim and Tromsø with time ashore to explore.

▷ **FULL STEAM AHEAD**
Captain Ernstsen, *M/S Nordlys*, and his crew, along with those of the other ships in the fleet, ensure generally smooth sailings in and out of the islands along the coast.

▷ **OUTWARD BOUND**
In the summer months the Hurtigruten take on the trimmings of cruise ships with dancing, film shows and day trips. Guides are on hand for hikes and vigorous climbs.

▽ **TEMPTING TREATS**
No matter what season, the meals on board offer a feast of Norwegian specialities, with abundant buffets, assorted cheeses and a mouthwatering selection of desserts.

◁ **STUNNING SCENERY**
Tranquil Trollfjorden: from fjords to open sea, fertile land to barren rock, fishing hamlets to cities, the voyage is a mix of the workaday and the spectacular.

△ **ARCHITECTURAL SIGHT**
Ishavskatedralen, the Arctic Ocean Cathedral at Tromsø, is a symbol of the north. Built in 1964, the cathedral features one of Europe's largest works of stained glass.

COMMUNICATIONS REVOLUTION

Over the past century more than 70 ships have served in the Hutigruten fleet.

These diverse vessels led a communications revolution, enabling the population and industries along the rugged Norwegian coast to keep in touch in a new way. Previously, it took three weeks in summer or five months in winter to send a letter from Trondheim to Hammerfest; the Coastal Express reduced this time to a few days.

Places such as the Lofoten Islands, Trollfjorden and the North Cape (symbol pictured above) became accessible to travellers who wanted to see the Midnight Sun, and so the tourist business began to grow. Nature lovers and bird-watchers are attracted by the scenery and the many bird colonies, which include puffins, kittiwakes and guillemots

As time went by, ships were built specifically with cold storage and freezer rooms, vehicle roll on/roll off capacity and conference facilities, as well as comfortable cabins.

Two companies now run 11 ships, ranging from the grand old *M/S Harald Jarl* to the *M/S Nordnorge*, built in 1997.

△ **VIEW FROM THE DECK**
With thousands of islands and skerries, mountains and glaciers, the landscape is constantly changing and no two days are alike.

◁ **NIGHT SKY**
The Northern Lights (Aurora Borealis) is a fascinating spectacle, whether a sparkling multicoloured vision or dancing white streaks.

THE NORTHWEST COAST

*North of Trondheim, Norway's religious and cultural capital,
lies a beautiful but often harsh landscape that crosses the Arctic
Circle into the land of the Midnight Sun*

Map
on page
206

T he northwest coast is where Norway gets thinner, from Trondheim – a large city for its latitude and the gateway to the north, up to Bodø, which lies beyond the Arctic Circle. The land along this narrow conduit is mostly forested, with the benign influence of the Gulf Stream ensuring temperate conditions persist far to the north.

Trondheim ❶ is a name rooted in Nordic mythology: *Trond* comes from the Old Norse *"throendr"*, the name of the people of the region and meaning "strong and virile", and *heim* comes from the word for habitation. It is a pleasant city, with clean air, wide streets, low buildings and a compact centre. Its relatively modest population of 147,000 swells by nearly a sixth in term-time, as this is a university town, as well as the country's leading hi-tech research centre. It is, as American sociologists have proclaimed, a most ideal city to live in.

As with all Norwegian cities, the outdoors is close at hand. Trondheim's back garden is Bymarka to the west, where **Gråkallen** (Old Man) at 520 metres (1,700 ft) high is a favourite walking and cross-country skiing area. Indeed, outdoor sports are a leading local pastime, and the city has acted as host to the World Nordic Ski Championships. The River Nidelva is known for the size of its salmon, and the fjord itself is ideal for sea fishing from boat or shore.

LEFT: overview of the city of Trondheim.
BELOW: Nidaros Cathedral, venue for Norwegian coronations.

NIDAROS CATHEDRAL

I n 997 the settlers of Nidaros could not have known, but the sheltered site they picked at the mouth of the Nid River was to become a pivotal city in Europe.

In the late 11th century, work started on a major church at Nidaros, erected over the grave of St Olav, the king who brought Christianity to the Vikings *(see page 209)*. Apparently the Pope found that fact auspicious, as he appointed an archbishop there and made the bishops of Greenland, Iceland, the Isle of Man, Orkney and the Faroe Islands, and the bishops in Norway responsible to him.

The church became a cathedral, one of the holy sites of Europe and the goal for many pilgrimages. It has become the national shrine and the venue for the coronation of Norwegian kings.

The name Nidaros endured; the cathedral is Nidarosdom (Nidaros Cathedral). The city that grew up around it became Trondhjem, a name rooted in Nordic mythology. In January 1930, when the city celebrated its 900th anniversary, the origin of the cathedral was honoured by changing the city name to Nidaros. The renaming triggered a debate that ended in March 1931 when the name reverted to Trondheim, with the spelling "*hjem*" amended to "*heim*" to please linguistic purists.

Viking city

The well-preserved buildings of the old harbour, the imposing **Nidarosdom** (Cathedral; *see box, page 205*; open daily: hours vary; entrance fee includes admission to adjacent Archbishop's Manor) and the statute of a Viking king, Olav Tryggvason, on a high pedestal in the centre of the city, belie the heritage of more than a millennium. Tryggvason founded the city in 997, and his successor, Olav Haraldsson, brought Christianity to the country (*see page 209*). It was Haraldson's martyrdom that triggered the building of the cathedral, where Norwegian kings are crowned, most recently King Harald V in 1991. The **Norwegian Crown Jewels** (open June–Aug: Mon–Fri 9.30am–12.30pm, Sun 1–4pm; Sept–May: Fri noon–2pm; free) are kept in the cathedral, and the regalia for king, queen and crown prince are on display in a chapel.

Through history, the cathedral also had influence on secular life. In pre-Reformation Europe, kings would often extend the powers of the clerics to civil and mercantile matters, including the issuing of coins. At Nidaros, that happened in 1222, when young King Håkon Håkonsson issued an edict empowering Archbishop Guttorm of Nidaros to mint and circulate coins. The archbishop and his successors exercised that right until 1537, when the Reformation ousted the last archbishop. Examples of the coins struck at the archbishop's mint were found in the following centuries, then in the early 1990s archaeologists discovered the mint beneath the ruins of a building that had burned down in 1640. The mint, the oldest found in Europe, forms part of the exhibits at **Erkebispegården** (the Archbishop's Manor) next to the cathedral.

Giving cyclists a lift

Trondheim has done much to relieve traffic congestion, including implementing a toll ring round the city. Cycling is encouraged on a network of dedicated bicycle paths. Yet topography challenges cycling: the flat centre is surrounded by steep hills. So in 1995, the resourceful city built **Trampe**, the world's first bicy-cle lift, 130 metres (426 ft) up Brubakken hill. The lift operates like a ski tow, and cyclists pay using keycards at the bottom of the hill. Not surprisingly, the annual **Styrkeprøven** (**Trial of Strength**) trans-mountain bicycle race held in June starts in Trondheim. It finishes 540 km (336 miles) south, in Oslo.

Map on page 206

And you can go to...

Some Norwegian words tempt double entendre in English, most notably the name of the village closest to Trondheim's Værnes airport. It's **Hell ❷**. Notwith-standing the derivation of the name from the Old Norse word for cavern, post-cards of the railway station at Hell sell astonishingly well. So when in Trondheim, you can indeed go to Hell; it's only 33 minutes east by commuter train. The station here must be one of the most photographed in the country. In September Hell hosts an annual blues festival which attracts international stars and fans to this otherwise quiet settlement.

St Olav's battleground

Many European countries claim histories highlighted by a decisive medieval bat-tle. For Norway, it's the **Battle of Stiklestad** on 29 July 1030, some 36 years before England's momentous Battle of Hastings. Unlike Hastings, which enabled the winning Normans to conquer the country, at **Stiklestad ❸** it was the loser who ultimately won. The forces of King Canute of Denmark and England were vic-torious and King Olav Haraldson of Norway was slain. Olav was later to become a saint *(see page 209)*. Stiklestad, located east of the E6 highway about 100 km (60 miles) north of Trondheim, is the venue for the annual *Olsokspelet* (St Olav's Play)

Northern road signs appear in Norwegian and Finnish.

BELOW: Bodø, port of call for the coastal steamers.

Map on page 206

The Arctic Circle at 66°N is defined not by temperature, but by light. It is the latitude at which the sun is above the horizon at noon on 21 June. At Bødo, the "Mørketid" (Arctic Night) lasts from 15 to 29 December.

BELOW: the bus runs whatever the weather.

performed every July in an open-air amphitheatre during the St Olav Festival. A 12th-century church marks the spot where King Olav died, and a museum (St Olav's Kulturhus) chronicles the events.

Trade essential

Despite their reputation as marauders, the Vikings were principally farmers and traders who settled and worked the land wherever they went. **Steinkjer ❹**, the first sizeable town north of Trondheim, reflects this. Its name comes from the Old Norse word for a river dam built to trap fish, and indeed in Viking times it was a trading centre. In 1857 it became an export port for timber and agricultural produce, a status that underscores the comparatively mild climate of the region, as here at 64°N the land is fertile and forests abound.

North of Steinkjer, the railway and the E6 highway follow the sheltered Namdalen valley to **Mosjøen ❺** at the head of the Vefsnfjorden and then to **Mo i Rana ❻** at the head of Ranafjorden. The word *Mo*, which means sand or gravel flats, is a common place name in Norway. Consequently, Mo at the head of Ranafjorden is called Mo i Rana to distinguish it from other towns named Mo. As for Steinkjer, trade triggered the first settlement of Mosjøen and Mo i Rana. Today the towns support heavy industries, starting in the mid-1950s with the **Norsk Jernverk** iron works at Mo i Rana and **Mosjøen Aluminumverk** aluminium plant at Mosjøen. From a business viewpoint, the locations of these industries in small, northern towns may be questioned. They are there as part of the government's efforts to provide jobs that keep people in the region. A similar effort is the more recent centralisation of the nine principal government registers at **Brønnøysund ❼**, on the coast south of Mosjøen. If, say, you take out a loan to buy a car anywhere in Norway, the relevant details will be registered at Brønnøysund.

Crossing the Arctic Circle

Most people experience an inexplicable thrill as they cross the **Polarsirkel (Arctic Circle)**. You cannot see it, but it's there. Perhaps the reason is celestial: unlike the Equator, set by geometry, or the International Date Line, drawn by timekeepers, the Arctic Circle delineates the southern boundary of a different sort of world, the land of The Midnight Sun.

The only building in this otherwise bleak landscape is **Polarsirkelsenteret ❽** (Arctic Circle Centre; open June–Aug: 9am–10pm; May, Sept: 10am–6pm; free). Situated on the Circle, alongside the railway and the E6 highway, it has a cafeteria, gift shop and exhibitions, including Europe's largest stuffed polar bear. Outside stands a memorial to the thousands of World War II prisoners of war who were used to build the railway and perished in the bitter winter conditions.

Farther north, **Bodø ❾** was founded as a trading centre, to compete with Bergen. It competed unsuccessfully, but today the Hurtigrute coastal steamers *(see Insight on Hurtigruten, page 202)* call on their way from Bergen. Bodø is the northern end of the rail network and a staging post for summer visitors. As the crow flies, it is as far from Kristiansand, the southernmost station, as Kristiansand is from Paris. ❑

STIKLESTAD: THE MAKING OF A SAINT

The site of the Battle of Stiklestad near Trondheim in 1030 marks a pivotal point in the history of the Norwegian nation and the adoption of Christianity

Stiklestad, north of Trondheim, is a name which is revered by Norwegians. This ancient battlefield is the place that saw the foundation of Norwegian unity and the adoption of the Christian faith.

In the 11th century Norway was a country constantly disrupted by disputes between rival chieftains. The ambition of the reigning king, Olav Haraldsson, was a united Norway. He also wanted to create a Christian country with Christian laws and churches and clergy.

He was not the first to attempt this. In the previous century Olav Tryggvason had been converted to Christianity in England. He returned to Norway in 995 with the express purpose of crushing the chieftains and imposing his new-found faith. But Olav Tryggvason's conversion had not swept away all his Viking instincts and in his zeal he used great cruelty to convert the populace. His chieftains became disenchanted and Olav was killed in the Battle of Svolder in the year 1000.

Olav Haraldsson ascended the throne in 1015, but like Olav Tryggvason he foolishly made too great a use of the sword to establish Christianity. King Canute of Denmark and England, with his eye on the Norwegian throne, gave support to discontented factions within the country and in 1028 invaded Norway, forcing King Olav to flee to Russia.

Undaunted, Olav returned with a few followers, but his support had dwindled. He met his end on 29 July 1030 at the Battle of Stiklestad. Olav's corpse was taken to the then capital, Nidaros, and buried on the banks of the Nidelva river. When the body was disin-

terred a year later, it showed no signs of corruption: his face was unchanged and his nails and hair had grown. This was taken as a sign of sanctity.

Following this revelation, Olav was proclaimed a saint and his body placed in a silver shrine in Nidaros Cathedral. Faith in the holiness of King Olav – St Olav – spread and his shrine became a centre of pilgrimage.

Canute's victory at the Battle of Stiklestad was brief. He ceded power to his son, Svejn, but as rumours of Olav's sanctity grew, popular support for Canute evaporated and Svejn was exiled to Denmark in 1035. Meanwhile, St Olav's son, Magnus, had been in exile in Russia. Norway now invited him to return and accept the crown.

From that time Stiklestad has been a place of pilgrimage. It now has a beautiful open-air theatre, and on the anniversary of the battle a cast of 300 actors, choristers, dancers and musicians re-enact the events of July 1030. ❑

TOP LEFT: statue of St Olav. **ABOVE LEFT:** a rune stone marks the place where King Olav died. **TOP RIGHT AND RIGHT:** the annual St Olav's Play.

NORWAY'S FAR NORTH

*Far removed from the rest of Europe, Norway's spectacular north
extends through Arctic latitudes from the rugged Lofoten Islands to
the Russian border. Beyond is the remote archipelago of Spitsbergen*

Map
on pages
212–213

T he far north of Norway, comprising Troms and Finnmark counties and the
Lofoten Islands, is unique in the Arctic, thanks to the warming currents of
the Gulf Stream. Here lies more than a third of the land of Norway, which
one resident in 20 calls home.

Imposing wall, tricky waters

Viewed from the mainland across Vestfjorden north of Bodø, the **Lofoten
Islands** present an imposing wall of rugged peaks rising from the sea. On the
west, these mountains form a mighty shield against the onslaught of Norwegian
Sea weather, so most of their habitation is along their east coasts, facing the
mainland. **Svolvær ❶**, the main town, has been a trading and fishing centre
since the 17th century. Fishing has long been the traditional calling of the
islanders, and today *Lofot torsk* (Lofoten Cod) remains choice throughout the
country. Between February and April, **Kabelvåg**, to the south, is the undisputed
fishing capital of northern Norway. Up to 10,000 vessels make for Vestfjord during these months for the colourful *Lofotfiske*, the annual cod-fishing event.

The southernmost of the larger Lofoten Islands, **Moskenesøya** is the most
photographed, perhaps because of the picturesque fishing village of **Reine ❷**.
Between Lofotodden, its southern cape, and the islet
of Mosken lies **Moskenstraumen ❸**, a 4-km (2½-
mile) wide, shallow channel. Here tidal currents reach
speeds of up to 6 knots in their alternating flow
between the Norwegian Sea and Vestfjorden, and
water always swirls around a submerged rock in the
middle of the channel. Sailing here is risky, as Dutch
navigators first noted on maps published in 1595 in
Mercator's Atlas, where the current was called "*Maelstrom*". Internationally, it has since been known by
that name, and writers, including the French novelist
Jules Verne and American poet Edgar Allan Poe, have
amplified it to a huge whirlpool that engulfs ships and
men. Maelstrom now is a synonym for a whirlpool
treacherous to navigation.

Paris of the North

Tromsø ❹ has long been a leading city in northern
Norway and now is regarded as the region's unofficial
capital. International trade and influence came early,
and by the 1860s the women of the town were so styl-
ishly dressed as to cause a visiting tourist to remark
that the city seemed to be "The Paris of the North".
That nickname persists, and now may apply as well to
Tromsø's abundant and varied nightlife, with an average of one seat in an eatery or place of entertainment
for every three residents. The city is built mostly on an
island between the mainland and the larger coastal

LEFT: sunset by a
frozen waterfall on
the Lofoten Islands.
BELOW: a tribute
to the explorer
Roald Amundsen.

For panoramic views of Tromsø, take the Fjellheisen cable car 420 metres (1,378 ft) above sea level. It even operates through the night when the Midnight Sun is shining.

island of **Kvaløya**. The sheltered location early made it a port for commercial operations in Arctic waters as well as the last port of call for polar expeditions.

The city's high latitude has made it a centre for Arctic research, such as on the spectacular Aurora Borealis, which can be viewed at the **Nordlysplanetariet** (Northern Lights Planetarium; open June–Aug: daily 10am–7pm; Sept–May: times vary; entrance fee; tel: 77 67 60 00). The University of Tromsø was opened in 1972, and to date is the most northerly university in the world. The **Tromsø Satellite Station** acquires images from polar-orbit meteorological satellites; the satellite weather map seen on television most likely came to earth here at Tromsø.

The city is the cultural centre of the North. The **Nordnorsk Kunstmuseum** (North Norway Art Museum; open Tues–Sun 11am-5pm; free; tel: 77 68 00 90) has fine collections of contemporary and applied art, and **Tromsø Museum** (open May–Sept: daily 11am–6pm; Oct–Apr: Mon–Fri 11am–3pm; entrance fee; tel: 77 64 50 00) has a splendid collection of Sami art.

Just over the bridge on the mainland, is the **Ishavskatedral** (Arctic Sea Cathedral; open June–Aug: 10am–8pm; Sept–May: 3–6pm; entrance fee), a daring and impressive modern work by the architect Jan Inge Hovig. Its entire east wall, 23 metres (75 ft) high, consists of a *dalle* (French for "flagstone") technique stained glass window by the artist Victor Sparre.

Tromsø is also home to Europe's northernmost brewery, **Mack** (tel: 77 62 45 00), established in 1845. Here you can sample its famous Arctic Ale, *Mackøl*.

Though it is in the Arctic, the city enjoys a benign climate. The average midday temperature in January is the same as in Oslo and summer temperatures are about the same as in Trondheim.

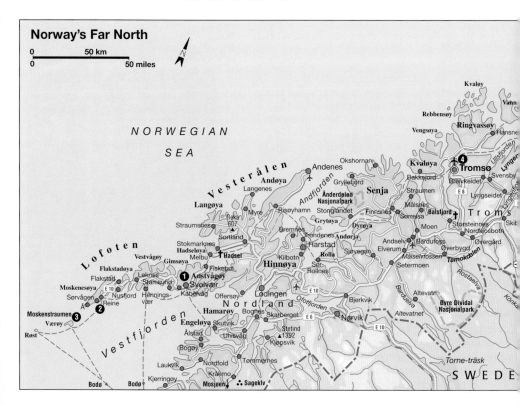

Norway's Far North

Heritage of the centuries

Alta ❺, the largest town in Finnmark, is known among fishermen for having one of the world's best salmon rivers. It is also home to the **Alta Museum** at **Hjemmeluft** (open June–Aug: daily 8am–11pm; Sept–May: times vary; entrance fee) on the southern outskirts, a collection of rock carvings dating from 4200 to 500 BC. These remarkable "stories in pictures" depicting people, animals (particularly reindeer), boats and weapons, are now a UNESCO World Heritage site.

South of Alta on the E93 lies **Kautokeino** ❻, a centre for the Sami, the indigenous people of northern Scandinavia and the Kola Peninsula of Russia. They are sometimes called Lapps, but prefer their own name Sami, which designates the land where they have lived for thousands of years. The size of the Sami population is not known, but is conservatively estimated at 70,000, of which about half live in Norway. Their native languages are related to Finnish, Hungarian and Estonian and have little in common with Norwegian. Traditionally, the Sami have been hunters, fishermen and reindeer herders. Some still follow the traditional callings, while others practise more modern trades. One of the more famous of them is film director Nils Gaup, whose *Pathfinder* (1987), the first feature-length Sami film, was nominated for an Academy Award. Like indigenous minorities elsewhere, the Sami were long suppressed, but now have their own flag and own parliament, *Sameting*, at **Karasjok** ❼.

Northernmost point

Nordkapp ❽ (The North Cape) at 71°10'21"N is considered to be the most northerly point of mainland Europe. It is, almost, as the tip of **Knivskjelodden**, a low, slim peninsula to its west, lies 47 seconds of latitude farther north. No

After two months of winter darkness, Vardø, Norway's easternmost town, celebrates the return of the sun around 20 January with a gun salute on the first day that the entire disk is visible above the horizon.

Map
on pages
212–213

*Part of the Children
of the World
Monument at the
North Cape.*

BELOW: polar bears
on Svalbard.
RIGHT: Sami woman
rounds up reindeer.

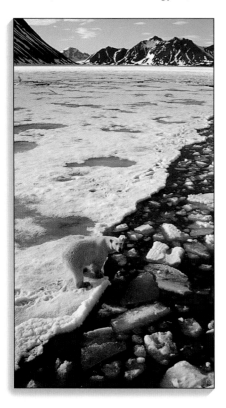

matter; the North Cape, a name first used in 1553 by English sailor Richard Chancellor, is the imposing headland that draws visitors from round the world. Residents further south know the annual signs: in early summer, a stream of cars with southern European number plates heads north, many of them with "To the North Cape" written on their boots. Later, the stream reverses, and the cars come south, reindeer horns strapped to their roof racks. They have attained their goal. Tablets attest that even royalty have been here, King Oscar II of Sweden in 1873, King Chulalangkorn of Thailand in 1907.

Nordkapphallen (North Cape Hall; open Apr–Sept: daily 9am–2am; entrance fee) has a café, restaurant and other facilities for visitors. The **Nordkappmuséet** (North Cape Museum; open June–Aug: 11am–8pm, closed Sat; Sept–May: Mon–Fri 12.30–4pm; entrance fee; tel: 78 47 28 33), near the Hurtigrute quay in **Honningsvag**, has a variety of displays about the cape and its history.

North to Svalbard

The **Svalbard** (**Spitsbergen**) archipelago lies 640 km (400 miles) north of the mainland. It was first mentioned in 1194 by Icelandic sailors. In 1596, the Dutch navigator Willem Barents, searching for the Northeast Passage, sighted the largest of its four main islands, which he called Spitsbergen (Pointed Peaks). Indeed, the terrain resembles that of the Alps, and Spitsbergen covers an area almost as large as Switzerland. In 1920, an international treaty gave Norway sovereignty over Svalbard and granted 35 signatory countries the right to exploit its resources. Only three countries have exercised their right on a commercial scale. In 1906, John Longyear, an American industrialist, founded the Arctic Coal Company on Spitsbergen. Today, the principal village, **Longyearbyen** (pop. 1,300) is named after him, but only Norway and Russia remain as mine operators.

The climate is relatively mild for the Arctic: midday temperatures at Longyearbyen average –7°C (19°F) in February and 7°C (45°F) in July. But permafrost prevails year-round. In 1998 it made the international news, when Canadian pathologists exhumed the well-preserved corpses of six Svalbard coal miners who had died in the 1918 influenza pandemic, to search for clues that might reveal its origin.

Today, hi-tech is supplanting mining as a leading livelihood. The **Svalbard Satellite Station** near Longyearbyen is positioned to download images from all earth observation satellites in polar orbits, and the **Svalbard Rocket Range** at **Ny Ålesund** is now instrumental in weather research.

With daily flights between Tromsø and Longyearbyen, tourism is growing. In summer, the stark mountains around the village are offset by a valley which has meadows spangled with flowers. Here you will find cassiope and purple saxifrage, and, perhaps, a patch of boreal Jacob's ladder, *Polemonium boreale*, an Arctic rarity. The polar winter is another matter. The sun does not rise above the horizon and everything is locked in darkness, lit only by the moon and the multicoloured rays of the **Aurora Borealis**, the Northern Lights. ❑

SWEDEN

From sophisticated Stockholm to mountain wilderness,
Sweden offers the traveller immense variety

A subtle change in Swedish attitudes has been emerging in recent years. Not so long ago the country was an introverted Fortress Sweden perched uneasily on the edge of Western Europe. Indeed, many Swedes still talked about travelling "to Europe" as if it was on a different continent. All that changed with the country's admission to the European Union in the 1990s and the opening in 2000 of the Öresund bridge across the straits separating Sweden from Denmark. The Swedes have finally become "good Europeans".

As such, Sweden is attracting many more visitors, not just to the bustling big cities and cultural centres of Stockholm, Göteborg and Malmö, but also to the rural regions and the vast wilderness areas of Lapland and the Bothnian coast. Where else can you stay in an hotel made entirely from ice, play golf under the Midnight Sun or dance with abandon around a maypole at Midsummer?

It is an ideal country for those who like the great outdoors and activities such as angling, golf, riding, fell-walking, skiing, sailing or canoeing. Even Stockholm, which covers a much wider area than you might expect for its 1.6 million population, is a city of sea, lake and open spaces, and never far from the thousands of islands that form its archipelago, reaching out into the waters of the Baltic.

The southern provinces, including Skåne, were for centuries part of Denmark and a faintly Danish accent persists. Much of south central Sweden is dominated by the great lakes of Vänern and Vättern, the heart of a network of waterways that make it possible to cross this widest part of Sweden by boat along the Göta Kanal, which links Stockholm to Göteborg.

Further north, the geographical centre of Sweden holds Dalarna, the folklore province where old customs linger. At the end of the long road or rail route north are the mountains. This is home to Scandinavia's second race, the Sami, whose wanderings with their reindeer herds take little account of national boundaries.

Culturally, well-preserved sites like the remains of the Viking capital of Birka, state-of-the-art museums, and the homes of artists such as Carl Larsson, who inspired the clean lines of contemporary Swedish design, are all open to the visitor. On the musical front, Göteborg's Symphony Orchestra is in the top rank of world orchestras. Sweden has even become a centre of gastronomic excellence.

This northern land is also a popular year-round destination. The winter climate is less harsh than many people imagine and the period around Christmas, with its traditional markets, brightly decorated streets and St Lucia processions, is a magical time of year. ❑

PRECEDING PAGES: the smooth rocks of the Bohuslän coast; Swedish paratroopers cool off after a sauna in Jukkasjärvi; Stockholm, city of islands.
LEFT: decorative ironwork at Stockholm's Royal Palace.

THE SWEDES

Beneath the cool, sophisticated exterior, the surprisingly mirthful Swede harbours a deep commitment to nature, tradition and schnapps

Contrary to popular opinion, Swedes do have a sense of humour. Armies of dissenters will no doubt beg to differ and sceptics will balk at the very idea. But the Swedish sense of humour is a peculiar thing: as elusive as Garbo and as fleeting as a Swedish summer. Blink and you'll miss it. Their reputation for being dry, sombre and painfully serious is itself the cause of much mirth for these Scandinavian jokers. And when the uninitiated confuse Sweden with Switzerland, it always raises an eyebrow and just the smallest trace of a knowing smile.

But don't let the cool exterior of this Scandinavian fool you. They may certainly seem calm and collected on the outside, but they're every bit as prone to hysterical fits as the next person. Even if they do recover much faster and the smile that flashed across those solemn features vanishes as quickly as it came.

Blonde and beautiful

When it comes to Sweden, popular misconceptions are rife. It is commonly held that most people in Sweden are blond, at least 6ft 3in tall and drive Volvos. In fact, only half the population are natural blonds, the average male is 5ft 10in and the BMW is the preferred mode of transportation for upwardly mobile Swedes today. Though the more stereotypical images of Sweden – leggy blonde beauties, pickled herring, meatballs and seemingly unflappable tennis players – certainly run true to form, Sweden today is a country of growing cultural and social diversity. A country in which the traditional mingles with the ultramodern and in which society and the political arena have been shaped by a strong democratic tradition.

First encounters with Swedes can be somewhat confusing. They are a baffling blend of the cosmopolitan and the provincial. For this sophisticated urbanite is every bit at home in the concrete jungle, sipping cappuccinos at a pavement café, as going barefoot at their place in the country. It's no exaggeration to say that Swedes are potty about nature. It's somehow a part of the Swedish soul. They are quick to wax lyrical about the grassy plains of Skåne, expound the virtues of lakeside Dalarna and

SWEDEN: THE ESSENTIALS

Population 8.9 million.
Capital Stockholm (pop.1.6 million).
Notable towns Göteborg, Malmö.
Climate Average afternoon temperatures in Stockholm in July are 22°C (71°F); in January, −1°C (30°F).
Top museums Vasamuseet, Nordiska Museet, Skansen, Stockholm; Rooseum, Malmö; Silvermuseet, Arjeplog.
Historic sights Drottningholm Palace, Gripsholms Slott, Uppsala Cathedral; Luleå; rock carvings, Tanumshede.
Best midsummer festivities Dalarna.
Outdoor activities watersports, hiking, fishing, skiing.
Tourist information www.visit-sweden.com.

LEFT: time off to unwind in the sauna, an essential part of Swedish life.
RIGHT: growing up in modern Sweden.

remind you that theirs is the only true wilderness left in all Europe. Ask any Swede to recount tales of their childhood and they'll dreamily recall summers spent in the country with a noticeable softening of facial expression, a voice tinged with more than just a hint of nostalgia and a faraway look in their eye.

National pride

Next to nature, there's nothing Swedes like to talk about more than Sweden itself. Get them started on this subject at your peril. This is not to say that Swedes are braggarts, far from it. A more humble, self-depreciating tribe you'd be hard pushed to find. But their modesty is a thin veil in the face of such obvious national pride. For all little Swedes are well versed in the achievements of their countrymen, be it Alfred Nobel or August Strindberg; even the exploits of their marauding ancestors are today taught in schools with pride.

At first glance a Swede may appear a very cool customer. But underneath that composed exterior and self-satisfaction with all things Swedish, you'll find a warm, friendly individual, who having decided to let their guard down and befriend you, will be a friend for life.

The image of the bloodthirsty Viking,

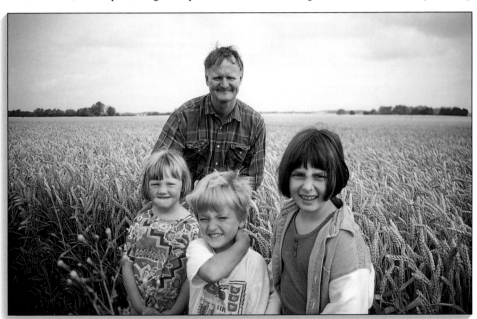

WINING AND DINING

Oddly enough, this "vodka-belt" nation has a rather uneasy relationship with alcohol. The liberalism that once made Sweden the envy of more conservative societies makes the prevailing attitude towards drinking, with its moral pontificating, all the more perplexing.

Despite EU membership and its initial effects, alcohol remains a contentious issue. Exorbitant prices and an unyielding state monopoly have conspired to create a sense of deprivation and prohibition. A Friday evening ritual is played out at state off-licences up and down the country, in which Swedes queue with stoical aplomb to buy a bottle of wine and a six-pack. It's not so strange then that when

the chance to indulge presents itself, Swedes have few qualms about throwing themselves into the fray.

Whatever your take on the Swedes' drinking habits, when it comes to dining their manners are impeccable. Be it state banquets or family get-togethers, Swedes are sticklers for etiquette. From arriving punctually to observing the niceties of fine dining, the formalities are upheld to the last drop of schnapps. At birthdays and anniversaries, coffee and cake are served with the precision of a military exercise. Yet Swedes will happily tuck into a crayfish feast, ripping off claws with their hands and clashing beer glasses in a fashion reminiscent of their Viking forebears.

plundering all in his path, is one the Swedes have taken centuries to live down. Nowadays the little red cottage is Sweden's most enduring image and there's nothing Swedes like better than to take off to the country for a spell. An affinity for the land runs deep within the Swedish soul and they are never happier than when they can kick off their shoes, swim naked and bond with nature.

Life in Sweden is intrinsically linked to the natural rhythms of the changing seasons.

SKÅL!

Friendships are often sealed over schnapps. Delicately flavoured with fruits or spices, schnapps is a perennial favourite and every Swede can name his or her tipple.

soaking up the first warming rays of spring. Summers are woefully short, often hot and always much longed for.

Swedes today come in a variety of creeds and colours. Immigration continues to influence the country's social, cultural and political landscape. During the turbulent 1990s Sweden was forced to re-evaluate its global position in the face of new economic challenges and growing questions of social inequality. The high standard of living once enjoyed by Swedes and

Swedish winters are famous for their longevity, Arctic temperatures and the sun's prolonged absence. But Swedes have learnt how to make the most of it and winter sports are popular with Swedes of all ages. They eagerly await the spring and the return of sunlight with all the excited anticipation of children at Christmas. Like hibernating animals re-emerging after winter, sun-starved Swedes are wont to stand on street corners, at crossings, in traffic lights, and any other spot with a south-facing aspect,

LEFT: Swedish fathers are more involved than their European counterparts in caring for their children.
ABOVE: male voice choir prepares for a performance.

their enviable cradle-to-the-grave welfare system has come under increasing pressure.

Looking to Europe

For years Swedes championed the causes of others, but their own increasingly precarious position has forced them to abandon, albeit unofficially, their policy of neutrality and take closer steps to the Continent. Sweden's entry into the European Union in 1995 was part of an effort to bring Sweden in line with a changing Europe. New social and economic policies are helping the country adapt to a global economy, while the Swedes themselves are learning to adapt to their new role – as Europeans. ❏

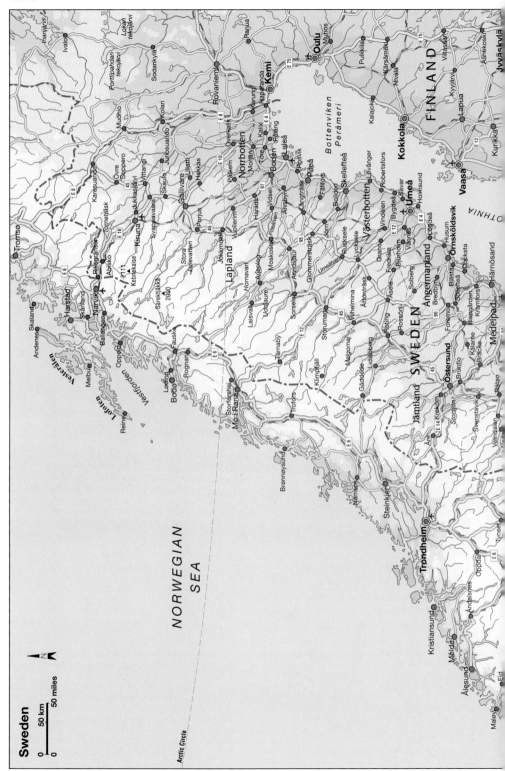

Sweden

0 50 km
0 50 miles

NORWEGIAN SEA

Östermalmsg.
Karlavägen
Karlavägen
Kommendörsgatan
Nybrogatan
Sibyllegatan
Lundagatan
Artillerigatan
Nybergsg.
Skeppargatan
Grevg.
Karlaplan
Karlaplan
Valhallavägen
Lindarängsvägen
Lindarängsvägen
DROTTNINGBERGET
Valhallavägen
Oxenstiernsgatan
Karlavägen
TV-huset
Radiohuset
Gärdesgatan
LADUGÅRDSGÄRDET
SKANSBERGET
Kaknästornet
(Kaknäs
TV Tower) ❶
Maximteatern
Berwaldhallen
Strandvägen
Nobelgatan
Djurgårdsbrunnsvägen
Statens
Sjöhistoriska
Museet
(National Maritime
Museum)
Tekniska
Museet
Folkens
Museum
Entografiska
Linnégatan
Artillerigatan
Grevgatan
Östermalmstorg
Öster-
malmstorg
Storgatan
Hedvig
Eleonora
ÖSTERMALM
Marie
Bebadelse
Marvavägen
Djurgårdsbrunnsviken
termalms
luhall
Styrmansgatan
Historiska Museet
(Museum of National
Antiquities) ❶❽
Armémuseum
Storgatan
Ladugårdsgärdet
Musik-
museet
Riddargatan
Grev Magnigatan
Storgatan
Ulrikagatan
DJURGÅRDEN
0 ___ 500 m
0 ___ 500 yds
Kungliga
Hovstallet
Kaptens-
gatan
Artillerig.
ipnargatan
Skeppargatan
Grevgatan
Torstensonsgatan
Riddargatan
Banérgatan
Marvavägen
Riddargatan
Storgatan
Berwaldhallen
Strandvägen
Engelska
Strandvägen
Strandvägen
Strandvägen
Djurgårds-
bron
NOBELPARKEN
Nobelgatan
Kaknästornet (Kaknäs TV Tower), Statens Sjöhistoriska Museet (National Maritime Museum)
ybrokviken
Strandvägen
Ladugårdslandsviken
Galärvarvsvägen
Djurgårdsvägen
Djurgårdsbrunnsviken
Junibacken ❶❸
Blasieholmen
JSEIPARKEN
ntional-
useum ❶❶
Musikajen
Nordiska
Museet
(Nordic Museum) ❶❻
Stockholms
Universitet
GALÄRPARKEN
Rosendalsvägen
Nybrokajen
Skeppsholmsbron
Slupskjulsvägen
Östasiatiska
Museet
Vasamuseet ❶❼
Hazeliusporten
Skeppsholms
Moderna Museet
(Modern Museum) ❾
Exercis-
plan
Arkitekturmuseet
Biologiska
Museet
DJURGÅRDEN
Hazeliusbacken
af Chapman ❽
Västra Brobänken
Svensksundsvägen
SKEPPSHOLMEN
Långa Raden
Östra Brobänken
Aquaria
Vattenmuseum
Alkärret
Falkenbergsg.
Liljevalchs Konsthall
(Liljevalch Art Gallery)
Cirkus
Skansen ❶❹
Seglora
Skogaholm
Tobaksmuseet
Akvarium
Strömmen
Södra Brobänken
Kastellholms-
bron
Kastellholmskajen
Örlogsvägen
Kastellholmskajen
Kastellet
Allmänna Gränd
Gröna
Lund ❶❷
Beckholmsvägen
Andréeg.
Djurgårdsvägen
Sollidsbacken
Prins Eugens Waldemarsudde ❶❺
Thielska Galleriet (Thiel Gallery)
Kastellholmen
Beckholms-
bron
Beckholmen
Vaxholm
S A L T S J Ö N
Birkaterminalen
Katrinavägen
glasbruksgatan
Stadsgårdsleden
ogbergsgatan
Fjällgatan
Stockholm
N
0 ___ 200 m
0 ___ 200 yds

STOCKHOLM

Sweden's capital is a city of islands where palaces and peaceful hideaways line the shores, and where cobbled streets lead to chic shops, cafés and lively cultural attractions

Map on pages 230-231

Stockholm

T he novelist Selma Lagerlöf called Stockholm "the city that floats on water". Nowhere do you see this more clearly than from the dizzy observation platform on top of the **Kaknästornet ❶** (Kaknäs Television Tower; open May–Aug: 9am–10pm; Sept–Apr: 10am–9pm; tel: 789 24 35), Ladugårdsgärdet, which rises 155 metres (508 ft). Below, Stockholm spreads out in a glinting panorama of blue water, the red of the old buildings contrasting with the stark white and glass of the new, cut through by swathes of trees and grass.

Fresh and salt water are separated by the island of Gamla Stan (Old Town) and the great lock gates of Slussen at the southern end. This island barrier is where Stockholm started some time before the 13th century. Today, with a population of 1.6 million, Stockholm is a modern and sophisticated metropolis, famous for Scandinavian design in furniture, textiles and interiors and a hotbed for innovation in information technology, Europe's Silicon Valley. The city features some of the most exciting cuisine in Europe. Stockholm's nightlife has exploded into an array of young, hip clubs and older, more sedate nightspots. Infusing the old with the new is a speciality of today's vibrant Stockholm.

Stockholm's history starts in **Gamla Stan** (Old Town), which still has the character of a medieval city. Its narrow lanes follow the same curves along

LEFT: Gamla Stan, the old town of Stockholm.
BELOW: outdoor café, Stortorget.

FACT FILE

Situation On a cluster of Baltic coast islands between the sea and Lake Mälaren.
Population 1.6 million people live in the Stockholm area.
Climate In summer the daytime temperature can reach 20–25°C (68–77°F); in winter −7°C to +2°C (19–36°F).
Transport Comprehensive bus and Tunnelbanen (underground) network; ferry services; sightseeing boats.
Best ferry ride Djurgårds ferry (Slussen to Djurgården).
Essential purchase Stockholmskortet (Stockholm Card), for free admission to museums and free public transport.
Top attractions Drottningholms Slott; Historiska Museet; Kungliga Slottet (Royal Palace); Moderna Museet; Stadshuset; Vasamuseet; Ekoparken.
For children Skansen; Junibacken; Aquaria; Gröna Lund.
Views Fjällgatan; Södermalm; Katarina Hissen; Slussen.
Annual festivities Walpurgis Night (end Apr); Midsummer celebrations, Skansen (late June); St Lucia celebrations (mid-Dec).
Best coffee Vete-Katten, Kungsgatan.
Best smörgåsbord Ulriksdals Slottspark; tel: 08 85 08 15.
Tourist information Stockholm Information Service, Sweden House, Hamngatan 27; tel: 08 789 2490/2495; www.stockholmtown.com

TIP

See more and pay less
with a Stockholm
Card, available from
Sverigehuset (Sweden
House), Hamnagatan
27. It offers free
admission to
museums and sights,
free travel, discounts
and a guide book.

which the seamen of former times carried their goods. The best place to start a tour is **Stortorget**, the centre of the original city, from which narrow streets fan out in all directions.

The Vasa capital

In medieval times, Stortorget was a crowded, noisy place of trade, where German merchants, stallholders, craftsmen, and young servant girls and boys jostled and shouted. In the cobbled square, people laze on benches or sit at one of the outdoor cafés, and it is hard to visualise that in 1520 the cobbles ran with blood during the Stockholm Bloodbath. Despite a guarantee of safety, the Danish King Kristian II, known as The Tyrant, murdered 82 people, not only nobles but innocent civilians unlucky enough to have a shop or a business nearby. This gory incident triggered the demise of the Kalmar Union, which had united Sweden with Denmark and Norway. Three years later, Sweden's first heroic king, Gustav Vasa, put an end to the union and made Stockholm his capital.

From the square, it's a short walk to **Storkyrkan ❷** (Cathedral; open Sept–Apr: daily 9am–4pm; May–Aug: 9am–6pm; free; tel: 723 30 16). This awesome Gothic cathedral is the oldest building in Gamla Stan, in part dating to the 12th century. It has high vaulted arches and sturdy pillars stripped back to their original red brick. Its most famous statue is St George and the Dragon, the largest medieval monument in Scandinavia, a wooden sculpture carved by Bernt Notke in 1489, which has retained its original colouring.

Gamla Stan's **Västerlånggatan** is a favourite shopping street for locals and tourists alike. Here and on nearly every other cobbled lane in the Old Town you will find shops, restaurants and cafés to suit every taste. Particularly enjoy-

BELOW: Stadshuset, the City Hall, on Lake Mälaren.

A CITY AND ITS SYMBOL

From any part of Stockholm that lies south of Lake Mälaren, Stadshuset (City Hall) dominates the skyline. Situated on the lake shore overlooking Riddarfjärden, Stadshuset is the work of architect Ragnar Östberg. A massive square tower rises 105 metres (450 ft) from one corner of the elegant building. Constructed of decorated brickwork with an open-fronted portico facing the lake, the building is topped with spires, domes and minarets. The roofs are clad in copper. Above them gleam the Tre Kronor, the three golden crowns that symbolise the city.

Östberg began work in 1911 and devoted the next 12 years of his life to the City Hall. It was formally opened in 1923 and used 8 million bricks and 19 million gilded mosaic tiles, the latter mostly in the famous Golden Hall. The effect is stunning. The walls are entirely clad in gilded mosaics. The gardens of the southern terrace feature a statue of the 15th-century Swedish patriot, Engelbrekt, who championed the peasants in his native Dalarna.

A procession of St George and the Dragon emerges twice a day as the bells play a medieval tune. Guided tours are available Oct–May: 10am, noon; June–Aug: 10am, 11am, noon, 2pm; Sept: 10am, 12pm, 2pm; entrance fee; tel: 08 508 290 59.

able are the cellar restaurants with their musty smell and stone walls. It's easy to imagine the Swedish troubador Evert Taube (1890–1976) raising a beer stein to his compatriots as he composed yet another lyric to the Swedish way of life.

The present **Kungliga Slottet** ❸ (Royal Palace; open May–Aug: daily 10am–4pm; Sept–Apr: noon–3pm; entrance fee; tel: 402 6130) was built on the site of the Tre Kronor Palace, which burnt down in 1697, some say not without the help of Nicodemus Tessin the Younger, who had already built a new northern wing and who obviously relished the glory of rebuilding the palace to his Renaissance designs. His father, Nicodemus the Elder, had been architect to the old Tre Kronor palace, and the grandson, Carl Gustaf, was responsible for supervising the completion of the new palace many years later. The palace comprises 608 rooms. Various suites are open to the public and the oldest interiors from the 1660s are in the north wing.

For more of Sweden's aristocratic heritage, head for **Riddarhuset** ❹ (House of Nobility; open Mon–Fri 11.30am–12.30pm; entrance fee; tel: 723 39 90) on the nearby island of **Riddarholmen**, built in 1641 as a meeting place for the nobles. It is arguably the most beautiful building in Gamla Stan, with two pavilions looking out across the water. Inside, the erstwhile power of the nobles is matched by the grandeur of the Main Chamber, where the nobles deliberated, watched from above by a painting of Mother Svea, who symbolises Sweden.

The refurbishment of the Swedish **Riksdaghuset** (Parliament building) on Helgeandsholmen to the north of Gamla Stan some years ago led to a remarkable archaeological find and a new museum. When the builders started to excavate the Riksdaghuset terrace to form an underground car park, they discovered layer upon layer of the past, including part of the medieval wall and the cellars

Map on pages 230-231

Royal guardsman on duty outside the Royal Palace.

BELOW: ceremonial display at the Royal Palace, Gamla Stan.

Doorman at Stockholm's famous Grand Hotel.

BELOW: gilded tiles decorate the walls of the Golden Hall, Stadshuset.

of an apothecary shop. Stockholm's **Medeltidsmuseum** ❺ (Medieval Museum, Strömparterren; open July–Aug: Tues–Thur 11am–6pm, Fri–Mon 11am–4pm; Sept–June: Tues–Sun 11am–4pm, Wed until 6pm; entrance fee; tel: 508 318 00), incorporates the old wall and other treasures uncovered during the excavations.

From the southern end of Gamla Stan it is worth making a detour to visit Stockholm's **Stadsmuseet** ❻ (City Museum, Ryssgården; open Tues–Wed, Fri–Sun 11am–5pm; June–Aug: Thur until 7pm; Sept–May: Thur until 9pm; entrance fee; tel: 508 31 600). While Stockholm received virtually no mention until the 13th century, the museum makes it clear that this strategic spot had been inhabited for many centuries. After the museum, it would be a pity not to make a quick trip up **Katarinahissen** ❼ (open Mon–Sat 7.30am–10pm, Sun 10am–10pm; entrance fee), a 19th-century lift rebuilt in 1935 that carries you to the heights of Södermalm.

Stockholm's playground

From Gamla Stan, it is just 10 minutes by boat across the harbour to the island of **Djurgården**. Once a royal deer park, much of Djurgården is still in its natural state, with paths and woods where you may spot small creatures, both everyday and rare, such as hares and the occasional deer. The island is part of **Ekoparken**, the world's first city national park. A good way to get around is to hire a bike at the bridge which forms the road entrance.

Between Djurgården and Gamla Stan lies **Skeppsholmen**. The sleek schooner moored off the island is the 100-year-old *af Chapman* ❽, now a youth hostel and a café. Also on the island is the spectacular new building of the **Moderna Museet** ❾ (Modern Museum; open Tues–Thur 11am–8pm, Fri–Sun 11am–6pm;

entrance fee; free first Tues of month, 5–8pm; tel: 519 552 82), designed by the Spanish architect Rafael Moneo, with a collection of 20th-century art that is considered one of the finest in the world, including works by Dali, Picasso and Magritte among others. Its large restaurant-café offers a beautiful panorama of the city skyline.

Heading northwest from Skeppsholmen is the waterfront of **Blasieholmen**, where the sumptuous big building is one of Scandinavia's most famous hotels, the **Grand ❿**. Nearby is the **Nationalmuseum ⓫** (National Museum of Fine Arts, Södra Blasieholmshamnen; open Tues 11am–8pm, Wed–Sun 11am–5pm; entrance fee; tel: 519 544 10/519 543 00) featuring Sweden's national collection of art, with most of the great masters from 1500–1900. Rembrandt is particularly well represented. In summer, the National Museum holds concerts in the evening, a lovely setting for music.

As the ferry slides into the Djurgården quay, there is no mistaking that this is an island devoted to enjoyment. On the right is **Gröna Lund ⓬**, an amusement park with its roots in the 18th century (open May–mid-Sept: hours vary; tel: 587 501 00; www.gronalund.com).

Fans of Astrid Lindgren's children books should not miss **Junibacken ⓭** (open June–Aug: daily 9am–6pm; Sept–May: Tues–Sun 10am–5pm; entrance fee; tel: 587 230 00), a museum dedicated to her life's work. An electrically operated indoor tram, with narration in English, allows the rider to experience *Astrid's World*, floating over miniature scenes from her books with moving figures, lights, and sound, as familiar figures pop suddenly out of corners.

Heading south on Djurgården, where the island rises in steps to a hilltop, is **Skansen ⓮** (open May: 10am–8pm; June–Aug: 10am–10pm; Sept–Apr:

Map on pages 230-231

Tunnelbanen, Stockholm's metro system, is described as the "world's longest art gallery". Many stations have paintings, sculptures, mosaics and engravings – and all can be seen for the price of a ticket.

BELOW: winter in the city.

Spinning is one of the many traditional skills still practised at Skansen, the open-air museum.

10am–4pm; entrance fee; tel: 442 80 00), the oldest open-air museum in the world. In 1891, Artur Hazelius decided to preserve the fast-disappearing Swedish way of life by collecting traditional buildings. Today there are some 150, including an 18th-century church, still used for services and weddings. Many of the houses and workshops are grouped together to form the town quarter along a steep cobbled street. They include authentic workshops where tradesmen once practised their craft. During the summer, many of the buildings revive their traditional use.

While on Djurgården it's worth visiting the lovely former home overlooking the sea and collection of the "Painter Prince" **Prins Eugens Waldemarsudde** ⓯ (Prins Eugens väg 6; open June–Aug: Tues–Sun 11am–5pm, Thur until 8pm; Sept–May: Tues–Fri 11am–4pm, Sat–Sun 11am–5pm; Thur until 8pm; entrance fee; tel: 545 837 00).

If you choose bus instead of boat and enter the island over Djurgårdsbron from Strandvägen, the first museum you come to is the **Nordiska Museet** ⓰ (Nordic Museum; open Tues–Sun 10am–5pm, Tues and Thur until 8pm; entrance fee; tel: 519 560 00), which depicts Nordic life from the 16th century. It has peasant costumes, a special collection of bridal gowns and the traditional silver and gold crowns worn by Swedish brides, Lapland culture, folk art, and more.

Marine treasure

BELOW: the *Vasa*, a remarkable work of restoration.

To the west of the Nordiska Museet on the waterfront is the huge, oddly shaped building of the **Vasamuseet** ⓱ (Vasa Museum, Galärvarvet; open mid-June–Aug: daily 9.30am–7pm; Sept–mid-June daily 10am–5pm, Wed until 8pm; entrance fee; tel: 519 548 00), which houses the *Vasa* warship, inaugurated in 1990). The warship was built in the 1620s for the Thirty Years' War, on the orders of Sweden's warrior king, Gustav II Adolf. She was a magnificent ship, decorated with 700 sculptures and carvings, but her oak was too solid. In 1628 she sank in Stockholm harbour on her maiden voyage. In 1956 the Swedish marine archaeologist, Anders Franzén, found her and, in 1961, brought her up from the depths. More than 24,000 objects have been salvaged from the sea bed, including skeletons, sails, cannon, clothing, tools, coins, butter, rum and many everyday utensils.

A short walk across the bridge is the spectacular **Guldrummet** (Gold Room), an underground vault featuring more than 3,000 prehistoric gold and silver arte-facts at **Historiska Museet** ⓲ (Museum of National Antiquities, Narvavägen; open mid-May–mid-Sept: daily 10am–5pm; Tues–Sun 11am–5pm, Thur until 8pm; entrance fee; tel: 519 556 00).

The King's Garden

It's anyone's guess what the Swedish sculptor John Tobias Sergel (1740–1814) might have thought of the huge illuminated obelisk, fountain and square that bear his name, and of the modern city around it. The heart of this business and commercial area is not large, but it sits somewhat uneasily with the rest. From **Sergels Torg** it is hard to miss the five towering office blocks on Sveavägen, which cast their shadow over the other buildings. In the 1960s, Stockholm City Council, like so many others, succumbed to the temptation to knock things down and build concrete and glass high-rise buildings.

The destruction of many fine old buildings continued until it threatened **Kungsträdgården** ⓳ (King's Garden) with the statue of the warrior king,

Map on pages 230-231

BELOW:
Prins Eugens
Waldemarsudde
art gallery and
former home of the
"Painter Prince".

OUTWARD-BOUND IN THE CITY

E koparken is the world's first national city park, a huge set of green lungs that stretch out in a 12-km (7-mile) long arch from Ulriksdals Slott (Castle) in the north to the archipelago islands Fjäderholmarna in the south. This green swathe is so large you'll need a full day of serious hiking to explore it, by foot during the warmer months or on skis or long-distance skates in the winter. The in-expensive Brunnsviken Runt (Around Brunnsviken) boat tour is an excellent way of seeing the Ekopark and includes free admission to many attractions.

The Ekopark includes three royal parks, Djurgården, Haga, and Ulriksdal, with palaces to tour (Ulriksdals Slott, Gustav III's Paviljong, Rosendals Slott). Visit the tropical Fjärilshuset (Butterfly House) where hundreds of colourful species land lightly upon your shoulder, or the Bergianska (Bergianska Botanical Gardens) and Naturhistoriska Riksmuseet (Museum of Natural History).

For a pleasant retreat on northern Djurgården, you'll find Rosendalsträgård (Rosendals Garden) with orchards, flowers and vegetables, garden shops and a café. For many Stockholmers this has become the ideal retreat after a day on Djurgården. For Ekoparken information, call Stockholm Information Service (tel: 08 789 2490).

*Prehistoric artefact
in the Gold Room,
Museum of National
Antiquities.*

BELOW: Stockholm's
underground is an
artistic wonder.

Karl XII on its southern side. At this point the Stockholmers had had enough. Normally placid and biddable, they mustered at the King's Garden, climbed the trees that were in danger of the axe, and swore that if the trees went so did the people. The City Fathers retreated and Kungsträdgården survives to soften the edges of the new buildings and harmonise with the older buildings that are left. This is the place to stroll or sit beside the fountains on a summer day and enjoy a coffee at its outdoor café. In summer it is the venue of many outdoor festivals and rock concerts. In winter, part of Kungsträdgården is flooded with water and becomes a popular ice rink, and the restaurant moves indoors.

At Hamngatan 27 is **Sverigehuset ⓴** (Sweden House; open June–Aug: Mon–Fri 8am–7pm, Sat–Sun 9am–5pm; Sept–May: Mon–Fri 9am–6pm; Apr, May, Sept: Sat–Sun 9am–3pm; tel: 789 2490), with Stockholm's main tourist information centre on the ground floor. The centre can advise and book tours and other entertainment, sells the Stockholmskortet (Stockholm Card), and has a well-stocked bookshop.

A short stroll east is the early 20th-century private palace housing one of Stockholm's most unusual museums, **Hallwylska Museet ㉑** (Hallwyl Collection, Hamngatan 4; open mid-June–mid-Aug: tours Mon–Fri hourly 11am–4pm, Wed 6pm; mid-Aug–mid-June: tours Tues–Sun noon–3pm, Wed 6pm, English tour Sun 1pm; entrance fee; tel: 519 555 99). It's the magpie collection of one person, Countess von Hallwyl, from her ornate piano, to china, beautiful furniture and personal knick-knacks.

On the southern side of Sergels Torg, **Kulturhuset ㉒** (Culture House; open Mon 11am–6pm, Tues–Sun 10am–7pm) is a popular meeting place and venue for lectures and entertainment. One block east on Hamngatan is **Gallerian ㉓**, a huge covered shopping arcade that stretches to Jakobsgatan. At the south end of Gallerian is the oldest auction house in the world, **Stockholms Auktionsverket** (Stockholm Auction House), Jakobsgatan 10, which has been in business since 1674 (open Mon–Fri 9.30am–6pm, Sat 10am–4pm; tel: 453 67 10). Everything from china to Chagall and furniture from the 7th century to the 20th is crammed into the storerooms. Many items are small enough to carry, and make unusual Stockholm mementoes.

To buy is easy: you just leave a bid in advance for the Tuesday and Wednesday auctions, or you can take part in the auction yourself, no Swedish required. Even if you don't care to bid, browsing among the showrooms sheds light on Swedish homes, the way Swedes live, and what they keep or discard.

Sweden's equivalent of Harrods is **Nordiska Kompaniet (NK)** ㉔, on Hamngatan (just opposite Sweden House), whose rooftop illuminated sign, constantly turning, is visible from far and wide. NK sells everything from shoes to sporting equipment, men's and women's clothing, glass, pottery and silver, jewellery and perfume; its services range from optician to post office and travel agency, and you can get your sightseeing shoes soled and heeled when you come to collect the high-speed prints of your latest roll of film.

Find a bargain

Shopping in Sweden is rarely cheap, but it is always good value. For a bargain, the words to look out for are *rea*, which means sale, and *extrapris*, which does not mean extra, but special low price.

Åhléns City ㉕ is on the corner of Sergels Torg and Drottninggatan. It has a similar range and quality to NK, and a visit to its supermarket food department

Map on pages 230-231

Swedish design is world renowned. Wherever you go in the city you'll never be far from shops selling crystal, china and ceramics, and the fashions of designers like Pia, Wallén, Filippa K and Anna Holtblad.

BELOW: enjoying an ice-cream break.

*Contemporary
Swedish crystal
design.*

is a sightseeing tour in itself. The third of this trio of stores is **PUB**, on Drottninggatan at Hötorget, which is a galleria featuring a variety of Swedish and international-brand shops.

Drottninggatan (Queen's Street), an old street which leads directly through the Riksdagshuset and over the bridge from the Royal Palace, is one of Stockholm's main pedestrian ways. In summer, it is full of casual crowds strolling or sitting at one of the outdoor cafés. Immigrants sell their wares on the pavement. This area is a haven for pickpockets, so be careful.

Not to be missed is **Strindbergsmuseet 26** (Strindberg Museum, Drottninggatan 85; open Tues–Sun noon–4pm; Sept–May: Tues until 7pm; entrance fee; tel: 411 53 54), housed in the top-floor flat of the **Blåtornet** (Blue Tower) where Sweden's greatest playwright spent his last years and wrote his last epic play, *The Great Highway* in 1908. Even at the end of his life, Strindberg was astonishingly prolific; he produced some 20 books in his four years in the Blue Tower. His study is just as he left it.

Fruit and finery

Walking south along Drottninggatan to Kungsgatan, on your left you'll come to **Hötorget 27**, with its open-air food stalls and indoor market. This is where Swedes shop for food. Here you can find Swedish delicacies such as elk steak and reindeer and the many varieties of Scandinavian cured herring.

In addition to exploring Gamla Stan's antique shops, take the Tunnelbanan (underground railway) south to Slussen station on **Södermalm**, once the great working class area of the city; the journey takes just 5–10 minutes. Nowadays, this district is a popular place for artists to live and work. It has become a trendy

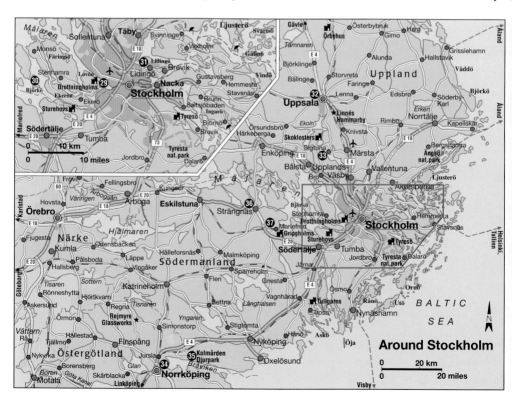

Around Stockholm

place to hang out, and new cafés, restaurants and boutiques seem to open daily. The steep slope of **Hornsgatan** ㉘ has a cluster of galleries.

Islands by the thousand

It is a rare city that has 24,000 islands on its doorstep and 100 km (60 miles) of lake at its heart, but this is Stockholm's eternal good fortune. Until the building of the Tunnelbanen, boats were the only means of getting around these vast expanses of water, and today boats are still part of Stockholm life. Waxholmsbolaget and Stromma Kanalbolaget transport passengers across Lake Mälaren and around the Archipelago *(see page 246)* in a variety of craft from old coalfired steamers to modern ferries.

The most popular place to visit in the archipelago is the royal palace, **Drottningholms Slot** ㉙ on Lovön *(see page 245)*, to the west of the city. West of Lovön is **Björkö** ㉚, the site of Sweden's oldest city, **Birka**. Between AD 800 and 975, Birka was the trading centre for the 40,000 inhabitants of the rich Mälaren area and the meeting point for traders. This was also where Christianity first came to Sweden, when Ansgar, the Saxon missionary, landed in the 9th century. Almost nothing is left of Birka above ground, but many archaeological digs have revealed the past at sites which include the old town. The **Birkamuseet** (open May–Sept: 10am–5pm; entrance fee; tel: 560 514 45) features the most recent finds.

In summer, take the boat to the island suburb of **Lidingö** ㉛, to visit **Millesgården**, the summer home of the sculptor, Carl Milles and his wife, the Austrian painter Olga Granner (open May–Sept: daily 10am–5pm; Oct–Apr: Tues–Sun noon–4pm; entrance fee; tel: 446 75 90). Here, Milles patiently

Maps:
City 230
Area 242

August is the time for a "kräftskiva" (crayfish party). Under the glow of paper lanterns, Swedes enjoy this beloved shellfish, once plentiful in freshwater lakes, but now imported.

BELOW: Stortorget, the square at the heart of Gamla Stan.

Map on page 242

A Carl Milles sculpture at Millesgården.

BELOW: Uppsala's Gothic cathedral.

reproduced the statues that had made him more famous in his adopted country of America than in Sweden. His creations appear to soar and fly, and step lightly over water, emphasised by their position on terraces carved from the cliffs.

North of Stockholm

Less than an hour's drive north of Stockholm on the E4 lies **Uppsala** ③, Sweden's ancient capital, last bastion of heathenism and seat of one of Europe's greatest universities. This is the birthplace of Ingmar Bergman and the setting for his film *Fanny and Alexander*. The town is also an Episcopal See and has the largest Gothic cathedral to be found in Scandinavia, **Domkyrkan** (open 8am–6pm). Its vaults, from 1435, house the shrine of Saint Erik, a former king and the patron of Sweden.

Across the town's lush parks rises **Uppsala Slott**, a fortress from the days of the Vasa dynasty (open June–Aug for tours; entrance fee; tel: 018 274 800). A few minutes north of the town lies **Gamla Uppsala** (Old Uppsala) the 5th-century bastion of the Yngling dynasty. The three huge grave mounds of kings Aun, Egil and Adils (described in the opening passages of *Beowulf*) dominate the evocative grave fields surrounding **Gamla Uppsalakyrkan** (parish church; open 9am–4pm; free; tel: 018 327 081).

Near Uppsala, where the sea meets the forest, you'll find **Sigtuna** ③, Sweden's oldest town. In the 11th century this was the commercial centre for the Svea and Vandal tribes. Merchant ships from as far away as Asia dropped anchor here; monasteries and abbeys competed with one another in building glorious churches. Today, Sigtuna is a picturesque town with crooked lanes, quaint wooden houses and a miniature town hall. Tant Brun's café on the main pedestrian lane is a lovely place to stop for a cup of strong Swedish coffee and a freshly baked cinnamon bun.

South to Södermanland

To the south of Stockholm is **Norrköping** ③, with its tree-lined avenues, outdoor café society, trams and elegant architecture. The town's main attraction is **Kolmården Djurpark** ③. This is Scandinavia's wildlife safari, natural habitat and amusement park supreme (open Apr–Sept: daily 10am–4pm, later in summer; entrance fee; tel: 011 249 000).

Heading north towards Lake Mälaren's bays and inlets you come to **Strängnäs** ③, a delightful small town dominated by a magnificent Gothic cathedral. Next to the church at **Boglösa**, 20 km (12 miles) north, are hundreds of Bronze Age rock carvings.

On the lake, about 15 km (9 miles) to the east, lies idyllic **Mariefred** ③ and **Gripsholms Slott** (Castle; open May–Aug: daily 10am–4pm; Sept: closed Mon; Oct–Apr: Sat–Sun only; entrance fee; tel: 0159 101 94), which contains the royal portrait collections and a marvellous theatre from the late 1700s. Best of all is the architecture of this fortress, begun in the 1370s and continually updated. Around the edge of the moat is a collection of rune stones carved with serpents, ships and magic inscriptions. Mariefred is a lazy, summer lake town, with cafés and restaurants to suit all tastes and ferry connections to Stockholm. ❏

A ROYAL TREAT: DROTTNINGHOLM PALACE

Often referred to as Sweden's "mini Versailles", the island palace of Drottningholm with its exquisite gardens and historic theatre is not to be missed

The most popular place to visit in Stockholm's archipelago is Drottningholms Slott (open May–Aug: 10am–4.30pm; Sept: noon–3.30pm; entrance fee; tel: 08 402 62 80) on Lovön. Now the main home of the Swedish royal family, the 17th-century palace is surrounded by formal Baroque and Rococo gardens of fountains, statues, flowerbeds, box hedges and a variety of trees.

The palace was built for Eleonora, the widow of King Karl X, by the Tessin family of architects headed by Nicodemus the Elder (1615–81). Work began in 1662 and was completed by his son, Nicodemus the Younger.

Although the royal family live at Drottningholm, much of the palace is open to the public. Interior highlights include a magnificent Grand Staircase with *trompe l'oeil* paintings by Johan Sylvius, the Baroque Karl X Gallery, Queen Hedwig Eleonora's State Bedroom with its richly painted ceiling, and the library of Queen Louisa Ulrika who married King Adolf Fredrik in 1744.

In the parkland stands the exotic pagoda roofs and ornamental balconies of the Kina Slott (Chinese Pavilion; open Apr–Oct: 1–3.30pm; May–Aug: 11am–4.30pm; Sept: noon–3.30pm; tours June–Aug: 11am, 2pm; entrance fee; tel: 08 402 62 70), a birthday present to Queen Louisa Ulrika from her husband in 1753. In one of four adjoining pavilions the king had his carpentry workshop.

The island's greatest treasure is undoubtedly the 18th-century Drottningholms Slottsteater (Court Theatre; open May: noon–4.30pm; June–Aug: 11am–4.30pm; Sept: 1–3.30pm; entrance fee; tel: 08 457 0600; Teatermuseet, open May–Sept: daily).

The theatre was designed for Queen Louisa Ulrika by Carl Fredrik Adelcrantz and opened in 1766. The queen's son, Gustav III, was an actor and playwright who became known as "The Theatre King". He invited French troupes of actors to perform at Drottningholm and the theatre soon became an influential centre for performing arts. Gustav went on to found Stockholm's Dramatic Theatre and hired Swedish talent to develop a native theatre and opera.

The building fell into disrepair in the 19th century, then in the early 20th century it underwent extensive restoration. Today it is the oldest theatre in the world still using its original backdrops and stage machinery for productions. Attending a performance of opera or ballet here on a summer evening is like experiencing magic from an earlier age. ❏

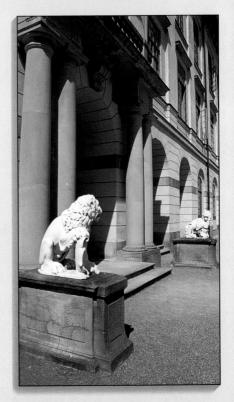

TOP LEFT: formal gardens at Drottningholm.
ABOVE LEFT: Chinese Pavilion. **TOP RIGHT:** ballet at the Slottsteater. **RIGHT:** palace entrance.

STEAMING OUT AMONG THE SKERRIES

When summer comes, the Swedes set off by boat to the thousands of idyllic islands that dot the waterways between Stockholm and the Baltic

Every summer thousands of Swedes in boats navigate carefully through waters loaded with 24,000 islands, rocks and islets in the Stockholm archipelago. The brackish waters start in the centre of Stockholm and extend 80 km (50 miles) out into the open Baltic Sea. Close to the mainland, the islands are larger and more lush, the bays and channels wider. Hidden here are idyllic island communities, farmlands and small forests. But as you travel further out, the scenery becomes more rugged, finally ending in sparse windblown islets formed by the last Ice Age.

ISLAND RETREATS

In the middle of the 19th century affluent Stockholm families began to build their second homes along the shores of the various islands in the archipelago. Over the years, "commoners" had more money and leisure time and soon they, too, sought their way to the archipelago. The combination of wilderness, sea, fresh air and closeness to the city satisfied many leisure needs. Today, Swedes either own their cottages or rent them, and enjoy swimming, fishing, boating, nature walks and socialising with friends.

▷ **YOUNG VOYAGER**
Dressed for the ferry ride and a deck-side view of the steam boats and yachts that ply the waters.

△ **ON THE WATERFRONT**
More than 50,000 chalets offering varying degrees of comfort are spread throughout Stockholm's inner archipelago.

▽ **LAZY DAYS**
The archipelago is such an important factor in the Stockholmers' leisure time, that every tenth resident now owns a boat.

▽ HOME FROM HOME
More than 10,000 people live year round on the 150 inhabited islands, working in farming, fishing, boat transport and retailing.

▽ WALK IN THE WILD
Escaping to the islands for summer weekends and holidays, mainly in July, is a perfect antidote to the bustle of city life.

A QUICK GUIDE TO ISLAND HOPPING

The archipelago can be explored on guided tours which can be picked up from Stockholm's city centre. But if you want to travel like the locals, then buy a *Båtluffarkort* (Inter-skerries card), which allows you to see as many islands as you can in 16 days, including:

● Sandön, with its attractive sailing centre village of Sandhamn, sandy beaches and some good restaurants (a 6-hour round trip).

● Fjäderholmarna, featuring a boat museum, aquarium, fish-smoking plant, restaurants and crafts shops (20 minutes by boat from Stockholm).

● Vaxholm, with its famous fortress (1 hour by boat).

● Utö, where a 12th-century iron mine is the principal attraction

△ ISLAND HARVEST
Berry and mushroom picking are popular pastimes enjoyed by all ages. Swedes also love nature walks, bird watching and picnicking.

▷ PADDLE POWER
Swedes take time to enjoy the scenery by water. Although sailing is a very popular water sport, canoeing and kayaking come in a close second.

This is a also a great place for bike-riding (3 hours by boat from the city).

SOUTHERN SWEDEN

Across the Öresund bridge from Denmark, southern Sweden is home to the lively city of Malmö. Castles and Stone Age sites abound, while bathers and birdwatchers head for Öland

Map on page 250

Stockholm

Skåne is Sweden's most southerly province, so close to Denmark across the narrow sound that even the accent is faintly Danish. This isn't surprising because for centuries Swedes and Danes fought over this area, along with the provinces of Halland and Blekinge, until Sweden established its sovereignty in 1658.

Since 2000, however, the two countries have been joined as one by the Öresund road and rail bridge that links Malmö and Copenhagen. The project has prompted a renaissance for southern Sweden as a centre of the Danish-Swedish Öresund region, with a total of 3 million people and one-fifth of the total combined GNP of Sweden and Denmark.

Skåne is often called Sweden's food store because of its rich farmland, mild climate and good fishing. Along the coast the landscape is undulating and lush and especially spectacular in the southeast corner, Österlen. Inland, there are lakes and three large ridges with lovely walks.

Skåne is renowned for its castles and manor houses. There are said to be 240 in the province, most of which are in private ownership, but it is usually possible to walk round the gardens such as at **Sofiero ❶**, 4 km (2½ miles) north of Helsingborg (open Apr–Sept; tel: 042 13 74 00). Built in 1857, Sofiero was used by King Gustav VI Adolf as his summer palace until his death in 1973. He was a keen botanist and made the gardens a real attraction.

Malmö: city of the south

Malmö ❷ is Sweden's third city, a lively place with a population of about 255,000. In the 16th century, Malmö competed with Copenhagen to be Scandinavia's leading capital. In those days it was an important port, not far from rich fishing grounds.

Today, the harbour is still busy and many of the old buildings remain. **Malmöhus**, the dominating castle built by King Christian III when Skåne was still part of Denmark, is Scandinavia's oldest remaining Renaissance castle. It houses the **Malmömuseer** (Malmö Museums; open June–Aug: 10am–4pm; Sept–May: noon–4pm; entrance fee; tel: 040 34 10 00), which includes the Art Museum, Museum of Natural History, City Museum, Science & Technology/Maritime Museum, and the **Kommendants Hus** (Commander's House), in Malmöhusvägen.

From the same period is **Rådhuset** (City Hall), which you will find in **Stortorget**, one of the largest squares in Scandinavia. **Stadshuset** (August Palms Plats; open Mon–Fri 8am–4:30pm; tel: 040 34 10 00) was built in 1546 in genuine Dutch Renaissance style. In 1860 it was given a facelift by the architect Helgo Zettervall, with niches, bays, allegorical paintings,

LEFT: markets are a focal point in many Swedish towns.
BELOW: Equestrian Week, Malmö.

Sweden leads the world in glassmaking. Many of the famous glassworks, such as Kosta and Boda, are located in the southeast of the country.

and colonnades. Northeast from Stortorget is **St Petri Kyrka**, Göran Olsgatan, built in the Baltic Gothic style and dating from the 13th century, although its towers were built in the 15th century and its copper spires in 1890. This elegant cathedral features a beautiful altar area created by sculptors in 1611.

A particularly idyllic place to sit and relax is **Lilla Torg** (Little Square), with its cobblestones, carefully restored houses and 16th-century charm. Through an arch on the south side of the square is Hemanska Gården. Once a merchant's home and trading yard, it now houses the **Form Design Center** (open daily), where Swedish industrial design and handicrafts are displayed.

When you get hungry, head for **Saluhallen** (open 10am–6pm; Sat 10am–2pm), on the northwest corner of Lilla Torg, where you can choose from fish restaurants, cafés, delicatessens and an abudance of fresh food.

Walking east from Lilla Torg, a rewarding visit can be made to **Rooseum**, (Stora Nygatan; open Tues–Wed 11am–5pm; Thur 11am–8pm; Fri–Sun 11am–5pm; entrance fee; tel: 040 12 17 16) founded in 1988 by the Swedish art collector and financier Fredrik Roos. Here you'll see the art currently at the centre of international debate, like that of Jean Michel Basquiat, Julian Schnabel and Susan Rothenberg.

Towards Helsingborg

Heading north from Malmö, **Lund ❸** is a university town with a fine cathedral, **Domkyrkan**, built in the 12th century. Don't miss the **Kulturhistoriska Museet** (Cultural History Museum, Tegnérs platsen; open May–Sept: 11am–5pm; Oct–Apr: Tues–Sun noon–4pm; entrance fee; tel: 046 35 04 00), an open-air museum with dozens of buildings, silver, textiles, ceramics and art. Along with the

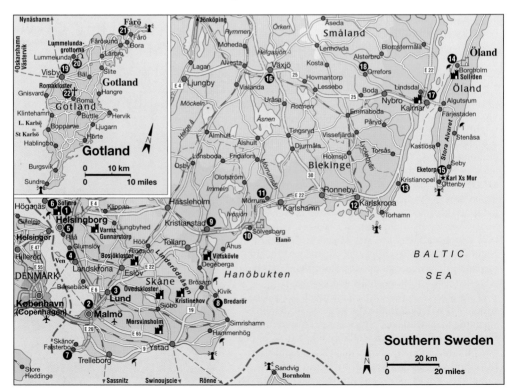

Southern Sweden

University of Uppsala, Lund is one of the two ancient Swedish universities. About 30 km (19 miles) north along the coast, **Glumslöv** offers memorable views. From the hill above the church, on a clear day you can see 30 churches and seven towns, including Copenhagen and Helsingør in Denmark.

Helsingborg ❺, 60 km (37 miles) north of Malmö, is an interesting town of cobbled streets, dominated by the remnants of an old castle, **Kärnan**, and with a bustling harbour. **Höganäs** ❻, 20 km (12 miles) north, is devoted to potters and artists. The large pottery is worth a visit.

Map on page 250

Along the south coast

Forty km (25 miles) southwest from Malmö are the summer idylls of **Skanör** and **Falsterbo** ❼. **Skanörs Ljung** is a must for bird lovers, particularly in September and October, when a large number of migrating birds gather.

Southeast of Kivik is **Bredarör** ❽, site of the Bronze Age **Kiviksgraven** (King's Grave). Scientists wonder about the mysterious markings on the stones. One theory is that Kivik may have been a Phoenician colony in AD 1200.

Kristianstad ❾ is the birthplace of the Swedish film industry, which started around 1910. The original studio is now a museum where you can watch some of the old films on video (**Filmmuseet**, Östra Storg 53; open 1–4pm; tel: 044 13 57 29). Nearby, the **Kristianstad Vattenriket** (Water Kingdom) is a rich wetland area on the Helge River, with a diversity of birds, wildlife and plants.

Blekinge is a tiny province with sandy beaches and Sweden's most southerly archipelago. It is excellent for sea fishing. You can enjoy peaceful angling in some of the lakes, or good sport for salmon in the Mörrum River. Canoeing is popular. Driving to Blekinge from Skåne, you first reach **Sölvesborg** ❿, and the ruins of 13th-century **Sölvesborg Slott** (Castle).

Mörrum ⓫, 30 km (19 miles) north of Sölvesborg, is noted for its salmon fishing: at **Laxens Hus** you can see salmon and trout at different stages of their development (open Apr–Sept: 9am–5pm; Oct: 9am–4pm; entrance fee; tel: 0454 501 23).

The biggest town in Blekinge is **Karlskrona** ⓬, a naval centre built in the 17th century, with wide streets and impressive buildings. In the Björkholmen district you'll find quaint 18th-century cottages built by ships' carpenters. The village of **Kristianopel** ⓭ is renowned for its smoked herring.

Öland: an ornithologist's delight

The island of **Öland**, off the east coast, is one of the most visited areas of Sweden and, with its diverse landscape and superb beaches, it is a paradise for bird-watchers, nature lovers and sun worshippers.

Once you've crossed the Öland bridge from Blekinge, you soon see the ruins of **Borgholm Slott** (Castle) rising above the main town of **Borgholm** ⓮, a once splendid residence from the 12th century (open Apr and Sept: 10am–4pm; May, June, Aug: 10am–6pm; July: 10am–9pm; entrance fee).

The island has many ancient burial places and there are remains of 16 fortified dwellings from earlier times. The most interesting is **Eketorp** ⓯, in the south, which has been partly restored. Sweden's prime

TIP

Råå, on the outskirts of Helsingborg, is a picturesque fishing village with an excellent inn.

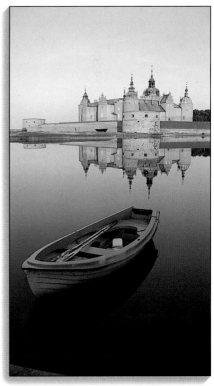

BELOW: Kalmar Castle, Småland.

Map on page 250

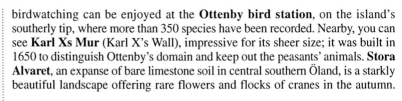

birdwatching can be enjoyed at the **Ottenby bird station**, on the island's southerly tip, where more than 350 species have been recorded. Nearby, you can see **Karl Xs Mur** (Karl X's Wall), impressive for its sheer size; it was built in 1650 to distinguish Ottenby's domain and keep out the peasants' animals. **Stora Alvaret**, an expanse of bare limestone soil in central southern Öland, is a starkly beautiful landscape offering rare flowers and flocks of cranes in the autumn.

Brightly painted timber buildings are a feature of southern Sweden.

The emigrants

During the late 19th and early 20th centuries, Sweden's population exploded, and many families could no longer eke out a living on the land. So began the years of migration to North America. A popular place to visit is **Utvandrarnas Hus** (House of the Emigrants; open June–Aug: Mon–Fri 9am–6pm, Sat–Sun 11am–4pm; Sept–May: Mon–Fri 9am–4pm; entrance fee; tel: 0470 201 20) in **Växjö** ⓰, 70 km (43 miles) west of Kalmar, which tells the story of the exodus.

Kalmar ⓱, one of Sweden's oldest cities, was of great importance in the Swedish–Danish wars. Sweden's best preserved Renaissance castle, **Kalmar Slott** (open June–Aug: 10am–6pm; Sept–May: 10am–4pm; entrance fee), was in fact begun in the 12th century but was completely renovated during the 16th century by the Vasa kings. The castle's coffered ceilings, panelled halls, fresco paintings and magnificient stonework have inspired the Renaissance Festival, held every July, featuring tournament games, market, music and theatre.

BELOW: glass-blowing is a highly valued skill in southern Sweden.

Kingdom of glass

Northwest of Kalmar, about 20 km (12 miles) is **Orrefors** ⓲, part of Sweden's Glasriket (Glass Kingdom). The first glass was melted in Sweden in 1556 but it was not established as an industry until 1742, when **Kosta**, the oldest works, was founded to the west of Orrefors. Anders Koskull and Georg Bogislaus Stael von Holstein took the first two syllables of their respective surnames to create "Kosta". The location was ideal because the dense forests provided the timber to keep the furnaces going.

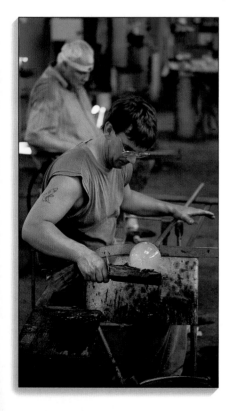

Orrefors started in the glass business by producing windowpanes and bottles. In 1913 the works was taken over by Johan Ekman, an industrialist from Göteborg. Ekman recruited two artists who with their creative flair were to transform Orrefors into one of the world's foremost glassworks: Simon Gate, a portrait and landscape painter, and Edvard Hald, a pupil of Matisse.

Most of the 17 major glassworks are open to visitors for demonstrations and many have shops (Mon–Fri 9am–6pm, Sat 10am–4pm, Sun noon–4pm; Orrefors Glasbruk, tel: 0481 341 95; Kosta Glasbruk, tel: 0478 345 32; Boda Glasbruk, tel: 0481 240 30).

Look out for *hyttsill* ("glassworks herring") evenings. In bygone times the glassworks were also a social centre where the locals would gather for a chat and bake herrings and potatoes in the furnace, with music provided by an accordionist or fiddler. Some of the works have revived these evenings for the benefit of visitors. ❑

GOTLAND: THE SUNSHINE ISLAND

With its medieval towns, sandy beaches and curious rock formations, tranquil Gotland – the largest island in the Baltic – is a favourite holiday spot

Gotland is an island of gaunt rocks, forests, wild flowers, cliffs and sandy beaches. Blessed with more hours of sunshine than anywhere else in the country, Swedes flock here for their summer holidays.

Gotland was created over thousands of years as the animals and plants of the ancient Silurian Sea slowly sank into the sediment that was to become the limestone platform of modern Gotland. Million-year-old fossils and the island's monumental sea-stacks (*raukar*), can still be found on the coast.

In the Viking Age the island was a busy trading post. **Visby ⑲**, the principal centre of population, later became a prosperous Hanseatic town. Great stone houses were erected, churches were founded, and a city wall was built. Today, 3 km (2 miles) of the medieval limestone wall remains virtually intact, interspersed with 44 towers and numerous gates. It is now a UNESCO World Heritage site.

Limestone has created one of the island's major attractions – the impressive subterranean tunnels and stalactite caves of **Lummelundagrottorna ⑳** (open May, June, Sept: 9am–4pm; July–Aug: 9am–6pm; guided tours only; entrance fee; tel: 0498 27 30 50), 13 km (8 miles) to the north of Visby, which should not be missed. Dress warmly, it's 8°C (46°F) inside.

About 50 km (30 miles) north of Visby lies **Fårö ㉑**, the "island of sheep". Take a ferry to the island from Fårösund, and enjoy sites such as Gamlehamn, a medieval harbour, and the ruins of a chapel to St Olof. You can

also see one of Gotland's most bizarrely shaped *raukar*, "The Camel", and visit the beach of Sundersand. After you have been here a while, you will begin to understand why Fårö is the favourite place of Sweden's leading film director, Ingmar Bergman.

Sweden's most primitive horse, the Russ, has lived in the forests of the island from time immemorial. The name Russ comes from the Old Norse *hross*, and it is thought that the horse is a descendant of the wild Tarpan. You can see them, only 123–126 cm (46–52 inches) tall, around the island.

Wherever you travel in Gotland you'll come across at least one of its 92 medieval churches. At **Romakloster ㉒**, in the centre of the island, there is a ruined monastery from the 12th century. There are many other relics of the past including runic stones and burial mounds. If you reach Gotland's southernmost tip, you'll see some of the most impressive *raukar* on the island. ❑

TOP LEFT: Gotland beach. **ABOVE LEFT:** Visby, a Hanseatic town. **TOP RIGHT:** Visby's medieval town wall. **RIGHT:** an unusual sea stack (*raukar*).

SWEDEN'S WEST COAST

*From the sandy beaches of Halland to the bustling city
of Göteborg and the rocky shores of Bohuslän, the west coast
has long been a summer playground for Swedes*

Map
on page
256

Stockholm

The west coast of Sweden, generously dotted with beaches and fishing villages, is 400 km (250 miles) of glorious coastline divided in two by the city of Göteborg (Gothenborg). It has been a favourite holiday spot since the early 20th century. The best beaches are in the southern province of Halland. North of Göteborg, in Bohuslän, is a majestic coast of granite rocks and islands.

The E6 connects all the larger cities, but follow the small coastal roads to discover the gems. Starting along the coast in the northwestern corner of the county of Skåne, a number of small towns offer views into the past. **Gamla Viken ①**, 15 km (9 miles) north of Helsingborg on highway 22, is a picturesque fishing village. **Torekov**, at the tip of the next peninsula, has a seaside golf course and is home to Kattegatt Gastronomi & Logi, whose chefs are two of Sweden's finest.

Sand and salmon

Halmstad ②, the largest town in Halland, lies on the River Nissan. **Halmstads Slott** (Castle), the provincial governor's residence, was built in the 17th century by the Danish king Kristian IV. In front of the castle is moored the old sail-training vessel *Najaden* (open June–Aug: Tues, Thur, 5–7pm, Sat 11am–3pm), built in 1897. Other sights include **St Nikolai**, a 13th-century church. **Tylösand**, 8 km (5 miles) west of Halmstad, is a popular holiday resort with a predominantly sandy beach and two golf courses. There are good beaches at **Östra Strand**, **Ringenäs** and **Haverdalsstrand**.

Falkenberg ③, 40 km (25 miles) north of Halmstad, is on the Ätran, a river famous for its salmon. The old part of the town with its 18th-century wooden houses and cobbled streets is centered on the 14th-century **St Laurenti Church**. There is an old toll bridge (*tullbron*) from 1756 and the oldest pottery in Sweden, **Törngrens Krukmakeri**, which has been run by the Törngren family since 1789 (open Mon–Fri; tel: 0346 103 54). Good beaches are found at **Olofsby** (north of the town) and **Skrea Strand** (south of the town).

Continue 30 km (19 miles) north on the E6 to **Varberg ④**, a bustling place combining spa, resort, port and commercial centre with a ferry service to Grenå in Denmark. **Varbergs Fästning** (Fortress) stands beside the water and houses a youth hostel, restaurant, apartments and a museum. Pride of place goes to the Bocksten Man, the only preserved figure in the world wearing a complete costume from the Middle Ages. Reminders of Varberg's late 19th-century development as a holiday resort include **Societetshuset** (1883), an elaborate wooden pavilion in the park,

LEFT: holiday
cottage on
Klädesholmen.
BELOW: rocky north
Bohuslän coast.

West Coast

0   20 km
0   20 miles

now a restaurant and a site for outdoor concerts. The bathing station (1903), is a rectangular wooden structure open to the sea in the middle. Around the sides are changing huts and deck chairs where, after a quick plunge in this early version of a sea-water swimming pool, bathers can relax over coffee and waffles.

A taste for Tudor

Heading 30 km (19 miles) north towards **Kungsbacka** you will pass the most out-of-character building along the entire coast. **Tjolöholm Castle 5** (open June–Aug: daily 11am–4pm; Sept, Nov–May: Sat–Sun only 11am–4pm; Oct: Sun 11am–4pm; entrance fee; tel: 0300 54 42 00) was built in the early 20th century in an English Tudor style, with a splendid Art Nouveau interior.

The moment you reach the little seaside resort of **Särö 6** (immediately north of Kungsbacka), you notice the coastline has changed. Instead of beaches, a dramatic landscape of rocks, inlets and islands takes over. In the early 19th century Särö was a fashionable resort, popular with the Swedish royal family. It remains in a time warp. You can walk along the Strandpromenaden and through **Särö Västerskog**, one of the oldest oak woods on the west coast.

Göteborg

Göteborg 7 (Gothenburg) is the second largest city in Sweden (450,000 inhabitants) and home to beautiful parks and a thriving cultural and industrial life. Dutch architects planned the city in the 17th century for King Gustav II Adolf, giving it an architectural character of its own. The shipping industry, particularly trade with the orient by the Swedish East India Company in the 18th century, shaped the history of the city. Today it is Scandinavia's largest seaport. The harbour area is its soul and a good place to start your sightseeing.

The bold new **Göteborgsoperan Ⓐ** (Opera House; tel: 031 10 80 00), opened in 1994, stands on the water just west of the commercial centre. Built in ship-like style, it is well worth a visit for its architecture alone. Near the Opera is Göteborg's **Maritima Centrum** (Maritime Centre; open Mar–Nov: 10am–4pm; July: noon–9pm; entrance fee; tel: 031 10 59 50), on Packhuskajen. Said to be the world's largest floating ship museum, it features 15 ships, including a submarine, destroyer and lightship.

The heart of Göteborg lies along Östra Hamngatan and Kungsportsavenyn. Start at the northern end of Östra Hamngatan; heading south you will pass **Nordstan**, one of northern Europe's largest covered shopping centres. Along the intersecting streets of Norra and Södra Hamngatan are dozens of small and inviting boutiques. Cross Stora Hamnkanalen (Great Harbour Canal) and continue south to **Kungsportsplatsen**, where you can pop into the **Göteborgs Turistbyrå** ☉ (Tourist Office; open daily June–Aug: 9am–6pm; Sept–May: Mon–Fri 9am–5pm, Sat–Sun 10am–2pm).

Across the street is **Saluhallen** ☉, a large indoor marketplace (1886–89) stocked with Swedish specialities such as seafood, cheese and meats. This is a good place to sit and enjoy a cup of coffee, a light snack or a full lunch.

Kungsportsplatsen is also the place to embark on a **Paddan** (Swedish for "toad"), one of the flat-bottomed sightseeing boats that cruise through the old moat, under some 20 bridges, along 17th-century canals, out into the harbour and back again (May–Sept: first departure 10am; tel: 031 60 96 70).

From Kungsportsplatsen, cross the moat into Kungsportsavenyn – more often known as "**Avenyn**" ☉ (The Avenue). The Avenyn, 40 metres (130 ft) wide and just under a kilometre long, is a boulevard lined with trees, restaurants, pubs and cafés as well as street musicians and peddlers of fruits and trinkets. Halfway along the Avenue, you are just a block away from the **Röhsska Museet** ☉ (Vasagatan 37–39; open noon–4pm, Tues noon–9pm, closed Mon; entrance

> **Maps:**
> **Area 256**
> **City 258**

A Göteborgskortet (Göteborg Card) gives unlimited travel on city buses and trams, a boat trip and free admission to many museums and to Liseberg.

BELOW: Göteborg's harbourfront and lookout tower.

fee; tel: 031 61 38 50), the Swedish museum for design and handicrafts. At the southern end of the Avenyn is Göteborg's cultural centre, **Götaplatsen**, with the imposing Poseidon fountain by the famous Swedish sculptor Carl Milles. Götaplatsen is flanked by the **Kunstmuseet G** (Art Museum; open 11am–4pm, Wed 11am–9pm, closed Mon; entrance fee; tel: 031–18 91 75), with an extensive collection of Scandinavian art, including Anders Zorn's *Bathers*, and work by Munch, Rembrandt and Pissarro. On the west side of the square is the **Konserthuset (Concert Hall) H**, home of the Gothenburg Symphony Orchestra.

Bohuslän is noted for its fine Bronze Age rock carvings. The "Bridal Pair" at Vitlycke, near Tanumshede, is among the best known of the carvings in the area.

Lisebergs Nöjespark I (open Apr–Sept; entrance fee; tel: 031 40 01 00), located in the middle of town, is the largest amusement park in northern Europe. Like most amusement parks, it is a great place to take children. For a calmer and non-commercial experience, explore the **Botaniska Trädgården (Botanical Gardens) J** or **Slottsskogen K**, two of the finer among Göteborg's 20 parks.

The rugged coast

The province of **Bohuslän** begins north of Göteborg. To see the coast, head 15 km (9 miles) west from Kungälv on road 168 past Tjuvkil, where you can catch a ferry to **Marstrand 8**. A town without cars, Marstrand is a popular holiday resort and sailing centre. In summer it is also a good place to buy crafts. **Carlstens Fästning** (Fortress) dominates the town and offers the best views of the island. King Oskar II (1872–1907) used to come here every summer to holiday and his statue stands in front of the Societetshuset.

Beyond Marstrand lie the islands of Tjörn and Orust, connected by bridge to the mainland. **Tjörn 9** is beautiful with some barren areas inland and a fascinating coastline. A magnificent curved bridge, which provides good views in either direction, links Tjörn and **Orust** . This island, the third largest in Sweden, has its quota of fishing villages, including Mollösund, Ellös and Käringön.

Returning to the mainland, take a ferry across the **Gullmarn**, Sweden's only genuine fjord, from **Fiskebäckskil** ⓫ to **Lysekil** ⓬. Lysekil comes to life in the summer with boat excursions to the islands and sea fishing trips. **Havets Hus** (Sea Aquarium; open 10am–4pm; entrance fee; tel: 0523 165 30) is one of the star attractions and includes sea life from Gullmarn and the Skagerrak. A tunnel aquarium holds creatures such as rays, sharks, halibut and cod.

North of Lysekil on the Sotenäs peninsula, the small harbour of **Smögen** ⓭ is a favourite stop for boats. The main attraction is the boardwalk, where you can shop, stroll and lounge. The other attraction is fresh shrimp. Watch a fish auction and then go round the corner to buy some of the catch.

At Åby **Säteri** ⓮, 17 km (11 miles) northeast of Smögen, is **Nordens Ark** (open 10am–4pm; June–Aug: 10am–6pm; entrance fee; tel: 0523 522 15), a nature park featuring endangered species and old breeds of Nordic farm animals.

Thrills for all:
Liseberg amusement
park in Göteborg.

Towards Norway

Near **Tanumshede** ⓯, a small town about 50 km (30 miles) north on route 168, is Europe's largest collection of Bronze Age rock carvings, including depictions of battles, ships, hunting and fishing scenes, and mating couples.

The last town before the Norwegian frontier is **Strömstad** ⓰. A health resort, it is also said to have more hours of sunshine than anywhere else in northern Europe. Strömstad shrimps are considered by the local inhabitants to be in a class of their own, with a distinctive mild flavour. The district has more than a touch of Norwegian about it having been part of Norway until 1717. ❑

BELOW: sailing competition on the island of Tjörn.

Maps:
Area 256
City 258

SWEDEN'S GREAT LAKES

Two of Europe's largest lakes, Vänern and Vättern, lie at the heart of southern Sweden. In this area of farmland and forests, painted churches, grand castles and literary hideaways abound

Map
on page
262

Two enormous lakes, Vänern and Vättern, dominate the map of Sweden. The larger of the two is Vänern, a vast stretch of water with an area of 5,585 sq km (2,156 sq miles). It is not only the biggest lake in Sweden but also the largest in Western Europe, and its western shore embraces two provinces, Dalsland and Värmland.

Dalsland is a province of neat farms and prosperous small towns and villages, with empty roads running through its forests. The greatest attraction here is nature and, thus, the most interesting activities are outdoors: namely, camping, hiking and canoeing. West of Mellerud is **Kroppefjällen ❶**, an upland area which is a nature reserve. One of the best ways to explore the region is to hike along the 15-km (9-mile) **Karl XIIs Väg** (Trail); maps obtainable from the tourist office in Mellerud (tel: 0530 183 08).

A local feature is the **Dalslands Kanal**, a network of interconnected lakes and rivers. It was designed by Nils Ericsson and built between 1864 and 1868 to provide better transport for the local ironworks and sawmills. Today, it is popular for sailing and canoeing. The aqueduct at **Håverud ❷**, 14 km (9 miles) north of Mellerud, is a dramatic piece of engineering. Made of iron and 33 metres (108 ft) long, it carries the canal over the rapids of the River Upperud.

LEFT: fishing on the tranquil waters.
BELOW: watery landscape.

Along the Klarälven

An old parish register in Western Värmland states: "Between Sweden and Norway lies Värmland." Even today, a certain rugged independence, plus a slight Norwegian accent, persists. The region has strong traditions and has produced a rich crop of writers of both prose and poetry. Spruce and pine forests cover the county and are often referred to as "Värmland's gold".

The province is crisscrossed with narrow lakes and rivers, and the **Klarälven** can claim to be among its most beautiful rivers. It begins turbulently in Norway, where it is called Trysilelva, but gradually becomes broader, winding and sluggish before emptying into Lake Vänern near the province's largest town, **Karlstad ❸**. Highlights in this 400-year-old town include the cathedral (1730), a school museum and a popular park, **Mariebergsskogen**.

The Klarälven was the last Swedish river used for floating logs. The practice ended in 1991, but in **Dyvelsten ❹**, 17 km (10 miles) north of Karlstad, the **Flottningsmuseet** (Log Rafting Museum; open June–mid-Aug: daily 11am–5pm; entrance fee; tel: 054 87 12 26) shows how it was done.

At **Ransäter ❺**, 40 km (25 miles) north of Karlstad on the Klarälven, the **Hembygdsgården** heritage village (open May–Aug: 9am–5pm, closed Sat–Sun; entrance fee; tel: 0552 303 43) includes museums devoted to mining, forestry, agriculture and rural life, which provide a fascinating picture of the Värmland of yesteryear. Ransäter hosts an annual folk music festival in June and the largest accordion festival in Scandinavia in July.

The Klarälven is no longer used for floating logs, but many Swedes holiday on the river – drifting along on the gentle current on a raft they assemble themselves. Contact Värmlands Turisttråd in Karlstad (tel: 054 22 25 50; www.varmland.org) for more details.

To the south of Lake Vänern, Lidköping's square is said to be the largest in north Europe. A big market is held here on Wednesday and Saturday mornings.

Nobel prize-winner

West of Ransäter, on the eastern shore of Mellan-Fryken, is **Mårbacka** ❻ (open May–Sept: 10am–5pm; Oct–Apr: guided tours on Sat; entrance fee; tel: 0565 310 27), the manor home of the Swedish writer Selma Lagerlöf, the first woman to receive a Nobel prize for literature, in 1909. Through her books, including *The Wonderful Adventures of Nils* and *The Story of Gösta Berling*, she made the Fryk valley and lakes famous. On the western side of the lake is

Rottneros Manor ❼ (open May–Aug: 10am–4pm; later in high summer; entrance fee; tel: 0565 602 95), which appears as Ekeby in Lagerlöf's *The Story of Gösta Berling*. One of Sweden's most beautiful parks, it has an arboretum and works by Scandinavian sculptors, including Milles, Eriksson and Vigeland.

Map on page 262

Inventive feats

North of Lake Vänern, the bedrock is rich in minerals and this area has long been associated with Sweden's early industrial development. Many Americans make the pilgrimage to **Filipstad** ❽, which has the mausoleum of John Ericsson, the gifted inventor and engineer.

    Björkborn Herrgård ❾, near Karlskoga, was the home of the Swedish inventor Alfred Nobel. The manor house is now a museum, **Nobelmuseet** (open June–Aug: 1–5pm; entrance fee; tel: 0586 818 94). At **Kristinehamn** ❿, 24 km (15 miles) to the west of Karlskoga, a 15-metre (49-ft) high sculpture by Picasso is the most striking navigational feature on Lake Vänern.

Mariestad Slot, on the eastern shore of Lake Vänern.

    To the east, in the province of Närke, is the town **Örebro** ⓫, with a dramatic **castle** (open June–Aug, daily tours; Sept–May, Sat tour 1pm; entrance fee; tel: 019 21 21 21). Despite its appearance, the building dates from only the late 1800s, but there has been a castle on the site since the 13th century.

Between the lakes

The region separating Lake Vänern from Lake Vättern offers rich pickings for the visitor. This is the province of Västergötland. In 1746 the indefatigable Linnaeus said: "Truly no one could ever imagine such splendour as in Västergötland who had not seen it for himself."

BELOW: ready with a smile.

    Heading south along the eastern shore of Vänern, you come to **Mariestad** ⓬, which is dominated by the spire of the 17th-century Renaissance-style cathedral, one of the few churches of this period remaining in Sweden.

    Most Swedes learn in school that the king who first united the Svea and Göta tribes, Olof Skötkonung (994–1022), was baptised in 1008 at Husaby Källa (Husaby Spring) at the southern tip of Kinnekulle. Despite disputes, historians would like to establish Husaby as the cradle of the Swedish state. **Husaby Church** ⓭ (open Apr–Sept, daily; tel: 0511 34 30 10) has an imposing stone tower with three spires.

    Nestled into Kinneviken (Kinne Bay), 51 km (32 miles) south of Mariestad, is **Lidköping** ⓮, a town founded in 1446 and renowned for its porcelain. **Rörstrand** (open Mon–Fri 10am–6pm, Sat 10am–2pm, Sun noon–4pm; tel: 0510 823 46), the second-oldest porcelain factory in Europe and maker of the Nobel china, has its own pottery museum featuring royal pieces, and a large shop. For such a modest-sized town, Lidköping has several fine cafés. The best is Garströms Konditori, established in 1859, on the main square (open daily).

    North of Lidköping on the Kållandsö peninsula, stands the 17th-century **Läckö Slott** ⓯ (open June–Aug: 10am–6pm; May, Sept: guided tours only; entrance fee; tel: 0510 103 20), one of the most

Map
on page
262

TIP

On the east of Lake
Vättern, historic sites
of note include the
stone of Rök at
Rökeskyrka with its
800 runes (E4 north of
Ödeshög) and Alvastra
Kloster, Sweden's first
Cistercian monastery
(Road 50 north of
Ödeshög).

BELOW:
cycling along
the Göta Kanal.

impressive castles in Sweden. In summer it is the venue for outdoor concerts and dramatic productions.

Trollhättan ⑯, at the southern tip of Lake Vänern, is the home town of Saab Automobile. Long before the invention of the motor car, the town was famous for the magnificent falls of the Göta River. The water level drops by about 32 metres (105 ft), and when the Göta Kanal was built a flight of locks was required to give ships access to Lake Vänern. Today, the river is diverted to generate electricity and the falls are silent. But during the annual Falls Festival in July it is released to follow the old course, providing an impressive spectacle.

The southern part of Västergötland was the heartland of Sweden's textile industry, with the focal point at Borås ⑰, where there is a **Textilmuseet** (Textile Museum; open Tues–Sat; entrance fee; tel: 033 35 76 72).

Around Lake Vättern

Lake Vättern, the second largest lake in Sweden, covers an area of 1,912 sq km (738 sq miles). Near the southern tip of the lake, on the west side, is the 14th-century timber-built **Habo Kyrka** ⑱ (Church), southwest of Habo village. It features an outstanding painted interior, the work of Johan Christian Peterson and Johan Kinnerus, both of Jönköping, between 1741 and 1743. Their paintings illustrate Luther's catechism and Biblical scenes.

Travelling north along the lake, stop at the small waterside resort of **Hjo** ⑲ to enjoy freshly smoked whitefish. Then tour the town in a horse-drawn carriage, or cruise on the lake in the 1892 steamer, *Trafik*. In the summer, Hjo hosts Scandinavia's largest handicraft festival. **Skara** ⑳, 50 km (31 miles) to the west of Hjo, has Sweden's second oldest cathedral (after Lund), dating from the 11th century. **Skara Sommarland** (open May–Aug: 10am–5pm; July–Aug: closes 6–7pm; entrance fee; tel: 0511 640 00), 8 km (5 miles) east of Skara on road 49, is a delight for children with numerous attractions from lunar vehicles to a giant water park.

For more relaxed pursuits, head 10 km (6 miles) southeast of Skara on road 184 to the lake of **Hornborgasjön**, a wildlife area with more than 100 species of birds. The biggest attraction is the annual mating dance of the crane, a graceful long-legged bird, best seen in April.

Mighty fortress

Karlsborg ㉑, on the western shore of Lake Vättern, 30 km (19 miles) north of Hjo, is dominated by its huge fortress, **Fästning** (open June–Aug: daily guided tours; entrance fee; tel: 0505 188 30). In 1809, when Sweden lost Finland to the Russians, the Swedes realised that a new defence strategy was required and decided to build two massive fortresses to house the government and the treasury. The first, at Karlsborg, was started in 1819 and required 250,000 tons of limestone. It was quarried by prison labour on the eastern side of the lake and ferried across by boat.

The castle has walls 2 metres (6 ft) thick with 5 km (3 miles) of ramparts, but by the time the building was finally finished, in 1909, fortresses were out of fashion. The second castle was never built. ❏

CROSSING SWEDEN BY CANAL

One of the most leisurely ways of sampling the country's history is to cruise along the Göta Kanal between Stockholm and Göteborg

The challenge of linking the lakes and rivers through the interior of Sweden, from Stockholm on the east coast to Göteborg on the west coast, had exercised the minds of many industrialists and kings before Baltzar von Platen succeeded at the beginning of the 19th century.

At the time, the country needed this new artery from east to west to transport timber, iron and food, and also to build up industry along its banks. For 22 years, 58,000 men laboured to build the **Göta Kanal** ㉒. In 1998, the canal was designated an "International Historic Civil Engineering Landmark", giving it the same status as the Golden Gate Bridge and the Panama Canal. Today, there is no commercial traffic on the canal, but many Swedes travel it in their own boats.

For the visitor, the classic way is to take a cruise between Stockholm and Göteborg on one of the vintage vessels operated by the Göta Kanal Rederiaktiebolaget (Göta Kanal Steamship Company). The oldest of the three vessels is *MS Juno*, built in 1874.

The four-day westbound cruise starts from Stockholm and enters the first lock on the canal at Mem – where the canal was officially inaugurated in 1832. On the second day the boat reaches Berg, with its flight of seven locks, where there is time to visit the historic monastery church at nearby Vreta, once the richest religious establishment in Sweden.

The route crosses two picturesque lakes, Asplången and Roxen, where there are good chances of spotting ospreys and herons during the breeding season. After Lake Roxen

the canal takes you through 15 locks in 3 km (2 miles), lifting you 37 metres (120 ft). The next night is spent at Motala, a town founded by Baltzar von Platen, who started the now thriving engineering industry.

On the third morning the boat crosses Lake Vättern to Karlsborg, site of a huge fortress built at the same time as the canal, and Forsvik, an old metal-working village and the site of the canal's first lock, built in 1813. Here, the boat is often greeted by a local family singing hymns and offering passengers wild flowers. This 100-year-old custom originated as a blessing for passengers as they embarked on what was then regarded as the hazardous crossing of Vättern. In the evening the boat reaches Sjötorp, marking the beginning of Lake Vänern.

At the south side of Lake Vänern, the boat enters the gorge at Trollhättan early the next morning for the last stage of the voyage down the Göta river to Göteborg. ❑

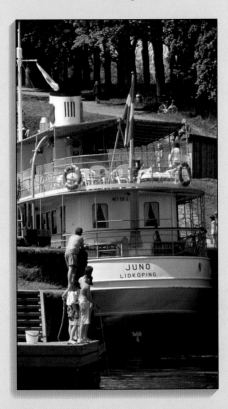

TOP LEFT: safety first. **ABOVE LEFT AND RIGHT:** two of the vintage vessels that cruise the Göta Kanal. **TOP RIGHT:** waiting for a catch.

DALARNA

Dalarna is Sweden's folklore province, as famous for its scarlet Dala horses as its music and merrymaking at Midsummer. Winter attracts skiers challenged by championship events

Map on page 268

Stockholm

Dalarna is often regarded as the heart of Sweden's folklore district, and indeed it represents all that is quintessentially Swedish. With its colourful costumes, centuries-old traditions of music and dance, Midsummer festivals, and evocative rural landscape, its folklore and beauty attract an increasing number of visitors each year.

Dalarna is the third-largest tourist site in Sweden, after Stockholm and Göteborg. The culture that gave us the red-painted Dalahäst (Dala horse) and inspired two of Sweden's most beloved artists, Carl Larsson and Anders Zorn, can best be experienced in the twilight of *fäbodar*, the old pasture cottages nestled in the hills of Dalarna; in the company of some elderly but amazingly energetic fiddlers; or at the magic of Midsummer, when a young woman places nine different flowers under her pillow to dream of the man she will marry.

Music-making

Music is one of the most defining characteristics of Dala culture. Music on Lake Siljan and the Falu Folk Music Festival are two annual festivals that attract visitors from all over Sweden and abroad. Distinctly Dala are the spelmansstämmor, folk musicians' rallies, particularly the one held each summer in **Bingsjö ❶**, 30 km (19 miles) east of Rättvik, where fiddlers in their eighties turn the classic polka into a musical performance that rivals any blues master.

An exotic setting for listening to music is **Dalhalla** (June–Aug: tours 10am–5pm; other times of year, by appointment; tel: 0248 79 79 50), a cavernous outdoor concert arena set in the depths of an abandoned limestone quarry near the town of **Rättvik ❷**. The quarry, abandoned in 1990, was inaugurated as a music arena in 1994, with the first performance, of Wagner's *Der Ring des Nibelungen*, held two years later. The annual summer festivals feature artists of international standing.

Pastoral scenes

For a change of pace, the gentle quiet of the region's *fäbodar* offer a taste of back-to-the-land living. These pasture cottages and surrounding buildings, dating from the 15th and 16th centuries, are found all over Sweden but are most often associated with Dalarna. They constitute a living museum, where cows are milked, butter is churned, *messmör* (a type of goats' cheese) is made, and the classic *tunnbröd* (thin bread) is baked. Many *fäbodar* are open to the public and sell products or serve food.

One worth visiting is **Ljusbodarnas Fäbodar** (open June–Aug; tel: 010 255 59 57/0247 330 80), about 20 km (12 miles) south of Leksand on Route

LEFT: Midsummer celebrations are an annual highlight.
BELOW: folk art telephone box.

70 towards Mockfjärd, where children can pet the cows, calves, hens, sheep and pigs, and you can enjoy a meal of *sill* (herring) on some nights.

If trying your own hand at 15th-century farming appeals, **Prästbodarna Fäbodar** (open June–Sept; book in advance; tel: 0248 141 59), near Bingsjö, has a variety of native Swedish farm animals, and offers one-day courses in butter churning, milking and cheese-making. The farming life seems a natural accompaniment to the breathtaking scenery of the province.

At the northern extremity of Dalarna is the deceptively gentle start of the mountain range which marches north, gaining height all the time until it culminates in the snow-topped peaks of the Kebnekajse range in Lapland. Dalarna is a transition zone between the softer landscapes of southern Sweden and the more dramatic, but harsher landscapes of the north. It is even divided within itself between the more densely populated area south and east of Lake Siljan (dense by Swedish standards) and the relatively uninhabited zones to the north and west of the lake.

Mora on Lake Siljan is best known as the home of the Swedish artist Anders Zorn (1860–1920). His house and studio, Zorngården, and the Zornmuseet are both worth visiting (open daily).

Industrial traditions

Dalarna is by no means exclusively rural. The provincial capital, **Falun ❸**, has been a centre of industry for 1,000 years, and is an attractive town, well worth a stroll to the central square. The **Bergslagen** area to the south developed as an important mining area when minerals including iron, copper and silver were discovered in the 17th century. The manufacture of steel has continued.

Hedemora ❹ claims to be the oldest town in Dalarna, with a charter dated 1459; its privileges as a market town go back even earlier than that, while parts of the church are 13th century. The locals have devised **Husbyringen**, a 56-km

BELOW:
local musician.

(35-mile) "museum trail" which you can take by car through the area northeast of the town to see a number of industrial archaeology sites.

Also worth visiting is **Säter** ❺, one of the seven best-preserved wooden towns in Sweden. Compared with Hedemora it is quite an upstart, with a town charter dated 1642. The ravines of the Säter Valley were created at the end of the Ice Age and are of interest for their flora.

Map on page 268

Traditional handicrafts

In the province that inspired the distinctive Dala horse, it is not surprising that the region is known for its abundance of carvers, potters, silversmiths, weavers, painters and bakers. This is a mecca for *hemslöjd* (crafts), all of which have their ancient roots in the farming culture. At **Säterglantan** ❻, 3 km (2 miles) south of Insjön lake, **Hemslöjdens Gård** (tel: 0247 402 73) offers a wide array of handicrafts as well as week-long courses. At **Nittsjö Keramik** (open daily Mon–Sat and Sun in June–July; tel: 0248 171 30), 6 km (4 miles) north of Rättvik, clay goods are made following a tradition that goes back 100 years.

The Dalahäst (Dala Horse), a more readily recognised Swedish symbol than the nation's flag.

Cross-country ski challenge

Dalarna's ski resorts are the principal winter tourist attraction, both for cross-country skiing and downhill. **Romme Alpin** ❼ is Sweden's most visited ski resort outside the proper mountain areas, with some 110,000 visitors annually. Together, **Sälen** ❽ and Idre, in northwest Dalarna, have almost half of Sweden's ski-lift facilities and Sälen is famous for being the starting point for a 53-mile (85-km) cross-country skiing race to **Mora** ❾: the Vasaloppet, the most popular sporting event in Sweden. ❑

BELOW: decorating the Maypole.

LARSSON

Carl Larsson (1853–1919) is Sweden's best-loved artist. The greatest source of inspiration for Larsson was the life he shared with his wife Karin, a textile artist, and their children at their home at **Sundborn** ❿ (open May–Sept: 10am–5pm; other times by appointment; entrance fee; tel: 023 600 53).

Carl Larsson was born to a poor family in Stockholm and during his youth he suffered all the deprivations of poverty, a period he later described as "hell on earth". He was determined to leave those hard times behind him and thus it was no coincidence that he became the artist who would best portray the happy, harmonious Swedish family, bathed in light, colour, and joyous celebration of home and hearth. In their wooden farmhouse, where Karin and Carl lived with their eight children, they created the simple interiors that were to influence so much of modern design. Stripped floors strewn with rugs, brightly painted furniture and hand-painted friezes were the key elements.

Larsson's paintings were strongly influenced by the local Dalarna folk-art traditions. In his autobiography, Larsson wrote, "My art: it is just like my home; there is no place there for fine furniture... it is simple, but harmonious. Nothing extravagant... just good, strong work."

CENTRAL SWEDEN

Brilliant blue lakes, rushing rivers, the mysterious outlines of mountains, and above all the space and silence beckon hikers and anglers to this untouched landscape

Map on page 272

Stockholm

Five provinces stretch across central Sweden. In the east are Gästrikland, Hälsingland and Medelpad, which share the long coastline known as Jungfrukusten (Virgin Coast). Further inland come Härjedalen and Jämtland, which stretch west to the Norwegian border, the land of lakes and coniferous or birch forests. Härjedalen marks the beginning of the great northern mountain ranges and the further north you go, the more dramatic the scenery.

The small province of **Gästrikland** has one major town, **Gävle ❶**, in the southeast corner of the region. Gävle was one of Sweden's great shipping towns, and the most treasured exhibit at the local museum, **Länsmuseet** (open Tues–Sun noon–4pm, Wed 4–9pm; entrance fee; tel 026 655 600), is the Björke boat, built in AD 100 and among the most notable finds in northern Europe.

Railway enthusiasts should make a point of visiting **Sveriges Järnvägsmuseum** (Railway Museum; open June–Aug: 10am–4pm; Sept–May: closed Mon; entrance fee; tel 026 144 615) on the outskirts of Gävle. The collection embraces 29 gleaming locomotives, 30 coaches and wagons and the 1874 coach of King Oscar II.

For children, **Furuviksparken** (open May–Aug: Mon–Fri 10am–4pm, Sat–Sun 10am–5pm; July: closes 6pm; entrance fee; tel: 026 199 000), 10 km

LEFT: thrill of the piste, western Jämtland.
BELOW: lynx, resident of northern Scandinavia.

THE INLAND RAILWAY

Atrip on the Inlandsbanan (Inland Railway) is an enjoyable way of seeing some of Sweden's most dramatic scenery. The route stretches through the Central Heartlands from Mora in Dalarna to Gällivare in Lapland.

The idea of building such a long railway through a harsh and inaccessible landscape was first promoted in 1894, but it was to take another 40 years of hard labour before it was completed. The 1,100-km (680-mile) line was finally inaugurated in Jokkmokk in Lapland on 6 August 1937, and a monument was erected to commemorate the event.

Today the train stops along the way so passengers can visit local artists and craftspeople or simply admire the views. Sometimes it has to halt to avoid running into herds of reindeer resting on the track. With luck, passengers may also spot elks or bears.

It is possible to make stopovers along the route and stay for a night or two in local towns and villages to do some walking in the mountains, or just enjoy the magnificent landscape. Various packages are available combining rail travel with hotel accommodation, or trekking. For more information contact Inlandsbanan AB, Box 561, SE-831 27 Östersund, Sweden. Tel: 063 108 672; fax: 063 108 670; www.inlandsbanan.se/england.html

(6 miles) south of Gavle, combines extensive zoological gardens with a variety of other attractions.

Grilled herring and potatoes with dill butter is a favourite dish all along the Virgin Coast. At **Bönan**, 10 km (6 miles) northeast of Gävle, visit **Engeltofta** to sample the town's famous golden-brown smoked herring, cured over spruce wood – in summer you can catch the boat over from Gävle.

Gästrikland is at the eastern end of the swathe of land which gave Sweden its early mining and smelting industries. Steam trains ply the 4.5 km (2¾ miles) from **Jädraås ❷**, northwest of Gavle, to **Tallås**. The railway is typical of those used to haul minerals or timber, and the coach used by King Oscar II (1872–1907) when he went hunting bears in Dalarna is still in service.

The good-time town

Follow the E4 north to **Söderhamn ❸**, the strarting point for boat trips around the archipelago. Söderhamn was founded in 1620 as an armoury for the Swedish army, and the museum is situated in part of what was the gun and rifle factory.

Around 120 years ago, when the timber industry was at its peak, **Hudiksvall ❹** had a reputation for high living. A reminder of the era is the town's theatre, opened in 1882. Hudiksvall also has a group of the best preserved 19th-century wooden buildings in Sweden, the **Fiskarstan**. About 10 km (6 miles) south, at **Iggesund**, is **Bruksmuseet** (open June–Aug: Mon–Sun 11am–5pm; Sept–May: by appointment; free; tel 0650 280 00), an impressive ironworks museum.

The interior of **Hälsingland** has the best scenery, particularly the valley of the Ljusnandalen river, which is laced with lakes along its entire length. West of **Ljusdal ❺**, where the Ljusnan meets the Hennan river, the forests begin.

*Relive the life of the charcoal burners of old at **Albert Vikstens Kojby** (Albert Viksten's Cabin Village) at **Lassekrog**, 40 km (25 miles) northwest of Ljusdal. Visitors can spend a night in a cabin and bake their own "charcoal bread" over the fire (tel: 0651 212 75).*

BELOW: folk dancers prepare for the Hälsingehambo festival at Järvsö.

Central Sweden

Dancing in the valley

About 12 km (7 miles) south of Ljusdal is **Järvsö ❻**, a small town in farming and forestry country. Once a year, its peaceful routine is broken by an unforgettable festival: the **Hälsingehambo**, a competitive event involving 3,000 folk dancers. At dawn on a July morning competitors in traditional costumes begin to dance to the tune *Hårgalåten* all the way up the Ljusnan valley, from **Bollnäs ❼** and Arbrå, to a grand finale 50 km (31 miles) away in Järvsö, in front of Stengård manor.

Bollnäs has a tradition of sweet-making. In 1919, in a little cottage at **Hållbo**, southeast of the town, Olof Käller invented a special peppermint sweet. Today you can still watch the sweets being boiled, rolled and stretched out in the old way at **Källers Karamellmuseum** (open July: 2–5pm; tel: 0278 800 23).

Of the mountains around Järvsö, **Gluggberget**, 515 metres (1,689 ft), has a viewing platform at the summit, while **Öjeberget**, 370 metres (1,314 ft), has the advantage that you can drive to the top.

To absorb this region you need to drive first along the minor road 30 km (18 miles) east from Järvsö to **Delsbo ❽**, which attracts large numbers of folk fiddlers for the annual **Delsbostämman**, and then on through Friggesund and Hassela and back to the coast. Surrounded by dark forests, this is **Dellenbygden**, rural Sweden at its best, and includes the Dellen lakes area, with boat trips and canoe trails, and walking trails.

Anglers' paradise

Together the provinces of **Härjedalen** and **Jämtland** are as big as Denmark, but with a population of only 135,000. To the east and southeast are extensive

Map on page 272

Snow scooters are the most practical form of transport in winter.

BELOW: the dense forests are a good hunting ground.

Map on page 272

The E14 from Östersund to the Norwegian frontier is an age-old route once used by pilgrims on their trek to the grave of St Olav at Trondheim (see page 205).

BELOW: Swedes take to their skis in the winter months. **RIGHT:** "fairy cottage" at Åre.

forests with hills, rivers and lakes. The higher mountains begin in Härjedalen. This heartland has four main rivers, the Ångermanälven, Indalsälven, Ljungan and Ljusnan, all well stocked with fish, especially trout and grayling. Perch, pike and whitefish are the most common in the forested regions, but many tarns have been stocked with trout. You may need a fishing permit, bought cheaply nearby or at the tourist offices. The vast tracts of near-uninhabited territory are also home to wildlife such as bears, wolverine, lynx and the ubiquitous elk.

When tourism was in its infancy, Härjedalen was one of the first Swedish provinces to attract skiers, who still return to pit their skills against its varied terrain, and come back in the summer for mountain walking. The scenery is impressive and, north of **Funäsdalen**, not far from the Norwegian border, the province has Sweden's highest road over the **Flatruet Plateau**, up to 1,000 metres (3,280 ft) high.

At the cross of the north–south route, Highway 45, and east–west, Highway 84, is **Sveg**, a small town but Härjedalen's largest at around 4,000 people. **Vemdalen ⑨**, 60 km (37 miles) northwest, has an eight-sided wooden church with a separate onion-domed bell tower. Beyond the village the road climbs between two mountains, **Vemdalsfjällen**, before entering Jämtland.

Jämtland is the biggest province in central Sweden, a huge territory of lakes, rivers and mountains. Its heart is the lake of **Storsjön**, the fifth largest stretch of inland water in the country, which is reputed to have its own monster, a Swedish version of Scotland's "Nessie". Present-day monster-seekers can take a cruise on the lake in the 1875 steamer *Thomee*. On the banks of Storsjön is Jämtland's largest town, **Östersund ⑩**, connected by a bridge to the beautiful island of **Frösön**. The island was home to the noted Swedish composer and critic Wilhelm Peterson-Berger (1867–1942). His most popular work, the opera *Arnljot*, is performed every summer on the island.

In Östersund, **Jamtli** (open July–Aug: 11am–5pm; Sept–June: closed Mon; entrance fee; tel 063 150 110), is one of biggest open-air museums in the country, comprising 18th- and 19th-century buildings including a *shieling* (summer farm), baker's cottage, smithy, and an old inn. The food in the café is recommended.

North of Storsjön, on the north bank of Lake Alsensjön at **Glösa ⑪** are a number of *hällristningar*, primitive rock carvings.

Mountains and canyons

In western Jämtland, the peaks rise up to nearly 1,800 metres (6,000 ft). It is a splendid area for trekking in summer and skiing in winter. Centuries ago, melting ice left many strange and unusual formations such as the deep canyon between the Drommen and Falkfångarfjället mountains. The region is also rich in waterfalls, such as **Ristafallet** near Hålland or **Storfallet**, northwest of Höglekardalen and **Tännforsen**, to the west of **Åre ⑫**.

Åre is a popular winter sports resort with a funicular railway that goes from the town centre part way up the local mountain, Åreskutan, and a cable car that continues almost to the summit. Lakes and mountains on every side make a superb view. ❏

NORTHERN SWEDEN

*Lapland, land of the Midnight Sun and home to the Sami, offers
a richly rewarding experience for the traveller. Fishing
villages and holiday islands dot the Bothnian coast*

Map
on page
278

I n the search for natural landscapes Lapland, which stretches across Northern Sweden and Finland, has become increasingly popular. The uplands, lakes and mountains of the region are among the finest in Europe, and although distances are great there are quality roads and a rail link. Anglers are attracted to the coast of Bottenviken (Gulf of Bothnia), the stretch of water that separates Sweden from Finland. There are excellent opportunities for both river and sea fishing along the coast; holiday-makers and sailors gravitate to its sheltered coves and islands.

The best way to absorb the immensity of Sweden's Lapland, is to take the inland Highway 45, from south to north. The first town across the border from Ångermanland is **Dorotea** ❶. Its claim to fame is the Dorotea Hotel, which is renowned for its cuisine. **Vilhelmina** ❷, 100 km (160 miles north) on the Ångermanälven river, is of greater interest. It is a well-preserved church village where travellers can find accommodation in its wooden houses.

West of Vilhelmina is the **Kittelfjäll** mountain region and the border with Norway. To the north lies an important road junction at **Storuman** ❸ where the 45 is bisected by the E12, known as the Blå Vägen (Blue Highway) because it follows a succession of lakes and the Umeälven river on its route from the east coast. It passes through **Lycksele** ❹ where there is a zoo, **Lycksele Djurpark** (open daily from 10am; closing times seasonal; entrance fee; tel: 0950 163 63), that has Nordic species including bear, elk, muskox, wolves and reindeer. From Storuman the E12 continues west through Tärnaby to Mo i Rana in Norway.

The Silver Road

From Slagnäs, on Highway 45, a secondary road leads through glorious lakeside scenery to **Arjeplog** ❺, one of Lapland's most interesting towns. The main attraction is the **Silvermuseet** (Silver Museum; open June–Aug: 9am–6pm; Sept–May: Mon–Fri 10am–4pm, Sat 10am–2pm; entrance fee; tel: 0961 612 90). Housed in an old school, it provides a fascinating insight into the region's history and the Sami people of Lapland. It owes its existence to Einar Wallqvist, "doctor of the Laplanders", who, besides his medical work, collected cultural objects. He established a museum which today has the finest collection of Sami silver in the world. Arjeplog's church is 17th-century and also worth a visit.

Arjeplog is roughly halfway along Highway 95, the Silvervägen (Silver Road) between Skellefteå in the east and Bodø on Norway's west coast. In the 17th century there were silver mines around **Nasafjäll** and the ore was transported, by reindeer and boat, to the east coast. Not until 1974 did it become an asphalted

LEFT: on top of the world in Lapland.
BELOW: Sami in traditional garb.

Northern Sweden

0 — 50 km E 6
0 — 50 miles

FINLAND

NORWAY

Lapland

Arctic Circle

Norrbotten

Perämeri

Bottenviken

Västerbotten

Jämtland

Ångermanland

Kåtölandet

Vaasa
Vasa

GULF OF
BOTHNIA

FINLAND

Medelpad

Karesuando 11
Kåarevaara 517
Palojoensuu
Raattama
Tepasto
Yli-Muonio
Muonio
Sirkka
Kittilä
Övre Soppero
Kangosjärvi
Äkäslompolo
Lainio
Kihlanki
Syväjärvi
Ylläsjärvi
Kurtakko
Lohiniva
Kolari
Ruokojärvi
Sieppijärvi
Meltaus
Pajala
Orajärvi
Konttajärvi
Pello
Raanujärvi
Mettosjärvi
Juoksenki
Mellakoski
Ylitornio
Karunki
Karungi
Kypasjärvi
Linkka
Haparanda
Tornio
Sangis
Kalix
Påläng
Ränéa
Haparanda
skärgårds   Sandskär
nat.park

Kistefjellet ▲1659
Skånland
Bjerkvik
Abisko   14
Torneträsk
E 10
Narvik
Riksgränsen
Abisko
nat.park
Ballangen
Kåtotjåkka
1991
98
Kurravaara
Jukkasjärvi   13
Vittangi
Kjöpsvik
Laukkuluspa   Kiruna
Kebnekaise
2117   Nikkaluokta   12
Kaalasjärvi
Kalixälven
Svappavaara
Masugnsbyn
Junosuando
Oppeid
Alitoaivi
1584
Skaulo
Nillvaara
Ullatti
Gautåive
1578
Stora
Sjöfallets
nationalpark
Satihaure
Kaitumjaure
45
Morsvikbotn
Sarektjåkkå
Padjelanta   2090 ▲
Kebnats
Sjöfallet
bryggan
Ruokto
Malmberget
Gällivare   10
Vastenjaure
Sareks
Stora
Lulevatten
820 ▲
Dundret
Hakkas
Ängesån
Rago
nat.park
Virihaure
nationalpark
Pårte
▲2006
Muddus
nat.park   9
Porjus
E 10
Nattavaara
Tjaktjajaure
Löding
Fauske
Isakkok Tarrekaise
1565   1829
Kvikkjokk
Skalka
Jokkmokk   8
Stora
Luleälven
Murjek
Råneälven
Vuottas
Svartbyn
Överkalix   25
Straumen
Rognan
Pieskehaure
Saggat
Karatj
Pärlälven
Vuollerim
Pålkem
Morjärv
Balvatnet
Mavasjaure
Tjeggelvas
Lakaträsk
Niemisel
Harads
Tjidtjakgaise
1587   Riebnes
Vuolvojaure
Puottaure
97
Luleälven
Boden   23
Ränéa
NORWAY
Pieljekaise
nat.park
Jakkvik
Gittun
Hornavan
Storforshei
Junkerfjellet
1459
Jutis
Laisvall
Storlaisan
Galtisbuouda
▲800
Arjeplog
45
Piteälven
Vidsel
Storforsen
Gammelstad
Älvsbyn
Luleå
Hertsön   22
Mo i Rana
Rerrogaise
1611
Björkfjället
Laisälven
Uddjaure
Moskosel
Vistheden
Sikfors
Junkön
Germandön
Rösvik
Överuman
N Storfjället
1767
Vindelälven
Ammarnäs
Storavan
Auktsjaur
Arvidsjaur   7
Kolerträsk
Långträsk
Piteå   21
Vargön
Mellerstön
Tärnaby
S Storfjället
1267
Fjällsjönäs
Storvindeln
Slagnäs
Abborrträsk
Fällfors
Åbyn
Byske
Forsmark
Storjuktan
Sorsele
Gargnäs
Skellefteälven
Malå
Glommersträsk
Jörn
95
Boliden
Skellefteå
Bureå
Abelvattnet
Gardiken
Gardfjället
1372
Dikanäs
Storuman
Gubbträsk
Björksele
Norsjö
E 4
Kittelfjäll
Daikanvik
Storuman   3
Gunnarn
Norsjön
Rusksele
Västerbotten
Åsträsk
Burträsk
Lövånger
Ransarn
Marsfjällen
Volmsjön
Kultsjön
Blåviken
Vindelälven
Sikån
Bygdeträsket
Klimpfjäll
1589
Malgomaj
45
Pautrask
Lycksele   4
Åmsele
Lidsjön
Robertsfors
Borgfjällen
1477
Vilhelmina   2
Norrbäck
Råberg
Hällnäs
Botsmark
Bygdeå
Larsmo
Luotoa
Jakobstad
Pietarsaari
Stöttingfjället
Åttonträsk
Siksjö
Skarda
E 12
Grand
Vindelen
E 4
Sand
Sävar
Nykarleby
Uusikaarlepyy
Längsele
Ångermanälven
Ormsjön
Åsele
92
Fredrika
Vännäs   Umeå   20
Holmön
Mickelsörarna
Mikkelinsaaret
Jämtland
Fiskåfjället
1198
Tåsjön
Dorotea   1
Svanabyn
Björnlandets
nat.park
Tegelträsk
Bjurholm
Nyåker
Hörnefors
Hössjö
Holmsund
Nordli
Lidsjöberg
Hoting
Hälla
Nyliden
Gideälven
Maxmo
Maksamaa
Flåsjön
Dragan
Rossön
Solberg
Björna
Lögdeå
Nordmaling
Jule
Stor-Ersfjället
919
Strömsund
Junsele
Ångermanland
Bredbyn
Husum
Vaasa
Vasa
Gloppet
Lahia   3
Rönnöfors
Ramsele
Hammerdal
90
Skorped
Örnsköldsvik   19
Bergö
Malax
Maalahti
Lillholmsjö
Boberg
Bjästa
Halsön
8
Solleftea
Ångermanälven
Skuleberget
295
Skuleskogen
nat.park   18
Korsnäs
Jürva
Trondheim
Krokom
Stugun
Bispgården
Forsmo
Docksta
Nordingrå
Peninsula   17
GULF OF
BOTHNIA
Närpes
Närpiö
Åre
Järpen
E 14
Frösön
Stugsjön
Östersund
Kälarne
Ytterlännäs
Kramfors
Visåsen
Sandö   16
Kaskinen
Kaskö
Kristinestad
Kristiinankaupunki
Hallen
Brunflo
E 14
Gällö
Nordanå
Hemsön
Härnösand   15
Sideby
Siipyy
Lunndörrsfjällen
1527
Kövra
45
Bräcke
Medelpad
Sundsvall

highway opening up an area of outstanding beauty. There are magnificent views from Galtisbuouda, 800 metres (2,620 ft) high, just north of Arjeplog.

West of Arjeplog at **Laisvall** ❻ is **Laisvallsgruvan** (July: guided tours Tues and Thur; no children under 15; entrance fee; tel: 0920 202 62), the biggest lead mine in Europe.

Arvidsjaur ❼, once a trading post, now a junction of roads and railways, has the atmosphere of a frontier town. The major attraction is **Lappstaden** (July: guided tours; tel: 0960 175 00), the oldest surviving example of a Sami village, with *kåtor*, tent-shaped wooden huts, and *härbren*, wooden storehouses. In summer, Arvidsjaur is a tourist centre and in winter, when it is intensely cold, both Arjeplog and Arvidsjaur are taken over by the motor industry to test products in sub-zero temperatures.

Map on page 278

Across the Arctic Circle

The **Arctic Circle** is 156 km (97 miles) north of Arvidsjaur and you can buy a certificate to prove you crossed the line at a nearby café. Further north is **Jokkmokk** ❽, the biggest *kommun* (municipal district) in Sweden covering an area of 19,425 sq km (7,500 sq miles) with a population of 7,000.

Jokkmokk is a centre for the Sami culture and in summer you can see nomadic Sami here. An annual outdoor winter market in February attracts thousands of people, although temperatures can drop to –35°C (–31°F). First held in 1605, the market soon became a meeting place for the Sami and merchants from the coastal communities. Today it is as much a social occasion as an opportunity to trade and events such as weddings and baptisms take place. The **Ajtte Svenskt Fjäll-och Samemuseum** (Swedish Mountain and Sami Museum; open June–Aug: 9am–6pm; Sept–May: times vary; entrance fee; tel: 0971 170 70) portrays the local culture as well as the mountain world, placing mankind in a natural, cultural and ecological perspective.

Highway 45 continues through a sparsely populated area to **Porjus** ❾, a major centre for hydroelectric power. **Stora Sjöfallet**, the largest waterfall in Sweden, is 180 km (112 miles) west of Porjus. To the east of the town is a wild area, **Muddus National Park** (certain areas are closed during the breeding season, mid-Mar–July; tel: 0971 121 40), home of bear, lynx and wolverine. **Dundret Mountain**, 820 metres (2,690 ft) high, northeast of the park, is a bustling holiday centre where you can ride, walk, windsurf, fish, play golf, go white-water rafting, or pan for gold. See the Midnight Sun in June and July from the summit.

Exploring Muddus National Park.

BELOW: the altar at Jukkasjärvi church shows Sami influences.

Gällivare

Gällivare ❿ (pop. 22,000), and its twin town, Malmberget, owe their growth to the discovery of iron ore. Gällivare is the end of the railway line, Inlandsbanan *(see box, page 271)*, that follows Highway 45 north from Östersund. It is a popular tourist route and jumping-off point for treks into the vast region that includes the Padjelanta and Stora Sjöfallet national parks. The town itself has a mining museum and an 18th-century Sami church. Beyond Gällivare, the 45 joins the E10 and continues north to **Svappavaara**, a former mining

Wolverines thrive in the national parks of Sweden's far north.

centre, and **Karesuando** , near the Finnish frontier. Place names in Sweden's northern Lapland owe more to Finnish than to Swedish. In Kiruna, for example, a fifth of the population are Finnish immigrants.

The most northerly church in Sweden can be found in Karesuando which also has the lowest average winter temperatures and Sweden's only tundra. From the top of **Kaarevaara Mountain**, 517 metres (1,696 ft) high, you can see three countries: Sweden, Finland and Norway.

Beyond Svappavaara, the E10 swings northwest to **Kiruna** (pop. 22,000). Mining began here in 1900 and is still the main industry. The **Kirunavaara Mine** is the world's largest deep mine with 400 km (250 miles) of underground roadways. In summer visitors can tour it by bus. With the decline in mining, Kiruna has turned to tourism and scientific research. There is a rocket testing station on the banks of the Vittangi river at Esrange. For a glimpse of Sami life and history, visit **Samegård** (open June–Sept: daily 8am–6pm; entrance fee. Oct–May: Mon–Fri 8am–4pm).

Ice Hotel

East of Kiruna, **Jukkasjärvi** has acquired fame for its Ice Hotel, which is rebuilt every winter. Activities in the region include dog-sledging in the snow-covered wilderness or white-water rafting in summer.

The E10 (Nordkalottvägen), from Kiruna via the Norwegian frontier to Narvik penetrates one of Europe's last wilderness areas. The mountains south-west of the highway can only be reached on foot or by pony and it is here that **Kebnekaise**, Sweden's highest peak at 2,117 metres (6,945 ft), reigns supreme. **Abisko** , 150 km (93 miles) from Kiruna, is a popular base from which to set

BELOW: creating art out of ice.

FISHING IN THE FAR NORTH

There is nothing quite like fishing against the impressive backdrop of Sweden's mountains. Creeping silently along a river bank and trying to tempt a shy trout or grayling to the fly is an unforgettable experience. Fishing is well organised in the north. If you are driving along the Northeast Coast there are plenty of opportunities to fish en route, particularly in the unspoilt Piteälven, Kalixälven and Torneälven rivers; just ask at the nearest tourist office.

Further afield, the Tjuonajokk fishing camp on the Kaitumälven river in northwest Lapland is renowned for its grayling fishing. South from there is the Miekak fishing camp, 100 km (60 miles) northwest of Arjeplog (accessible by helicopter from Tjärnberg at Silvervägen, or by snowmobile in winter from Silvervägen), providing arguably the best char fishing in Lapland. At the northernmost extremity of Sweden the fishing centre on Rostojaure lake is renowned for its char and grayling. It is accessible in summer only by helicopter.

Not surprisingly, transport can be expensive, but the cost of fishing permits is relatively low compared with other countries. Permits can be bought at a number of outlets, including tourist offices and some fuel stations. The best month for fishing is usually August.

out along the **Kungsleden** (King's Trail) which enables even inexperienced walkers to see the mountains.

The High Coast

For the most part the Bottenviken (Gulf of Bothnia) coastline is low lying and ranges from polished rock to sand and shingle beaches. The major towns along the coast have grown up from trading settlements. Islands form an almost continuous archipelago – a playground for holidaymakers to indulge the Swedish passion for sailing and the sea. Inland, lakes provide tranquil blue oases in the dense forests.

Starting in the south, the main coastal town of Ångermanland is **Härnösand** ⓕ, which is modern except for the town hall, the Domkyrkan (cathedral) and some 18th-century wooden houses. Overlooking the harbour at Murberget there is a large open-air historical museum (open June–Aug: daily 11am–5pm; free).

Travelling north, the Höga Kusten (High Coast) Bridge, modelled partly on San Francisco's Golden Gate Bridge, is an impressive structure, 1.8 km (1.1 miles) long. It has a restaurant and visitor centre. Northwest of Härnösand, is **Kramfors** ⓖ, a leading centre for accordionists. The 13th-century church, near **Ytterlännäs** on Highway 90, is an antiquarian wonder.

The heart of the High Coast is the **Nordingrå Peninsula** ⓗ, where the bedrock is an intense red *rapakivi* granite. Scenic treasures include **Omne bay**, the villages of **Måviken** and **Norrfällsviken**, and the view from the church over Vagsfjärden. **Bönhamn** is a tiny place among the rocks, where **Arne's Sjöbod** is renowned for fresh fish and mashed potatoes and **Café Mannaminne**, near **Häggvik**, provides home-baked delicacies, handicrafts and musical

Map on page 278

TIP

The mosquitoes are rapacious in summer in northern Sweden, so don't forget to pack insect repellent.

BELOW: Bönhamn, on the High Coast.

Map on page 278

A traditional Sami hut made from wood and reindeer skins.

BELOW: catch of the day.
RIGHT: winter scene in the frozen north.

evenings. The **Höga Kusten walk**, 25 km (16 miles), starts at Fjordbotten with bathing places at Storsand, Norrfällsviken, Hörsång and Noraström.

Between the E4 and the coast lies **Skuleskogen National Park** ⑱ (open all year), which is noted for its rare birds and mammals.

Örnsköldsvik ⑲, known as Övik, is an industrial town and one of Sweden's leading winter sports areas, particularly for ice hockey and ski jumping. The islands offshore include **Södra Ulvön** with one of the oldest fishermen's chapels in Sweden; **Trysunda**, a favourite with the sailing fraternity; and **Norra Ulvön**, accessible by boat from Docksta and ferry from Trysunda.

Umeå ⑳ is the principal town of Västerbotten. The main attraction here is **Gammlia Friluftsmuseum**, an open-air museum (open July–Aug: daily 10am–5pm), which includes the provincial museum of Sami culture (open July–Aug: Mon-Fri 10am–5pm, Sat, Sun: 10am–4pm; Sept–June: Tues–Fri 10am–4pm, Sat noon–4pm, Sun noon–5pm, closed Mon; tel: 090 171800).

Continuing north, **Piteå** ㉑ can come as a culture shock after the rural landscape. Some narrow lanes and wooden houses remain from the 17th century but today it is an industrial centre with timber, paper and pulp industries and a large holiday resort. Norwegians come in flocks from their calm northern fjords.

From Piteå, the road leads northwest through Älvsbyn to Bredsel and **Storforsen**, Europe's highest natural waterfall with a 81-metre (265-ft) drop.

World Heritage site

Luleå ㉒, the most northerly major town in Sweden, was moved 10 km (6 miles) by the king in 1649 and stands now at the mouth of the Luleälven river. The old church town, **Gammelstad**, was left on its original site and is a fascinating place to visit with its 400 red-painted cottages and a 15th-century church, still used on important religious occasions. The town is a UNESCO World Heritage site. Beside the original harbour there is an open-air museum, **Friluftsmuseet Hägnan** (open all year; entrance free; tel: 0920 29 35 81), which includes a farming hayshed typical of Norrbotten. The **Norrbotten Museum** (open Mon–Fri 10am–4pm, Sat–Sun noon–4pm; entrance free; tel: 0920 24 35 00) in Hermelin Park provides a picture of the province and has Sami artefacts.

Boden ㉓, 35 km (22 miles) inland from Luleå on the Luleälven river, is the largest garrison town in Sweden. At the end of the 19th century, it was referred to as "one of the strongest fortresses of Europe – that is to say, in the whole world". The **Garnisonsmuseet** (Garrison Museum; open June–Aug: daily 11am–4pm) portrays 400 years of Sweden's military history.

Sweden's easternmost town, **Haparanda** ㉔, was built opposite Finnish Tornio on the Torneälven river, which forms the border between the two countries.

Road 400 goes north along the river on the Swedish side into the Tornedalen valley to the Kukkolaforsen waterfall. West of the falls, on the Kalixälven river, is **Överkalix** ㉕ with fine views from the top of Brännaberget. At the end of June, this is the place to come and see the spectacular tradition of netting whitefish and salmon. ❏

FINLAND

The urban scene may have undergone a transformation, but the serenity of Finland's lakes and forests remains timeless

From the moment your plane lands at Helsinki airport you are confronted with a scramble for mobile phones. Reserved and reticent Finns? You'd never guess it from the constant telephone prattle. The stereotype of the hesitant, sullen Finn was always questionable, but now Finns are really starting to open up.

In the late 20th century Finland's capital, Helsinki, underwent rapid expansion, draining the enormous, sparsely populated rural areas and maturing into a distinctive and vibrant metropolis with its own identity. Startling new buildings, such as the weird and wonderful Kiasma (Museum of Contemporary Art) and the gleaming National Opera, transformed the city's silhouette; restaurants multiplied; and pavement cafés now open at the first glimpse of spring sunshine, bringing life and colour to the streets.

By the time they celebrated Helsinki's 450th birthday and its status of European City of Culture in 2000, the city's residents had found their place in the European scheme of things. Technological innovations, from the ubiquitous phones to state-of-the-art medical equipment and progressive Internet services, have begun to catch up on, and even overtake, Finland's still substantial pulp and paper industry in terms of economic prestige and significance.

For a country of 5 million people, Finland has produced an astonishing number of architects, artists, sculptors and designers – and it shows. In Helsinki, in particular, almost every corner reveals an intriguing detail: an elegantly carved façade, a statue, a curved window. In cities such as Turku or Porvoo, where the Swedish influence was strongest, some of the oldest buildings remain. Cultural festivals and artistic events are commonplace.

Finland has seemingly endless expanses of untouched landscape, crossed by straight roads running between tall trees. Nobody has managed to count with any degree of certainty how many lakes and islands there are in the country – almost enough, it seems, for every Finnish family to have an island or lake of its own, with plenty of space for visitors, too. No wonder an ideal Finnish summer is based on a waterside wooden cabin and nearby sauna house. With some fishing, swimming, and a small boat, this is Finnish perfection.

As the road heads north, you scarcely realise at first that the rolling farmland of the south has moved into boundless forests and that, gradually, the dark green gives way to the peat and tundra of Lapland. This is the territory of reindeer, bear, wolf, elk and lynx. Along the west coast of the Gulf of Bothnia, the beaches and surprisingly warm waters are ripe for exploration. ❑

PRECEDING PAGES: Sami life as captured by the Sami artist Alariesto; with the onset of winter, artists turn their hand to making ice sculptures; reindeer transport. **LEFT:** lakeside sauna near the town of Jyväskylä.

THE FINNS

*Cool, but not humourless, the innovative Finns have fought hard
to preserve their identity and move with the times*

People tend mistakenly to describe Finns and their Scandinavian neighbours as cold characters when, in fact, their demeanour can be better described as cool and calm. When one spends some time with Finns in either a social situation or doing business, their dry sense of humour starts to emerge – and it doesn't necessarily need the lubrication of alcohol to loosen things up. Though, of course, the Finns are more at ease away from the work place, in the comfort of their weekend retreat in the country or relaxing in a pub or café.

Finland has come of age since it became a member of the European Union in 1995, taking a more visible, if not more vocal stance. It served a six-month EU presidency in 1999 and Helsinki was chosen as a European Cultural Capital for 2000, attracting international recognition as a city to visit rather than just a stopover en route to Russia or other Scandinavian destinations. Helsinki has taken on a more colourful demeanour in recent years, attributable in part to Finland's more relaxed policy towards immigration, which has boosted the foreign population to nearly 5 percent, many of whom are from Vietnam and Senegal.

Well-travelled Finns have long considered themselves cosmopolitan, but they were in the minority. Many younger Finns, shedding their parents' unease, go on to study, work and travel abroad, as well as welcoming all things foreign to Finland.

City versus country

For a traditionally rural country, Finland is becoming more urbanised. Some 80 percent of Finns live on 2 percent of the land. Domestic emigration is accelerating – Finns are moving from small towns to greater Helsinki, Tampere, Turku and Oulu, although many Helsinki business types are relocating to other countries with warmer climates and lower taxes. The much publicised "*etäyöy*" (distance working via the Internet) has its attractions, but most people still try to escape to the cities.

Nature is sacred

The Finnish state of mind owes a lot to the land itself and the abundance of lakes and forests:

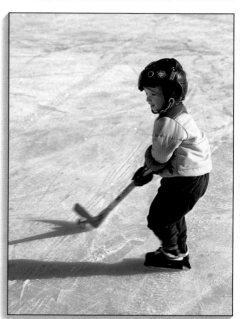

FINLAND: THE ESSENTIALS

Population 5.2 million.
Capital Helsinki (pop. 547,000).
Notable towns Turku, Tampere, Rovaniemi, Oulu.
Climate Northern winters average −13°C (9°F); in the south −5°C (23°F). Summer temperatures average 20°C (68°F).
Top museums Kiasma, Helsinki; Alvar Aalto Museo, Jyväskylä; Suomen Lasimuseo (Finnish Glass), Riihimäki.
Famous homes Hvitträsk (Saarinen); Ainola (Sibelius).
Top events Helsinki Festival; Savonlinna Opera Festival.
Natural wonders Around 190,000 lakes.
Outdoor activities Water sports, hiking, fishing, skiing.
Tourist information www.mek.fi

LEFT: Thick furs protect the Sami against winter cold.
RIGHT: ice hockey, Finland's national sport. Champions start training at an early age.

more than 400,000 Finns own a plot of forest and everyone has the right of access to the land, which is why Finns take to the woods every summer. Nature is sacred and full of mystery as well as a place of renewal and preparation for the cold, dark months to follow. Which causes one to contemplate whether Finns are manic-depressive by nature, as more suicides are committed after the springtime thaw.

SPORTING PROWESS

As a nation, Finns are great lovers of the outdoors and of sport, and some young Finns, following in the footsteps of the great Finnish runner Paavo Nurmi, live for little else but their athletic activities.

Sisu is a word synonymous with the Finnish character. It mean guts or fortitude, a descrip-

Russian regime more than 100 years ago and being long dominated by Sweden. These days Finns are feeling more self-confident. Although they may not forget, they are willing to forgive: across the eastern border, Finnish trucks carry emergency assistance to the struggling Russians who not so long ago were dictating internal issues within Finland.

The Finns are well used to change; it is so deep-rooted in the Finnish soul that the nation accepts almost any new innovation with little resistance, be it

tion which aptly fits the heroic, patriotic and noble warriors of Finland's national epic, the *Kalevala*. Yet, in private, these strong men are shy and uncertain, and have great difficulty in waxing poetic when they set out to woo and win the girl. The women, in contrast, are strongheaded, matriarchal, and family-orientated. Perhaps this is why Finland has had so many women in political power in recent years, including their latest president, Tarja Halonen, who was elected for a six-year term in 2000.

No more identity crisis

In the past, Finland struggled to keep its identity, defending its language against the

the Euro, or the latest technological advances in mobile phones.

Change is most visible in nature. With spring in the air everything grows rapidly, the summer months are light and hot, then winter arrives and for a few weeks around the solstice nature stops, frozen, for a pause. Finns prepare for Christmas and their New Year's resolutions. The big wheel keeps turning, another year means new opportunities for change. "The only constant is change," Finns will tell anyone who asks, but despite this, traditions are never completely forgotten.

Indeed, there are so many paradoxes in the Finnish character that it would be hard to convince the sceptical foreigner that there isn't more than a dash of schizophrenia in the national psyche. For every ranting drunk, there's a raving teetotaller. For every patriotic Finn, there's one who leaves as soon as he can afford the fare, never to return. For every shrinking violet, there's an arrogant, cigar-smoking bombast who's never happier than when showing off his possessions and singing his own praises.

Nordic links

The "typical Finn" is the result of a genetic combination that is 75 percent identical to that whose ancestors merged with the gargantuan Vikings. Most Finns are fair-haired (though, overall, Finns are the "darkest" of the Scandinavians). Some of the most famous Finns are sportsmen and women, taking advantage of their generally strong and healthy physiques.

Finns have entered the 21st century with both style and class. By nature, they are peace-makers. At war, Finns tend to lose, but at peace, Finns certainly seem to be winning. Pinning down their personality is not easy, but if you go to Finland with preconceived stereotypes at the ready, you will no doubt be able to satisfy any or all of them. ❏

of other Scandinavians, but 25 percent is thought to be derived from tribes that migrated to Finland from east of the Ural Mountains. This more Oriental strain accounts for certain physical traits that set Finns apart from their Nordic neighbours – finely pronounced cheekbones and quite small slatey-grey or blue eyes.

Laplanders tend to be smaller in stature and sturdily built. Karelians are stockier and have sallower complexions. They are slightly smaller in stature than people from the west coast,

LEFT: with the first sign of summer, cafés spill out onto Helsinki's streets and squares.
ABOVE: enjoying a crisp winter's day in Lapland.

ROMANY GYPSIES

One of the oldest groups in Finland who are not ethnic Finns are the Romany gypsies, whose womenfolk are instantly recognisable by their elaborate embroidered lace blouses and voluminous skirts. Although today most speak only Finnish, few have intermarried, so their dark good looks stand out against fairer Finns.

Most gypsies are no longer nomadic and live instead in houses and flats, subsidised by the government. Some families still tend to wander, especially in autumn, from one harvest festival to another. Little horse-trading is done these days, however, and the gypsies' appearance at these fairs is little more than a vestige of nostagia.

Finland

50 miles

50 km

Pukkisaaret
Bockholmarna

Seurasaarentie

Fö15sundet

Seurasaarensalmi

MEILAHDEN PUISTO

Humallahti
Hummelviken

Ulkomuseo
★ (Open-Air Museum)

Seurasaari
Fölisön

Variskari
Kråkören

Rajasaari
Råholmen

KAUPUNGIN
PUUTARHA

Messeniuksenk

Olympia-
stadion

Urheilukatu

M. Lybeckink

Tavaststjernank

Stenbackinkatu

Topeliuksenkatu

Nordenskjöldinkatu

Mannerheimintie

Idrottsgatan

KAUPUNGIN
TALVIPUUTARHA

Tahkontie

Paavo Nurmen tie

Mäntymäent

Linnankoskenkatu

Humalistonkatu

Eino Leinon k.

Rajasaarent.

SIBELIUKSEN
PUISTO ③③

Merikannontie

Topeliuksenkatu

Töölönkatu

Runeberginkatu

Helsinginkatu

Sibeliusmonumentti

Sibeliuksenk.

Suomen
Kansallisooppera
(Finnish National O
Hou.

⑧

TAKA-TÖÖLÖ
BORTRE TÖLÖ

Mechelininkatu

Vaskiniemi

Kivelänk

Runebergsgatan

Mannerheimintie

Töölönla
Tölövike.

Kesäk.

Pohj. Hesperiankatu

Norra Hesperiagatan
Södra Hesperiagatan

Eläinen Hesperiankatu

Finlandiatalo
(Finlandia Hall)

Apollonk.

⑦

Taivalluoto
Edesgrundet

Kansallismuseo
(National Museum)

⑥

Museokatu

Hakasalmi Villa

Seurasaarenselkä
Fölisöfjärden

Mechelingatan

Hietaniemenkatu

Caloniuk.k

Oksasenkatu

Museokatu

Tunturik.

Tunturik.

Nervanderinkatu

Temppelik.

Runeberginkatu

Eduskuntata
(Parliament Buil

⑤

Porsas
Grisen

Hiekkarannantie

Hietaniemenkatu

Kremanatorinte

Sammonk.

⑨

Temppelinaukion
kirkko

Pieni-Porsas
Lilla Grisen

Ourit
Órarna

HIETANIEMEN
HAUTAUSMAA †

Sandudd

Sanduddsgatan

Luonnontieteellinen Museo
(Natural History Museum)

Perhonk.

Hietaniemenk

Runebergsgatan

Tennispalatsi

④

Lapinlahti
Lappviken

Eteläinen Hesperiankatu

Leppäsuonk

Malminkatu

Kamppi

Fredrikinkatu

Pohj. Rautatiekatu

Lapinlahdenk.

Lapinlahdenk

Salomonk.

Mustasaari

Västerleden

Länsiväylä

SALMISAARI
SUNDHOLMEN

Pässink.

Lapinlahdentie

Mechelininkatu

Lastenk.

Ruoholahdenk

Abrahamink

Eerikink

Kalevank

Ruoholahdengatan

Pohjoiskaari

Norrsvängen

Porkkalankatu

Porkalagatan

Arenranta

Spaarens.

Suomen Valokuvataiteen
museo & Teatterimuseo
(Photography &
Theatre Museums)
⑬

Östersjögatan

Ruoholahti ⓜ

Kellosaarenk.

Selkämerenk.

Santakatu

Ruoholahdenp.

Hietalahdentori
(Hietalahti Market)

㉕

Sinebrychoffin
museo

PUNAVUOF
RÖDBERGE

Pungvuor

ⓜ Kaisaniemi

Kansallisarkisto
(National Archives)

Vironkatu

Rauhankatu

Fredsgatan

Siltasaarenk.

Tammasaarenranta

Jaalaranta

Messityönk.

Lavapajankatu

Skeppsgossegatan

Hietalahti
Sandviken

Fabianinkatu

Unionink

Unioninkatu

Spelmanninkatu

Mariankatu

Maariankatu

Riktarinkatu

Selkämerenk.

Jaalaranta

Hietalahdenranta

Pinlitanikuja

RUOHOLAHTI
GRÄSVIKEN

Yliopiston kirjasto
(University Library)

Kirkkokatu

Kyrkogatan

Säätytalo
(House of Estates)

Tuomiokirkko
(Cathedral)

㉑

KRUUNUNHAKA
KRONOHAGEN

Vuorikatu

Yliopistonkatu

Regeringsgatan
Senaatintori

Hallituskatu

Ritarihuone
(House of Nobility)

Meritullintori
(Sjötullstorget)

Mattaankuja

Läntinen vaihdekatu
Itäinen vaihdekatu

Läntinen Tarmonk

MUNKKISAARI
MUNKHOLMEN

Hyl. Munkkis. k.

Munkkisaarenk

Munkkisaarenk

Hernesaarenk.

Kluuvikatu

Yliopisto
(University)

Aleksanteri II ⭐ ⑳

Alexandersgatan

Valtioneuvoston linna
(Council of State)

Aleksanterinkatu

Bockin talo
(Bock House)

Sederholmin talo
(Sederholm House)

Katariinank

Helenank.

Uspenskin
katedraali

㉓

Poseidoninkuja

LÄNSISATAMA
VÄSTRA HAMNEN

Länsi-
terminaali

Kaupungin
matkailutoimisto
(Helsinki Information Office)

⑮ ⓘ

Kaupungintalo
(City Hall)

⑱

Presidentinlinna
(Presidential Palace)

⑲

KATAJANOKKA
SKATUDDEN

HERNESAARI
ÁRTHOLMEN

Hernesaarenkatu

Hernesaarenranta

Pohjoisesplanadi

Norra   Esplanaden

Kappeli

⑯

Kauppatori
Salutorget

⑰

Kanavakatu

Katajanokan laituri

Kalliosaarenkuja

Matasalmenk.

Matasalmenk

J.L.
Runeberg

⑭

ESPLANADIN
PUISTO

Fabianinkatu

Havis
Amanda

Obeliski Keisarinnan kivi
(Czarinas Obelisk)

Kanavaterminaali

Tulli-ja
Pakkahuone
(Customs)

㉔

Matkailun edistämiskeskus
(Finnish Tourist Board) ⓘ

KAARTINKAUPUNKI
GARDESSTADEN

Etelärana

Södra kajen

Vanha Kauppahalli
(Old Market Hall)

Eteläsatama
Södra hamnen

Tallinn

0   200 m

0   200 yds

P. makasiinikatu

Kasarmikatu

Kasarmitori
(Kaserntorget)

E. makasiinikatu

Suomenlinna, Korkeasaari

Tallinn

⑰ Pihlajasaari

Työväen kotimuseo
(Museum of Worker Housing)

Linnanmäki

Porvoonk.

HARJU
ÅS

Fleminginkatu

Vaasankatu

Harjukatu

L.Brahenk.

Sturegy

Sturenkatu

Helsingegatan

Sörnäinen

M

Lautatarhank.

Pääskylänkatu

Työpajakatu

Varastokatu

Itäväylä

Österleden

N

0   500 m
0   500 yds

Helsinginkatu

Vilhonvuorenk.

Sörnäs strandvägen

SÖRNÄINEN
SÖRNÄS

SÖRNÄINEN
SÖRNÄS

M

Helsingkatu

Aippikatu

Kaarlenkatu

Franzenin k.

Torkkelinkatu

Penger katu

Tavastvägen

Käenkuja

Sörnäs Parrukatu

Kaasutehtaankt.

Hopeasalmi
Silversundet

Ensi linja

Wallininkatu

Castreninkatu

Neljäs linja

Vides linja

Agricolank.

Linnaisten rantatie

Hanasaarenranta

SOMPASAARI
SOMPARN

Sompasaarensalmi
Sumparssundet

MUSTIKKAMAA
BLÅBÄRSLANDET

Kolmas linja

Toinen linja

KALLIO
BERGHÄLL

Siltasaarenkatu

Linja

Kaupunginteatteri
(City Theatre)
Djurgårdsvägen

Hämeentie

Näkinkuja

HANASAARI
HANAHOLMEN

Mustikkamaansalmi
Blåbärssundet

Eläintarhanlahti
Djurgårdsviken

Hakaniemi

Hakan ranta

Näkinsilta

MERIHAKA
HAVSHAGEN

Hagnäskajen

Korkeasaaren
eläintarha
(Zoo)

31

KORKEASAARI
HÖGHOLMEN

Palosaari
Paloholmen

SANIEMI
JSANIEMI

Säästöp. ranta

M

Hakaniemen torik.

Hakaniemenranta

Pitkänsillanrt.

HAKANIEMI
HAGNÄS

Kaisaniemenranta

Sittavuorenranta

Sörnäisten satama
Sörnäs Hamnen

Vrakholmssundet

Kaisaniemenranta

Töölönlahdenk.

KASVITIETEELLINEN
PUUTARHA
(UNIVERSITY BOTANICAL
GARDENS)

Kristianink.

Ruiskumestarin talo
(Burgher's House)

Sotamuseo
(Military Museum)

Norra kajen

Tervasaarenkannas

Tervasaari
Tjärholmen

Pohjoissatama
Norra Hamnen

Hylkysaarensalmi

Hylkysaari
Vrakholmen

allonki

Töölönlahdenk.

Rautatieasema
(Railway Station)

Kiasma   1
G.E. Mannerheim

Postik.
sipalatsi
ss Palace)

M Rautatientori

Kaivokatu

Kaisaniemi

Liisankatu

Maneesik.

Elisabetsgatan

Vironk.

Rauhankatu

Maurink.

Mariank.

Kristianink.

Mertullinkatu

Norra kajen

Ateneum   2
(National Gallery)

Aleksanterinkatu

Yliopistonkatu

Tuomiokirkko

Yliopisto

Senaatintori

Rltarik.

Kirkkokatu

KRUUNUNHAKA
KRONOHAGEN

Stockmann   10
Pohjoisesplanadi

Svenska   12
teatern
(Swedish Theatre)

Vanha
kirkko

Aleksanterinkatu

Alexandersgatan

Norra Esplanaden

ESPLANADIN PUISTO

Eteläesplanadi

Eteläranta

Presidentinlinna

Uspenskin
katedraali

Laivastokatu

Luotsikatu

Kaup.k.

Kanavakatu

Katajanokankatu

Kruunuvuorenkatu

Vyökatu

Kanalgatan

Merikasarmi
(Ex-Naval Barracks)

Maringatan

Merikasarmink.

Mansk.

Annik. Skatuddsstranden

KATAJANOKKA
SKATUDDEN

Uudenmaankatu

Erottajankatu

Korkeavuorenkatu

Uusonrtinkatu

Kasarmikatu

Uniongatan

Makasiini
terminaali

Kanavatermi-
naali

Katajanokanranta

Katajanokan
laituri

Katajanokanluoto
Skatakobben

Taideteollisuusmuseo
(Museum of Art & Design)

Suomen Rakennustaiteen
Museo
(Museum of Finnish
Architecture)

26 27

Johanneksen
kirkko
Tarkk ampujank.

Tähtitorni
(Observatory)

Katajanokan
terminaali

Eteläsatama
Södra Hamnen

Kruunuvuorenselkä
Kronbergsfjärden

Rostock, Stockholm, Tallinn, Mariehamn

Jääkärinkatu

Vuorimiehenk.

ULLANLINNA
ULLRIKASBORG

Fabriksgatan

Pyhän
Henrikin
kirkko

Cygnaeuksen
galleria

Mannerheim-
museo

29 Olympia-
terminaali

Valkosaari
Blekholmen

34

Luoto
Klippan

Ryssänsaari
Ryssholmen

Merimiehenk.

Pietarinkatu

Iso Puistotie

Bergmansgatan

Tähtitorninkatu

Kapteenink.

Laivanvar.k.

28

KAIVOPUISTO
BRUNNSPARKEN

Puolimatkansaari
Halvvägsholmen

Huvilakatu

Neitsytpolku

Itäinen Puistotie

Siltatie

EIRA

binderintiek.

Merisatamanranta

Ehrenströmintie

Ehrenströmsvägen

Pormestarinluodot
Borgmästargrunden

ardintie

favsgatan

Merisatama
Havshamnen

Lonna
Lonnan

Sirpalesalmi

Sirpalesaari
Flisholmen

36 Uunisaari
Ugnsholmen

Liuskasaari
Skifferholmen

Harakka
Stora Räntan

35 Särkkä
Långören

Pikku-Musta
Lilla Östersvatö

Vanha-Räntty
Gamla Räntan

Länsi-Musta
Västersvartö

SUOMENLINNA
SVEABORG

30

Iso-Mustasaari
Stora Östersvartö

HELSINKI

*An intriguing mix of Swedish and Russian influences combine
with an ultramodern architectural stamp to make
Finland's capital a gem of the northern Baltic*

Map
on pages
298–299

Flying over Helsinki, one sees nothing but lakes and forests. Arriving in the city centre, there are stately granite buildings and people bustling along, purposefully conversing into mobile phones. Although it appears at first glance to be a city in motion, the Finnish capital is surprisingly quiet, except for the buzz of a skateboard, or a tram making its way across town. In recent years, once the spring light and summer sun appear, pavement cafés have become a pleasant addition to city life.

After a complex 450-year history, Helsinki has grown from a picturesque village with a harbour to a modern, confident capital where the quality of life has been ranked as among the highest in Europe. The "Daughter of the Baltic" has gained her own identity.

Building a capital

Before gaining independence in 1917, Finland lived through 500 years of Swedish rule, and more than 100 years under the Russians. These diverse influences from the west and then from the east have contributed to Helsinki's character. Helsinki was founded in 1550 by the Swedish King Gustav Vasa, but the monumental city centre was built in the early 19th century, thanks largely to

LEFT: monument to Jean Sibelius.
BELOW: young sailor at the harbour.

FACT FILE

Area 338,000 sq km, of which 10 percent is water.
Situation Helsinki is the centre of the Greater Helsinki Area, a region with some 1.2 million inhabitants.
Population 547,000.
Climate July is the warmest month, average temperature: 20°C (68°F); January is the coldest: –5.7°C (22°F).
Finest building Finlandia Hall by Alvar Aalto.
Biggest attraction Annual Helsinki Festival which takes place at the end of August and beginning of September. The festival offers a range of international culture, including classical music, dance, theatre and exhibitions (tel: 6126 5100; www.helsinkifestival.fi).
Newest attraction City Art Museum and Museum of Cultures in Tennispalatsi, the former tennis palace, which also contains a 14-screen cinema complex.
Best excursions City Bus Tour departing from Esplanadi Park, Viking and Olympia terminals (tel: 2288 1222); and the 50-minute round trip by Tram 3T.
Best view of the city From the lookout tower and bar of the Hotel Torni, Helsinki's tallest building at 13 storeys.
Meeting place Kappeli café-restaurant, Eteläesplanadi 1.
Tourist information Helsinki City Tourist Office, Pohjoisesplanadi 19 (tel: 169 3757).

Rautatieasema, the railway station designed by Eliel Saarinen in 1905.

the talents of the German-born architect Carl Ludwig Engel. Engel's first commission was a new administrative centre, followed by the cathedral, senate building, university and university library. Engel's neo-classical work can also be seen in St Petersburg and Tallinn. At the same time, Helsinki became the seat of a nationalist movement. Native architects, such as Eliel Saarinen and Alvar Aalto emerged and, after independence in 1917, Finnish Functionalism replaced Art Nouveau as Helsinki's predominant architectural style *(see page 306)*.

Nothing could completely protect the city from the massive Russian air raids of 1944 – nor from fervent, and not always lovely, post-war reconstruction. But Helsinki's position on the sea soon helped it to regain and then increase its stature, not only as a major port, but also as the important site for shipbuilding and international meetings it is today.

Helsinki today

Modern Helsinki is a tranquil but still growing city with some 547,000 occupants. The heart of the city pulses around **Rautatieasema ❶**, the Railway Station, which also contains a metro station and an underground shopping complex. Designed by Eliel Saarinen in 1905 and completed in 1919, it links two of Helsinki's most prevalent styles: National Romanticism and Functionalism.

To the east of the station on the opposite side in another stately building is the **Ateneum ❷** (Museum of Finnish Art, Kaivokatu 2; open Tues, Fri 9am–6pm; Wed–Thur 9am–8pm, Sat–Sun 11am–5pm, closed Mon; entrance fee; tel: 173 36224), built in 1887. The museum's collection of Finnish paintings, sculpture and graphic art covers the years 1750 to 1960 and includes works by such notable Finns as Akseli Gallén-Kallela and Albert Edelfelt.

BELOW: fresh produce on sale in a city market.

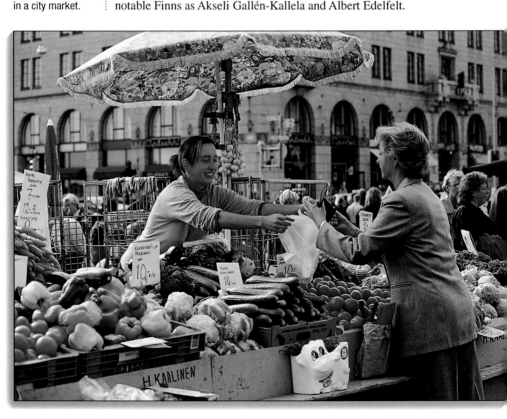

Aalto's plan

To get around Helsinki, just remember that all roads lead to **Mannerheimintie**, the city's main thoroughfare and the longest street in Finland. This neighbourhood is evolving based on a plan by Alvar Aalto, which is finally being realised perhaps in ways the great designer would not have anticipated.

From the railway station turn north into Mannerheimintie and on your right you'll see **Kiasma** ❸ (open Tues 9am–5pm, Wed–Sun 10am–10pm; entrance fee; tel: 173 36501), a new museum of contemporary art, opened in 1998. This remarkable gleaming white structure by the American architect Steven Holl is a symbol of the new Helsinki. Outside, the building's close proximity to the bronze statue of Field Marshal Mannerheim atop his steed, makes a striking reflection at night.

Behind Kiasma is a brand new glass building, **Sanomatalo**, which is headquarters for Helsinki's two daily newspapers. Within this striking complex that resembles a space station, is the **Design Forum** (open Mon–Fri 10am–6pm, Sat–Sun 11am–4pm), which hosts free exhibitions, and an innovative new restaurant called **Pulp**.

Joining Kiasma to create a triangle of Functionalist architecture are two other cultural institutions: **Lasipalatsi** (Glass Palace) across Mannerheimintie and the former **Tennispalatsi** ❹ (Tennis Palace) at the other end of the bus station area. Lasipalatsi has been rejuvenated with utmost care to create a media centre which includes an Internet library, television studios, cinema, and fine cafés and restaurants. Tennispalatsi was used during the 1952 Olympic Games and now houses Finland's largest cinema complex (14 screens) and two museums, the **City Art Museum** (open Tues–Sun 11am–8.30pm, closed Mon; entrance

Map on pages 298–299

TIP

See the best of Helsinki with a Helsinki Card, which can be purchased from the Tourist Office, Pohjoisesplanadi 19, hotels and R-kiosks. The card includes free museum admission and free travel on city buses, trams, trains and metro.

BELOW: Kiasma, the Museum of Contemporary Art.

Traditional Finnish dolls are popular souvenirs.

fee; tel: 169 3166), and the **Museum of Cultures** (open 10am–8pm, closed Mon; entrance fee; tel 40 501).

Opposite Kiasma is the **Eduskuntatalo ❺** (Parliament Building), built between 1925 and 1930 and distinguished by an impressive row of steps and a façade of 14 columns of grey granite. Statues of former Finnish presidents scatter the area between the Parliament Building and the **Kansallismuseo ❻** (National Museum; closed for renovation at the time of writing) two blocks to the north. The museum's decoration, its collection and the stone bear by the entrance is the work of Emil Wikström. The frescoes on the foyer ceiling, depicting scenes from Finland's national epic, the *Kalevala*, are by Gallén-Kallela. The City Museum branch in the fine **Hakasalmi Villa** (tel: 169 3444) across Mannerheimintie houses a special exhibition on Helsinki's history.

Finlandiatalo ❼ (Finlandia Hall; tel: 40 241), opposite the National Museum, is undoubtedly the most famous building in Helsinki. Alvar Aalto designed it both inside and out, completing the main section in 1971. Home to the Helsinki Philharmonic Orchestra, it is used regularly for concerts and events.

Around the corner is the **Sibelius Academy** (Pohjoinen Rautatiekatu 9; tel: 405 4662), Helsinki's famous musical conservatory, where concerts are given by top students. Continuing north along Mannerheimintie to where Hesperia Park and Töölö Bay come to an end, the **Suomen Kansallisooppera ❽** (Finnish National Opera House; www.opera.fi), which opened in 1993, offers an ambitious season with many international performers.

Nestling, literally, into a small hill west of the Parliament Building behind Mannerheimintie and the winding streets of Töölö, is the ultramodern church, **Temppelinaukion Kirkko ❾** (open Mon–Fri 10am–8pm, Sat 10am–6pm, Sun

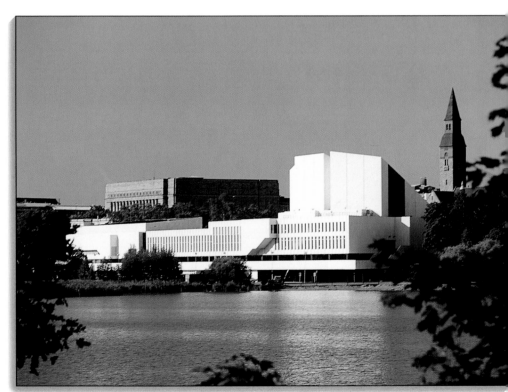

noon–1.30pm and 3.15–5.45pm). It is not only an architectural oddity – built as it is directly into the cliffs, with inner walls of stone – but it is also the site of many good concerts. A service for English speakers is held Sundays at 2pm.

Shopping and entertainment

Heading south, back to town on Mannerheimintie, you'll find **Stockmann** 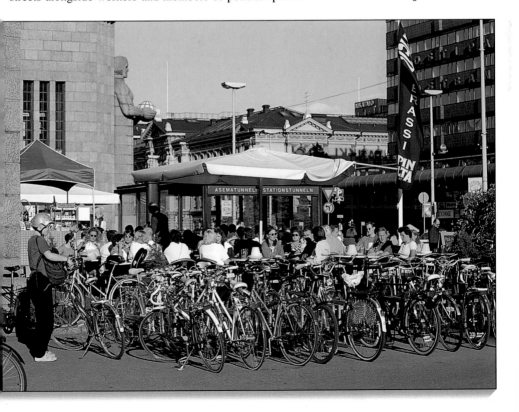, Finland's largest department store, which has an excellent food hall on the lower level. Behind it, on Keskuskatu, is Scandinavia's largest bookshop, **Akateeminen Kirjakauppa**, a great place to browse or to take a break in the stylish café designed by Alvar Aalto. The bookshop faces another Helsinki landmark, **Esplanadin Puisto** (Esplanade Park), which was first laid out in 1831 and runs east–west between Mannerheimintie and South Harbour.

The **Svenska Teatern** (Swedish Theatre), an elegant semi-circular stone building dating from 1866, commands Esplanade Park's western head on Mannerheimintie. In front of the theatre, Bus 20 will take you just five minutes out of town to the **Ruohalahti** area and the Kaappeli Cable Factory complex, where the **Suomen Valokuvataiteen Museo** and **Teatterimuseo** (Photography and Theatre Museums, Tallberginkatu 1) are located.

The **Esplanadi**, an old-fashioned promenade leads from the theatre across the length of the park, past the central statue of J.L. Runeberg, Finland's national poet, to **Kappeli** (Eteläesplanadi 1; tel: 179 242) a café-restaurant. The park is a very popular meeting place and is often the scene of animated fairs, such as the Christmas Fair in December or Night of the Arts in late August. On May Day Eve it is given over to general lunacy as students wearing white caps revel in the streets alongside workers and members of political parties. Two boulevards

Map on pages 298–299

Helsinki lies at latitude 60°N, and experiences lengthy summer days as a result. At the summer solstice on 22 June, the sun only drops below the horizon for 1 hr 20 mins.

BELOW: two-wheeled transport, a popular way to get around Helsinki.

ON THE TRAIL OF JUGENDSTIL

Helsinki offers a wealth of interest for lovers of architecture, especially among its flamboyant Art Nouveau buildings

For those who love architecture, Helsinki has lots to offer. After becoming Finland's capital in 1812, the Senate Square, designed by Carl Ludwig Engel (1778–1840), was a bold example of the early period of autonomy after Russian rule. Engel's Graeco-Roman-inspired work is found throughout the city in churches, government buildings and the university.

During the second half of the 19th century, the number of architects and designers grew and building styles became more diverse with references to Classicism and Rationalism.

It was after the turn of the 20th century that a younger generation of architects, inspired by

the Arts and Crafts movement, rose in revolt against Classicism and Eclecticism. These included: Lars Sonck (1870–1956), Bertel Jung (1872–1946), and the trio Herman Gesellius (1874–1916), Armas Lindgren (1874–1929) and Eliel Saarinen (1873–1950), who were committed to creating "a more domestic, freer and more authentic world" with their work.

This Art Nouveau, or Jugendstil, as it is called in Finland, is also known as National Romanticism. It is distinguished by its use of stained glass and murals, timber and bronze accents, interesting windows, heavy ornamentation, grey granite, natural colours, and castle-like features. Some of the most famous tourist attractions in Helsinki are Art Nouveau. Their roots go back to the national epic, the *Kalevala*, which inspired the composer Sibelius and the artist Gallén-Kallela. There are many such buildings to be seen in the Katajanokka area near the harbour and in the stylish Eira quarter – look out for Lars Sonck's hospital, Laivurinkatu 27; Lindahl and Thomé's Lord Hotel, Lönnrottinkatu 29, with a granite facade and romantic turrets, and their Otava publishing house at Uudenmaankatu 10. The Pohjola House, Aleksanterinkatu 44, is by Gesellius, Lindgren and Saarinen, as is the National Theatre. Do not miss spending time at the railway station, which is one of Saarinen's masterpieces, especially the murals in the Eliel restaurant.

Private villas were also prominent in this movement and it is worth making an excursion to Hvitträsk *(see page 318)* at Kirkkonummi, just outside Helsinki, which was designed by the architecture trio as a shared living and studio space for themselves and their families. The best-preserved rooms are essentially a museum to Saarinen, who is buried in the wooded, lakeside environs, along with Gesellius. ❑

TOP LEFT: Eliel Saarinen's railway station.
LEFT: Hvitträsk studio. **TOP RIGHT:** Art Nouveau detail, Korkeavuorenkatu. **ABOVE:** owl motif.

stretch east–west alongside either side of the park. Nowadays, the fine 19th-century stone buildings along **Pohjoisesplanadi** mostly house design shops including Marimekko, Arabia and Aarikka, known respectively for their colourful clothing, distinctive glassware and wooden jewellery. At number 19, the **Helsinki Information Office** and the **City Tourist Board ⑮** occupy the first floor. Both offer extensive selections of maps and brochures.

In 1999 the **Hotel Kamp**, Pohjoiseplenadi 29, a popular rendezvous in Helsinki at the end of the 19th century, reopened its doors as a luxury hotel. The **Kamp Galleria** is an exclusive shopping complex on the lower level.

Map on pages 298–299

Market days

Across the road from the Kappeli restaurant is the **Havis Amanda Fountain ⑯**, which created quite a stir when it was first erected in 1908. Surrounded by four sea lions spouting water, the bronze statue represents the city of Helsinki rising from the sea, innocent and naked.

Kauppatori market is the place to look for Sami handicrafts, such as this novel hat.

Opposite the fountain, is the bustling **Kauppatori ⑰** (Central Market Square; open Mon–Sat 7am–2pm and in summer 3.30pm–8pm). Shoppers wander from stand to stand looking for the perfect new potato, salmon fillet, bunch of dill or flowers. The small tents serve tasty cinnamon or meat pastries and the ubiquitous coffee which seems to fuel the Finns. Other stands proffer interesting goods and handicrafts, many from Lapland.

To the south of the square at the 100-year-old, yellow-and-red brick **Vanha Kauppahalli** (Old Market Hall), one can buy salmon, reindeer cold-cuts, rounds of Oltermanni cheese, or even Vietnamese *loempia* (egg rolls).

Opposite the market stands the long blue **Kaupungintalo ⑱** (City Hall) designed by Engel in 1833, and **Presidentinlinna ⑲** (Presidential Palace), designed in 1818 as a private home and turned into a tsarist palace by Engel in 1843. The Finnish president no longer resides here.

Another major landmark, **Senaatintori ⑳** (Senate Square), stands one block north of here, on the busy **Aleksanterinkatu** shopping street. Over the centuries the square has remained a very impressive spot. Nowadays it functions principally as a byway or as the occasional backdrop for an important event. **Tuomiokirkko ㉑** (Helsinki Cathedral), at the top of a flight of treacherously steep steps on the north side, is a point of pride for Finns, and the exterior – with its five green cupolas, numerous white Corinthian columns and sprinkling of important figurines posing on its roof – is certainly impressive.

The city's oldest stone building, dating from 1757, is the small blue-grey **Sederholmin Talo ㉒** on the corner of Aleksanterinkatu and Katariinankatu. Across the street is the **Bockin Talo** (Bock House), also 18th-century, which became the meeting place for Helsinki's City Council in 1818.

BELOW: Helsinki's fine cathedral, Tuomiokirkko.

Beyond the centre

After exploring Helsinki's centre, venture into one of the surrounding districts, each of which has its own very particular character. **Katajanokka** lies on a small promontory sticking out into the sea a few blocks east

The interior of the Uspensky Cathedral.

from Senate Square, connected by two short bridges. The spires and onion-shaped domes of the Russian Orthodox **Uspenskin Katedraali ㉓** (Uspenski Cathedral), built in 1868, tower above a popular restaurant complex across the street. Helsinki's first Russian restaurant, the **Bellevue**, established in 1917, sits at the base of the cathedral, across from Katajanokka Park.

Jugendstil (Art Nouveau) architecture rules in **Luotsikatu** street, just east of the cathedral. Don't miss the charming griffin doorway at No. 5.

On the southern side of Katajanokka the huge Silja and Viking Line ships from Stockholm tie up, and stylish catamarans ply the route to medieval Tallin, the Estonian capital. In recent years, many of the old warehouses have been converted to restaurants, shops and a hotel. The **Tulli-ja Pakkahuone ㉔** (Customs and Bonded Warehouse, Katajanokan Laituri 5) from 1900 remains the same, with its inventive Jugendstil architecture.

Finding your way back to Esplanadi, head west on **Bulevardi** and the neighbouring streets like Eerikinkatu, Fredrikinkatu and Uudenmaankatu, which in recent years have become filled with fashionable galleries, boutiques, antique bookshops and restaurants. At the end of Bulevardi, past the old opera house, don't miss the flea market, **Hietalahdentori ㉕** (open Mon–Fri 8am–2pm, Sat 8am–3pm).To the south of Bulevardi are the exclusive **Eira** and **Ullanlinna** districts. The **Taideteollisuusmuseo ㉖** (Museum of Art and Design, Korkeavuorenkatu 23; open 11am–6pm, closed Mon; entrance fee; tel: 622 0540) is a showcase for Finland's renowned skills in design, including Alvar Aalto furniture and Lapponia jewellery.

BELOW: Kappeli, a popular meeting place on Esplanadi.

In the same block is the **Suomen Rakennustaiteen Museo ㉗** (Museum of Finnish Architecture, Kasarminkatu 24; open 10am–4pm, closed Mon; entrance fee; tel: 8567 5100), which has an excellent archive of architectural drawings and changing exhibitions focusing on Finnish architectural movements.

The southernmost end of the peninsula is lined by parkland, frequented by joggers, skaters and cyclists. In summer, the city sponsors free concerts in **Kaivopuisto ㉘** (park). In winter, when the sea is frozen, you can actually walk out to some of the closer offshore islands. On the eastern point, embassies fill the chic Ullanlinna district. **Olympiaterminaali ㉙** (Olympia Quay) is a stopping place for Silja and Viking liners and a popular promenade for walkers who find refreshment at **Café Ursula** or **Carousel**.

Islands abound

Literally hundreds of islands dot the Helsinki coastline. **Suomenlinna ㉚** (Finland's Castle) is undoubtedly the most important. In reality it consists of five islands, over which the ruins of a naval fortress and its fortifications are spread. Suomenlinna has played an integral part in Helsinki's life since its construction started in 1748. It has been listed by UNESCO as a World Heritage site, and functions today as a thriving local artists' community with the restored bastions being used as studios and showrooms. Water buses ferry visitors here from Market Square every half-hour. They dock on **Iso Mustasaari**, from where a hilly path leads up through **Rantakasarmi** (Jetty Barracks), which house art exhibitions and an interesting restaurant and microbrewery known as **Panimo**.

There are several museums on the island (island open daily; entrance to fortress free; museums and restaurants open daily May–early Oct; entrance fee to museums; tel: 668 880). The **Nukke-ja lelemuseo** (**Museum of Dolls and Toys**) has a charming café and excellent apple pie. The large **Suomenlinna**

Map on pages 298–299

Helsinki has a number of public saunas, but the only wood-heated one is Kotiharjun Sauna in Harjutorinkatu (near Sörnäinen metro station; open Tues–Fri 1–8pm, Sat noon–6pm; tel: 735 1535).

BELOW LEFT: taking a break on the harbourside. **BELOW RIGHT:** quiet place for a chat.

Map
on pages
298–299

Museum is the main historical exhibition of the islands, as well as the main information centre for Suomenlinna. The **Military Museum Manege** exhibits heavy equipment mainly from the war period 1939–45.

Cross the bridge to the rambling remains of the **Kruunulinna Ehrensvärd** (Ehrensvärd Crown Castle) and gardens. The castle courtyard is the best-preserved section of the fortress and contains the 1788 sarcophagus of Count Ehrensvärd himself. His former home is now a museum, with old furniture, arms and lithographs. Try to visit the atmospheric summer restaurant **Walhalla**, where on a clear day it is sometimes possible to see Estonia, some 80 km (50 miles) away. There is also the **Rannikotykisto Museo** (Coast Artillery Museum), and the **Vesikko Submarine** to see.

Korkeasaaren Eläitarha ㉛ (open May–Sept: daily 10am–6pm; tel: 169 5969) is one of those rare zoos in the world set entirely on an island. In summer you can reach it by boat from Market Square. The zoo, perhaps not surprisingly, specialises in "cold climate animals" although there's an interesting enclosure of South American animals. If you want to learn about indigenous Finnish fauna, you'd do just as well at the **Luonnontieteellinen** (Natural History Museum, Pohjoinen Rautatiekatu 13; open Mon–Fri 9am–5pm, Sat–Sun 11am–4pm; entrance fee; tel: 191 7400), known for its excellent exhibitions.

The island of **Seurasaari** ㉜ is eminently more atmospheric. A pretty, forested place with a national park (open all year), its northeastern side has been made into an **Ulkomuseo** (Open-air Museum; open June–Aug daily until 5pm; entrance fee; tel: 40 501) containing wooden buildings from provinces all over Finland from the 17th to 19th centuries. The island is connected to the Helsinki shore by a wooden footbridge. Take either bus No. 24 from Erottaja (in front of the Swedish Theatre), or cycle along the Meilahti coastal drive which takes you past **Sibeliuksen Puisto** ㉝ (Sibelius Park) and the silvery tubular **Sibeliusmonumentti** (Monument) to the bridge.

BELOW: military
might at the castle
of Suomenlinna.
RIGHT: café life,
central Helsinki.

Off the beaten track

Less well known are the smaller islands that form a string around Helsinki's southern peninsula. Across the "Olympic Harbour" are **Luoto** ㉞ and **Valkosaari**, restaurant islands with romantic villas. A long pier outside Kaivopuisto offers a boat service to **Särkkä** ㉟, another island with a popular restaurant.

Uunisaari ㊱ is accessible at the southern end of Neitsytpolku street. It's a popular recreational island with a beach, sauna and restaurant.

The **Finnish Sauna Society** situated on the beautiful island of **Lauttasaari** offers wood-heated and smoke saunas and massage (open 11.30am–4pm for men, 4.30–8pm for women; tel: 678 677).

Helsinki's favourite island for swimming is undoubtedly **Pihlajasaari** ㊲. It actually comprises two islands, with a sandy beach, café and changing cabins on the larger island's western shore. Helsinki's only nudist beach is on the smaller island. Boats to Pihlajasaari depart in summer every 15 to 30 minutes from outside Café Carousel in Eira. The former military island of **Harakka** ㊳, south of Kaivopuisto, is now a wildlife reserve. ❑

THE TRADITIONAL FINNISH SAUNA

An old Finnish proverb says: "First you build the sauna, then you build the house." Even today, there's nothing so uniquely Finnish as a sauna

There are some things along the way which a traveller does not forget – and a real Finnish sauna is one of them. Although its origin is obscure, the sauna came to Finland over 2,000 years ago, and it is a rare Finn who admits to not liking one. Official statistics estimate that there are over 625,000 saunas in Finland, not counting those in private houses or summer cottages that dot the shoreline of the country's lakes. The actual figure could easily be over 1 million in a country of just 5 million people – but then, the sauna is a national institution.

BUSINESS AND PLEASURE

The sauna outgrew its rural roots long ago. Today, be it city or village, you will find public saunas, and it is safe to assume that every new apartment block has a sauna for its tenants. Many companies also have saunas for its employees.

A Finnish sauna is not a meeting place for sex, as it is in some countries; codes of behaviour are strict. Titles and position are, they say, left hanging in the changing room with the clothes. It is not unusual for board meetings and government cabinet meetings to be held in a sauna – perhaps because it's "not done" to swear or raise one's voice. A sauna also leaves you relaxed yet alert.

▽ **FRIENDS AND FOLIAGE**
Tying up birch leaves for the sauna is a social event in summer.

▽ **MORAL CODE**
Despite the nudity, a Finnish sauna is a moral place. Generally, saunas are same-sex only; a mixed sauna is solely a family affair.

▽ **HOT GOSSIP**
There is more to the sauna than just getting clean. It is a happening – a time to meet friends, or to make business deals.

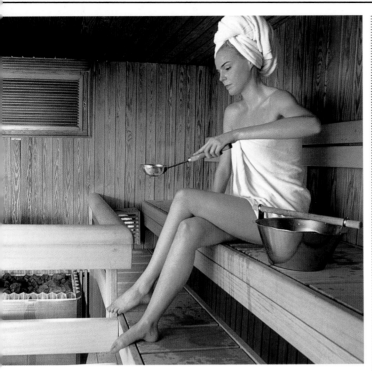

HOW TO TAKE A SAUNA

There is no "right way" to take a sauna – temperature and style vary. The ideal temperature is between 60–80° C (140–175° F) although it can be a cooler 30° C (85° F) on the bottom platform, reserved for children. A common practice is to brush oneself with a wet birch switch, called the *vihta*. This not only gives off a fresh fragrance but increases blood circulation and perspiration.

How long you sit in the sauna is entirely up to you. When you have had enough, you move on to stage two: cooling off. A cold shower is the most common way but, if the sauna is by a lake or the sea, a quick plunge into the cool water is stimulating.

The final stage is to dry off, which should be done naturally, to avoid further perspiration. It is also time for a beer or coffee and a snack to complete the ritual.

△ **STEAM HEAT**
Water thrown over the hot stones creates a dry steam *(löyly)*, which makes the heat tolerable and stimulates perspiration.

◁ **COOLING OFF**
In the winter, brave souls jump through holes in the ice or roll around in the snow – not recommended practice for people with high blood pressure.

◁ **SAUNA FASHIONS**
The sauna has become such an integral part of Finnish life, that there are even "designer" outlets specially geared towards sauna accessories.

▷ **ANCIENT USES**
In olden days in rural Finland the sauna was not just the place in which to get clean, but also where babies were born and sausages smoked.

SOUTHERN FINLAND

*Follow the route of the Nordic kings from west to east across
Southern Finland through a gentle landscape with painted
villages, ancient castles and an island-studded coast*

Map
on page
316

To follow the south coast of Finland from west to east is to follow a route once travelled by Nordic kings and princes to St Petersburg. Known as The King's Road, the route passes through mainly flat coastal country covered with farmland and dense forest. The area is heavily settled, and it is also heavily Swedish-speaking. From Pargas (Parainen), south of **Turku ❶** *(see page 323)* at the head of the Turunmaa archipelago island chain, through Hanko (Hangö), Ekenäs (Tammisaari), Karis (Karjaa), and further east via Porvoo (Borgå) through a cluster of small villages on the approach to Kotka, you will hear a great deal of Swedish being spoken and read it as the first language on signposts. This is all part of the democracy of bilingualism in Finland.

The eastern portion of the coast, past Helsinki, is riddled with fortifications. For the Swedes, then the Russians, and finally the independent Finns, the Russian border has been a crucial dividing line. The Finnish-Soviet borders still have a no-man's-land running between them, and although travel between the two countries has become far easier and more popular since the break-up of the USSR, there is no mistaking the sterner attitude of the Russian customs guards and immediate deterioration of road conditions as soon as one crosses over the border to the east.

LEFT: models of
ships traditionally
grace the windows
of Loviisa's
wooden houses.
BELOW:
a summer treat.

Exploring the islands

Richly vegetated but sparsely populated, the archipelago of **Turunmaa ❷** is quieter than the Alands *(see page 321)* in terms of tourism, and the islands are reached more quickly from the mainland. They are linked by a series of bridges and then ferries. Ferries also service some of the smaller islands that spin off south from the main chain. Local buses connect the larger towns. Many Finnish families have their own islands – the ultimate refuge.

Turunmaa's finest harbour is on the northern spur of **Nagu**. An old wooden house overlooking the marina has been made into a guesthouse-style hotel. Also to be found in Nagu is the **Borstö Folk Museum** and the 14th-century **St Olof's Church**.

As you approach **Pargas (Parainen) ❸** from west or south you come to **Sattmark**, on the island of Stortervolandet. This tiny log cabin was once a sailor's quarters. It now serves light meals in its prettily furnished rooms and outside on the dock.

Continuing east towards Piikkiö, it is worth making a detour to **Kuusiston Linna ❹** on the Kuusisto peninsula. This medieval bishop's castle stood stoutly until Gustav Vasa ordered its demolition in 1528, but enough remains to have encouraged restoration.

Salo ❺, to the east on the mainland in the heart of the apple-growing Salojoki Valley, has a lively market

Åland Islands

Stockholm, Norrtälje, Kapellskär

Gulf of Bothnia

RUSSIA

Gulf of Finland

Southern Finland
and the Lakes

0 ⎯ 50 km
0 ⎯ 50 miles

and is set off by a triad of churches – the Lutheran **Uskela** (1832) by C.L. Engel, the Greek Orthodox **Tsasouna** at its foot, and the stunningly modern **Helisnummen** (Helisnummi Church) about 4 km (2 miles) outside the town. Many of the world-famous Nokia phones are manufactured in Salo. At **Sammatti ❻**, 48 km (30 miles) east of Salo, look out for the sign to **Paikkarin Torppa** (Paikkari Cottage), the home of Elias Lönnrot who collected the legends and tales for the *Kalevala (see page 58).*

Map on page 316

Marina life

Due south of Salo is **Hanko (Hangö) ❼**, Finland's southernmost town, once a popular spa resort, and now frequented for its annual regatta and its beaches. Hanko is distinguished by an abundance of turreted villas in pastel shades which grace the stretch of beach behind a line of charming white changing huts. These stately homes were built at the turn of the 19th century for the Russian nobility who came for health cures; several offer bed and breakfast accommodation.

Hanko's **Linnoitusmuseo** (Frontline Museum; open May–Sept: Tues–Sun; Oct–Apr: Sat, Sun and Wed afternoons only), with its wartime bunker is a reminder of the town's strategic history, such as the destruction of the fortifications during the Crimean War. The Municipal Library and Gallery offers a range of exhibitions and there are several art galleries, notably **Loft Gallery E. Pinomaa**, Satamakatu 1, which exhibits contemporary art. **Alan's Cafe**, Raatihuonentori 4, is run by an Englishman who makes divine pastries and shares a charming garden complex with an antiquarian book shop and crafts gallery. At the harbourfront, housed in some renovated warehouses, are a couple of restaurants featuring locally caught fish. On 26 August, the annual Night of the Bonfires takes place in the main harbour area and launches the Hanko Days Weekend Festival (note that at the end of August hotels and restaurants virtually shut down).

There are boat excursions to **Bengtskär Lighthouse**, 25 km (15 miles) south of Hanko, which make a memorable day's adventure. Built in 1906, the massive stone structure is Scandinavia's tallest lighthouse at 52 metres (170 ft) high. The walk to the top (252 steps) is worth the extra breaths for the view. There is a café and chapel, and it is possible to lodge here.

Ekenäs (Tammisaari) ❽ is the next main coastal stop along the King's Road. It is a finely laid out old town, with 18th- and 19th-century cobbled streets and charming wooden buildings, and is a great place for a stroll and some delicious Finnish ice cream (*jäätelö*). Just to the south is the **Tammisaaren Saariston Kansallispuisto**, a national park, resplendent with marshes, forests and water birds.

There is an extremely active boating life in and around Ekenäs, and numerous outdoor concerts in summer. The **Knipan** summer restaurant and the steeple of the old granite church (1680) are the town's main landmarks. For an historical background on the town, visit **Porvaristalo** (Ekenäs Museum, Gustav Vasas Gata 13; open daily in summer; winter: Tues–Thur evening and Fri–Sun afternoon; tel: 19 263 3161). There are four-hour boat tours from the

Setting off for a sail from the marina at Hanko.

BELOW: the flat landscape of southern Finland is ideal for cycling.

Windmills are a feature of the islands and low-lying districts of the south.

North Harbour in July and early August. A few kilometres eastwards is **Snappertuna**, a farming village 15 km (10 miles) from the late-14th-century ruined castle at **Raasepori** ❾. The outdoor theatre in the Raseborg dale stages dramatic and musical evenings and in July you may catch a re-enacted medieval duel. Further east beyond Snappertuna is **Fagervik** ❿, the site of a tremendous old manor overlooking an inlet. This is the place to picnic, horse ride or enjoy good walking paths.

Approaching Helsinki from the west it would be a shame to miss Eliel Saarinen's home at **Hvitträsk** ⓫ (open June–Aug: Mon–Fri 10am–7pm, Sat–Sun 10am–6pm; Nov–May: Tues–Sun, times vary; entrance fee; tel: 9 297 5779). The stone and timber buildings seem to blend with the forest, the great cliffs and the White Lake that give the house its name. The main studio, now a museum, saw the planning of 70 projects by the great three architects in recent Finnish history: Saarinen, Herman Gesellius and Armas Lindgren.

Tarvaspää ⓬ was the home of Finland's national artist Akseli Gallén-Kallela (1865–1931). His Jugendstil-inspired studio has been converted into the **Gallén-Kallela Museum** (open June–Aug: Mon–Thur 10am–8pm; Sept–May: Tues–Sat 10am–4pm, Sun 10am–5pm, closed Mon; tel: 9 513 388) displaying the artist's paintings, stained glass, tools and objects collected on his travels.

Medieval town

BELOW: the former home of Finland's national poet, J.L. Runeberg, Porvoo.

East of Helsinki, **Porvoo** (**Borgå**) ⓭ is one of Finland's most important historical towns. The Swedish king, Magnus Eriksson, gave Porvoo a royal charter in 1346; from this point on it became a busy trading post and, ultimately, it was the place where the Diet of Porvoo (1809) convened to transfer Finland from Swedish to Russian hands. The striking **Porvoo Cathedral**, where this momentous event took place, dates from the 15th century.

Map on page 316

While its rich history made the town important, Porvoo's writers and artists gave it its real character. The home of Finland's national poet, **J.L. Runeberg** (open May–Aug: Mon–Sat 10am–4pm, Sun 11am–5pm; Sept–Apr: Wed–Sun, times vary; entrance fee; tel: 19 581 330) has been restored to its original condition. **The Edelfelt-Vallgren Art Museum** (open May–Aug: daily; Sept–Apr: Wed–Sun; entrance fee; tel: 19 574 7589) occupies a 1792 merchant's house, formerly the Town Hall, on Rahtihuoneentori (Town Hall Square). It features paintings by Albert Edelfelt – one of Finland's finest 19th-century artists – and works by sculptor Ville Vallgren, as well as a fine Art Nouveau furniture collection. The **Albert Edelfelt Atelier** in Haikko, 6 km (4 miles) south of Porvoo, also exhibits much of Edelfelt's work.

For scenery, the medieval atmosphere of **Old Porvoo** has few rivals: its riverbanks are lined with red-ochre warehouses and the pastel-coloured wooden houses from the 16th century provide a charming backdrop. Today, they house museums, boutiques, cafés and restaurants, as well as private residences. A fine excursion is to take a river cruise to Porvoo from the main harbour in Helsinki.

Good stopping points on the journey east from Loviisa to Kotka are the excellent sandy beaches of Pyhtää and the holiday island of Kaunissaari with its interesting fishing village.

Towards the border

East of Porvoo, the landscape becomes more rural and less populated. In summer, the grassy hillocks bristle with wildflowers. **Loviisa ⑭** is a pretty coastal town with an esplanade headed by the New Gothic Church. A town museum tells the local history, including the role of the Rosen and Ungern bastions, built in the 18th century to protect the important trade route between Vyborg and

BELOW: wooden home typical of southern Finland.

Map
on page
316

*Tsar Alexander III,
whose hand-crafted
timber fishing lodge
at Langinkoski
was a gift from the
Finnish state.*

BELOW:
strawberries
for sale at a
roadside stall.

Turku. The Old Town buildings survived the fire of 1855 and tours can be made of the last spirits factory, which today is an artist's atelier. Just 10 km (6 miles) from the centre of town on an island at the mouth of Loviisa Bay is the **Svartholma** sea fortress, built in 1748.

Kotka ⑮ is the next important destination on the King's Road and is considered one of the most beautifully situated cities in Finland. It is around Kotka that the Kymi River breaks up into five branches before rushing off into the sea, making for perfect salmon and trout fishing. The closest of the spray of islands along the coast can be reached by bridges, the rest by ferry.

Kotka centre is based on an esplanade. One street to the northwest, at Kirkkokatu and Koulukatu, is the main Lutheran church with tremendous brick buttresses; the imposing Orthodox St Nicolai Kirkko complex and park runs along Papinkatu. Kotka has frequent boat services to nearby islands, some of which have old fortifications. The pleasant **Sapokka Harbour** has one of the finest parks in Finland, with a high artificial waterfall. Step aboard a water bus for a tour of this beautiful archipelago.

Apart from the Kotka islands, the **Kymenlaakso** (Kymi river valley) extends further inland, where there are gorgeous forest paths. Details are available from the Kotka Tourist Office at Keskuskatu 17, tel: 5 234 4424.

Imperial lodge

The impressive Imperial Fishing Lodge of Tsar Alexander III (1845–94), is at **Langinkoski** ⑯ (open May–Aug: daily 10am–7pm; Sept–Oct: Sat–Sun only; entrance fee; tel: 5 228 1050). The tremendous log building with simple furnishings was crafted by the Finns for the Tsar. Several nature paths begin from Langinkoski. If you walk north for 5 km (3 miles), you'll pass the Kyminlinna fortification, over the Hovinkoski rapids in Huumanhaara, on a branch of the Kymijoki river to Keisarin Kosket. These "tsar's rapids" course around Munkkisaari Island, with its Orthodox chapel (Tsasouna). The spot is also ideal for fishing and rapids-shooting. On the bank is **Keisarin Kosket Lodge**, an Orthodox monastery site from 1650 to 1850, with café, boats, and cabins for hire; fishing licences are also sold (tel: 5 260 9301).

In summer, **Kärkisaari**, just to the west of Kotka, makes for a lovely excursion. The former youth hostel here (originally a villa from the beginning of the 20th century) now provides stylish bed and breakfast accommodation. The long swimming dock leads into the island-filled inlet of the Gulf of Finland. On the adjacent peninsula is **Santalahti**; the crescent-shaped beach has grassy knolls at the edge of a sandy bay.

Kotka is only 70 km (45 miles) from the nearest Russian city, Viipuri (Vyborg) and 270 km (170 miles) from St Petersburg; all varieties of Finland–Russia trips can be arranged with the Kotka Tourist Board, but remember to plan overnight trips well in advance so that your visa will be ready.

Hamina ⑰ is the last of the large Finnish towns before the Russian border. Further east lies **Vaalimaa**, a busy border station with huge supermarkets selling goodies to Russians and Finns alike. ❏

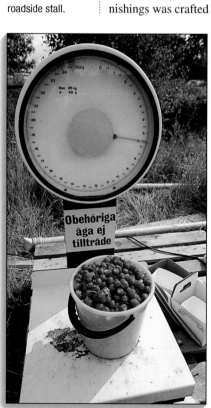

Obehöriga
äga ej
tillträde

ÅLAND ISLANDS: THE ULTIMATE RETREAT

To the west of Finland, the Ålands are a perfect island-hopping destination. Catch a ferry, hire a bike and discover this little-known paradise

The Åland Islands (Ahvenanmaa in Finnish) are a collection of granite skerries comprising some 6,500 islands off the west coast of Finland.

Ålanders have inhabited their islands for thousands of years, and have a strong ethnic culture and a formidable pride in their identity. The population of 25,000 has had its own flag since 1954 and its own postage stamps since 1984. Today, the islands are an autonomous demilitarised zone represented both in the Finnish parliament and the Nordic Council, with Swedish being the official language. Although part of the EU, Åland remains outside the tax union agreement so tax-free shopping is available to travellers.

June to August is the ideal time to visit. Take a Viking or Silja Line ferry from Turku, Helsinki, or Stockholm to **Mariehamn** ⑱, sailing through the maze of skerries en route. There are also Finnair flights from Helsinki.

Mariehamn is the capital of the main island, Åland, and with 11,000 inhabitants, it is the only town-sized settlement. In the West Harbour, the four-masted museum ship *Pommern*, built in Glasgow in 1904, is worth a visit, as is the nearby Maritime Museum (open daily Apr–Oct; entrance fee). Other museums feature exhibitions on prehistoric and Ice and Bronze Age life, hunting, fishing and even delivering mail.

The islands are a paradise for hiking, fishing, cycling, golfing, swimming and other water sports, and are best explored by bicycle and ferry. From Åland, there is a daily bike ferry to **Prästö** ⑲. You can hire bicycles from the Mariehamn harbours. Most notable in Åland's northeast are the historic Kastelholm and Bomarsund fortresses. **Kastelholm** ⑳, (open mid-Apr–Sept) was once the administrative centre for the islands and dates from the 1300s. The Russians began fortifying it in 1829. Adjacent are the Cultural History Museum and Jan Karlsgärden Open-Air Museum (open May–Sept: daily; Oct–Apr: Mon–Fri; entrance fee).

To the southeast of Åland lies **Föglö** ㉑, once an important vodka smuggling destination. In the eastern part of the island there is a natural bird reserve.

Midsummer celebrations are held in almost every village with the traditional raising of the Midsummer pole and dancing.

Hotels, guest houses, cottages and camping facilities are available. For information, contact Ålands Turistinformation, Storagatan 8; tel: 18 240 00; fax: 18 242 65; Website: www.info.aland. ❑

TOP LEFT: figurehead, Åland Maritime Museum.
ABOVE LEFT: Åland flags. **TOP RIGHT:** riding on the islands. **RIGHT:** sauna on the water's edge.

TURKU

Ancient and modern coexist in Turku, Finland's former historic capital. Colourful restaurant boats line the river; museums, bars and galleries intermingle in the city centre

Map on page 324

Surrounded by islands, river and sea, Turku (Åbo in Swedish) is a summer paradise, yet it is also worth a visit during other seasons. The River Aura divides the modern city in two and you can cross its five main bridges or take the little ferry that still carries pedestrians and bicycles free of charge.

Turku is Finland's oldest city and yet many of the buildings go back only to the Great Fire of 1827 which destroyed a town then largely made of wood. In 1300, when it acquired a new cathedral, Turku became the spiritual centre of Finland. Around the same time, the solid lines of a castle began to rise near the mouth of the River Aura as the heart of royal power in Finland, where the Swedish governor lived and visiting dignitaries paid their respects.

After the Great Fire, the market and town moved away from the cathedral to the west bank of the Aura, much of it designed and built to the plan of Carl Ludwig Engel. Turku had the first university in Finland, founded by the 17th-century Governor General of Finland, Count Per Brahe.

Today, **Turun Linna** Ⓐ (Turku Castle; Linnankatu 80; open daily; entrance fee; tel: 2 262 0300) looks towards the modern town centre, some 3 km (2 miles) away. Many of its rooms have been preserved as the Turku Historical Museum.

LEFT: Turku's 14th-century cathedral.
BELOW: market day in the main square.

Exploring the town

Begin your walking tour in the colourful market square. Just adjacent is the **Ortodoksinen Kirkko** Ⓑ (Orthodox Cathedral), built in 1838 on the orders of Tsar Nicholas I. Be sure and visit the 19th-century **Kauppahalli** Ⓒ (Indoor Markethall), across the street in Eerikinkatu.

Turning down Aurakatu, the Auransilta (bridge), gives the first view of the numerous restaurant boats and the sleek white hull and complicated rigging of the *Suomen Joutsen*, which once plied the ocean between South America and Europe. Nearby at Luostarinmäki is the open-air **Käsityöläismuseo** Ⓓ (Handicrafts Museum; open Apr–Sept: daily 10am–6pm; Oct–Mar: Tues–Sun 10am–3pm; entrance fee; tel: 2 262 0350) which features traditional crafts people at work. Coming down the hill, detour via the Observatory on Vartiovuori, now the **Merenkulku-Museo** Ⓔ (Turku Art Museum; open Tues, Fri, Sat 10am–4pm; Wed, Thur 10am–7pm; Wed closes 4pm in winter; Sun 11am–6pm; entrance fee; tel: 2 274 7570) until 2004, when it will return to its former location on Puolalanmäki. It houses a comprehensive collection of Finnish art.

Tuomiokirkko Ⓕ (Turku Cathedral; open daily) maintains a stately presence. Consecrated in 1300, it is Finland's most important medieval structure. In the Cathedral Park a statue depicts Governor Per Brahe in

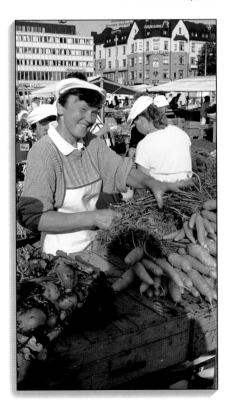

a classically proud pose. A complex of cream-hued buildings at Vanha Suurtori 7, houses the **Turku Cultural Centre** with a cosy Book Café and restaurant, Teini (tel: 2 233 0203), offering a reasonably priced luncheon buffet. To the north stands the **Rettig Palace**, today the museum complex, **Aboa Vetus and Ars Nova ©** (open May–Aug: daily 10am–7pm; Sept–Apr: closed Mon; entrance fee; tel: 2 250 0552). The main house exhibits 20th-century art and the courtyard (with ruins of a medieval town) provides a glimpse of Turku's history.

Along the riverbank

For a riverbank tour, visit **Qwensel House**, named after a judge, J.W. Qwensel, who bought the plot of land in 1695. This is Turku's oldest wooden building, with a popular courtyard café , and now houses the atmospheric **Apteekkimuseo ①** (Pharmacy Museum; Läntinen Rantakatu 13; open Apr–Sept: 10am–6pm; Oct–Mar: Tues–Sun 10am–3pm; entrance fee; tel: 2 262 0280). From the front of the museum, the horse-cab *Musta-Hilu* provides a leisurely view of the city.

Walk past Myllysilta (Mill Bridge) to the next bridge, Martinsilta, where the *SS Ukkopekka* steamship is moored, and still offers pleasant excursions through the archipelago. Depending on how far you care to walk, you can continue on this side of the river as far as Turku Castle and the modern harbour areas, with merchant tugs and tankers and the terminals of the Viking and Silja Lines.

On your way to the harbour at Linnankatu 74 is the **Forum Marinum ①** (Maritime Centre; open daily; entrance fee), home of the excellent Maritime Museum and Turku's museum ships, including the barque *Sigyn*.

Heading back towards the centre you come to the **Wäinö Aaltonen Museo ①** (Itäinen Rantakatu 38; open Tues–Sun 11am–7pm; entrance fee; tel: 2 235

TIP

A dining experience not to be missed: The Angel Restaurant, Kauppiaskatu 16 (tel: 2 231 9088) serves heavenly meals in a series of dining rooms all featuring seraphic decor. Live music in the evening.

5690). The modern structure contains works by one of Finland's most important sculptors, Wäinö Aaltonen (1894–1966). In **Urheilupuisto K**, the surrounding park, the windmill on Samppalinnanmäki is the last of its kind in Turku. Next to it is the running track where the champion long distance runner and Olympic gold medallist Paavo Nurmi (1897–1973) trained. His statue stands on Auransilta. The polished granite stone on the slopes of Samppalinnanmäki is Finland's independence memorial, unveiled in 1977 on the 60th anniversary.

Ruissalo Island

Boat services depart several times daily for **Ruissalo Island L**. An ideal excursion for cyclists, walkers and nature lovers, Ruissalo also has the area's best beaches. The 19th-century **Villa Roma** is typical of the "lace villas" (so-called because of their latticed balconies and windows) built by wealthy merchants. Its owner, the Procultura Foundation, shows summer exhibitions of top-quality Finnish art. In summer, the island is home to Ruisrock, the annual rock festival.

One of the most civilised ways to see the archipelago is with a morning, afternoon or supper cruise aboard the *SS Ukkopekka*, which retains something of its steamship past. The bearded skipper, Captain Kangas, is everyone's image of a sea captain and a couple of musicians sing old Finnish sailing songs as the islands glide by. The steamship cruises to different islands and towns, including Captain Kangas's home town of **Naantali**, a charming place north of Turku. In summer Naantali comes alive as people move into their summer houses in the narrow winding streets of the old town and yachts moor in the harbour. Children are attracted by **Moomin World** (open mid-May–mid Aug: 10am–8pm), based on the characters made famous by the Finnish author Tove Jansson. ❑

Map on page 324

Turku has become known for its quartet of bars in the city centre, all housed in buildings that have been converted from a pharmacy, bank, schoolhouse, and even a public toilet.

BELOW: boats moored on the Aura river.

FINLAND'S LAKELAND

*A labyrinth of lakes and pine-covered islands extends north
from Helsinki. The landscape that was home to Sibelius
rewards exploration by lake steamer and canoe*

Map
on page
316

Helsinki

With some 33,000 islands and peninsulas, the Great Lakes of Saimaa and Päijänne in Central Finland provide a diverse waterscape of lakes, rivers and canals to form Europe's largest inland waterway system. This varied landscape owes its beauty to the Ice Age when glaciers carved out the shape of lakes and ridges. Excellent holiday facilities are offered for most kinds of water sports throughout this region.

The best approach to the lakes is via industrial **Kouvola** ㉒, about 140 km (86 miles) northeast of Helsinki and a junction of road and rail routes into Saimaa. Although not the most interesting town in Finland, Kouvola's Kaunisnurmi quarters house quaint handicraft shops and several museums.

To capture the spirit of Saimaa, ignore the direct routes to Kuopio in the north of the region and head east on Road 6 to **Lappeenranta** ㉓, South Karelia's main town. The fortress next to the harbour was built by the Russians in 1775. Nearby, the suburb of Linnoitus is the most interesting part of the town, where you will find Finland's oldest **Orthodox Church** (1785) and the **Etelä-Karjalan Museo** (South Karelian Museum; open Mon–Fri 10am–6pm, Sat–Sun 11am–5pm; Sept–May: closed Mon, Fri; entrance fee; tel: 5 616 2255), with a fascinating section on the old city of Vyborg (just a few miles south in Russia). The **Ratsuväkimuseo** (Cavalry Museum; open June–Aug: Mon–Fri 10am–6pm, Sat–Sun 11am–5pm; entrance fee; tel: 5 616 2255) details the history and distinctive red uniforms of Finland's proud soldiers. Day cruises to Russia operate from Lappeenranta for which Western visitors do not require visas, although they are obligatory for other visits.

A few miles further east is the industrial city of **Imatra** ㉔, once erroneously described as the "Niagara of Finland", but worth a brief visit to see the impressive **Imatrankoski** (rapids).

High on the ridges

About 50 km (30 miles) north of Imatra, Road 6 passes within a few hundred metres of the Russian border. Switching to Road 14, you soon come to **Punkaharju** ㉕, one of Finland's best-loved beauty spots. Punkaharju is one of countless ridges bequeathed to Finland by the last Ice Age. It's around 7 km (4 miles) long and in places is just wide enough to carry the road; elsewhere it widens to accommodate magnificent pine and birch woods.

Lusto, the superb Forestry Museum (open May–Sept: daily; Oct–Apr: Tues–Sun; entrance fee; tel: 15 345 1030) has a comprehensive exhibition on Finland's forests and associated subjects such as design, wilderness trekking, forestry industry and research. Tucked away among Punkaharju's ridges are well-

LEFT: peaceful Lakeland waters.
BELOW: composer Jean Sibelius was born in the town of Hämeenlinna.

The Retretti Arts Centre, Punkaharju, is housed in caverns literally blasted out of the rock to provide a remarkable exhibition space for Finnish art and design, and an atmospheric underground area with a concert hall.

equipped holiday centres and the **Kesämaa (Summerland) Leisure Centre** for family fun. The **Retretti Arts Centre** (open June–Aug: daily 10am–5pm, July until 6pm; entrance fee; tel: 15 775 2200), built into the bedrock on the ridge, is well worth a visit. Its annual exhibition, featuring four usually quite different, internationally acclaimed artists, is a major event in Finland. In summer, a lake steamer sails between Punkaharju and Savonlinna from Retretti. The two-hour trip is a delightful mini-voyage through the islands.

Operatic odyssey

Savonlinna ㉖ ("the castle of Savo") is the most charming of Finland's main lakeland towns and the best base in Saimaa for making trips. It has the medieval castle of **Olavinlinna** (open for tours, June–Aug: 10am–5pm; Sept–May: 10am–3pm; entrance fee), which is the site of the annual International Opera Festival that takes place throughout July. Tickets for, and accommodation during, the festival should be booked well ahead (tel: 15 47 6750; fax: 15 47 67540; e-mail: info@operafestival.fi). With its massive granite walls, ramparts and shooting galleries topped by three great round towers, Olavinlinna has everything you might expect from a medieval castle.

Near the castle, the museum ship *Salama*, a steam schooner built in 1874, shipwrecked in 1898 and raised from the lake in 1971, is one of three converted old ships that form the inland navigation section of the **Savonlinnan Maakuntamuseo** (Savonlinna Provincial Museum, Riihisaari; open July–Aug: daily 11am–8pm; Sept–June: Tue–Sun 11am–5pm; entrance fee; tel: 15 571 712).

From Savonlinna to Kuopio by lake steamer is a full day's journey. Road travellers have a choice of continuing west from Savonlinna on Roads 14 and 5 to Mikkeli or staying with Saimaa to its northern limits beyond Kuopio.

Mikkeli ㉗, a pleasant provincial capital, is a historic army town. Some 5 km (3 miles) north of Mikkeli, the **Visulahti Family Leisure Centre** is set in a park populated with an automobile exhibition, waxworks and the Dinosauria amusement centre.

Convent culture

The recommended way to Kuopio from Savonlinna is via Varkaus on Road 464, a particularly attractive and watery route. Then take Road 23 heading northeast towards Joensuu in north Karelia, passing by the Orthodox monastery of **Valamon Luostari** ㉘ (open daily 8am–9pm; tel: 17 570 111) and the convent of **Lintulan Luostari** (tel: 17 563 106). On all three counts of history, culture and scenery, these merit a visit. Monastery cruises run from Kuopio in summer.

The clue to the monastery's history lies in its name. Valamo is the large island on Lake Ladoga, across the Russian border to the east, on which an Orthodox religious foundation was established in the Middle Ages. During the Finn-Russian Winter War, 1939–1940, the handful of elderly monks was forced to leave and eventually settled in the present site of Uusi ("New") Valamo, originally an old manor house. Valamon Luostari has experienced something of a renaissance in recent years. There is a fine church, completed in

BELOW: the lakes attract windsurfers.

1977, a cafeteria, wine shop, souvenir shop and a modern hotel. The Lintulan Luostari, a few kilometres away, has a similar but shorter history.

Music and dance

Kuopio ㉙ has a crowded summer calendar, the highlight of which is the International Dance and Music Festival in June. The town's daily market fills most of the central **Tori** (Market Place) and is one of the most varied outside Helsinki. Sights to see include the **Kuopion Kortellimuseo** (Kirkkokatu 22; open May–Sept: 10am–5pm; Oct–Apr 10am–3pm; entrance fee; tel: 17 182 625), comprising a number of original dwellings complete with authentic furniture, warehouses, and even gardens dating from the 18th century to the 1930s. The **Kuopion Museo** (Kauppakatu 23; open Mon–Sat 10am–4pm, Sun 11am–6pm; Sept–Apr: closed Sat; entrance fee; tel: 17 182 603) houses regional collections of a cultural and natural history order in a castle-like building.

Icons – many from the 18th century and some from the 10th century – and sacred objects are on view at the **Ortodoksinen Kirkkomuseo** (Orthodox Church Museum, Karjalankatu 1; open May–Aug: Tues–Sun 10am–4pm; Sept–Apr: noon–3pm; entrance fee; tel: 17 287 2244). The treasures were brought here from Valamo and Konevitsa monasteries in Karelia and a few from Petsamo in the far north, all territories ceded to the Soviet Union.

At **Iisalmi** ㉚, 80 km (50 miles) north of Kuopio on Road 5, **Evakkokeskus** (Kyllikinkatu 8), a Karelian-Orthodox Cultural Centre, displays valuable relics recovered from territory now in Russia. You can dine on the harbour at **Kuappi**, "the smallest restaurant in the world", or at **Olutmestari**, Savonkatu 18, a popular summer restaurant with an attractive terrace.

Map on page 316

The 19th century re-created in Lappeenranta.

BELOW: Olavinlinna, a dramatic setting for opera.

Street corner kiosks offer everything from culinary delights to fast food.

The western lakes

To the west of the region lies Päijänne, Finland's deepest lake and its longest at 119 km (74 miles). At the southern and northern ends of the lake system are two of Finland's more substantial towns, Lahti and Jyväskylä respectively, which are linked to the west of Päijänne by one of Europe's main highways, E24, and to the east of it by a network of slower more attractive routes.

Lahti ❸ lies 103 km (64 miles) north of Helsinki on Road 4 (E75). The **Lahden Urheilukeskus** sports centre, offers some of Finland's best winter sports facilities, and is the venue for the annual Finlandia Ski Race and the Ski Games. Lahti is a modern place, one of its few older buildings being the **Kaupungintalo** (Town Hall) designed by Eliel Saarinen in 1912. Three blocks to the north is the market, and two blocks further north, at Kirkkokatu 4, the highly individualistic **Ristinkirkko** (Church of the Cross; open daily), built in 1978, and the last church in Finland designed by Alvar Aalto.

The **Lahden Historiallinen Museo** (Lahdenkatu 4; open Mon–Fri 10am–5pm, Sat–Sun 11am–5pm; entrance fee; tel: 3 814 4536) in Lahti Manor is an exotic late 19th-century building with very good regional ethnographical and cultural history collections, as well as art and furniture. A few kilometres northwest to Tiirismaa, is the tourist centre of **Messilä**, combining an old manor house, downhill skiing in winter and camping.

From Lahti it's only 35 km (21 miles) northeast on Road 4 to the pleasant little town of **Heinola** ❷. Taking the popular summer lake route, it is a lovely four-and-a-half hours by steamer.

The **Jyrängönkoski** (rapids) provide good sport for local canoeists and for fishermen casting for lake and rainbow trout. Rent a rod at the **Siltasaari**

BELOW: dancers perform at Kuopio's annual festival.

Fishing Centre by the rapids and have your catch smoked to eat on the spot or take it away.

An attractive route to Jyväskylä is to leave Lahti to the north on Road 24 and after 25 km (15 miles), soon after crossing the Vääksy canal at Asikkala, branch right onto minor Road 314. This will take you along the **Pulkkilanharju** (ridge), which vies with that of Punkaharju for magnificent views. Continue via Sysmä and Luhanka, through various waterscapes that make up Päijänne's contorted eastern shore. To rejoin Road 9 (E63) at Korpilahti for the final leg to Jyväskylä you can use the enormous bridge across Kärkistensalmi, one of Päijänne's many narrow straits. Road 24, of course, provides a more direct main road link all the way from Lahti to Jyväskylä in 174 km (107 miles).

A particular beauty spot inside the **Päijänteen Kansallispuisto** (Päijänne National Park) is the long, slender island of **Kelvenne** ㉝, about 60 km (37 miles) north of Lahti, with its lakes, lagoons and curious geological formations. You can reach it from the Ravintola Laivaranta camping area (tel: 40 512 0645) at Padasjoki.

Alvar Aalto's city

Jyväskylä ㉞ is situated on the northern shore of Lake Päijänne. Alvar Aalto grew up here and there are no fewer than 30 major buildings by him around the area, including the university, theatre and the Museum of Central Finland. Don't miss the **Alvar Aalto Museo** (7 Alvar Aallonkatu; open Tues–Sun 11am–6pm; entrance fee; tel: 14 624 809) with its collection of architectural plans, photographs, scale models and Aalto's furniture designs. There are a number of winter and summer sports facilities in Jyväskylä, but the town is best known

Map on page 316

BELOW: a boat is an essential part of Lakeland life.

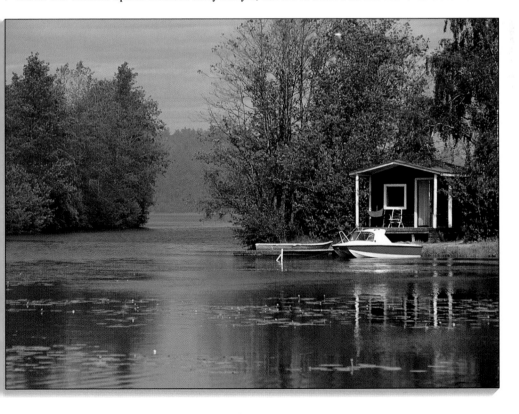

internationally as the venue for the well-attended 1,000 Lakes Rally in August, Finland's premier motor racing event. The Jyväskylä Arts Festival is a major cultural event held every June, always with a different theme.

With over 200 lakes in the area, make sure to take a boat journey from Tampere, either south on the Silverline route, or north on the Poet's Way, or hop on a boat to Viikinsaari to retreat into nature.

Tampere

Tampere ㉟, Finland's industrial capital, lies 150 km (94 miles) southwest of Jyväskylä. It was officially founded in 1779 by King Gustav III of Sweden-Finland and owes its fortunes to the Tammerkoski (rapids), which first brought power and industry to the area. The Tammerskoski have largely lost their working factories, and in their place are hotels, shopping centres and museums.

Significant churches, museums and buildings include the 20th-century **Kirjasto Ⓐ** (City Library) by husband and wife architects, Reima and Raili Pietilä, the design of which is said to be based on the open wings and spread tail feathers of a wood grouse; and **Tampere-talo Ⓑ** (Tampere Hall), a spectacular blue-white structure designed in 1990 by Esa Piiroinen and Sakari Aartelo.

Tuomiokirkko Ⓒ (Tampere Cathedral, Tuomiokirkonkatu 3), designed by Lars Sonck in National Romantic style and completed in 1907, contains some of the best of Finnish art, including Magnus Enckell's altar fresco of the Resurrection and Hugo Simberg's masterpiece, *The Wounded Angel*.

In a park on the eastern side of town is another Pietilä design, the stark-looking **Kalevan Kirkko** (Church; Liisanpuisto 1). Built in 1966, its most striking feature is the organ with 3,000 pipes shaped like a sail.

The Tampella foundry, built in 1850, was transformed in 1996 into an impressive museum centre and renamed **Tehdasmuseo Vapriikki Ⓓ** (Veturiaukio 4; open Tues, Thurs–Sun 10am–6pm, Wed 11am–8pm, closed Mon; entrance fee;

tel: 3 3146 6966). It features exhibitions on the Tampere region from archaeology to technology. There is a café-restaurant, and museum shop.

Across the northern harbour entrance from Näsinpuisto (park) is the highest viewpoint in Finland, the **Näsinneula Observation Tower** **E** (open summer: 10am–8pm; entrance fee). It stands 120 metres (400 ft) high at the centre of Särkänniemi Park. The park is a favourite place for children with its aquarium, dolphinarium, planetarium, children's zoo and amusement park (for opening hours, tel: 3 248 8212; www.sarkanniemi.fi). In the same complex is the **Sara Hildénin Taidemuseo** **F** (Sara Hildén Art Museum; open daily 11am–6pm; entrance fee; tel: 3 214 3134) located in a beautiful building housing Hildén's collection of modern Finnish and foreign art.

South of Tampere

From Tampere, the 175-km (110-mile) route back to Helsinki passes through the industrial centre of **Valkeakoski** **36**. In the Middle Ages, Valkeakoski was no more than a hamlet, later a mining village in the important parish of Sääksmäki; but, even then, it had the rapids that meant water power, first to grind corn and then to make paper. In contrast, the 19th-century National Romantic movement brought artists to Sääksmäki and these two ingredients – industry and art – still combine today.

The old **Voipaalan Kartano** (Voipaala Manor; open May–Sept: daily; Oct–Apr: closed Mon; entrance fee; tel: 3 543 6528) on Rapola Hill has become an art centre. It was once the home of the sculptor Elias Ilkka who owned the manor and farm where the Valkeakoski Summer Theatre performs. Make your way to **Visavuori**, the studio home of one of Finland's best-known sculptors,

Maps:
Area: 316
City: 332

Tampere Library houses "Moomin Valley", an exhibition of the characters from Tove Jansson's popular books.

BELOW: Kaleva Church, Tampere.

Map on page 316

Emil Wikström (1864–1942). At the age of 29, he won a competition to design the frieze for Helsinki's House of Estates and in the same year designed this house overlooking the lake, complete with rooftop observatory.

Glass-blowing centre

Of all Finland's glassmakers, **Iittala 37** is probably the most famous. In the **Iittalan Lasimuseo** (museum; open May–Aug: 9am–8pm; Sept–Apr: 10am–6pm; entrance fee; tel: 2 0439 3521) beautiful functional glassware and *objets d'art* such as glass birds and fruit shapes are on display, along with designs by Alvar Aalto and Timo Sarpaneva. Visit the Iittala shop where seconds are often indistinguishable to the inexpert eye and less than half the price of perfect work.

It's also worth visiting the **Suomen Lasimuseo** (Finnish Glass Museum; open May–Aug: daily 10am–6pm; Sept–Apr: Tues–Sun 10am–6pm, closed Mon; entrance fee; tel: 19 741 7494) in **Riihimäki 38**, just off Road 3, 35 km (26 miles) south of Hämeenlinna. The museum is housed in an authentic glassworks from 1914. Exhibits trace the history of glassmaking from the early days of windowpane production to the era of glass as a fine art in the 20th century.

Häme Castle, Hämeenlinna, built by the Swedes in the 13th century.

BELOW: keeping up the glassmaking tradition at Iittala.

Sibelius country

Continuing south from Iittala, Road 57 leads to the lake of Hattula and **Hattulan Pyhän Ristin Kirkko** (Hattulan Church of the Holy Cross), one of Finland's best known and oldest churches, built in 1320. Just off the E12, **Aulangon Puisto** (Aulanko Forest Park) is ideal for a break, overlooking Aulankojärvi (lake). Jean Sibelius, who was born in nearby **Hämeenlinna 39**, is said to have commented on Aulanko: "I was thinking of these scenes from my childhood when I composed *Finlandia*."

Hämeenlinna has two claims to fame: first, the early 13th-century Häme Castle (open May–Aug: 10am–6pm; Sept–Apr: 10am–4pm; entrance fee; tel: 3 675 6820) and, second, the fact that it was the birthplace of Jean Sibelius. Sibelius was born in December 1865 in the little timberboard house of the town physician, Christian Gustaf Sibelius, now the **Sibeliuksen Syntymäkoti Museo** (Sibelius Home Museum, Hallituskatu 11; open May–Aug 10am–4pm; Sept–Apr: noon–4pm; closed Jan; entrance fee; tel: 3 621 2755). The big dining room is used for recitals, and the house is full of memorabilia.

Heading south through Hyvinkää to **Järvenpää 40**, you are only 45 km (30 miles) from Helsinki. The area's **Tuusulanjärvi** (lake) attracted late 19th-century artists and intellectuals away from their city haunts to build studio-villas on the eastern side, just beyond Järvenpää. Among them was the portrait painter Eero Järnefelt, noted for his rural and folk scenes, and Jean Sibelius and his wife Aino.

Museon Nimi Ainola 41 was the Sibelius home for 53 years (open June–Aug: Tue–Sun 11am–5pm; May and Sept: Wed–Sun 11am–5pm; entrance fee; tel: 9 287 322). Designed by Lars Sonck, the house is still furnished as it was in Sibelius's time and the drawing room holds the composer's piano. Floral tributes adorn the couple's grave in the garden. ❏

CANOEING THE OPEN WATERS

Paddling a canoe on the lakes and rivers of Finland is one of the most pleasurable ways to explore the country. For the energetic there are annual races

One of the more testing annual events on the European canoeing calendar is the Arctic Circle Race which takes place every summer north of the Arctic Circle from Kilipsjärvi to Tornio along 537 km (334 miles) of the border rivers between Finland and Sweden. Another is the six-day 700-km (430-mile) Finlandia Canoe Relay each June, usually through the complex Saimaa system.

With 187,888 lakes (at the last count) and innumerable rivers, it's surprising that canoeing has only become popular in Finland in recent years. There is a growing range of packages whereby you can canoe well-tried routes of varying lengths with the option of hiring equipment, camping or staying in farmhouse accommodation.

A particularly well-tried series of routes forms an overall 350-km (217-mile) circuit beginning and ending at Heinola. This needs 10–15 days, but can also be divided into shorter sections. Another, along 320 km (200 miles) of the Ounasjoki river in Lapland from Enontekiö to Rovaniemi, features sections of true Arctic wilderness; the rapids are mainly Grade I, but it is possible to portage round the most daunting of these. Yet another follows a 285-km (180-mile) lake-and-river route taken by the old tar boats from Kuhmo to Oulu.

If you're attracted to the idea of pioneering across the lakes the possibilities are legion. Any of the 19 road maps which cover the entire country on a scale of of 1:200 000 will be sufficient for general planning, but absolutely essential for more detail are the

special inland water charts, for example, for Saimaa on a scale of 1:40 000/1:50 000. It's not until you are in your canoe, however, that navigation problems become clear. From water level one island of rock and pine trees looks like another with few helpful landmarks. You will appreciate those other vital aids to canoeing the Finnish lakes: a compass and a pair of binoculars.

The greatest inconvenience you are likely to encounter is wind. Squalls blow up quickly and across these great expanses, waters are soon whipped up into turbulence. Head for shelter at the first sign.

Seek permission to camp whenever possible, since the right to pitch your tent anywhere has been abused by some foreigners and is no longer permitted. Often, of course, there is no one to ask. It is one of the joys of canoeing in Finland that you may travel for days without sign of humanity, other than a tugboat hauling timber, or a fisherman. ❏

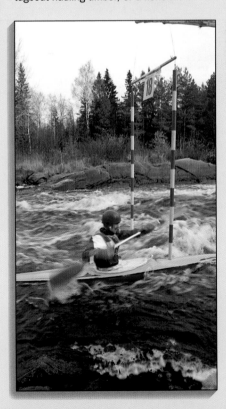

TOP LEFT: canoeists stop for a well-earned rest. **ABOVE:** kayakers in action. **ABOVE RIGHT:** paddle power. **RIGHT:** slalom competitor.

FINLAND'S WEST COAST

The beautiful Bothnian coastline preserves its rich
maritime heritage and its blend of Finnish-Swedish culture
in the islands and towns along the road to Lapland

Map
on page
338

T he west coast of Finland is a fascinating mixture of past and present: stately churches and old wooden houses, museums and modern industry. With its close proximity to Sweden, Swedish remains the first language for many communities and some towns have both Swedish and Finnish names.

The first main town north of **Turku** *(see page 323)* on Road 8 is **Uusikaupunki (Nystad) ❶**. The **Kulttuuruhistoriallinen Museo** (Museum of Cultural History; open June–Aug: Tues–Sun; entrance fee; tel: 2 8451 5399) is in the house of F.W. Wahlberg, a former shipowner and tobacco manufacturer. **Myllymäki Park** is a reminder that many retired sailors became millers and the countryside was once dotted with windmills; four windmills and a tower remain.

Palaces and timber homes

Rauma ❷ is the largest medieval town in Scandinavia, listed as a UNESCO World Heritage Site with 600 or so wooden buildings painted in traditional pastel shades. Many of these are still private homes. Although the dwellings and shops are 18th- and 19th-century buildings, the pattern of narrow streets dates back to the 16th century.

Pori ❸, some 47 km (37 miles) north of Rauma, was founded by Duke Johan of Sweden in 1558. With a population of 76,600, it is one of Finland's chief export harbours and hosts a jazz festival every July. Interesting sights include the **City Hall**, built in the style of a Venetian Palace. More off-beat is the **Jusélius Mausoleum** (open May–Aug: daily noon–3pm; Sept–Apr: Sun only noon–2pm; free) at Käppärä Cemetery, built by a Pori businessman in memory of his young daughter. Inside is one of the artist Akseli Gallén-Kallela's masterpieces.

Satakunta Museo (open Tues–Sun 11am–5pm; entrance fee; tel: 2 621 1063), dating from 1888, is the largest Finnish cultural history museum and includes a fine collection of 19th- and- 20th century Finnish art. The **Porin Taidemuseo** (Pori Art Museum, Eteläranta; open Tues–Sun; entrance fee; tel: 2 621 1080), features contemporary art.

The peninsula leading from Pori to **Reposaari** has a long sandy beach and is one of Finland's best resorts. **Kristinestad (Kristiinankaupunki) ❹**, 95 km (59 miles) to the north was founded by the Swedish governor, Count Per Brahe, in 1649. A master of diplomacy, he gave the town the name of both his wife and Queen Kristina of Sweden-Finland. **Merimuseo** (open May–Sept: Tues–Sun; entrance fee; tel: 2 128 59), is set in the house of former shipowner S.A. Wendelin and displays his memorablilia.

Vaasa (Vasa) ❺, established in the 14th century, has been devasted by wars and fire. Today it is a hand-

LEFT: sparkling water in the Gulf of Bothnia.
BELOW: Rauma's Franciscan monastery.

West Coast

| 0 | 50 km |
| 0 | 50 miles |

some town with wide, attractively laid-out streets and a large market square. Notable buildings include the Orthodox Church, the Court of Appeal (1862), and the Town Hall (1883). For the best view of the town, clamber up the 200 steps in the tower behind the police station headquarters.

Vaasa is well-endowed with museums, the most important being the **Pohjanmaan Museo** (Ostrobothnian Museum; Museokatu 3; open daily; entrance free Wed; tel: 6 325 3800), which covers local history and art. **Bragen Ulkomuseo** (Brage Open-Air Museum; open June–Aug: Tues–Sun; entrance fee; tel: 6 312 7166) features Ostrobothnian farm life in the 19th century. **Wasalandia** is the town's colourful amusement park (open May–Aug: daily; entrance fee). Offshore islands add to the charms of Vaasa.

Jakobstad (Pietarsaari) ❻ gained repute as the pre-eminent Finnish shipbuilding centre, producing vessels that opened new trade routes around the world. One of the town's best known sailing ships *Jakobstads Wapen*, a 1767 galleon, still makes cruises. Some 300 or so restored wooden houses may be seen in the old part of town.

Road of seven bridges

From Jakobstad to **Kokkola** ❼, take the attractive route called the "road of seven bridges", which runs from island to island across the archipelago. Kokkola's Town Hall was designed by Carl Ludwig Engel, who has left his mark on so many Finnish towns, and there is an English park and boathouse commemorating an episode in the Crimean war with the British fleet. On the 230-km (140-mile) road north between Kokkola and Oulu, the town of **Kalajoki** ❽ is a popular spot for fishing, bathing and sailing.

Oulu ❾ is the largest city in northern Finland, with a population of 115,500. **Turkansaaren Ulkomuseo** ❿ (Turkansaari Open-Air Museum; open June–Sept: daily; entrance fee; tel: 8 5586 7191) can be found on a small island in the Oulujoki, 14 km (8 miles) east of Oulu. It has an interesting collection of Ostrobothnian buildings, including a church, farm buildings and windmills. In town, the **Tietomaa Science Centre** (open daily; entrance fee; tel: 8 5584 1340), offers a wealth of hands-on exhibits. The elegant **Oulun Taidemuseo** (open Tues–Sun 11am–6pm, Wed 11am–8pm; entrance fee; tel: 8 5584 7463) has a permanent exhibition of Finnish contemporary art. Visit **Koskikeskus** (Rapids Centre) on the mouth of the Oulujoki, with 12 fountains.

Map on page 338

Snow and the Midnight Sun

From Oulu to **Kemi** ⓫, one begins the approach to Lapland. Kemi lies at the mouth of the Kemijoki River and is known as the seaport of Lapland. In winter, you can take an excursion on the 1961 icebreaker, *Sampo*. A sight not to miss is **Lumilinna** (Snow Castle; tel: 16 259 502) with its dazzling white walls and illuminated towers. The castle is rebuilt every year and opens in February.

Lumilinna, the annual snow castle at Kemi, makes an impressive sight.

On the border a short distance west is **Tornio** ⓬, near the mouth of the Tornionjoki. The **Aineen Taidemuseo** (Aine Art Museum; open Tues–Sun; entrance fee; tel: 16 432 438) houses a fine collection of Finnish art from 1814 to the present. For a great view, visit the **Vesitorni** water tower (open daily mid June–mid Aug).

At the **Green Zone Golf Course** (open June–Oct) on the Finnish-Swedish border, you can play nine holes in Sweden and nine in Finland. It is a rare delight to play a night round in summer, thanks to the Midnight Sun.

If you drive 9 miles (15 km) north of Tornio off Road E78, you will come to **Kukkolankoski** ⓭, the longest free-flowing rapids in Finland at 3,500 metres (11,150 ft). Fishermen here still use the traditional long-handled net.   ❏

BELOW: tranquil scene on the West coast.

Map
on page
342

KARELIA AND KUUSAMO

*Easterly Karelia with its distinctly Orthodox heritage is the
setting for Finland's epic poem, "Kalevala". Traditions
abound, the air is pure and the landscape untouched*

BELOW: the
Evakkokesus
Orthodox Centre;
many Karelians
belong to the
Orthodox Church.

Karelia is the general name for the area whose westernmost part is still in
Finland and the larger, easternmost part – which was ceded to the Soviet
Union as a result of the Treaty of Paris in 1947 – is in Russia. There are
many holiday options, including renting a cottage or log cabin by the water or
staying in a "working" farmhouse. Depending on the season, one can enjoy a
range of water or winter sports, fishing, hiking, and berry-picking.

Joensuu ❶, the "capital" of North Karelia, is famous for its Festival of Song
every June. The **Pohjois-Karjalan Museo** (North Karelia Museum, Koskikatu
5; open Tues–Fri noon–4pm; Sun 10am–6pm; entrance fee; tel: 13 610 0670)
features exhibits on the history and the folk culture of this part of Karelia. The
museum is housed in the Carelicum tourist centre (tel: 13 267 5223). Along
the same street there is the **Taidemuseo** (Art Museum, Kirkkokatu 23; open
Tues–Sun 11am–4pm; entrance fee; tel: 13 267 5388), containing an icon collection and Finnish paintings from the 19th and 20th centuries.

Before turning north, go east to **Ilomantsi** ❷. Ilomantsi is the oldest inhabited area of North Karelia and a stronghold of the Orthodox Church. Easter is
the most impressive festival here, and other colourful events are held throughout the summer. Ilomantsi was one of the main battle grounds in the wars of

1939–45 and the **Fighter's House** on Hattuvaara Hill has exhibitions about that period. Nearby in the village of **Runokylaå** at the Singers Lodge on Parppeinvaara Hill, the ancient folk poems of the *Kalevala* are still sung by women in traditional costume (accompanied by the *kantele*, a zither-like instrument). The **Parppei Pirtti** restaurant (tel: 13 881421) on the hill features Karelian cuisine, including tiny fish (*vendace*), cold smoked whitefish, hearty meat casseroles and pies, *pirakka* pastries, and baked cheese with cloudberry jam.

Gateway to the wilderness

Heading north from Joensuu, take Route 6 and the eastward fork to Route 73 to **Lieksa ❸**, where the **Ruuankoski** (rapids) must be seen, and possibly experienced, under the supervision of a guide. Lieksa, one of the many forest centres in Finland, is only about 20 years old and has a population of 19,000 in an area larger than London. The **Pielinen Museo** (Pielinen Open-Air Museum, Pappilantie 2; open May–Sept: daily; entrance fee; tel: 13 520 2402) has 70 buildings, some dating to the 17th century, which document local settlement.

At **Vuonisjärvi ❹**, 29 km (18 miles) from the centre is **Paateri** (open June–Aug: daily; entrance fee), the studio of Eeva Ryynänen, a wood sculptor noted for her spectacular Wilderness Church.

Lieksa is the gateway to Finland's wilderness. "Never go hiking on your own" is the warning motto of this region, whose dense forests are inhabited by bears, wolves, elk and reindeer. At **Kaksinkantaja**, 40 km (26 miles) from the centre, there is an exhibition of bear skulls and stuffed animals by Väinö Heikkinen, a renowned bear hunter (open June–Aug: daily; entrance fee). From Lieksa, Road 73 leads to **Nurmes ❺**. First mentioned in documents in 1556, Nurmes is a beautiful

TIP

Mountain biking is a popular way to explore Karelia. Hire a bike locally, or join a week-long guided trail bike expedition from Lieksa (details from Lieksa Tourist Service, tel: 13 520 2400).

BELOW: traditional way of life on a Karelian farm.

KARELIA: SOUL AND SAUNA

If Finland has a soul, that soul lives on in Karelia. When Finns have gone to war, it has concerned Karelia. A Karelian theme runs through the music of Sibelius and his *Karelian Suite* reaches sublime heights of patriotism.

The Karelians were one of the earliest of the Finnish communities; they are evident in Bronze and Iron Age discoveries. The *Kalevala*, the great epic saga of ancient life in the far north, is really about Karelians. The poem, which in the 18th and 19th centuries became the cornerstone of the struggle for national culture, recounts everyday events and rituals and finally the heroes' joy as they celebrate in song the salvation of the land of Kalevala from its enemies.

True Karelia exists only as a fragment of its former self. The greater part of the region lies east of the Russian border, lost to Finland after the Winter War (1939–40). As a result 400,000 Karelians had to be resettled in the 1940s. Since then, people of Karelian origin can be found in all parts of Finland. They tend to be lively and talkative, in contrast with the more taciturn nature of other Finns.

It is they who are responsible for the sauna. Early Karelians cleared woodland to grow crops and used steam heat to dry their grain. The therapeutic benefits of this heat were later realised and so the sauna was born in Finland.

Karelia and Kuusamo

town. The **Bomba House** (Suojårvenkatu 1; tel: 13 687 200) is a traditional wooden Karelian house at Ritoniemi, about 2 km (1¼ miles) from the town, surrounded by a "Karelian village" which provides visitors not only with comfortable accommodation, but also with delicious meals of local specialities.

Nurmes is the place to leave the car and take a scenic ride on Finland's largest inland waterway ferry down Lake Pielinen to **Kolin Kansallispuisto** ❻ (Koli National Park). Here you will see views that inspired some of Finland's greatest painters as well as the composer, Sibelius.

Before reaching the Oulu area, if your choice is Road 6 north you could detour to the remote national park, **Tiilikkajärven Kansallispuisto** ❼, near Rautavaara. It was established to conserve the uninhabited area of Lake Tiilikka and the surrounding bogs.

Another national park, **Hiidenportin Kansallispuisto** ❽, is southeast of Sotkamo and also best reached from Road 6. This is a rugged area with the narrow Hiidenporti Gorge, a rift valley with rock sides dropping 20 metres (70 ft) to the floor. There are well-marked trails and camp sites in the park.

Both in and outside the parks you may find reindeer. These animals are the main source of income for many people living in the region and it is very important to take special care on roads when reindeer are around, especially at dusk.

The Finnish frontier

Kuhmo ❾ is a frontier town surrounded by dense forests in the wilderness area of Kainuu. It is known for its annual Kuhmo Chamber Music Festival. A fascinating re-created **Kalevala Village** (open June–Aug: daily; entrance fee; tel: 8 655 4500) in a wooded park on the outskirts of Kuhmo displays numerous local folk traditions. The aim is to give modern-day visitors an idea of Finnish culture as it was immortalised in Finland's epic poem, *Kalevala*. The **Hotel Kalevala** specialises in regional cuisine (tel: 8 655 4100).

A long straight road through some of

Finland's darkest forests leads west out of Kuhmo to Sotkamo and then onwards to **Kajaani** ⑩, the area's main town, on the eastern edge of Oulujärvi (lake). Kajaani still has the ruins of the 1604 castle and its town hall was designed by Carl Ludwig Engel, who was responsible for so much of early Helsinki. The road from Kajaani towards **Oulu** hugs the shores of Oulujärvi, plunging first into thickly wooded hill country. Before entering Oulu, the route goes through **Muhos** which has the second-oldest church in Finland, dating from 1634.

Kuusamo

The only other main centre in this scantily populated area is **Kuusamo** ⑪, almost at the Russian border, some 360 km (225 miles) northeast across the breadth of the country along Road 20. The Kuusamo region is marvellous wilderness country, ideal for canoeing and fishing, and the main sound in these parts is a mixture of rushing water and the wind high in the pines. This is also berry country, with several varieties growing in great profusion on the Arctic tundra. The only snag is the number of mosquitoes: take plenty of protection.

    Karhuntassu Tourist Centre (tel: 8 850 2910) provides information on every activity, accommodation and most other aspects of the region. In winter, the area is excellent for skiing and snowmobiling. There are two national parks: the largest, **Oulangan Kansallispuisto** ⑫, to the north, covers a largely untouched region bordering the Oulanka river. **Karhunkierros**, the most famous walking route in Finland, stretches some 100 km (60 miles) through the Oulanka canyon to the **Rukatunturi Fells** ⑬. A smaller national park, **Riisitunturi**, lies to the southwest of Oulanka. Moving further north approaching Lapland, the landscape and culture change from the traditions of Karelia to the ancient ways of the Sami people. ❑

The Museum of North Karelia at Joensuu traces the region's social history.

BELOW: white water expedition.

FINLAND'S LAPLAND

*For some travellers, Lapland is the land of the Midnight Sun,
a haven for fell-walkers and anglers. For others, it's the land
of Father Christmas, reindeer racing and dog sledging*

Map
on page
346

W hatever the season, Lapland offers a variety of interesting natural phenomena and cultures, from the mysterious Northern Lights and the dark Kaamos skies to the magical contrast of the Midnight Sun. However you choose to arrive – by air, sea, train, or car, be prepared to experience Lapland and the Arctic Circle on foot, whether reindeer spotting, cross-country skiing, snowmobiling, ice-golfing, salmon-fishing, gold-panning, discovering the Sami culture, or simply hiking the rich swampland in search of cloudberries. These activities will only whet your appetite for the delicious Lappish cuisine.

Two main roads bore their way northwards through the province of Lapland (Lappi). Road 4, sometimes called the Arctic Road, links Kemi (coming from Oulu) with Rovaniemi before continuing northeastwards into Norway at Utsjoki. The other is Road 21 (E8), which follows the Tornio Valley upstream from Tornio, continuing beside various tributaries that form the border with Sweden, eventually to cross into Norway near Kilpisjärvi.

When exploring this region, the need for proper clothing and equipment cannot be over-stressed: climatic changes are rapid and, for all its magnificence, the Arctic wilderness can be a ruthless place. In summer take plenty of mosquito repellent, preferably purchased from a local *apoteeki* (pharmacy), which will be able to recommend the most effective product.

LEFT: a Laplander.
BELOW: tending reindeer.

Rovaniemi, Lapland's capital

From Kemi, Road 4 follows the valley of the Kemi-joki. You reach **Rovaniemi ❶** within 115 km (70 miles). This administrative capital of Lapland, on the cusp of the Arctic Circle, is the launching point for most trips into the province.

The town has been completely rebuilt since World War II, almost quadrupling its population to 34,500 in the process. The reconstruction plan for Rovaniemi was made by Alvar Aalto who also designed the fine **Lappia House** complex on Hallituskatu, containing a theatre, library and congress facilities.

Half underground, the eye-catching **Arktikum** (Pohjoisranta 4; open May–Aug: daily 10am–6pm; Sept–Apr: closed Mon; entrance fee; tel: 16 317 840) houses the Arctic Centre and the Provincial Museum of Lapland. The Arctic Centre has exhibits illustrating Arctic history and culture; the museum gives a good introduction to Lapland's flora and fauna, Sami traditions and Rovaniemi's history. You'll get a better feeling for bygone days in the 19th-century farm buildings at the **Pöykkölä Museum** (open June–Aug: Tues–Sun 1–4pm; entrance fee; tel: 16 181 095), by the Kemi river, 3 km (2 miles) to the south.

Rovaniemen Taidemuseo (Rovaniemi Art Museum, Lapinkävijäntie 4; open Tues–Fri and Sun noon–5pm;

Lapland

0 ——————— 50 km
0 ——————— 50 miles

NORWAY

SWEDEN

RUSSIA

Lappi

Pohjois-Pohjanmaa

Gulf of Bothnia

Hammerfest, Nordkapp

Varangerbotn
Polmak
Nuorgam
Lakselv
Terojoki
Utsjoki
Ailigas 342
Kevo
Galddoaivi 430
Villavaara 344
Jiesjavrre
Paistunturi 619
Kevon luonnonpuisto
Guorboaivi 443
Näätamö
Alta
Altaelva
Guivi 641
Ailigas 620
Masi
Karasjok
Karigasniemi
Sevettijärvi
Iijärvi
Punta
Goldden
Muotkatunturit 520
Partakko
Biedjovággi
Sarggejok
Kaamanen
Skibotn
Halti 1328
Harroaivi 828
Mutusjärvi
Inarijärvi
Saana 1029
Kilpisjärvi
Kautokeino
Vaskojoki
Angeli
Inari
Nellim
Ropi 945
Ropinsalmi
Urtivaara 660
Porrastunturi 588
Menesjärvi
Viipustunturit 599
Hammastunturit 531
Ivalo
Järämä
Kaaresuvanto
Leppäjärvi
Enontekiö
Hetta
Jänispää 459
Kultala
Ivalojoki
Raja-Jooseppi
Karesuando
Vuontisjärvi
Korsatunturi 462
Kuttura
Saariselkä
Kaunispää 438
Kiilopää 546
Sokosti 718
Talkkunapää 693
Palojoensuu
Ketomella
Ounastunturi
Outtakka 723
Pallas- ja Ounastunturin kansallispuisto
Tankavaara
Sompion luonnonpuisto
Urho Kekkosen kansallispuisto
Övre Soppero
Nedre Soppero
Lannavaara
Pallastunturi
Taivaskero 807
Raattama
Pallasjärvi
Tepasto
Pokka
Porttipahdan tekojärvi
Vuotso
Loka tekojärvi
Yli-Muonio
Muonio
Jerisjärvi
Pomovaara 421
Lokka
Vittangi
Kitkiöjoki
Kangosjärvi
Sirkka
Levi 530
Koitelainen 402
Painopää 526
Kangos
Aakenustunturi 570
Äkäslompolo
Ylläs 718
Kittilä
Kumputunturi 581
Petkula
Kihlanki
Ylläsjärvi
Sattasvaara 368
Taohua
Martti
Maltiotunturi 478
Äkäsjokisuu
Kaukonen
Sodankylä
Savukoski
Kurtakko
Tärendo
Kolari
Kierinki
Syväjärvi
Kairala
Nousu
Pajala
Ruokojärvi
Lohiniva
Unari
Luosto 514
Suvanto
Pelkosenniemi
Ullatti
Sieppijärvi
Raudanjoki
Pyhätunturi 540
Ahvenselkä
Kelloselkä
Hakkas
Orajärvi
Meltaus
Pyhätunturin kans. puisto
Vuostimo
Salla
Korpilombolo
Pello
Konttajärvi
Raanujärvi
Sinettä
Kemijärvi
Kursu
Arctic Circle
Juoksenki
Juoksenki
Meltosjärvi
Vikajärvi
Kemijärvi
Isokylä
Joutsijärvi
Vuottas
Aavasaksa 242
Mellakoski
Rovaniemi
Joulupukin pajakylä (Santa Claus' Workshop Village)
Suomutunturi
Arctic Circle 408
Vännäsberget
Övertorneå
Ylitornio
Ounasvaara
Oikarainen
Luusua
Maaninkavaara
Överkalix
Muurola
Vanttauskoski
Pirttikoski
Suolijärvi
Morjärv
Kemijoki
Koivu
Riisitunturin kansallispuisto
Karungi
Karunki
Portimo
Perä-Posio
Posio
Yli-Kitka
Råneå
Töre
Kukkolankoski
Kukkola
Tervola
Simojoki
Boden
Kalix
Sangis
Tornio
Itäkoski
Ranua
Kuolio
Kostonjärvi
Pyhitsvaara 422
Gammelstad
Hapanda
Haaparanta
Keminmaa
Sarajärvi
Luleå
Luulaja
Kemi
Simo
Kuivaniemi
Oijärvi
Pärjänsuo
Iso-Syöte 431
Taivalkoski
Umeå
Veitsiluoto
Oulu
Tannila
Kajaani
Oulu

entrance fee; tel: 16 322 2822) has the Wihuri collection of modern Finnish art and various changing exhibitions.

Rising up from the confluence of the Ounasjoki and Kemijoki to the south of Rovaniemi are the wooded slopes of **Ounasvaara**, a well-developed skiing area and the site of annual international winter games. It's also a favourite gathering place on Midsummer Night.

Map on page 346

Land of Santa Claus

About 8 km (5 miles) from the town on Road 4, soon after the turn-off for Rovaniemi airport, **Joulupukin Pajakylä** ❷ (Santa Claus' Workshop Village; open June–Aug: daily 8am–8pm; Sept–May: Mon–Fri 11am–7pm, Sat 10am–4pm; free) straddles the Arctic Circle. Its post office annually handles thousands of letters from children. There are some good shops, a puppet theatre, art exhibitions, a glass factory, a few reindeer and, of course, Santa Claus.

At Syväsenvaara, 5 km (3 miles) from Rovaniemi, is **Santapark** (open June–Aug: 11am–6pm: May–Sept: times vary; entrance fee; tel: 16 333 0000), an amusement park which provides fun rides and attractions for children.

You will notice that the landscapes – predominantly forested – are becoming progressively emptier as you travel north. However, there are reindeer aplenty and the occasional elk, so do drive slowly; keep your eyes open and your camera handy – they say white reindeer bring good luck. One of the best fell areas east of Road 4 is centred on **Pyhätunturi**, about 135 km (84 miles) northeast of Rovaniemi. Another, just north of it, is **Luostotunturi**, south of Sodankylä.

Sodankylä ❸, 130 km (80 miles) from Rovaniemi, is the first substantial place along this route. It is the home of the Midnight Sun Film Festival held each June. Next to its 19th-century stone church, its wooden predecessor is Lapland's oldest church, dating from 1689.

Rovaniemi lies just 8 km (5 miles) south of the Arctic Circle.

BELOW: Santa Claus out for a stroll.

Gold country

Northwards, there's little to detain you for the next 100 km (60 miles) or so until, a few miles beyond Vuotso, you reach **Tankavaara** ❹. Gold panning has been practised in various parts of Lapland for well over a century, and at **Tankavaara Gold Village**, its **Kultamuseo** (Gold Museum) not only chronicles man's historical endeavours to find gold, but for a modest fee gives tuition and allows you to pan for gold. There are cabins where you may lodge and a simple restaurant (tel: 16 626 171; fax: 16 626 271).

About 40 km (25 miles) further north there is more self-catering accommodation, together with modern hotels and sports facilities, centred on **Laanila** and **Saariselkä** ❺, an immensely popular winter sports centre with good facilities.

Ivalo and Inari

Another 23 km (14 miles) north is the turning for Ivalo airport, Finland's northernmost. **Ivalo** ❻ is the largest community in northern Lapland, though in terms of Sami culture it is much less important than Inari. There is, however, an attractive wooden Orthodox church tucked away in the woods, serving the

TIP

Ranua, south of Rovaniemi, is the cloudberry capital of Finland. These unusual berries grow on peat bogs and pine marshes and are ripe for picking in July. Taste them at Ranua's cloudberry markets in early August.

Skolt Sami, a branch of the Sami people who formerly lived in territory ceded to the Soviet Union in 1944. They have different costumes, language and traditions from the Finnish Sami, and some now breed sheep as well as reindeer. Ivalo's Lutheran Church stands near the bridge which carries Road 4 over the Ivalojoki; then it's a further 39 km (27 miles) to **Inari ❼**, much of it a delightful route along parts of the shores of Inarijärvi. Inari village is an excellent base for wilderness exploration; you can lodge at the traditional Hotel Inarin Kultahovi (tel: 16 671 221).

Though smaller than Ivalo, Inari is the administrative centre for a vast if sparsely populated area, and a traditional meeting place for colourfully costumed Sami people, especially during the church festivals of Lady Day and Easter Day.

Inarijärvi is Finland's third largest lake, covering 1,300 sq km (808 sq miles) and is dotted with 3,000 islands, some of them considered sacred according to Sami tradition. Boat trips and sightseeing flights are available during the summer to the holy **Ukko Island**.

Inari's excellent **Saamelaismuseo** (Siida Sami Museum; open June–Aug: daily 8am–10pm; Sept–May: times vary; entrance fee; tel: 16 665 212) comprises a modern museum building and an open-air section (*skansen*) with old buildings and equipment illustrating the traditionally nomadic way of life. There are also some exhibits on early Skolt Sami culture and modern Sami life. The Siida building also houses the **Ylä-Lapin Luontokeskus** (Northern Lapland Visitor Centre), which sells fishing permits and assists in hiking plans for those wishing to explore the wilderness. Be sure to leave time to shop at Inari's many fine handicraft shops that include a silversmith's shop and a knife-making studio.

BELOW: reindeer sledging is a popular activity.

SLEDGING

The easiest way to get across Lapland's vast, icy and largely flat landscape has always been on skis or sledges; the latter less exhausting for longer distances. There are many types of sledging, but the most popular and readily associated with northern Finland is the dog sledge. Four or six husky dogs, hardy beasts naturally acclimatised to snow and ice, are harnessed to the front of the sledge, with passengers standing on the back runners. Unlike horses, the huskies are not readily controllable, so keeping the sledge stationary is done with a hook wedged deep in the snow. Once the hook is withdrawn, the dogs lurch forward.

Reindeer sledging, as epitomised by images of Santa and his sleigh at Christmas, is another method of getting around, with the advantage that these animals can cover longer and more snowy distances, although they travel more slowly than dogs.

Many centres in Lapland now offer the chance of sledging excursions for tourists – contact tourist offices in main towns for more details. It is essential that the right equipment is worn: thermals, waterproofs, hats and goggles are necessary to combat the dampness and bitterness of the snow.

Towards Norway

Road 955 from Inari leads 40 km (25 miles) southwest to **Menesjärvi** , a Sami settlement from which one can continue by road then river boat or on foot up the wild and beautiful **Lemmenjoki Valley** ("river of love") to a remote gold prospectors' camp. From Menesjärvi, Road 955 continues across Lapland to join Road 79 at Kittilä. Around Inari and north of it, the road passes a number of attractive holiday centres, mostly of the self-catering variety. After 26 km (16 miles) you come to Kaamanen from which a minor road branches northeast 100 km (60 miles) to **Sevettijärvi** ❾, the modern main settlement for the Skolt Sami. An interesting time to be there is during the Easter Orthodox festival. While there, visit the Sami graveyard, with its unusual turf-covered graves.

A couple of kilometres north of Kaamanen take the minor road to **Utsjoki** ❿, 94 km (58 miles) away on the border with Norway, passing a series of beautiful lakes close to the eastern fringes of the **Kevon Luonnonpuisto** (Kevo Nature Park). Utsjoki is an important Sami community close to Finland's northernmost point. Its church (1860) is one of the few pre-World War II churches still standing in Lapland.

The village and road follow the Utsjoki downstream to join with the Tenojoki, a renowned salmon river. As you approach the Norwegian border at **Kirkenes**, the landscape changes dramatically. You can connect with a variety of routes, eventually returning into western Lapland at Kilpisjärvi or Enontekiö.

Leather goods and "puukko" knives are among the best buys in Lapland.

Western Lapland

Your route through western Lapland is likely to begin at **Tornio** about 80 km (50 miles) south of the Arctic Circle. The earlier stretches of the **Way of the Four Winds** (E8) present a very different face of Lapland from the Arctic Road, for the lower section of the Tornio valley is much more populated, and served by Finland's northernmost railway branch to Kolari.

In its southern stages the road passes through a string of small communities mainly based, in these marginally milder and more fertile conditions, on agriculture and dairy farming. The Tornionjoki is a good salmon river. Perch, whitefish, grayling, trout and even Arctic char can be found in Lapland's waters. Local travel agencies will organise guided fishing trips complete with gear and permits. At **Kukkola** ⓫ look out for the **Kukkolankoski rapids**; people used to ride the rapids while standing on a log.

About 70 km (43 miles) north of Tornio, beyond Ylitornio, is the 242-metre (794-ft) high **Aavasaksa Hill** ⓬, the most southerly point from which the Midnight Sun can be seen, attracting considerable throngs for Midsummer Eve festivities. A few miles nearer Juoksenki, you cross the Arctic Circle. The scenery becomes wilder as you pass between Pello and Kolari.

Fell country

About 10 km (7 miles) north of Kolari, a detour by Road 940 to the right leads to **Akäslompolo** ⓭. This well-equipped tourist resort and skiing centre, on the shores of a small lake, is set among magnificent forested hills and bare-topped fells; the highest is

BELOW: panning for gold, Tankavaara.

Map on page 346

Map on page 346

In northern Lapland the sun stays above the horizon from late May to late July. Autumn is known as "Ruska", when the leaves turn explosive shades of red, yellow and orange.

BELOW: traditional wooden cabin.
RIGHT: Lemmenjoki National Park.

Ylläs, at 718 metres (2,355 ft), served by chair lifts. A marked trail follows the chain of fells stretching northwards from here, eventually leading in about 150 km (90 miles) to the **Pallastunturi** ⓮ fell group. It's a glorious trail with overnight shelter available in untended wilderness huts. Off-road biking is also a possibility with trails for various levels of expertise.

From Akäslompolo you can continue north along minor roads and in 31 km (19 miles) turn left onto Road 79. This is the main road from Rovaniemi, providing an alternative approach to western Lapland. Road 957 to the right is recommended as the best approach to Enontekiö. A further branch left off this route leads from Road 79 to the lonely hotel complex of **Pallastunturi**, magnificently cradled in the lap of five of the 14 fells which make up the Pallastunturi group. From here the choice of fell walks includes the long-distance 60-km (37-mile) trail north from Yllästunturi across the fells to Enontekiö. At **Ketomella** ⓯ on Road 957 there's a car ferry across the river.

Enontekiö ⓰, sometimes known as Hetta, sprawls along the northern shore of Ounasjärvi (lake), looking across to the great rounded shoulders of the Ounastunturi fells. Most of Enontekiö's buildings are modern, including the pretty wooden church which has an altar mosaic depicting Sami people.

Soaring mountains

From **Palojoensuu**, Road 21 continues northwest along the Muonionjoki and Könkämäeno valleys, the scenry becoming even wilder and more barren. A little north of Kaaresuvanto you cross the coniferous tree line and pass the last of the spindly pines.

At **Järämä** ⓱, 10 km (6 miles) further from the tiny settlement of Markkina, German soldiers built fortifications during a standstill in the Lapland War of 1944. Many of these bunkers have been restored and are now open to the public. South and north of **Ropinsalmi**, the mountains reach ever greater heights; the highest, **Halti**, soars up to 1,328 metres (4,357 ft) on the Norwegian border at Finland's northwesternmost point. More accessible and distinctive is Saana, 1,029 metres (3,376 ft), above the village and the resort of **Kilpisjärvi** ⓲.

Kilipisjärvi is an excellent launching pad for wilderness enthusiasts. There is a lake of the same name whose western shore forms the border with Sweden, and a marked trail which takes about a day and leads to the boundary stone marking the triple junction of Finland, Sweden and Norway.

Motorboats take visitors to the **Mallan Luonnenpuisto**, a nature reserve to the north of the lake (entry permit required: details from Kilipsjärven Retkeilykeskus, tel: 16 537 771). Within, there is a pleasant 15-km (9-mile) trek.

The rest of these immense, empty, rugged acres are as free to all comers as the elements – and as unpredictable. Never set off without proper equipment and provisions and, unless you are experienced in such landscapes, a guide; always inform someone where you are heading and when you expect to return. Simple advice, but it cannot be said often enough. ❏

INSIGHT GUIDES

Travel Tips

TIMBUKTU KALAMAZOO

AT&T Direct® Service

AT&T Direct Service access numbers are the easy way to call home from anywhere.

Global connection with the AT&T Network

AT&T
direct
service

www.att.com/traveler

AT&T **Direct**® Service

The easy way to call
home from anywhere.

AT&T Access Numbers

Argentina .0800-555-4288	Czech Rep.▲.00-42-000-101
Australia...1-800-881-011	Denmark........8001-0010
Austria●....0800-200-288	Egypt●(Cairo) ...510-0200
Bahamas..1-800-USA-ATT1	France.....0800-99-00-11
Belgium● ..0-800-100-10	Germany ..0800-2255-288
Bermuda✚ 1-800-USA-ATT1	Greece● 00-800-1311
Brazil 000-8010	Guam 1-800-2255-288
Canada...1 800 CALL ATT	Guyana○ 165
Chile 800-225-288	Hong Kong .800-96-1111
China, PRC▲ 10811	India▲ 000-117
Costa Rica .0-800-0-114-114	Ireland 1-800-550-000

AT&T **Direct**® Service

The easy way to call
home from anywhere.

AT&T Access Numbers

Argentina .0800-555-4288	Czech Rep.▲.00-42-000-101
Australia...1-800-881-011	Denmark........8001-0010
Austria●....0800-200-288	Egypt●(Cairo) ...510-0200
Bahamas..1-800-USA-ATT1	France.....0800-99-00-11
Belgium● ..0-800-100-10	Germany ..0800-2255-288
Bermuda✚ 1-800-USA-ATT1	Greece● 00-800-1311
Brazil 000-8010	Guam 1-800-2255-288
Canada...1 800 CALL ATT	Guyana○ 165
Chile 800-225-288	Hong Kong .800-96-1111
China, PRC▲ 10811	India▲ 000-117
Costa Rica .0-800-0-114-114	Ireland 1-800-550-000

Global
connection
with the AT&T
Network

AT&T
direct
service

The best way to keep in touch when you're traveling

overseas is with **AT&T Direct®** Service. It's the

easy way to call your loved ones back home from just

about anywhere in the world. Just cut out the wallet

card below and use it wherever your travels take you.

For a list of AT&T Access Numbers, cut out the attached wallet guide.

AT&T

Israel 1-800-94-94-949	Portugal ▲ 800-800-128
Italy ● 172-1011	Saudi Arabia ▲ 1-800-10
Jamaica● 1-800-USA-ATT1	Singapore 800-0111-111
Japan ● ▲ 005-39-111	South Africa 0800-99-0123
Korea, Republic ● ...0072-911	Spain 900-99-00-11
Mexico ▽ ● ..01-800-288-2872	Sweden............020-799-111
Netherlands● ..0800-022-9111	Switzerland● 0800-89-0011
Neth. Ant. ▲⊛001-800-USA-ATT1	Taiwan............0080-10288-0
New Zealand ● 000-911	Thailand❬......001-999-111-11
Norway...............800-190-11	Turkey● 00-800-12277
Panama 00-800-001-0109	U.A. Emirates ● 800-121
Philippines ● 105-11	U.K. 0800-89-0011
Poland ● ▲...00-800-111-1111	Venezuela 800-11-120

FOR EASY CALLING WORLDWIDE
1. Just dial the AT&T Access Number for the country you are calling from.
2. Dial the phone number you're calling. *3.* Dial your card number.*

For access numbers not listed ask any operator for **AT&T Direct®** Service.
In the U.S. call 1-800-222-0300 for **AT&T Direct** Service information.
Visit our Web site at: **www.att.com/traveler**
Bold-faced countries permit country-to-country calling outside the U.S.
● Public phones require coin or card deposit to place call.
✚ Public phones and select hotels.
▲ May not be available from every phone/payphone.
○ Collect calling only.
▽ Includes "Ladatel" public phones; if call does not complete,
  use 001-800-462-4240.
⊛ From St. Maarten or phones at Bobby's Marina, use 1-800-USA-ATT1.
❬ When calling from public phones, use phones marked Lenso.
* AT&T Calling Card, AT&T Corporate, AT&T Universal, MasterCard®,
  Diners Club®, American Express®, or Discover® cards accepted.

When placing an international call *from* the U.S., dial 1-800-CALL ATT.
WW   © 6/00 AT&T

Israel 1-800-94-94-949	Portugal ▲ 800-800-128
Italy ● 172-1011	Saudi Arabia ▲ 1-800-10
Jamaica● 1-800-USA-ATT1	Singapore 800-0111-111
Japan ● ▲ 005-39-111	South Africa 0800-99-0123
Korea, Republic ● ...0072-911	Spain 900-99-00-11
Mexico ▽ ● ..01-800-288-2872	Sweden............020-799-111
Netherlands● ..0800-022-9111	Switzerland● 0800-89-0011
Neth. Ant. ▲⊛001-800-USA-ATT1	Taiwan............0080-10288-0
New Zealand ● 000-911	Thailand❬......001-999-111-11
Norway...............800-190-11	Turkey● 00-800-12277
Panama 00-800-001-0109	U.A. Emirates ● 800-121
Philippines ● 105-11	U.K. 0800-89-0011
Poland ● ▲...00-800-111-1111	Venezuela 800-11-120

FOR EASY CALLING WORLDWIDE
1. Just dial the AT&T Access Number for the country you are calling from.
2. Dial the phone number you're calling. *3.* Dial your card number.*

For access numbers not listed ask any operator for **AT&T Direct®** Service.
In the U.S. call 1-800-222-0300 for **AT&T Direct** Service information.
Visit our Web site at: **www.att.com/traveler**
Bold-faced countries permit country-to-country calling outside the U.S.
● Public phones require coin or card deposit to place call.
✚ Public phones and select hotels.
▲ May not be available from every phone/payphone.
○ Collect calling only.
▽ Includes "Ladatel" public phones; if call does not complete,
  use 001-800-462-4240.
⊛ From St. Maarten or phones at Bobby's Marina, use 1-800-USA-ATT1.
❬ When calling from public phones, use phones marked Lenso.
* AT&T Calling Card, AT&T Corporate, AT&T Universal, MasterCard®,
  Diners Club®, American Express®, or Discover® cards accepted.

When placing an international call *from* the U.S., dial 1-800-CALL ATT.
WW   © 6/00 AT&T

CONTENTS

DENMARK

The Place

Area 43,094 sq km (16,659 sq miles).
Capital Copenhagen.
Population 5,330,020, of whom 1,796,335 live in the Copenhagen area, 284,846 in Århus and 183,584 in Odense.
Life expectancy 74 years for men and 79 for women.
Language Danish.
Religion 89 percent of Danes are registered as belonging to the Evangelical Lutheran Church, although few attend services.
Time zone Central European Time Zone. One hour ahead of Greenwich Mean Time (GMT), six hours ahead of Eastern Standard Time (EST).
Currency Danish krone (crown); plural kroner; marked kr in shops or DKK internationally; and split into 100 øre.
Weights and measures Metric.
Electricity 220 volts AC, two-pin round plugs.
International dialling code +45.

Geography

The Kingdom of Denmark – the word originally meant "border district of the Danes" – lies between the North Sea on the west and the Baltic Sea on the southeast. Germany borders to the south for 69 km (43 miles), and Sweden is 25 minutes to the east.

Jutland, which makes up about 70 percent of the country, is a peninsula jutting into the North and Baltic Seas. The rest of the land consists of islands, 405 in all. The major islands are Bornholm, Zealand (where Copenhagen is situated), Falster, Fyn and Lolland.

Flat or gently undulating,

Denmark has been covered by ice sheets at least four times over the past two million years. The natural vegetation is a mixed forest covering one-eighth of the country. Around seven-tenths of the land is used for farming, with most farms family run. Barley, used for cattle feed, is the main crop. There are few valuable minerals, but limestone and gravel are widely mined. Oil and gas have both been found in the Danish sector of the North Sea.

Greenland and the Faroe Islands are also part of the kingdom of Denmark. Both are self-governing and have their own languages.

Climate

Denmark's temperate marine climate keeps the weather mild, with the North Atlantic Drift, part of the Gulf Stream, providing a warming influence. Average rainfall is 660 mm (26 in) a year.

The swimming season starts (except for true masochists) in the middle of May and ends in September.

Be prepared for a variable climate and remember to dress for cold and wet weather in the winter and spring.

Max. Temperatures

January	2°C (36°F)
February	2°C (36°F)
March	5°C (41°F)
April	10°C (50°F)
May	16°C (61°F)
June	19°C (66°F)
July	22°C (71°F)
August	21°C (69°F)
September	18°C (64°F)
October	12°C (54°F)
November	7°C (45°F)
December	4°C (39°F)

The People

Most Danes are Nordic Scandinavians, although a German minority can be found in south Jutland. Around 85 percent of the population lives in towns or cities.

There is a growing number of foreign residents (in all 6.8 percent of the population).

Economy

A member of the European Union, Denmark is one of the world's great trading nations. Grain was the major export until the 19th century; dairy products then became dominant. Although they remain the best-known exports, dairy products account for only 30 percent of export turnover, with light industrial goods accounting for the rest.

Denmark has a growing environmental development industry, inventing and producing a wide variety of products that span energy-saving light bulbs to high-tech windmills, which are sold locally and internationally.

As elsewhere in western Europe, service industries provide an increasing proportion of work, and only one-fifth of workers are now engaged in manufacturing.

The average income and benefits provided by the social welfare system are still among the highest in the world – but so are personal income taxes. The average family spends about 30 percent of its net income on rent, 20 percent on food and 15 percent on transport.

Government

Denmark has been a kingdom for over 1,000 years and is therefore the oldest monarchy in the world. The reigning monarch, Queen Margrethe, has no real political power or influence, yet no laws or governments are recognised without her signature.

The majority of governments since World War II have been coalitions, yet the Social Democrats remained the most influential political party throughout the greater part of the 20th century. The Danish parliament has 179 members, including two from Greenland and two from the Faroe Islands (Færøerne).

Planning the Trip

Visas and Passports

A valid passport entitles you to a stay of up to three months. Visas are not required for EU citizens, and those from Canada and the US. Other nationalities may need a visa before arriving. If in doubt, ask at a Danish Embassy or Consulate.

If you arrive from a Scandinavian country, your passport probably won't be checked. If you intend to stay longer than three months you have to obtain a resident's permit.

Customs

Danish customs formalities are usually painless. The rules about limits on goods/gifts allowed through customs depend on whether you are coming from an EU country. If in doubt, check with a local Danish consul. Money and cheques may be brought in freely.

DUTY FREE

Visitors from countries outside Scandinavia and the EU are entitled to claim back value added tax moms) when leaving Denmark.

Many shops can mail goods home to you, avoiding VAT payment. For visitors wishing to take goods with them straight away, shops displaying Global Refund Denmark emblems offer tourists a personal export service with VAT refunds on purchases of over 300DKK. You must declare your purchase and get a stamp from customs from the last EU country you leave.

There are Global Refund outlets at almost every international airport in Europe and on some ferry lines.

Information Before You Go

● **UK** The Danish Tourist Board, 55 Sloane Street, London SW1X 9SY. Tel: 020 7259 5959. Fax: 020 7259 5955. Website: www.dtb.dt.dk E-mail: dtb.london@dt.dk
● **US** The Danish Tourist Board, 655 Third Street, 18th Floor, New York, NY 10017. Tel: 212-885 9727. Fax: 212-885 9726. Website: www.visitdenmark.com E-mail: ac@dt-nyc.com
Scandinavian Tourist Board, 150 North Michigan Avenue, Suite 2110, Chicago, Il 60601. Tel: 312-726 1120.
Scandinavian Tourist Board, 8929 Wilshire Blvd, Beverly Hills, CA 90211. Tel: 213-854 1549.

● **Canada:** The Danish Tourist Board, PO Box 115, Station N, Toronto, Ontario M8V 3S4. Tel: 416-823 9620.
● **Australia/New Zealand** The Danish Consulate/Embassy supplies information.

The following websites provide useful information:
● **Danish Tourist Board** www.denmark.dt.dk
● **Denmark Hotel list** www.dkhotellist.dk
● **Wonderful Copenhagen** Guide to the city: www.woco.dk
● **The Faroe Islands Tourist Board** www.tourist.fo
● **Greenland Tourism** www.greenland-guide.dk

Health

Standards of hygiene in Scandinavia are among the highest in the world. Visitors often comment upon how clean Denmark is. There are no major health hazards and the tap water is safe to drink.

The Danish medical system will assist anyone in an emergency; however you should take out travel insurance before you leave. British nationals should take a form E111. You will be charged for doctors' consultations and prescriptions. To get a refund, take the receipts together with your E111 and passport to the local health office.

Money Matters

Currency

Notes come in 50, 100, 200, 500 and 1,000 denominations. There are 25 and 50 øre coins (both copper coloured), 1 krone, 2 krone, 5 krone (silver coloured with a hole in the centre), and 10 and 20 krone (solid gold-coloured coins that are similar except the 20 krone piece is a little bigger than the 10 krone).

Changing money

Exchanges are open outside normal business hours at the Copenhagen Central Railway Station, and in the centre of the city.

Den Danske Bank (tel: 33 12 04 01) is open Monday to Sunday 8am–8pm; and Forex Monday to Sunday 8am–9pm.

There are three 24-hour exchange machines near Copenhagen City Hall.

How to pay

Visa and MasterCard are widely accepted in shops. Diner's Club is accepted in many restaurants. American Express cards can sometimes be used in major hotels and shops. All banks and a few shops take travellers' cheques.

What to Bring

The time of year you are most likely to encounter good weather is mid-May to mid-June. Even if you are lucky enough to travel in a year with a fine summer, you should still expect some cold and rainy days. Yet it can also be very hot. Whatever time of year you are visiting, it is wise to bring a sweater and a raincoat.

Danes dress casually both in their free time and at work. When going out for the evening men rarely have to put on a suit and tie.

Getting There

BY AIR

The two main airports in Denmark are Copenhagen Kastrup Airport and Bilund Airport in Jutland. Denmark's national carrier is SAS (Scandinavian Airlines System), which is primarily for international traffic. Maersk Air and Cimber Air serve most of the domestic routes. British Airways flies five times daily from Heathrow to Kastrup Airport. Among the low-cost operators, GO flies daily from London Stansted to Copenhagen.

From the UK
British Airways Tel: 0345 222111.
Website: www.british-airways.com
GO Tel: 0845 6054321
Website: www.go-fly.com
Maersk Air Tel: 020 7333 0066.
SAS Tel: 0845 60727727.
Website: www.sas.dk

From the US
SAS Tel: 1-800-221 2350.
Website: www.sas.dk

BY SEA

From Germany and Poland
From Germany, ferries connect Puttgarden and Rødby (Lolland). Ferries also run between Warnemünde and Gedser, and in the summer, Sassnitz and Rønne (Bornholm). Swinoujscie in Poland sends a daily ferry to Copenhagen.

From Sweden
Sweden operates several lines from Helsingborg to Helsingør (North Zealand) and from Helsingborg to Grenå (East Jutland); other ferries go from Varberg to Grenå and from Göteborg to Frederikshavn (North Jutland); ferries bound for Copenhagen go from Landskrona to Tuborg Havn, from Malmö to Nyhavn (Copenhagen), and from Limhamn to Dragør; from Rønne (Bornholm) there is a ferry to Ystad.

From Norway
Boats go from Oslo to Copenhagen or to Hirtshals and Frederikshavn in North Jutland; from Hirtshals there are ferries to Bergen, Egernsund, Kristianssand and Stavanger. Ferries from Larvik and Moss (Norway) go to Frederikshavn.

From the UK
Ferries run from Harwich to Esbjerg and in summer from Newcastle.

BY RAIL

Trains arrive daily from Germany, Britain and Sweden.
● For trains from Britain:
Tel: 0990 186186.
Website: www.eurostarcom
● For information in Denmark on international trains:
Tel: 70 13 14 16.
E-mail: tlfsalg@-dsb.int.dk
● For Denmark's inland trains:
Tel: 70 13 14 15.
Website: www.dsb.dk

BY BUS

Eurolines is the leading operator of scheduled coach services, including 11 destinations in Denmark with regular departures from London to Copenhagen, Hirtshals, Ålborg, Århus, Padborg and Rødby.
● **Eurolines** Tel: 0990 143219 or 020 7730 8235.
Website: www.eurolines.co.uk

Tour Operators

● **Scantours**
47 Whitcomb St, London WC2H 7DH.
Tel: 020 7839 2927.
Fax: 020 7839 5891.
Website: www.scantoursUK.com
All-inclusive to Denmark, Greenland and the Faroe Islands.
● **Scandinavian Travel Service**
2 Berghem Mews, Blythe Road, London W14 0HN.
Tel: 020 7559 666.
Fax: 020 7371 4070.
● **DFDS Seaways**
Scandinavia House, Parkeston, Harwich, Essex CO12 4QG.
Tel: 0990 333 666 (brochure line).
Tel: 0990 333 111 (reservations).

Practical Tips

Media

NEWSPAPERS AND MAGAZINES

English-language newspapers are widely available at all main train stations, as well as kiosks. You can also read them free at the Central Library, Krystalgade 15 or Café Europa, Amagertorv 1, Copenhagen.

The English-language weekly *The Copenhagen Post* has information, news, entertainment and restaurant guides (from tourist offices).

BOOKS

Many of the public libraries have a good selection of books in English, and Copenhagen has bookshops that specialise in foreign literature (*see Shopping, page 366*).

TELEVISION

There are many satellite/cable channels featuring CNN, BBC and MTV in English. In addition, there are often movies in English without subtitles on the national channels DR1, DR2 and TV2.

RADIO

A high percentage of music on Danish radio is in English. For news

Useful Numbers

● **Police, ambulance, fire** 122
● **Danish directory enquiries** 118
● **International directory enquiries** 113

Public Holidays

- **1 January** New Year's Day (1)
- **March/April** Easter
- **1 May** Workers' Day
- **May/June** Whit Monday
- **May/June** Ascension Day
- **5 June** Constitution Day
- **24–26 December** Christmas

A floating holiday is Prayer Day (*Store Bodedag*), which falls on a different day each year. All shops and businesses close all day on major holidays, and for half a day on Prayer and Ascension Days.

in English, tune to Radio Denmark, programme 3 at 93.8MHZ, Monday to Friday at 8.31–8.36am.

Postal Services

For opening hours of most post offices, *see Business Hours, below.* The railway station office in Copenhagen is open Monday to Friday 8am–10pm, Saturday 9am–4pm and Sunday 10am–5pm.

Telecommunications

Phone calls to foreign countries can be made from Statens Teletjeneste offices, above the post office in the Central Railway Station, and next door to the post office in Købmagergade in Copenhagen.

Tourist Offices

There is a tourist office in almost every city, with knowledgeable and friendly staff. They can assist in planning a trip, make reservations, or provide directions and leaflets.

For access to websites and information about all tourist offices in Denmark, visit the central website: www.visitdenmark.com. Some of the tourist bureaus are:

Copenhagen
Bernstorffsgade 1, 1577
Copenhagen V (at the main entrance of Tivoli)
Tel: 33 25 38 44. Fax: 70 22 24 52
Website: www.woco.dk

North Zealand
Havnepladsen 3, 3000 Helsingør
Tel: 49 21 13 33. Fax: 49 21 15 77
Website: www.helsingerturist.dk

Southwest Zealand
Fondens, Bro 3, Postboks 278,
4000 Roskilde
Tel: 46 35 27 00. Fax: 46 35 14 74

Bornholm
Munch Petersensvej 4, 3700 Rønne
Tel: 56 95 95 00. Fax: 56 95 95 68
Website: wwwbornholminfo.dk

Funen
Rådhuset, 5000 Odense C
Tel: 66 12 75 20. Fax: 66 12 75 86
Website: www.odenseturist.dk

East Jutland
Rådhuset, 8000 Århus C
Tel: 89 40 67 00. Fax: 86 12 95 90
Website: www.aarhus-tourist.dk

North Jutland
Østerå 8, 9000 Ålborg
Tel: 98 12 60 22. Fax: 98 16 69 22
Website: www.tourist-aal.dk

West Jutland
Nytorv 5, 8800 Viborg
Tel: 86 61 16 66. Fax: 86 60 02 38

South Jutland
Torvet 3–5, 6760 Ribe
Tel: 75 42 15 00. Fax: 75 42 40 78

Greenland
Greenland Tourism, PO Box 1552,
DK-3900 Nuuk, Greenland
Tel: 299 32 28 88
Fax: 299 32 28 77
E-mail: info@visitgreenland.com
Website: www.greenland-guide.dk

The Faroe Islands
The Faroe Islands Tourist Board,
Gongin, PO Box 118,
FO-110 Tórshavn, Faroe Islands
Tel: 298 31 60 55
E-mail: tourist@tourist.fo
Website: www.tourist.fo

Travelling with Kids

Denmark is a peaceful, safe country with many suitable attractions, such as amusement parks, playgrounds, parks and children's theatres. Many museums have opened children's sections, and music festivals are often arranged so kids can take part. Highlights include:

Copenhagen
Experimentarium (Science Centre)
Tuborg Havnevej 7
Tel: 39 27 33 33. A hands-on science museum. Open Monday to Friday 9am–5pm (Tuesday until 9pm); Saturday and Sunday 11am–5pm.
Zoologisk Have (Zoo)
Roskildevej 32. Tel: 36 30 20 01. Open daily 9am–4pm or 6pm.
Puppet Theatre
Over the summer there are free puppet shows in Kongens Have (the Royal Gardens) near Rosenborg Palace. At 2pm and 3pm, Tuesday to Sunday.
Tivoli
Vesterbrogade 3. Tel: 33 15 10 01. The world-famous amusement park, Tivoli, just across from Central Station, is a delight, with Italian-style *Commedia dell´Arte* twice daily and an endless variety of rides and amusements. Open April to

Business Hours

Offices: 8/9am–4/5pm.
Shops: Monday to Thursday until 5.30pm; Friday until 7pm (8pm in Copenhagen); Saturday 9am–noon or 5pm. All are closed on Sunday except for bakeries and kiosks, some of which are open around the clock.
Pharmacies: As shops except Steno Apotek in Copenhagen

(across the street from the train station) which opens all hours.
Supermarkets: until 7/8pm, at least in Copenhagen. The one at the railway station opens all hours.
Banks: Monday to Friday 9.30am–4pm, some till 6pm Thursday.
Post offices: 9am–5pm weekdays, Saturday 9am–noon.

Lost Credit Cards

- **MasterCard/Visa**
  44 89 25 00 (24 hours)
- **American Express** 80 01 00 21
- **Diners' Club** 36 73 73 73

September, Sunday to Thursday
11am–12pm, Friday and Saturday
11am–1am.

Outside Copenhagen

Bakken
A traditional amusement park in the
beautiful Dyrehaven area near
Klampenborg. This is also a perfect
place for a walk in the countryside,
or for a ride in a horse-drawn
carriage. Open daily 25 March to 30
August, noon–midnight.
Benneweis Circus
The largest circus in northern
Europe, in Dronningmølle.
Website: www.cirkus-benneweis.dk
Legoland
An amusement park in Jutland, built
out of 33 million Lego brick blocks.
Open daily May to mid-September.
Tel: 75 33 13 33 and 32 54 06 06.
Lejre Research Centre
Historical-archaeological centre in
Zealand with a reconstructed Iron
Age village. Children can grind their
own flour, cut wood and make
Viking bread. Tel: 46 48 08 78.

Babysitters

- **Studenternes Babysitters**
  Lykkesholmsallé 33 C,
  1902 Frederiksberg C.
  Tel/fax: 70 20 44 16.
  Monday–Friday 10am–3pm,
  Thursday until 6pm.
- **H-H Babysitting**
  Open daily 6.30am–10pm
  Tel: 38 74 81 51. Fax: 38 76 17 17.
  E-mail hh.baby@hh-baby.dk

Business Travellers

The Danes are not excessively
formal when it comes to business
dress. Punctuality is appreciated
and it's probably best to make
business appointments for morning
or early afternoon. Offices are often
deserted on Friday afternoons. July
and August is holiday-time.

Travellers with Disabilities

The Danish Tourist Board publishes
*Access in Denmark – A Travel Guide
for the Disabled*. Tourist offices
have lists of restaurants and
businesses, and the free *Denmark
Accommodation Guide* lists hotels
with special facilities.

Medical Services

Health care is generally free in
Denmark. Acute illnesses or
accidents will be treated at the
casualty department of the nearest
hospital. Outside normal business
hours you can contact a doctor at
38 88 60 41 or 32 84 00 41.

PHARMACIES

Most operate normal business
hours. But there is also a 24-hour
pharmacy in every region, the name
and address of which is posted on
the door of every pharmacy (or look
in the *Yellow Pages* telephone
directory under *Apotek*).

DENTAL SERVICES

Dental care is available by
appointment only. Check the listings
under *Tandlæger* in the *Yellow
Pages*. Outside normal business
hours you can call Tandlægevagten,
tel: 35 38 02 51.

Religious Services

Services are normally on Sunday at
10am, and they are often repeated

Copenhagen Card

We recommend that you buy a
Copenhagen Card at your hotel,
the central railway station or the
Copenhagen tourist information
office. The card gives you free
entry to Tivoli and discounts to
other sights, plus free bus/train
rides in the city and an
informative 114-page guide.

at 2pm. There are several foreign
congregations in Copenhagen.
English Church
At Esplanaden near Amaliegade.
Sankt Petri Church
On the corner of Nørregade and Skt
Pedersstræde. In German.
Church of the Reformation
At Gothersgade across the street
from Rosenborg Castle. Shared by a
German and French congregation.
Jewish Synagogue
Krystalgade.
Nusrat Jahan Mosque
Eriksminde Alle 2.
Roman Catholic Church
Skt Ansgars, Bredgade 64.

Security and Crime

Denmark is generally very safe, but
you should not take risks. To
recover lost or stolen property,
contact the nearest police station
for assistance, or try the lost and
found offices at railway stations.
  Police stations in Copenhagen
can be found on Central Station,
tel: 33 15 38 01, and at
Polititorvet, tel: 33 14 14 48.

Tipping

Service is included in all bills, but a
sign of appreciation is often
welcomed. In restaurants it is a
friendly gesture to pick up the notes
but leave the coins. Cab drivers
appreciate it if the fare is rounded
up to the nearest 5 or 10DKK.

Consulates

The following embassies and
consulates are in Copenhagen.

- **Australia**
  Strandboulevarden 122
  Tel: 39 29 20 77
- **Canada**
  Kristen Bernikowsgade 1
  Tel: 33 13 22 99
- **Ireland**
  Ostbanegade 21
  Tel: 35 42 32 33
- **UK**
  Kastelsvej 40. Tel: 35 44 52 00
- **US**
  Daghammarskjolds Allé 44
  Tel: 35 55 31 44

Getting Around

On Arrival

Almost all international flights arrive and depart from Copenhagen Airport. Trains run three times an hour directly from Terminal 3, the international terminal at Copenhagen Airport, to the Central Station. They take 12 minutes and leave at 15, 35 and 55 minutes past the hour, running from 4.55am to 12.15am.

An intercity express train runs from the airport daily to Frederikshavn, Struer, Herning and Esbjerg.

Buses run between the airport and all major Swedish cities. Contact Combus Denmark for details, tel: 32 52 66 31.

There is a taxi stand next to Terminal 3.

The new Øresund bridge connects Denmark and Sweden. Starting near Kastrup Airport, you can reach the Swedish city of Malmø in 20–30 minutes.

By Air

If you fly you can be on the other side of Denmark in less than an hour. Maersk Air and Cimber Airways have daily flights from Copenhagen to Bornholm, Odense, Århus (Tirstrup) and several other destinations in Jutland.
Maersk Air
Tel: 70 10 74 74 or 32 31 41 00
Fax: 76 50 26 50
Cimber Air Tel: 70 10 12 18
Website: www.cimber.dk

By Bus

There is an extensive network of buses throughout Denmark. For details contact HT Customer

Service, tel: 36 13 14 15.
Website: www.ht.dk
Open daily 7am–9.30pm.

By Train

There is a very efficient train service linking all major cities and some of the smaller towns.
There is a boat-train link from Copenhagen to Rønne, Bornholm.

Useful numbers
General information
Tel: 33 14 17 01
Website: www.dsb.dk
Trains going out of the country
Tel: 70 13 14 16
Inland trains
Tel: 70 13 14 15

By Car

Rules of the road
Remember to drive on the right, and drive politely. Always give way at pedestrian crossings and look out for bicycles when turning right. Look over your left shoulder every time you open the doors on the driver's side – bicycles are everywhere. Overtake on the left only.

Drivers and passengers must wear seat belts at all times, and dipped headlights are required.

Speed limits
These are standard speed limits, which are enforced:
Built-up areas 50 kph (30 mph)
Main roads 80 kph (50 mph)
Motorways 110 kph (70 mph)
For a car with a trailer, the limits are 50 kph (30 mph), 70 kph (40 mph) and 90 kph (55 mph) respectively.

Roadside assistance
If you break down, use the emergency telephones by roads to call FALCK, the Danish motorists' aid organisation, tel: 70 10 20 30. If FALCK can't repair your car on the spot it will be towed to a garage, for a fee. Open 24 hours a day.

Car rental
It pays to shop around. Ask travel agents about special offers, or try

Yellow Pages. **Avis** (tel: 33 15 22 99) and **Hertz** (tel: 33 17 90 27) have offices all around the country, but it is often possible to get a better deal with smaller firm like **Europcar** (tel: 33 55 99 00) and **Lej et Lig** (tel: 39 29 85 05). You need a valid international driving licence and must be 20–25 years old.

By Bike

In the centre of Copenhagen you can use bikes free of charge. You pay 20DKK, which is refunded when you deliver the bike back.

Information and advice
Dansk Cyklistforbund
Romersgade 7, 1362
Copenhagen K. Tel: 33 32 31 21

Bike rental in Copenhagen
Cyklebørs
157 Gothersgade. Tel: 33 14 07 17
Dan Wheel
Colbjørnsgade 3. Tel: 33 21 22 27

By Taxi

Taxis are available at airports, central train and bus stations and in the centre of all major cities.
● **Copenhagen Taxi**
Tel: 35 35 35 35
● **Øbrotaxi** Tel: 32 51 51 51
● **HS Taxi** Tel: 38 77 77 77

Tour Operators

Throughout Denmark
Copenhagen Excursions
Tel: 32 54 06 06. Fax: 32 57 49 05.
Website: www.copenhagen-excursions.dk
Auto Paaske
Tel: 32 66 00 00. Fax: 32 66 00 25.

Copenhagen
● To hire an authorised guide to the city, contact: Wonderful Copenhagen, 1 Gammel Kongevej, 1610 Cph.V. Tel: 33 25 38 22.
● Copenhagen This Week (website: www.ctw.dk free at most hotels and tourist agencies) has a list of tours.

Where to Stay

Choosing a Hotel

Danish hotels are not cheap, but have first-class facilities and are very much business-orientated. They are classified by one to five stars by HORESTA (Danish Hotel, Restaurant and Tourist Employers' Association). Rooms have showers more often than baths, so If you want a bath ask before you book.

Greenland
In Greenland hotels come into the expensive category and there is not a wide selection of alternatives. Make sure of your accommodation before you go.
Greenland Tourism Tel: 299 32 28 88. Website: www.greenland-guide.dk

Faroe Islands
Hotels here were until recently largely designed for visiting sailors. Apart from a few in Torshavn (of which at least two have good facilities), modern hotels are not plentiful. Private houses and youth hostels provide an alternative.
Faroe Islands Tourist Board Tel: 298 31 60 55. Website: www.tourist.fo

Information and reservations
The *Denmark Accommodation Guide* is available free from the Danish Tourist Board in London, tel: 020 7259 5959, website: www.dtb.dt.dk. This lists hundreds of hotels, holiday centres and inns.
You can book a hotel at the tourist information office opposite Central Station in Copenhagen (open daily 9am–4pm; tel: 33 25 38 44). For further information try the Danish Tourist Board in your home country (*see page 355*).

Hotel Listings

Hotels are grouped by area, starting with Copenhagen. Within each city or region, they are listed alphabetically in price order, with the most expensive first.

COPENHAGEN

Hotel d'Angleterre
Kongens Nytorv 34, DK-1050
Tel: 33 12 00 95. Fax: 33 12 11 18
E-mail: anglehot@remmen.dk
Website: www.remmen.dk
Often entertains European royalty and the famous. Its pavement café is popular. 243 beds, suites available. **$$$**
Savoy Hotel
Vesterbrogade 34, DK-1620
Tel: 33 26 75 00. Fax: 33 26 75 01
Carefully restored 1906 building in a garden courtyard. **$$–$$$**
Copenhagen Admiral Hotel
Toldbodgade 24–28
Tel: 33 11 82 82. Fax: 33 32 55 42
E-mail: admiral@admiral-hotel.dk
Website: www.admiral-hotel.dk
Conversion of a 1787 granary with excellent facilities. 815 beds. **$$**
Sophie Amalie Hotel
Sankt Annæ Plads 21, DK-1250
Tel: 33 13 34 00. Fax: 33 11 77 07
E-mail: anglehot@remmen.dk
Website: www.remmed.dk
Well-renovated building not far from the quay near Nyhavn. Some rooms have a harbour view. Quiet. **$$**
Hotel Amager
Amagerbrogade 29, DK-2300
Tel: 32 54 40 08. Fax: 32 54 90 05
On the way to the airport but only five minutes' bus ride to the centre. A traditional *pension* hotel. **$**
Hotel 9 Små Hjem
Classensgade 38–42, DK-2100
Tel: 35 26 16 47. Fax: 35 43 17 84
Website: www.9smaahjem.dk
In the quiet embassy area just 10 minutes from the centre of town. **$**
Hotel Fy and Bi
Valby Langgade 62, 2500 Valby
Tel: 36 45 44 00. Fax: 36 45 44 09
A charming 100-year-old hotel and restaurant built around a courtyard and painted in traditional Danish yellow. **$**

Price Guide

$$$ 955–2,995DKK
$$ 725–1,050DKK
$ under 450–835DKK
Price categories are based on the average cost (including tax) of a double room, usually with breakfast.

ZEALAND

Fredensborg
Hotel Store Kro
Slotsgade 6, 3480
Tel: 48 48 00 47. Fax: 48 48 45 61
Delux and romantic with Fredensborg Castle as its neighbour. **$$**

Frederiksværk
Hotel Frederiksværk
Torvet 6, 3300
Tel: 47 72 22 88. Fax: 47 72 01 13
235 years old and in the centre. **$**

Helsingør
Hotel Hamlet
Bramstræde 5, 3000
Tel: 49 21 05 91. Fax: 49 26 01 30
E-mail: hotelhamlet@internet.dk
Website: www.hotelhamlet.dk
A charming old-fashioned building near Kronborg Castle only two minutes from the train station. **$$**

Køge
Hotel Hvide Hus
Strandvejen 111, DK-4600
Tel: 56 65 36 90. Fax: 56 66 33 14
Modern hotel with sea views. **$$**

Næstved
Mogenstrup Krog
Præstø Landevej 25, DK-4700
Tel: 55 76 11 30. Fax: 55 76 11 29
First-class hotel and resort. **$$**

Rødby
Landmands Hotel
Vestergade 6, 4970
Tel: 54 66 07 67. Fax: 55 66 07 67
Quaint roadside inn near ferry. **$**

Roskilde
Hotel Prindsen
Algade 13, DK-4000
Tel: 46 38 80 10. Fax: 46 35 81 10

Royal-style building 305 years old, newly renovated and central. **$$**

Slagelse
Hotel Frederik d.11
Idagårdsvej 3, DK-42200
Tel: 58 53 03 22. Fax: 58 53 46 22
A modern red-brick building near the Antvorskou ruins. **$$**

Stege
Præstekilde Kro & Hotel
Klintevej 116, Keldby DK-4780
Tel: 55 86 87 88. Fax: 55 81 36 34
Modern hotel in a pretty area 20 km (12.5 miles) from Møn cliffs. **$–$$**

Tisvildeleje
Strandhotel "Højbohus"
Hovedgaden 75, 3220
Tel: 48 70 71 19. Fax: 48 70 71 77
On the beach. Popular with both Danes and tourists in summer. **$$**

Vedbæk
Hotel Marina
Vedbæk Strandvej 391, 2950
Tel: 45 89 17 11. Fax: 45 89 17 22
E-mail: marina@hotelmarina.dk
Website: www.hotelmarina.dk
Modern, overlooking the marina. **$$**

FUNEN

Odense
Hotel H.C. Andersen
Claus Bergs Gade 7, DK-5000
Tel: 66 14 78 00. Fax: 66 14 78 90
Good, modern hotel in the old part of town. Conference facilities. **$$$**
City Hotel Odense
Hans Mulesgade 5, DK-500
Tel: 66 12 12 58. Fax: 66 12 93 94
Moderately priced three-star with all modern comforts. **$$**
Odense Congress Hotel
Ørbækvej 350, DK-5220
Tel: 66 15 55 35. Fax: 66 15 50 70
E-mail: konf@occ.dk
Website: www.occ.dk
Both a congress centre and four-star hotel with 218 beds. **$$**
Motel Brasilia/Blommenslyst Kro
Middelfartvej 420
DK-5491 Blommenslyst
Tel: 65 96 70 12. Fax: 65 96 79 37
Beautiful motel, 8 km (5 miles) west of Odense, added to an old

kro (inn) with lovely garden. Excellent traditional food. **$$**
Hotel Ærøhus
Vestergade 38, DK-5970
Tel: 62 52 10 03. Fax: 62 52 21 23
Website: www.sima.dk/arohus
Holiday apartments and live music at weekends. **$–$$**
Det Lille Hotel
Dronningensgade 5, DK-5000
Tel: 66 12 28 20. Fax: 66 12 28 21
A charming little family hotel on a quiet street near the centre. **$**
Missionhotellet Ansgar
Østre Stationsvej 32, DK-5100
Tel: 66 11 96 93. Fax: 66 11 96 75
One of the old mission hotels with all the facilities. 70 rooms. **$**
Pjentehus Bed and Breakfast
Pjentedansgade 14, DK-5000
Tel: 40 31 76 12
E-mail: pjentehus@teliamail.dk
Beautiful villa with a relaxed atmosphere and pleasant rooms. **$**
Ydes Hotel
Hans Tausensgade 11, DK-5000
Tel: 66 12 11 31
Website: www.ydes.dk
Small hotel. English breakfast. **$**

Rudkøbing
Rudkøbing Skudehavn
Havnegade 21, DK-5900
Tel: 62 51 46 00. Fax: 62 51 49 40
Modern hotel with many facilities. Overlooking the harbour. **$**

Svendborg
Hotel Tre Roser
Fåborgvej 90, DK-5700
Tel: 62 21 64 26. Fax: 62 21 15 26
Family-friendly hotel. One-night stopovers, mini-holidays or week-long stays in holiday apartments. **$**

JUTLAND

Ålborg
Park Hotel
J.F. Kennedys Plads 41, DK-9000
Tel: 98 12 31 33. Fax: 98 13 31 66
Built in 1900 in the centre just five minutes' walk from the station. **$$**

Århus
Hotel Royal
Store Torv, Box 43
Tel: 86 12 00 11. Fax: 86 76 04 04

Beautiful building, more than 150 years old, but modernised with a fine conservatory restaurant. **$$$**
SAS Radisson
Margrethepladsen 1, DK-8000
Tel: 86 12 86 65. Fax: 86 12 86 75
A large steel and glass building and major conference centre. **$$$**
Hotel Marselis
Strandvejen 25, DK-8000
Tel: 86 14 44 11. Fax: 86 11 70 46
Between a beach and forest. With a café and restaurant. Conference facilities and live music. **$$–$$$**
Hotel La Tour
Randersvej 139, DK-8200
Tel: 86 16 78 88. Fax: 86 16 79 95
200 beds, all private facilities. **$$**
Hotel Ritz
Banegårdsplads 12, Postboks 37
Tel: 86 13 44 44. Fax: 86 13 45 87
Very central and close to the station with interesting decor. **$$**
Plaza Hotel
Banegårdspladsen 14, DK-8100
Tel: 87 32 01 00. Fax: 87 32 01 99
E-mail: post@plaza-hotel-aarhus.dk
Website: www.plaza-hotel-aarhus.dk
Central, with a bar, fitness centre, Jacuzzi and indoor parking. **$$**

Christiansfeld
Hos Gert Sørensen
Lindegade 25, DK-6070
Tel: 74 56 17 10. Fax: 74 56 36 40
Website: www.sima.dk/hos-gert-s
Old guesthouse with a restaurant that specialises in desserts. **$**

Esbjerg
Palads Hotel
Skolegade 14, DK-6700
Tel: 75 18 16 00. Fax: 75 18 16 24
Nice, newly renovated. Central. **$**

Fanø
Sønderho Kro
Kropladsen 11, 6720
Tel: 75 16 40 09. Fax: 75 16 43 85
E-mail: sonderho@relaischateaux.fr
Built in 1722 in idyllic surroundings perfect for a romantic break. **$$**

Frederikshavn
Hotel Frederikshavn
Tordenskjoldsgade 14, DK-9900
Tel: 98 43 32 33. Fax: 98 43 33 11
E-mail: hotel.frh@post3.tele.dk

Website: www.hotel-frederikshavn
Modern. Central. Good facilities. **$$**

Hirtshals
Hotel Strandlyst
Tornby Strand, DK-9850
Tel: 98 97 70 76. Fax: 98 97 70 76
Cosy 100-year-old hotel 10 minutes
from the beach. Open summer. **$**

Ribe
Hotel Dagmar
Torvet 1, DK-6760
Tel: 75 44 00 33. Fax: 75 42 36 52
The oldest hotel in Denmark,
established in 1581. Across the
street from the cathedral. **$$**

Skagen
Danhostel Skagen
Rolighedsvej 2, DK-9990
Tel: 98 44 22 00. Fax: 98 44 22 55
E-mail: danhostel.skagen@adr.dk
Website: www.danhostelnord.
dk/skagen
Clean, cosy and near the beach. **$**

Vejle
Munkebjerg Hotel
Munkebjergvej 125, DK-7100
Tel: 79 42 79 10. Fax: 79 42 79 01
Website: www.munkebjerg.dk
Modern hotel in the middle of forest
with marvellous views. **$$–$$$**

BORNHOLM

Allinge
Hotel Pepita
Langebjergvej 1 Sandvig, DK-3770
Tel: 56 48 04 51. Fax: 56 48 18 51
Cosy family-run hotel near beach. **$**

Gudhjem
Hotel Casa Blanca
DK-3760
Tel: 56 48 50 20. Fax: 56 48 50 81
Modern family hotel with a fantastic
view of the sea. Outdoor pool. **$$**

GREENLAND

Illulisaat
Hotel Arctic
Box 1501, DK-3952
Tel: 299 94 41 53
Fax: 299 94 39 24

Good-quality modern hotel with a
superb view over the bay and Disko
Island. The best way to reach it is
by helicopter from Søndrestrømfjord
Airport. **$$$**

Kangerlussuaq
Hotel Kangerlussuaq
Box 1006, DK-3910
Tel: 299 84 11 80
Fax: 299 84 12 84
On the tip of one of Greenland's
longest fjords with 269 rooms, and
numerous amenities. **$$**

Narsarsuaq
Hotel Narsarsuaq
The Airport, DK-3921
Tel: 299 66 52 53.
Fax: 299 66 53 70
The airport hotel with 192 rooms,
around 16km (10 miles) from the
start of the inland ice. **$$$**
Hotel Perlen
Box 8, DK-3291
Tel: 299 66 17 13/57 20 17
Fax: 299 66 17 13
Family-run hotel with good food and
beautiful views of the sound. **$$**

Nuuk
Hotel Hans Egede
Aqqusinersuaq 1–5,
Box 289, DK-3920
Tel: 299 32 42 22
Fax: 299 32 44 87
E-mail: hhe@greennet.gl
Website: www.greenland-guide.dk
Modern conference hotel. Has 250
beds with private facilities. **$$$**

Qaanaaq
Hotel Qaanaaq
Box 88, DK-3971
Tel: 299 97 12 34
Fax: 299 97 10 64
A small, simple hotel on the remote
northwest coast of Greenland. **$**

Price Guide

$$$ 955–2,995DKK
$$ 725–1,050DKK
$ under 450–835DKK
Price categories are based on
the average cost (including tax)
of a double room, usually with
breakfast.

● For further information contact:
Greenland Tourism
Tel: 299 32 28 88.
Fax: 299 32 28 77.
E-mail: info@visitgreenland.com
Website: www.greenland-guide.dk

THE FAROE ISLANDS

Bordoy, Klaksvik
Klaksvikar Sjomansheim
Vikavegur, FR-700 Klaksvik
Tel: 298 45 53 33
Fax: 298 45 72 33
Handy for the ferry. 61 rooms,
some en suite. Restaurant. **$$**

Eystoroy, Eidi
Hotel Eidi
Tel: 298 42 34 56
Fax: 298 42 32 00
Has 31 beds without private
facilities but with mini-bars. **$**
● Eystoroy also has two youth
hostels, as do many other islands.
Details from: **Færøernes Touristråd**
Tel: 45 33 14 83 83
Fax 45 33 93 85 75

Mykines
Kristianshus
Tel: 298 31 09 85
Open May to September. **$**

Torshavn
Hotel Borg
Oggjarvegur, PO Box 105, FR-110
Tel: 298 31 75 00
Fax: 298 31 69 19
Modern but built in traditional style,
looking across to the island of
Nolsoy. All private facilities. **$$$**
Hotel Hafnia
Aarvegur 6 1B, FR-110
Tel: 298 31 12 70
Fax: 298 31 52 50
By the harbour, with 76 beds all
with private facilities. Sauna. **$$**
Hotel Vagar
Sørvagar, FR-380
Tel: 298 33 29 55
Fax: 298 33 23 10
Restaurant serving Faroe food;
conference facilities. **$$**
Torshavn Sjomansheim
Torsgata 4, PO Box 97, FR-110
Tel: 298 31 35 15
Fax: 298 31 32 86

Comfortable, with 72 rooms, some with private facilities. Restaurant. **$**

● For further information contact:
The Faroe Islands Tourist Board
Tel: 298 31 60 55
E-mail: tourist@tourist.fo
Website: www.tourist.fo

Family Holidays

Camping/caravanning
You can hire stationary caravans or huts on many camp sites (all high standard), or take your own tent. For a list of sites, ask the Danish Tourist Board or contact:
Camping Rådet Tel: 39 27 88 44.
Fax: 39 27 80 44.
Camping Club Denmark Horsens Tourist Bureau. Tel: 70 10 41 20.
Fax: 75 60 21 90.

Farm Holidays
For details contact: **Horsens Tourist Board**. Tel: 70 10 41 20.
Fax: 75 60 21 90.

Youth Hostels

Denmark has around 100 youth hostels. You need to be a member of the Youth Hostel Association in your home country. For details:
Denmarks Vandrerhjem
Vesterbrogade 39, DK-1620, Copenhagen V. Tel: 31 31 36 12.
Danish tourist offices also have a free list of sites.

Where to Eat

What To Eat

Within the past couple of decades the Danish kitchen has gone through a quiet revolution. Not only have the traditional hearty meals of pork and beef seen new low-calorie, high-fibre varieties, but words like pizza, pasta, quiche and kebab have also gone into the everyday vocabulary.

However, the food that is usually associated with Denmark has not suffered from this clash of cultures: open sandwiches (*smørrebrød*) are still most common for lunch. *Smorgåsbord* is a lunch buffet of cold dishes, where you can pick and choose from a range of Danish specialities. Beer and an aquavit are also traditional.

Take advantage of the varieties of fish from the Baltic and North Seas. Fowl and game are common, especially in autumn.

Many restaurants offer "a two-course meal of good, Danish food". This is where one finds pork roast, minced beef, meat or fish balls, and other traditional dishes.

Restaurant Listings

Restaurants are grouped by area, starting with Copenhagen. Within each city or region they are listed in price and alphabetical order starting with the most expensive.

COPENHAGEN

Danish
Krogs Fiskerestaurant
Gammel Strand 38, 1202 K
Tel: 33 15 89 15
Fax: 33 15 83 15
Possibly the best (and priciest) fish restaurant in town. **$$$**

Peder Oxe
Grobrødretorv 11
Tel: 31 11 99 11
Good for lunch, with an excellent salad bar and *smørrebrød*. **$$$**
St Gertrude's Kloster
Hauserplads 32d
Tel: 33 14 66 30
Specialises in medieval dishes. **$$$**
Dockside Steak and Lobster
Langelienekaj 5
Tel: 35 55 75 80
Excellent fish. Great views. **$$–$$$**
Bjælkehuset
Valbylanggade 2
Tel: 36 30 35 96
A beautiful place for a traditional Danish lunch. Closed in winter. **$$**
Ida Davidsen
Stor Kongensgade 70, 1264 K
Traditional *smørrebrød*. **$$**

International
San Giorgio
Rosenborggade 7
Tel: 33 12 61 20
One of the best Italian (Sardinian) restaurants in Copenhagen. **$$$**
El Gusto
Havnegade 47
Tel: 33 11 32 16
Oldest, largest Mexican in town. **$$**
Indian Taj
Jernbanegade 3–5
Tel: 33 13 10 10
Traditional Indian. Good value. **$$**
Mitsu
Jagtvej 101
Tel: 35 85 79 97
Excellent Japanese food. **$$**
Pasta Basta
Valkendorfsgade 22 (between Stråget and Gråbrødretorv), 1151 K
Tel: 33 11 21 31
Try the first-rate buffet of hot and cold pasta dishes. Reasonable prices. **$**

Price Guide

Price categories are based on an average cost of a two-course meal (excluding drinks but with tax) per head:
$$$ 120DKK or more
$$ 70–120DKK
$ less than 70DKK

ZEALAND

Lyngby
Restaurant Brede Spisehus
I.C. Modewegsvej, 2800 Kongens
Tel: 45 85 54 57.
Fax: 45 85 57 67
Danish/French cuisine. **$$$**

Humlebæk
Sletten Kro
Gl. Humlebækvej, 3050
Tel: 49 19 13 01.
Fax: 49 19 13 91
Danish specialities. **$$$**

Nysted
The Cottage
Skansensvej 19, 4880
Tel: 54 87 16 00.
Fax: 54 87 16 44
Danish cuisine. **$$$**

Hillerød
Slotskroen
Slotsgade 67, 3400
Tel: 48 26 01 82.
Fax: 48 24 08 82
Typical Danish lunch. **$/$$**

BORNHOLM

Fredensborg
Strandvejen 116, Rønne
Tel: 56 95 44 44. Fax: 56 95 03 14
High gastronomic standard with a
view of the forest and the sea.
$$$

ODENSE

Den Gamle Kro (The Old Inn)
Overgade 23
Tel: 66 12 14 33
Fax: 66 17 88 58
International cuisine in a building

Price Guide

Price categories are based on an
average cost of a two-course
meal (excluding drinks but with
tax) per head:
$$$ 120DKK or more
$$ 70–120DKK
$ less than 70DKK

dating back to 1683. **$$$**
Restauranten Søhesten
Pantheonsgade 5B
Tel: 66 91 46 96
Specialises in seafood. **$$–$$$**
Kreta
Vestergade 98
Tel: 66 19 44 40
A three-course menu of excellent
Greek food at inexpensive prices. **$**
Olivia
Vintapperstræde 37
Tel: 66 17 87 44
Cosy café with home-made pies. **$**

JUTLAND

Aabenraa
Krusmølle
Krusmøllevej 10, Feldstedskov
Tel: 74 68 61 72
Fax: 74 68 62 10
Serves Danish and international
cuisine. **$$**

Ålborg
Restaurant "Mortens Kro"
Algade 37, 9000
Tel/fax: 98 12 48 60
Both Danish and French cuisine.
$–$$

Arden
Rold Gammel Kro
Hobrovej 11, 9510
Tel: 98 56 17 00
Fax: 98 56 25 11
Traditional Danish dishes. **$$**

Århus
Latin Brasserie & Crêperie
Klostergade 2
Tel: 86 13 78 12
Elegant, romantic French restaurant
with chefs of the highest calibre. An
arty, bohemian-type setting. **$$$**
Le Canard
Frederiksgade 74
Tel: 86 12 58 38
Top-class classic French food. **$$$**
Chez Tony
Tordenskjoldsgade 25
Tel: 86 16 88 30
Popular Greek restaurant. **$$**
Emmery's
Guldsmedegade 24
Tel: 86 13 04 00
Gourmet bakery and tapas. **$$**

Copenhagen's Cafés

Café Chips
Øster Farimagsgade 53
Tel: 35 38 47 91
Cosy. Music some Sundays. **$**
Café Dan Turell
Store Regnegade 3, 1110 K
Tel: 33 14 10 47
Artists often frequent this café. **$**
Café Norden
Østergade 61, 1100 K
Tel: 33 13 59 59
Pretty upstairs, with paintings. **$**
Krasnapolsky
Vestergade 10, 1456 K
Tel: 33 32 88 00
Popular with the young. **$**
Park Café
Østerbrogade 79, 2100 Ø
Tel: 35 42 6248
Often has live music. **$**

Pind's Café
Skolegade 29
Tel: 86 12 20 60
An Århus institution serving
traditional Danish fare. **$$**

Christiansfeld
Den Gamle Gæstgivergård
Lindegade 25, 6070
Tel: 74 56 17 10
Fax: 74 56 36 40
Top-class restaurant specialising in
classic Danish cuisine. **$$$**

Nykøbing Mors
Sallingsund Færgekro
Sallingsundvej 104
7900 Nykøbing Mors
Tel: 97 72 00 88
Fax: 97 72 25 40
French cuisine. **$–$$**

Randers
Slotskroen
Slotsgade, 8900
Tel: 86 43 56 64
Fax: 86 42 69 41
Danish, French and Italian. **$$$**

Skagen
Brøndums Hotel
Anchersvej 3, 9990
Tel: 98 44 15 55
Established in 1840. Good-quality
wine and traditional cuisine. **$$**

Nightlife

Information

The best entertainment is found in Copenhagen, Århus and Odense. Check the local newspapers or call tourist information offices.

BILLETnet is an information network where you can reserve tickets and get details on entertainment events. Tel: 70 15 65 65. Website: www.billetnet.dk

For details about musical events, contact **Danish Music Information Centre**: Tel: 33 11 20 66. Fax: 33 32 20 16. Website: www.mic.dk

Listings

COPENHAGEN

Theatre

Most theatre is in Danish even though the piece may have been written in another language.

The London Toast Theatre, Kochsvej 18. Tel: 33 22 86 86. The only English-language theatre in Copenhagen, showing plays of a high standard.

Det Konglig Teater (The Royal Theatre), Kongens Nytorv. Tel: 33 69 69 33. Website: www.kgl-teater.dk Major operas and symphonies.

Live music

Café Baptof
Nodre Fasanvej 46
Tel: 38 86 90 67
Folk, Irish, American.

Copenhagen Jazz House
Niels Hemmingsensgade 10
Tel: 33 15 26 00
The place for jazz.

Mojo
Løngangsstræde 21C
Tel: 33 11 64 53
Live blues every night.

Pumpehuset
Stidiestræde 52. Tel: 33 93 14 32
Big names in modern music.

Café Svejk
Smallegade 31. Tel: 38 86 25 60
Blues, rock and folk.

ODENSE

Badstuen
Østre Stationsvej.
Tel: 66 13 48 66
Rock, blues, Latin and pop.

Brandts Klædefabrik
Bradnst Passage 37–43
Music, dance and theatre.

Odense Koncerthus
Claus Berg Gade 9
Tel: 66 12 44 88
Classical music.

Rytmeposten
Østre Stationsvej 35
Tel: 66 13 60 20
Rock blues and pop.

ÅRHUS

Nightlife is centred around Skolegade. Many cafés and bars are near the cathedral and in the streets leading to Guldsmedegade. You should also stroll through Vestergade and Jægersgårdgade.

Bent J
Nørre Allé 66. Tel: 86 12 04 92
Famous jazz bar.

Fatter Eskild
Skolegade 25. Tel: 86 19 44 11
Blues music.

Glazzhuset
Åboulevarden 35. Tel: 86 12 13 12
Live jazz.

Musikcaféen
Mejlgade 53. Tel: 86 76 03 44
Rock, blues, folk all kinds.

Musikhuset Århus
Thomas Jensens Allé
Tel: 89 31 82 10
All music, dance and theatre.

Cinema

All foreign films are shown with their original soundtrack. Local newspapers have all the details of what's on where.

Sport

Angling

Anglers must have fishing permits, which can be obtained at any post office or tourist office.

Fishing rights in lakes and streams are usually privately owned but can often be hired from the local tourist office.

Golf

There are more than 125 golf courses to choose from in Denmark. Guests are welcomed at Danish golf clubs on presentation of a valid membership card from their home club. Two worth trying are:

Smørem Golf Centre
Skebjerg 46.
Tel: 44 97 01 11.

Furesø
Tel: 42 81 74 44.

Hiking

There are many beautiful places for hiking in Denmark. Local tourist offices have maps of tested walks and will help you to plan routes. Try walking along the lovely chalk-white cliffs of Stevens or through the peaceful forest of Bøgeskov, just an hour south of Copenhagen.

Sailing

Boats and yachts are available for hire on a weekly basis. Visitors should ask to see a certificate from the Shipping Inspection office before hiring a boat. Try:

Nordia Boat Charter
Tel: 97 20 99 22.
Fax: 97 11 88 70.

Maritim Camping
Tel: 46 73 28 28.
Fax: 46 73 28 11.

Shopping

What to Buy

Danish design is famous all over the world, especially in kitchenware, furniture and stereo equipment.

Beautiful amber necklaces are to be found in all jewellery stores, along with exquisite replicas of ancient Viking jewellery in silver and gold.

Ceramics and glassware are a tradition in Denmark and, in addition to Royal Copenhagen Porcelain, there are many small ceramic studios scattered throughout the country.

Danish furs are very popular among tourists and countless shops specialise in traditional and modern knitwear.

Lego bricks are known throughout the world, but most children's toys are made of strong, durable wood with designs and functions that are based on educational principles.

Feather bedding is a Danish speciality and many stores sell down duvets, eiderdowns, quilts and pillows and can arrange shipment of bulky items.

Danish pipe makers carve wood and meerschaum pipes with excellent craftsmanship.

Tax-free Shopping

Part of the reason for the high prices is a value-added tax (called MOMS) of 25 percent, added to all sales and services.

Visitors can avoid making this contribution to the Danish state by having their purchases shipped home or, for non-EU residents, by shopping in stores that offer a tax-free service (*see Customs, page 355 for further details*).

Shopping in Copenhagen

The main shopping in Denmark's capital are the pedestrian streets, and first among them Strøget. When there, take a look inside **Illums Bolighus** (at Amagertorv). It sells everything from high quality furniture to kitchenware. Nearby is **Georg Jensen**'s silver shop at Strøget and Pilestræde.

Visit **Krea** in Vestergade and **BR** across the street from **Magasin** (said to be the largest department store in Scandinavia) for toys and gifts for children. Around the corner in Lars Bjørnstræde are street fashion and secondhand shops.

Pistolstræde is more pricey, and you will notice the influence of Birger Christensen, the owner of **Café Bee Cee**, **Birger Christensen Furs** and several other food and fashion shops in the neighbourhood.

Hennes & Mauritz, originally a Swedish company, is now an enormous success with the younger generation in Denmark.

HANDICRAFTS

There is an information centre for Danish handicrafts on Amagertorv 1,1160 Kbh. K.
Tel: 33 12 61 62.
Website: www.craftsdk.com.

BOOKS

The following shops are worth trying for foreign-language literature:
Arnold Busck
Købmagergade 49
Tel: 33 73 35 00
Fax: 33 73 35 35
English Books and Records
Fredriksalle 53
Tel: 86 19 54 55
GAD
At Central Station and Fiolstræde 31–33
Tel: 33 12 91 48
Website: www.gad.dk
Books in English, German and French.

Language

Pronunciation

The old joke says that Danish is not so much a language as a disease of the throat, and so it sometimes seems. To make it even more difficult, Danish has three extra letters – æ, ø, and å – plus unpronounceable sub-glottal stops, and myriad dialects and accents. Here are a few simple rules of thumb for pronouncing vowels:
a = a, as in bar
å = aw, as in paw
æ = e, as in pear
e = e, as in bed
i = ee, as in sleep
ø = u, as in fur

General

yes/no ja/nej
big/little stor(t)/lille
good/bad god(t)/dårlig(t)
possible/impossible muligt/umuligt
hot/cold varm/kold
much/little meget/lidt
many/few mange/få
and/or og/eller
please/thank you vær så venlig/tak
I jeg
you (formal) du (de)
he/she han/hun
it den/det
we vi
you (plural, formal) I (de)
they de
foreigner udlænding
foreign fremmed

Medical

pharmacy (et) apotek
hospital (et) hospital
casualty (en) skadestue
doctor (en) læge

Food and Drink

breakfast morgenmad
lunch (break) frokost (pause)
dinner middag
tea te
coffee kaffe
beer fadøl

Getting Around

left venstre
right højre
street (en) gade/vej
bicycle (path) (en) cykel (sti)
car (en) bil
bus/coach (en) bus
train (et) tog
ferry (en) færge
bridge (en) bro
traffic light (et) trafiklys
square (et) torv
north nord
south syd
east øst
west vest

Numbers

1	*en/et*
2	*to*
3	*tre*
4	*fire*
5	*fem*
6	*seks*
7	*syv*
8	*otte*
9	*ni*
10	*ti*
11	*elleve*
12	*tolv*
13	*tretten*
14	*fjorten*
15	*femten*
16	*seksten*
17	*sytten*
18	*atten*
19	*nitten*
20	*tyve*
21	*enogtyve*
30	*tredive*
40	*fyrre*
50	*halvtreds*
60	*tres*
70	*halvfjerds*
80	*firs*
90	*halvfems*
100	*hundrede*

Buying a Ticket

ticket billet
adult voksen
child barn
single enkelt
return retur

Money

How much is it? Hvad koster det?
Can I pay with... Må jeg betale med...
traveller's cheques rejsechecks
money penge
notes/coins sedler/mønter
Please may I have... Må jeg få...
the bill? regningen?
May I have a... Må jeg få en...
receipt? kvittering?
bank (en) bank
exchange veksle
open åben
closed lukket

Time

good morning godmorgen
good day/evening goddag
goodnight godaften/godnat
today i dag
tomorrow i morgen
yesterday i går
morning formiddag
noon middag
afternoon eftermiddag
evening aften
night nat
What time is it? Hvad er klokken?
It's five Den er fem

Place Names

Copenhagen København
Elsinore Helsingør
Zealand Sjælland
Funen Fyn
Jutland Jylland
MOMS value-added tax (VAT)

Days of the Week

Monday mandag
Tuesday tirsdag
Wednesday onsdag
Thursday torsdag
Friday fredag
Saturday lørdag
Sunday søndag

Further Reading

General

A History of Denmark by Palle Lauring (Høst; Copenhagen, 1986). An authoritative account of Danish history.
Our Nordic Heritage (KOM, 1997). Explores the World Heritage Sites of the Nordic countries.
An Account of Denmark as it was in the Year 1692 by Robert Molesworth (Wormanium Publishers; Århus, Denmark).
Country Report: Denmark (Reuters News Agency, London electronic database).
Danmark Fra Luften (Denmark from the Air) by Torkild Balslev (Bogan's Forlag A/S; Viborg, 1984). In Danish; English edition available.
The Art of Scandinavia, Volumes 1 & 2, Pby eter Anker and Aron Andersson (translated by Vivienne Menkes from the French original).

Other Insight Guides

Over 200 titles in the acclaimed Insight Guides series cover every continent. Titles in the region include *Denmark, Norway, Sweden*, and *Finland*. Insight Pocket Guides, with an itinerary-based approach, include *Denmark* and *Oslo & Bergen*. Insight Compact Guides to the region include *Denmark, Copenhagen, Norway* and *Finland*.

NORWAY

Area 386,958 sq km (150,000 sq miles).
Capital Oslo.
Population 4.47 million, of whom 495,000 live in Oslo, 222,000 in Bergen, 106,000 in Stavanger and 145,000 in Trondheim.
Language Norwegian, of which there are two variations: *bokmål* and *nynorsk*. The Sami in north Norway speak Lappish. English is widely understood.
Religion Around 94 percent are Evangelical Lutheran Church of Norway. Other churches, mostly Protestant and Roman Catholic, represent about four percent.
Time zone Central European Time, 1 hour ahead of Greenwich Mean Time, 6 hours ahead of Eastern Standard Time. The clock is set forward an hour in March, and back an hour in September.
Currency Norwegian krone (NOK), divided into 100 øre.
Weights and measures Metric. Distances are given in kilometres (km) but Norwegians often refer to a *mil* which is 10 km (so 10 mil is 100 km). When talking about land area you will also often hear the word *mål*. This old measure of 984.34m^2 has been rounded up to 1,000m^2 (or 1 decare).
Electricity 220 AC (two-pin plug).
International dialling code +47.

Topography

Norway is a narrow country 2,600 km (1,600 miles) long. At points it narrows down to as little as 6 km (4 miles). Most of the country's 21,465-km (13,330-mile) continental coastline lies along the North Sea. Norway has common borders with Sweden, Finland and Russia. It also has sovereignty over a few islands within the Arctic Circle, the largest being Svalbard (Spitsbergen).

The south is hilly and partially forested. The most fertile food-growing region is the southern quarter. Although indented with fjords all around its coast, the west coast from Stavanger to Bergen and Bergen to Trondheim contains the most-visited fjords.

The Glomma is Norway's longest river, with its source in South Trøndelag and outflow into the Oslofjord. Norway has thousands of glacial lakes, the largest of which is Lake Mjøsa in the southeast.

Climate

Oslo is one of the warmest places in Norway during winter; in January the average 24-hour high is -2°C (28°F) and the low is -7°C (19°F). Up north it's a different story, with sub-zero temperatures reigning for months and a good number of roads shut over winter due to long-term snow. February and March are the best skiing months. March, April and early May are the wet spring months when roads are buckled due to thaws and refreezes; through this period the temperature slowly lifts from about 4°C (39°F) to 16°C (61°F).

Come summertime and the season of the midnight sun, Oslo enjoys average temperatures in the low-to mid-20s°C (70s°F), while the sunlight-bathed north has a perfect hiking temperature, around 20°C (68°F). October is the time for autumn rains as temperatures dip below 10°C (50°F), then continue

Aurora Borealis

The Northern Lights, or Aurora borealis, are most often seen from November to February during the long Arctic nights. It's best to head north of the Arctic Circle, which cuts Norway just south of Bodø on the Nordland coast.

their slide towards zero. The first snow arrives mid-October.

Government

Norway's national assembly, *Stortinget*, is the mainstay of its political system. There are 165 members who sit in two chambers (*Odelsting* and *Lagting*); elections occur every four years. There are 19 major local government counties (*fylke*), divided into smaller municipalities (*kommune*). The government is headed by a prime minister who leads the majority party or a coalition of parties in the *Stortinget*. The Norwegian monarch is the symbolic head of state.

Across the political spectrum from left to right are the Red Electoral Alliance (RV), the Socialist Left Party (SV), the Labour Party (A), the Centre Party (SP), the Liberal Party (V), the Christian Democratic Party (Kr.F), the Conservative Party (H) and the Progress Party (Fr.P). Norway's constitution dates from 17 May 1814.

Economy

Norway has been a member of NATO and the OECD since 1949, and is a founder member of the UN. The nation spends more money per capita on foreign aid than any other country. It is also a member of the Council of Europe and the EEA (the country turned down European Union membership in referenda in 1972 and 1994).

With Denmark, Sweden, Iceland, Finland, the Faroe Islands and Greenland, Norway is also a member of the Nordic Council (founded in 1952).

Norway's economy has boomed due to North Sea oil. Other long-established industries include timber, pulp and paper, hydro-electric power, gas, shipping and some mining. Fish and agricultural products have long been staples of the economy. The revenue from ocean fisheries has now been surpassed by fish farming, particularly salmon. Commercial whaling is carried out on a modest scale (roughly 600 minke whales a year) against the wishes of the International Whaling Commission (IWC). Newer industry revolves around computers and business services. Tourism is a continually increasing source of capital, too. Some of Norway's most successful ventures include Statoil, Norsk Hydro, Kværner, Aker RGI and Royal Caribbean Cruise Lines.

The People

Norwegians are pleasantly polite. Whenever strangers meet, there is always a handshake and exchange of full names. Whenever you are served you will hear the phrase *Vær så god* ("You are welcome" and "It is a pleasure to serve you" rolled into one). The only equivalent to "please" in Norwegian is *vennligst*, which is formal and not frequently used. Nor do they say *takk* (thank you) as frequently as English-speaking people.

The only thing remotely unruly in Norwegian manners occurs in the busy streets of Oslo. People jostle each other with impunity: don't be offended if there's no apology.

Doing Business

Norwegians have all the state-of-the-art props. Don't be caught out without a good-looking business card, a laptop and mobile phone.

People take work seriously, but also know how to maintain a relaxed business atmosphere. Liquid lunches are unusual, and the work day ends at 3.30 or 4pm. Norwegians take their summer holiday very seriously: from mid-June to the end of July/first week in August, offices and factories empty, and it is almost impossible to do business. May can also be a tricky month.

Norwegians are rarely duplicitous. They may well mention the bad points of something first, to get them out of the way; then it's on to the sell. You won't be drowned in a sea of hype, but the honesty may be hard to get used to.

Planning the Trip

Visas and Passports

A valid passport is all that is necessary for citizens of most countries to enter Norway. Visas are not required. Tourists are generally limited to a three-month visit; it is possible to stay longer, but you must apply for a visa after the initial three months.

Customs

The following can be imported:
● **Money** Notes and coins (Norwegian and foreign) up to nok 25,000 or equivalent. If you intend to import more, you must fill in a form (available at all entry and exit points) for the Customs Office.
● **Alcohol** 1 litre wine (up to 22 percent proof) and 1 litre of spirits (up to 60 percent proof) or 2 litres wine if no spirits. 2 litres beer. On top of the tax-free quota you may bring in 4 litres wine or liquor against payment of duty.
● **Tobacco** 200 cigarettes or 250 g of other tobacco goods.

Health

The are no major health hazards in Norway. No vaccinations are necessary and the tap water is (generally) good.

Treatment

Norway has reciprocal treatment agreements with the UK and many other European countries; your own National Insurance should cover you to receive free treatment at public hospitals (you will have to pay towards medicine, however). EU members should obtain the relevant documentation to entitle them to

this (for British citizens a form E111 from post offices). People from countries without such agreements, and those without an E111, will have to pay a small fee.

Money Matters

The Norwegian krone (NOK) is divided into 100 øre. Notes come in denominations of NOK 50, 100, 200, 500 and 1,000 and coins 50 øre and NOK 1, 5, 10 and 20.

You can change currency at post offices, the Oslo S-train station, international airports, some hotels and commercial banks. Public telephones take phone-cards (from kiosks) or coins.

Road toll stations are sometimes unmanned and require coins to be inserted (usually NOK 10) to lift the barrier.

How to pay

Use of credit cards is widespread, with Eurocard, Visa, American Express and Diner's Club the most common. Traveller's cheques are accepted. In most banks you can also get cash on a Visa card, up to a certain limit.

What to Bring

Norway is protected by the Gulf Stream so it can get even warmer than its southern neighbours. In the south, temperatures in the upper 20s°C (80s°F) are not unusual. The average temperature for the country as a whole in July is about 16°C (60°F).

Pack the clothes you would normally wear in northern Europe, including jumpers and a raincoat and walking shoes. You are not usually required to dress formally for dinner at Norwegian resort hotels.

Spring and autumn are rainy so an umbrella is useful. In winter bring very warm clothing: mittens or gloves and hats (covering the ears) are strongly advised.

A first aid kit is recommended for those making trips to remote parts. Include potions for preventing and treating mosquito bites.

Tour Operators

● **Activity holidays**
Inntravel, Hovingham,
York YO62 4ZR. Tel: 01653
629010.
JMC Holidays, 29-31 Elmfield
Road, Bromley, Kent BR1 1LT.
Tel: 0870 511 4113

● **Arctic voyages/dog-sledging/whale watching**
Arctic Experience & Discover the
World, 29 Nork Way, Banstead,
Surrey SM7 1PB.
Tel: 01737 218800.

● **Norway specialists**
Bridge Travel Service, 55-59 High
Road, Broxbourne, Herts EN10
7DT.
Tel: 01992 456300.
Norsc Holidays, South Winds,
Lower Sea Lane, Charmouth
DT6 6LR.
Tel: 01297 560033.
Taber Holidays, 30A Bingley
Road, Saltaire, Shipley, West
Yorkshire BD1 2SX.
Tel: 01274 594642.
Yes, Broadway, Peterborough,
PE1 1RS.
Tel: 01733 340345.

● **Tailormade holidays**
Specialised Tours, 4 Copthorne
Bank, Copthorne, Crawley, West
Sussex
RH10 3QX.
Tel: 01342 712785.

● **Tours**
Explore Worldwide, 1 Frederick
Street, Aldershot GU11 1LQ.
Tel: 01252 319448.

Page & Moy, 136–140 London
Road, Leicester LE2 1EN.
Tel: 0116 250 7979.
ScanMeridian,
28b Hampstead High Street,
London NW3 1QA. Tel: 020 7431
5393.
Scantours, 47 Whitcomb Street,
London WC2H 7DH.
Tel: 020 7839 2927.

● **Fjord tours**
DFDS Seaways, Scandinavia
House, Parkeston, Harwich, Essex
CO12 4QG.
Tel: 0990 333 666.
Fjord Line,International Ferry
Terminal, Royal Quays, North
Shields, Tyne & Wear NE29 6EG.
Tel: 0191 296 1313
Taber Holidays, 30A Bingley Road,
Saltaire, Shipley, West Yorkshire
BD18 4RS
Tel: 01274 594642
Scandinavian Travel Service,
2 Berghem Mews, Blythe Road,
London W14 0HN
Tel: 020 7559 6666
(brochure line tel: 01443 82222)

● **Skiing/Walking**
Crystal Holidays, Crystal House,
Arlington Road, Surbiton, Surrey
KT6 6BW.
Tel: 01235 824324
Mountain & Wildlife Ventures,
Brow Foot, High Wray, Ambleside
LA22 0JE.
Tel: 015394 33285.
Waymark Holidays, 44 Windsor
Road, Slough
SL1 2EJ.
Tel: 01753 516477.

Getting There

BY AIR

Scandinavia's flagship carrier,
SAS, runs a wide range of
flights between Oslo
Gardermoen Airport and other
world capitals, with many direct
services to and from Bergen,
Oslo, Stavanger, Tromsø and
Trondheim.

From the UK

SAS offers daily non-stop flights
from Heathrow to Oslo and
Stavanger. During the summer
months there is a twice-weekly
non-stop service from Heathrow to
Tromsø and daily (except Saturday)
flights from Manchester to Oslo and
from Aberdeen to Stavanger.
● SAS Scandinavian Airline
Services, Star Alliance Office, 7–8
Conduit Street, London W1R 0AY.

Tel: 0845 60727727.
Website: www.flysas.co.uk.
Braathens operates daily
flights from Stansted to Oslo
and Stavanger/Bergen, and
six days a week from Newcastle
Airport to Oslo and Stavanger.
● Braathens, Newcastle
International Airport, Woolsington,
Newcastle upon Tyne NE13 8BZ.
Tel: 0870 5074074 (UK only).
Website: www.braathens.se.

British Airways operates several
flights a day from London to Oslo
(out of both Heathrow and
Gatwick).
● British Airways, Speedbird House,
PO Box 10, Heathrow Airport,
Hounslow TW6 2JA.
Tel: 0345 222111.
Website: www.british-airways.co.uk

Air UK operates scheduled flights
Monday to Friday from Aberdeen,
Humberside and Teeside to
Bergen.
● Air UK, Stansted House, Stansted
Airport, Essex CM24 1AE.
Tel: 0870 5074074.

British Midland operates from
several UK airports via London
Heathrow to Oslo and Bergen.
● British Midland Airways,
Donnington Hall, Castle Donnington,
Derby DE74 2SB.
Tel: 0870 6070555.
Website: www.britishmidland.co.uk

RyanAir offers cut-price flights from
Stansted to Torp near Sandefjord,
two hours by coach to Oslo.
● RyanAir, Enterprise House,
Stansted Airport, Stanstead, Essex
CM24 1QW.
Tel: 0541 569569.
Website: www.ryanair.com

Charter flights There are also
charter flights to various airports in
Norway (check with your travel
agent for details).
   All airports are served by
buses and taxis and Oslo
Gardermoen Airport has a high-speed rail link to Sentralstasjon
(known as Oslo S, the city's
central railway station).

From the US
● **SAS** c/o United Airlines, 437 Madison Ave (enter on 50th St), NY. Tel: 1-800-221 2350.

BY SEA

From the UK
Fjord Line operates the only direct year-round service from the UK with sailings from Newcastle to Stavanger, Haugesund and Bergen.
● Fjord Line, Norway House, International Ferry Terminal, Royal Quays, North Shields, Tyne & Wear NE29 6EG. Tel: 0191 296 1313.

DFDS Seaways sail from Newcastle and Harwich to, among other places, Gothenburg in Sweden.
● DFDS Seaways, Scandinavia House, Parkeston Quay, Harwich, Essex CO12 4QG.
Tel: 0990 333 666.
Website: www.scansea.com/UK

BY RAIL

Numerous rail services link Norway with the rest of Scandinavia and Europe. From the Continent, express trains operate to Copenhagen, where inter-Scandinavian trains connect to Oslo. There are train connections in Oslo to other cities in Norway.
Norwegian State Railways (NSB) operates trains from Stockholm and Copenhagen to Oslo usually twice a day. You can also get to northern Norway from Stockholm, with Trondheim and Narvik the principal destinations.
   International arrivals and departures are at Oslo S station. Gardermobanen, the high-speed rail link from/to Oslo Gardermoen Airport, has a terminal at Oslo S.
● For tickets and information, contact NSB Reisesenter, PO Box 673, N-5001 Bergen, Norway.
Tel: 55 96 60 52.
Fax: 55 32 72 70.
● When in Norway, you can contact NSB directly, tel: 81 50 08 88 and dial 4 to be connected to an English-speaking operator, or

Info Before You Go

AUSTRALIA
The embassy deals with tourist information.
17 Hunter Street, Yarralumia, Canberra ACT 2600.
Tel: 062 733444.

UK
Norwegian Tourist Board
Charles House, 5 Lower Regent Street, London
SW1Y 4LR.
Tel: 020 7839 6255.
Fax: 020 7839 6014.
E-mail: infouk@ntr.no
Website: www.visitnorway.com

USA/CANADA
Norwegian Tourist Board
655 Third Avenue, Suite 1810, New York 10017.
Tel: 212-885 9700.
Fax: 212-885 9710.
E-mail: usa@nortra.no
Website: www.norway.org

contact the nearest railway station. Website: www.nsb.no.

BY ROAD

Most major shipping lines to Norway allow passengers to bring cars. Petrol is expensive in Norway. For further information contact:
Norges Automobil Forbund (NAF or Norwegian Automobile Association), Storgt 2, 0105 Oslo.
Tel: 22 34 14 00.
Fax: 22 33 13 73.
Kongelig Norsk Automobilklub (KNA or Royal Norwegian Automobile Club), Drammensv. 20C PO Box 2425 Solli, 0201 Oslo.
Tel: 22 56 19 00.

Practical Tips

Media

NEWSPAPERS

Most larger kiosks (like the Narvesen chain at railway stations, airports and so on) and some bookshops sell English language newspapers.
   Deichmanske Bibliotek, the main public library, is at Henrik Ibsen's Gate 1 in Oslo, where you'll find a selection of international papers and periodicals.

RADIO

English broadcasts on short wave can be picked up if atmospheric conditions are favourable. Best results can usually be heard on short wave frequency 9410.
   During winter BBC Radios 1, 2, 3 and 4 can sometimes be received on AM. Radio 5 can be picked up on 909 and 693 medium wave (best reception in the evening). On Sunday Radio Norway (93 FM) broadcasts news in English.

TELEVISION

Norway has three main television stations: NRK (Norsk Rikskringkasting), TV2 and TVNorge (TVN). Cable TV is widespread.

BOOKS

Oslo has several bookshops with English sections, including:
Erik Qvist, Drammensveien 16.
Tel: 22 54 26 00.
Tanum Karl Johan, Karl Johansgate 37/41. Tel: 22 41 11 00.

Postal Services

The central post office in Oslo, at Dronningensgate 15 (the entrance is on the corner of Prinsensgate), is open Monday to Friday 8am–8pm and Saturday 9am–3pm. Other post offices are open weekdays 8am–4pm, Saturday 8am–1pm.

Telecommunications

Calls abroad can be made from hotels – with a surcharge – or from phone booths or the main telegraph office at Kongensgate 21 (entrance Prinsensgate), Oslo.

You can also send faxes and telegrams from here.

Norwegian pay-phones take 1, 5 and often 20-kroner pieces; the minimum charge is NOK 2. Phonecards, which can be used in the green phone booths, can be bought in Narvesen kiosks and at post offices. Credit cards (Visa, American Express, Diners, Eurocard and Mastercard) are accepted in some card phones. Cheapest calling time is 5pm–8am.

Local Tourist Offices

General information
The Norway Information Centre, Vestbaneplassen 1 (between the Oslo City Hall and Aker Brygge), 0250 Oslo.
Tel: 82 06 01 00 (in Norway) or 22 83 00 50 (from abroad).
Fax: 22 83 81 50.
NORTRA (Norwegian Tourist Board), Drammensveien 40, 0230 Oslo.
Tel: 22 92 52 00.

Useful Numbers

- **Fire** 110
- **Police** 112
- **Ambulance** 113
- **Medical problems**
For emergency treatment in Oslo ring 22 11 70 70.
- **Internal directory enquiries** 180
- **International directory enquiries** 181
 No coin required in phone boxes

Website: www.tourist.no
Regional information
Regional tourist offices are not open to callers, but supply information in writing or by phone.

Oslo/Oslofjord
Oslo Promotion AS
Vestbaneplassen 1, N-0250 Oslo
Tel: 82 06 01 00 (when in Norway)
Tel: 22 83 00 50 (from abroad)
Fax: 22 83 81 50
Website: www.oslopro.no
Akershus Tourist Board
Schweigaardsgt 4, N-0185 Oslo
Tel: 22 05 58 75
Fax: 22 05 58 99
Destinasjon Vestfold AS
St Olavsgt. 4, N-3110 Tønsberg
Tel: 33 44 36 60
Fax: 33 44 34 47

East Norway
Olympia Utvikling
Troll Park AS, PO Box 373, N-2601 Lillehammer
Tel: 61 28 99 00
Fax: 61 26 92 50
Hedmark Tourist Board
Grønnegt 11, N-2300 Hamar
Tel: 62 52 90 06
Fax: 62 52 21 49
Oppland Tourist Board
Kirkegt 76, N-2600 Lillehammer
Tel: 61 28 91 86
Fax: 61 28 94 98
Fjell og Fjord Ferie
DBC-senteret, N-3550 Gol
Tel: 32 07 45 44
Fax: 32 07 55 09
Website:
www.tellus.no/fjellogfjord/fff-e.htm
Buskerud Adventure
Dronninggt 15, N-3019 Drammen
Tel: 32 89 00 90
Fax: 32 83 47 51
E-mail: opplevel@online.no

South Norway
Syd Norge AS
PO Box 91, N-4601 Kristiansand
Tel: 38 07 10 08
Fax: 38 07 11 01
www.sydnorge.no
Telemark Travel
PO Box 2813 Kjørbekk, N-3702 Skien
Tel: 35 53 03 00
Fax: 35 52 70 07

Public Holidays

- **1 January** New Year's Day
- **March/April** Palm Sunday, Maundy Thursday, Good Friday, Easter Sunday, Easter Monday
- **1 May** Labour Day
- **17 May** National Independence Day
- **May** Ascension Day (6th Thursday after Easter)
- **May/June** Whitsun and Whit Monday (7th Sunday / Monday after Easter)
- **25 December** Christmas Day
- **26 December** Boxing Day

E-mail: destination.telemark @nano.no
Aust-Agder Tourist Board
Fylkeshuset, N-4800 Arendal, c/o Info-Sr, N-4993 Sundebru
Tel: 37 15 85 60
Fax: 37 15 85 65

Fjord Norway
Fjord Norway
PO Box 4108 Dreggen
N-5023 Bergen
Tel: 55 31 93 00
Fax: 55 32 60 20
Website: www.fjordnorway.no
Rogaland Tourist Board
PO Box 798,
N-4001 Stavanger
Tel: 51 51 66 00
Fax: 51 51 68 85
Hordaland/Bergen Tourist Board
Slottsgt 1, N-5003 Bergen
Tel: 55 31 66 00
Fax: 55 31 52 08
Sogn/Fjordane Tourist Board
PO Box 299,
N-5801 Sogndal
Tel: 57 67 23 00
Fax: 57 67 28 06
Møre/Romsdal Tourist Board
PO Box 467,
N-6501 Kristiansund N
Tel: 71 67 39 77
Fax: 71 67 00 70

Central Norway
Central Norway Travel
(Sør/Nord-Trøndelag), PO Box 65, N-7001 Trondheim
Tel: 73 92 93 94
Fax: 73 52 04 30

North Norway
Top of Europe Norway
PO Box 771, N-9001 Troms
Tel: 77 61 05 80
Fax: 77 61 05 79
Website: www.tellus.no/finnmark/
Nordland Reiseliv
PO Box 434, N-8001 Bod
Tel: 75 52 44 06
Fax: 75 52 83 28
Website: www.nordlandreiseliv.no
Email: Ntravel@sn.no
Finnmark Travel Association
PO Box 1223, N-9501 Alta
Tel: 78 43 54 44
Fax: 78 43 55 59
E-mail: finnoppl@barentsnett.no

Medical Services

DOCTORS/HOSPITALS

Even in remote areas you should have no problem getting medical help. In emergencies EU members will receive free treatment at state hospitals (see page 369 for details of reciprocal arrangements), but have to pay towards non-hospital costs and for prescriptions.

If you are ill, ask your hotel, tourist office or a pharmacy for the address of an English-speaking GP. Private doctors are in the directory under Leger (doctors). Keep receipts if you have insurance.

PHARMACIES

For minor problems, head for a pharmacy, or Apotek. Most larger cities have all-night pharmacies. In other cities enquire at your hotel; or try the emergency number in the phone book under Legevakt or Lækjarvakt (doctor on duty).

DENTISTS

Emergency dental treatment in Oslo is available from:
Oslo Kommunale Tannlegevakt, Tøyen Senter, Kolstadgata 18 (near Tøyen T-bane station).
Tel: 22 67 30 00.
Open every day 7am–10pm, Sunday and public holidays 11am–2pm.

Religious Services

Services are held in English at the American Lutheran Church and the Anglican/Episcopalian Church (St Edmund's, Møllergate 30; tel: 22 69 22 14).

The Jewish synagogue is at Bergstein 13, near St Hanshaugen, tel: 22 67 23 83).

Oslo's Protestant cathedral or domkirke (at Storgate, tel: 22 41 27 93) puts on concerts for tourists at 8pm every Wednesday). For up-to-date information, consult the daily press, or latest Oslo Guide.

Security and Crime

The streets of Oslo are relatively safe compared with the bigger cities of Europe and North America. Crime against tourists is rare. Park safely and hide valuables.

Norwegian cities late at night are often full of young people who are drunk, but you're more likely to meet verbal harassment than bodily harm. Most bars have good bouncers, and police patrols are supplemented by private-sector security personnel and Nattravnene (Night Ravens, a Guardian Angel-type patrol).

Worse than the drunks are drug abusers. Give them and the areas they frequent a wide berth (these are usually the cheaper bars and cafés around railway stations).

Tipping

Hotels include a service charge and tipping is generally not expected. Restaurants usually include the service charge, in which case it's your choice to add anything (5–10 percent is customary). The same applies to taxi drivers. Table service in bars requires tipping.

Travellers with Disabilities

Visitors in need of guidance could contact the Norwegian Association for the Disabled, PO Box 9217, Grønland, N-0134 Oslo. Tel: 22 17 02 55. Fax: 22 17 61 77.
Hotel listings in accommodation guides have symbols denoting disabled access and toilets. In the Oslo Guide under Outdoor Activities you'll find some listings that mention accessibility for the disabled.

The Norwegian State Railways (NSB) have carriages specially furnished for the disabled and the new Coastal Express ships have elevators and cabins for disabled people. The Euro Booking Service AS, at Rådhusgt 17, N-0158 Oslo, offers brochures on coach tours for wheelchair users, and provides hotel bookings and hire cars.
Tel: 22 00 77 20. Fax: 22 33 38 44.

Travelling with Kids

Norway is welcoming and safe for children. Family attractions include:

In and around Oslo
Barnekunstmuseet (International Children's Art Museum; exhibits and workshops), Lille Frøensveien 4. Tel: 22 46 85 73.
Horse riding, mini-golf and Mini-zoo Ekeberg near Ekeberghallen.
Tel: 22 68 26 69.
Puppet Theatre Frognerveien 67. Tel: 22 42 11 88 (open May–Sept).
TusenFryd Amusement Park Ås, Østfold. Tel: 64 94 63 63. Open June–Aug (May and Sept weekends only). Transport by bus 541 from Oslo-S or Rådhuset. Attractions

Business Hours

● **Offices** 9am–4pm or 8am–4pm; lunch is taken early, 11.30am–12.30pm, or 12–2pm at a restaurant.
● **Shops** Monday to Friday 9am–5pm, Thursdays until 8pm, Saturday from 9am until 1, 2 or even 3pm.
● **Shopping centres** Until 8 or 9pm on weekdays, 6pm on Saturday.
● **Banks** 9am–3.30pm weekdays, Thursday until 5pm.
● **Pharmacies** Monday to Friday 9am–5pm, Saturday mornings and on a rota basis in larger cities.

include roller-coaster, Spaceshot, flume ride, carousel, magic carpet and climbing wall.
VikingLandet, adjacent to Tusenfryd. Tel: 64 94 63 63. Live like a Viking for a day. Open June to September.

Around Norway
The Troll Family Park near Lillehammer. Tel: 61 27 72 22. Attractions include: the World's Largest Troll, Fairy Tale Cave, Supervideograph, Photo Adventure, Energy Centre (exhibition centre for oil and gas), Wax Museum and Experience Centre for Ice Cream.
Kongeparken near Stavanger. Tel: 51 61 71 11. More than 40 attractions, including life-sized model of The Giant Gulliver (85 x 7.5 metre), riding tracks, bob track, farm, car track, Wild West City, birds and fun fair.
Sommarland Bø in Telemark. Tel: 35 95 16 99. Norway's biggest water park, including many waterslides and Stuka, a 26 metre (85-ft) water chute and a floating river. Plus live entertainment, pony rides, Wild West City and playground.
Kristiansand Dyrepark Tel: 38 04 97 00. Norway's largest wildlife park and most-visited tourist attraction. The park has many other attractions: amusement park, water park, show and entertainment park, leisure park and Cardamomaby – a tiny village from a well-known children's book.
Youth Information, at Møllergata 3, Oslo, provides information on all subjects for young people. Open Monday to Friday 11am–5pm. Tel: 22 41 51 32.
Website: www.unginfo.oslo.no

Embassies in Oslo

Canada
Wergelandsvn 7
Tel: 22 99 53 00
UK
Thomas Heftyesgate 8
Tel: 23 13 27 00
United States
Drammensveien 18
Tel: 22 44 85 50

Getting Around

Public Transport

Norway has an excellent network of public transport services. Although covering great distances can be expensive, there are discount tickets for tourists such as the Fjord Pass and Bonus Pass (for all Scandinavia), plus pan-European budget passes such as InterRail and Eurail. Within larger cities, tourist passes cover urban transport and many museums.

From the Airport

Oslo's Gardermoen Airport is roughly 50 km (30 miles) north of the city. The airport bus runs every 15 minutes from the airport to downtown Oslo, taking 47 minutes. A taxi or private vehicle takes 30 minutes. A high-speed rail link runs to Oslo S station in 20 minutes.

If you are coming from London's Stansted you will arrive at Torp Airport (which is at Sandefjord, almost two hours' drive south along the west side of the fjord). From there buses and trains connect with central Oslo.

All other major city airports are served by buses and taxis.

By Air

Considering its size, Norway is well served by airlines, with about 50 airports and airfields. The three domestic airlines are SAS, Braathens and Widerøe.

Discount tourist passes
SAS offers a Visit Scandinavia Pass, Braathens a summer Visit Norway Pass (discount-rate flight coupons) and Widerøe the Summer Pass.

SAS Scandinavian Airlines
0080 Oslo
Bookings Tel: 81 00 33 00
Info Tel: 67 59 67 19
Main office Tel: 67 59 60 50
Braathens
Oksenøyveien 3, 1330 Oslo
Tel: 67 59 70 00
Fax: 67 59 13 09
Widerøe's Flyveselskap ASA
Vollsv. 6, Pb 131, 1324 Lysaker
Bookings Tel: 67 11 14 60
Fax: 67 11 14 56
Info Tel: 67 11 14 70
Tel (main office): 67 11 60 00
Fax: 67 11 61 95

By Rail

Rail services are far more comprehensive in the south than in the north, and tend to fan out from Oslo, so you will have to supplement your trip with ferries and buses. The Oslo–Bergen line is regarded as one of the world's most spectacular for its scenery.

Oslo S is Norway's busiest railway station, located in central Oslo at the eastern end of Karl Johansgate on Jernbanetorget. Long-distance, express and local suburban trains arrive and depart here. The end of the line in Norway is at Bodø, but the most northerly station is at Narvik, which is reached through Sweden by train or by bus from Fauske.

Most trains are modern and efficient, but the older rolling stock has a touch of nostalgic luxury. New inter-city express (ICE) trains offer one class only. If you plan to take special fast trains, you must book ahead. Ticket sales are from the main hall of the train station.

For information about timetables, ticket prices, bookings and seat reservations, tel: 81 50 08 88 + 1 for operator, or fax: 22 36 64 58. Or contact Trafikanten (see *Tickets and Info, right*).

Discount tourist passes
The Norway Railpass offers one or two weeks of unlimited rail travel in Norway, or three travel days over one month. The Scanrail Pass offers unlimited travel all over Scandinavia,

as well as discounts on certain ferries, buses and hotel chains.

By Bus/Coach

Where the rail network stops, the bus goes further: you can get to practically anywhere you want by bus. Usually it is not necessary to book in advance, but pay the driver when you board.

Discount tourist pass

The NOR-WAY Bussekspress (bus pass) guarantees a seat for all passengers. On sale only outside Norway through the company's agents, the pass is valid all year round and offers two categories for travel on the national network: either unlimited travel within seven consecutive days, or unlimited travel within a 14-day period.
NOR-WAY Bussekspress AS
Karl Johans gt. 2, N-0154 Oslo.
Tel: 23 00 24 40. Fax: 23 00 24 49.

By Boat

Ferries

Ferries are an invaluable means of transport that allow short cuts across fjords to eliminate many road miles. In Oslo, ferries to the fjord islands leave from the quay near Aker Brygge.

Long-distance boats

Hurtigruten, the Norwegian coastal express service, is a vital means of water transport for Norwegians, and a superb way for visitors to see Norway's dramatic coast. In summer, boats leave daily, travelling between Bergen and Kirkenes in 11 days and putting in at 35 ports.

Travel agents can give details, and sell special Coastal Passes to 16–26-year-olds. The steamers take cars, and should be booked well in advance. Either contact your local travel agent or:
Troms Fylkes Dampskibsselskap AS Bookings Tel: 77 64 82 00
Fax: 77 64 81 80
E-mail: booking@tfds.no
Ofotens og Vesteraalens Dampskibsselskab asa

Narvik Tel: 76 96 76 00
Fax: 76 96 76 01
Bookings Tel: 76 96 76 96
Fax: 76 96 76 11
E-mail: booking@ovds.no
Website: www.hurtigruten.com

City Travel Cards

Oslo

The Oslo Card (*Osloskortet*, issued for one, two and three days, with half price for children) is your ticket to unlimited public transport (including city ferries) and free entry to many museums.

If you want a card for travel only, passes include the Minikort (four rides at a discount) and Maxikort (14 rides at a discount).

The Oslo Card may be purchased at the Oslo S railway station, Trafikanten (*see Ticket and Info, opposite*), Narvesen kiosks, hotels, camp sites and tourist offices.

Bergen and elsewhere

Other cities offer similar tourist travel cards: for example, the Bergen Card (24-hour and 48-hour passes from tourist information offices, the railway station, hotels, camp sites and the Hurtigruten terminal) and the Bergen Package (details in the *Official Bergen Guide* from the Bergen Tourist Board).

City Travel

By bus and tram

Oslo has a comprehensive bus and tram system. There are detailed timetables at every stop. There are night buses on some routes and morning buses (starting at 4am).
Bergen and Trondheim also have tram systems.

Tickets and Info

For tickets, routes, times and all queries about public transport, Trafikanten at Oslo S Station offers an information and booking service. Tel: 22 41 70 30.
Open weekdays 7am–11pm, weekends 8am–11pm.

By underground

Oslo's underground is called the T-bane and is very simple to use. There are eight lines, four from the east and four from the west that converge under the centre of Oslo. You can catch any train to any of the far-flung suburbs from any of the stations between Tøyen and Majorstuen. Station entrances are marked with "T". Trafikanten has route maps. The most scenic route is T-bane 1 up to Frognerseteren.

By Taxi

Taxis are widely available. In Oslo, telephone 81 54 48 15 and you will be transferred to the nearest taxi rank. Taxis can also be booked for up to four people, tel: 22 38 80 90, and mini-buses, tel: 22 38 80 70. Otherwise, you can take a taxi from one of the many ranks around the city. All registered taxis carry a registration number on the roof, which is lit when the taxi is free.

In Oslo taxis are more expensive at night or if ordered by phone. When everyone leaves the bars and restaurants around 3am, long queues build up at ranks. This has given rise to "pirate" taxis. These either cruise up out of the blue or a "dummy" (usually a foreigner) asks you if you want a taxi without queuing. These taxis, which do not carry a taxi sign on the roof, are not recommended; if you want to take the risk agree a price beforehand.

By Car

Norway's roads are extremely good, particularly in view of the treacherous weather conditions encountered in winter. Be prepared for long tunnels. EU driving licences are valid in Norway, but drivers from other countries must carry an International Driving Licence.

You drive on the right, and traffic regulations are strictly enforced (*for guidelines, see page 376*).

Winter driving

With Norway's winters, you should never assume all roads are passable. Small roads in the north

Norway in a Nutshell

This is a unique trip that takes you through some of Norway's most beautiful scenery, ascending to altitudes of 866 metres (2,850 ft) with breathtaking views. The usual tour comprises: train from Oslo to Myrdal/Flåm, boat to Gudvangen, bus to Voss and train back to Oslo. But it is also possible to start at Oslo and finish in Bergen or vice versa. Tickets are available from railway stations.

are often closed and even the E6 highway from Oslo to Trondheim closes occasionally.

Breakdown and accidents

The AA and RAC are affiliated to the AIT (Alliance Internationale de Tourisme), so members receive free assistance (with journey planning as well as backup in case of breakdown or accident) from Norway's rescue service, NAF (Norges Automobilforbund). Comprehensive repairs can also be carried out at NAF-contracted garages (for which you will have to pay), and NAF patrol Norway's main roads and mountain passes from 16 June to 14 August.

NAF, Storgt 2, N-0155 Oslo
Tel: 22 34 14 00
Fax: 22 33 13 73
24-hour emergency service (for members of RIT clubs):
Tel: 22 34 16 00. Fax: 22 42 88 30.

If you are involved in an accident where there are no injuries but you need help, you can phone two 24-hour assistance firms on these freephone numbers:
Falken Redningskorps AS
Tel: 80 03 00 50/22 95 00 00.
Viking Redningstjeneste AS
Tel: 80 03 29 00/22 08 60 00.
It is not necessary to call the police for minor accidents, but drivers must exchange names and addresses; leaving the scene without doing so is a crime. Only call the police (112) or an ambulance (113) in emergencies.

Tolls

Several roads have moderately expensive tolls, and you have to pay to enter larger cities.

CARAVANNING

For information contact:
The Norsk Caravan Club,
Solheimveien 18, N-1473 Skårer.
Tel: 67 97 49 20.
Fax: 67 90 13 13.

CAR HIRE

Hiring a car can be expensive. Watch for special weekend and summer prices. Hire firms include:
Avis Bilutleie/Liva Bil AS
PO Box 154, N-1361 Billingstad (near Oslo).
Tel: 66 77 11 11. Fax: 66 77 11 22.
Oslo reservations Tel: 22 83 48 00.
Fax: 22 83 18 24.
Bergen reservations
Tel: 55 32 01 30.
Trondheim Tel: 73 52 69 15.
Fax: 73 52 64 66.

Rules of the Road

Some of Norway's driving regulations vary significantly from those elsewhere. Here are a few tips, but for further guidance get *Velkommen på norske veier* (Welcome to Norwegian Roads), which has an English section and is available at tourist offices.
• **Speed limits** The maximum speed limit is usually 80 kph (50 mph), though 90 kph (55 mph) is permitted on dual carriageways. The limit is 50 kph (30 mph), and even 30 kph (20 mph) on certain residential roads. On-the-spot fines are given for speeding.
• **Giving way** Roads marked at intervals by yellow diamond signs indicate that you have priority. On all others you must give way to traffic from the right. Some have a series of white triangles across them at junctions: stop and give way.

Europcar/Interrent
Box 7041 Homansbyen, N-0306 Oslo
Tel: 22 60 70 22. Fax: 22 60 82 44.
Hertz Bilutleie
Box 331, N-1324 Lysaker/Oslo.
Tel: 67 16 80 00. Fax: 67 16 81 00.
Oslo reservations Tel: 67 12 55 55.
Fax: 67 58 02 22.
Bergen Tel: 55 96 40 70.
Trondheim Tel: 73 50 35 00.

By Bike

A lot of people cycle in Norway. Proceed with caution, however; although there are a few cycle routes, it is not an integrated system. In the countryside cycling is easier as you'll find surfaced cycle paths.

Cyclists are not permitted to travel through the larger road tunnels, but bikes are allowed on most trains and buses for a small charge. There are even special cycle trains in summer. Tourist offices have details of tours and can provide suggestions and maps of cycling routes.

On roundabouts priority is from the left. Always give way to trams, buses and taxis. Many roads have a lane for buses and taxis only.
• **Documentation/equipment** You must always have the following with you in your car: driving licence, car registration documents, European accident statement form, insurance policy and a reflective warning triangle. A snow shovel and tow rope are useful in winter.
• **Lights** It is obligatory for all vehicles to drive with dipped headlights during the day all year round. Carry spare bulbs.
• **Seat belts** must be worn, both front and back.
• **Tyres** It is obligatory to use winter tyres from October to April. These are either tyres with studs (*piggdekk*) or specially designed tyres for use in ice and snow.

Information
The Syklistens Landsforening
(Cycling Association), Storg 23C Pb.
8883 Youngstorget, 0028 Oslo.
Tel: 22 47 30 30. Fax: 22 47 30 31.
E-mail: slf-bike@online.no

Cycle rental
Bikes can be hired from hotels,
camp sites, tourist offices or sports
shops, as well as small cycle hire
shops. In Oslo, contact:
Vestbanen AS, Vestbaneplassen 2
(near Aker Brygge).
Tel: 23 11 51 00. Fax: 23 11 50 70.
Off-road and mountain bikes are for
hire in Oslo from:
White Water AS, Cort Adelers g 27.
Tel: 22 55 11 07. Fax: 22 55 11 48.

On Foot

Norway is a nation of devout
walkers. You can walk wherever you
want in forests, mountains, the
seashore and other non-cultivated
regions. This should be done with
consideration, though – use paths.

Information
The Touring Association (Den
Norske Turistforening), Storgate 3,
Pb. 7 Sentrum, 0101 Oslo
(weekdays only). Tel: 22 82 28 00.
Fax: 22 82 28 01.
Provides maps and information.
Membership gives you rights to use
the association's huts.
The Norwegian Tourist Board
publishes *Mountain Hiking in
Norway*, with itineraries for
mountain walks and details of
where to stay (from Nortrabooks
Scandinavia Connection, 26
Woodsford Sq, London W14 8DP).
For details on walking in national
parks, contact local tourist offices.
The Ministry of Environment
Information Centre, Myntgt 2,
N-0030 Oslo.
Tel: 22 24 57 87. Fax: 22 24 27 56.
The Ministry has a leaflet about
walking in the national parks.

Where to Stay

Norwegian hotels are notoriously
expensive, but they cut rates in
summer and most weekends.
Accommodation ranges from hotels
(luxurious to comfortable), to more
modest guesthouses, camp sites,
cosy self-catering chalets, and
youth/family hostels. Facilities and
service are international standard.

Choosing a Hotel

There is no central hotel booking
service, so you have to go through
travel agents and tour operators, or
book direct (as practically everyone
speaks English this is easy).
In Oslo, the tourist offices at the
Information Centre at Brynjulf Bulls
Plass 1 and at Central Station will
book accommodation for those
arriving in person. It is open every
day 8am–11pm.
The *Accommodation in Norway*
brochure, available from Norwegian
embassies and consulates or
Norwegian Tourist Board (NORTRA) in
Oslo, is useful.
The *NRI Guide* is a free book with
around 1,000 establishments, ferry
timetables and the coastal express
steamer. It is available from tourist
offices, or contact:
Norsk Reiseinformasjon AS, Karl
Johansgt. 12A, N-0154 Oslo.
Tel: 22 47 73 40. Fax: 22 47 73 69.

Hotel Chains

The major hotel chains are all well
represented in the five main
congress towns of Oslo, Stavanger,
Bergen, Trondheim and Tromsø.
Most offer discount cards.
Best Western Hotels Norway, Cort
Adelers g 16, N-0254 Oslo.
Tel: 22 55 09 10. Fax: 22 55 61 23.
Free booking number: 80 01 16 24.

Choice Hotels AS, Olv V's g 6 Pb.
1936 Vika, 0125 Oslo.
Tel: 22 40 13 00. Fax: 22 40 13 10.
First Hotels
Tel: 800 104 10 (in Norway)
Tel: 8 692 44 50 (international)
E-mail: first.res@firsthotels.se
Website: www.firsthotels.com
Norlandia
2060 Gardermoen.
Tel: 22 98 97 00
Radisson SAS International Hotels
PO Box 185, N-1324 Lysaker.
Tel: 67 12 02 20. Fax: 67 12 00 11.
Rica Hotel og Restaurantkjede AS,
Løkketangen 10, Bærum.
Tel: 67 80 72 00. Fax: 67 80 72 50.
Scandic Hotels AS
Sjølyst pl 5, PO Box 173 Skøyen,
0212 Oslo.
Tel: 23 15 50 00. Fax: 23 15 50 49.

Hotel Listings

Hotels are grouped by area, starting
with Oslo. Within each city or
region, they are listed alphabetically
in price order, with the most
expensive first.

Price Guide

$$$ More than NOK1,700
$$ NOK1,100–1,700
$ Less than NOK1,100
Price categories are based on
the average cost (including tax)
of a double room with breakfast.

OSLO

Grand
Karl Johansgate 31, N-0159
Tel: 22 42 93 90. Fax: 22 42 12 25
Luxurious hotel opposite the
Stortinget. Spacious rooms. **$$$**
Radisson SAS Scandinavia Hotel
Holbergsgate 30, N-0166
Tel: 22 11 30 00. Fax: 22 11 30 17
Luxurious, with fine restaurants and
a rooftop bar. Airport buses. **$$$**
Bristol
Kristian VII's Gate 7, N-0164
Tel: 22 82 60 00. Fax: 22 82 06 01
Patronised by the wealthy, with a
superb lobby and antiques. Situated
close to the main shopping
street. **$$**

Clarion Royal Christiania Hotel
Biskop Gunnerus' Gate 3, N-0106
Tel: 23 10 80 90. Fax: 23 10 80 80
Magnificent atrium, spacious rooms,
good service. Near station. **$$**
Continental
Stortingsgaten 24–26, N-0161
Tel: 22 82 40 40. Fax: 22 42 96 89
Established in 1909, this is where
Norwegian guests of state stay. **$$**
Holmenkollen Park Hotel Rica
Kongveien 26, N-0390
Tel: 22 92 20 00. Fax: 22 14 61 92
In a leafy district, this grand old
wooden building overlooks a famous
ski jump. Excellent facilities. **$$**
Radisson SAS Plaza Hotel
Sonja Henies pl 3, N-0134
Tel: 22 93 87 95. Fax: 22 17 73 00
This is the tall glass structure
between Oslo S and Oslo Spektrum.
Popular among rock stars. **$$**
Golden Tulip Rainbow Hotel Stefan
Rosenkrantz Gate 1, N-0159
Tel: 22 42 92 50. Fax: 22 33 70 22
One of a chain. Couldn't be more
central; buffet lunches are great. **$**
Norrøna Hotell
Grensen 19, N-0159
Tel : 22 42 64 00. Fax: 22 33 25 65
Completely renovated three-star but
century-old atmosphere. Central. **$**
Norum
Bygdøy Allé 53, N-0265
Tel: 22 44 79 90. Fax: 22 44 92 39
Beautiful old building just west of
the centre; quiet, with cosy bistro. **$**

AROUND OSLO

Clarion Oslo Airport Hotel
N-2060 Gardermoen
Tel: 63 94 94 94
The first of many chain hotels near
Oslo Gardermoen Airport. **$$**
Quality Airport Hotel
N-2050 Jessheim
Tel: 63 97 30 11
Well situated for the airport. **$$**
Gardermoen Gjestegård
2060 Gardermoen
Tel: 63 97 85 30
Small family-run hotel. Restaurant. **$**
Rica Hotel Oslofjord
Sandviksvn 184, 1330 Sandvika
Tel: 67 54 57 00. Fax: 67 54 27 33
Set in a handsome fjord town
15 km (9 miles) from Oslo, with

Fjord Pass

This pass gives 20 percent
discount at 236 hotels,
guesthouses, apartments and
holiday cottages, plus several
hotel chains. It is available from
travel agents or tourist offices,
as well as hotels and Mix kiosks.

great views over the fjord and
islands. **$**
Scandic Hotel Høvik/Oslo
Drammensvn 507, N-1322 Høvik
Tel: 67 12 17 40. Fax: 67 53 52 83
Attractive hotel with good dining and
bar; 6 km (4 miles) from Oslo. **$**

BERGEN

Clarion Admiral
C. Sundtsgate 9–13
Tel: 55 23 64 00
Part of the Choice chain and one of
Bergen's finest. The restaurant has
superb views and cuisine. **$$**
Radisson SAS Hotel Norge
Ole Bulls Plass
Tel: 55 57 30 00
One of Bergen's best-loved hotels
and meeting places, in the centre,
with 350 quality rooms/suites, four
restaurants, garden and pool. **$$**
Radisson SAS Royal Hotel
Bryggen
Tel: 55 54 30 00. Fax: 55 32 48 08
The classic Norwegian building style
makes this an unusually handsome
hotel. With high-grade facilities. **$$**
Rainbow Hotel Rosenkrantz
Rosenkrantz 7
Tel: 55 31 50 00. Fax: 55 31 14 76
Comfortable and central with
restaurant and nightclub. **$$**
Victoria Hotel
Kong Oscarsgate 29
Tel: 55 31 50 30. Fax: 55 32 81 78
Once a staging-post inn. Central and
full of character with bar. **$$**
Fagerheim Pension
Kalvedalsveien 49A
Tel: 55 31 01 72
A friendly, central *pension*. **$**
Hotel Park Pension
Harald Hårfagresgt 35
Tel: 55 32 09 60. Fax: 55 54 44 44
Rooms with or without facilities. **$**

Strand Hotel
Strandkaien 2B
Tel: 55 31 08 15. Fax: 55 31 00 17
Family-run with restaurant and bar. **$**

STAVANGER

Radisson SAS Royal Hotel
Løkkeveien 26
Tel: 51 56 70 00
SAS's usual excellent services. **$$**
Scandic Hotel
Eiganesvn 181, PO Box 570 Madla,
N-4040 Hafrsfjord
Tel: 23 15 50 00. Fax: 23 15 50 01
One of the quality Scandic hotels,
ideal for conferences. Includes
"environmental" rooms made from
97 percent recyclable material. **$$**
City Gjestehuset
Lagårdsvn 47, N-4010
Tel: 51 52 04 37
Guesthouse with basic facilities. **$**
Commandør Hotell
Valberggt 9, N-4006
Tel: 51 89 53 00. Fax: 51 89 53 01
Cosy with home comforts. **$**
Havly Hotel
Valberggt 1, N-4006
Tel: 51 89 67 00. Fax: 51 89 50 25
Modest well-appointed rooms. **$**
The Little House
Vaisenhusgt 40, N-4012 Stavanger
Tel: 51 89 40 89
Home-from-home rooms (each with
bath). Central. **$**

TROMSØ

Rica Ishavshotel Tromsø
Fr. Langesgt 2
Tel: 77 66 64 00. Fax: 77 66 64 44
First rate, specialising in
conferences and comfort. **$$$**
Grand Nordic
Storgt 44
Tel: 77 68 55 00. Fax: 77 68 25 00

Price Guide

$$$	More than NOK1,700
$$	NOK1,100–1,700
$	Less than NOK1,100

Price categories are based on
the average cost (including tax)
of a double room with breakfast.

4 km (2.5 miles) from airport with conference facilities. **$$**
Saga Tromsø
Richard Withs Plass 2
Tel: 77 68 11 80. Fax: 77 68 23 80
Small conference hotel. **$$**
Scandic Tromsø
Heiloveien 23
Tel: 77 67 34 00. Fax: 77 67 67 40
Modest conference hotel in Tromsø suburb close to the airport. Well-appointed rooms. Outside pool. **$$**
With Home Hotel
Sjøgata 35–37, N-9000
Tel: 77 68 70 00. Fax: 77 68 96 16
First-class hotel with beautiful view to the Tromsø Bridge and cathedral. Feels like a maritime museum. **$$**
Tulip Inn Rainbow Tromsø Hotell
Grønneg 50
Tel: 77 75 17 20. Fax: 77 75 17 30
Small, informal and central. **$**

TRONDHEIM

Grand Olav Hotel
Olavskvartalet
Tel: 73 53 53 10. Fax: 73 53 57 20
Top-class in the heart of town. **$$**
Radisson SAS Royal Garden Hotel
Kjøpmannsgt 73
Tel: 73 52 11 00
Well-appointed rooms plus pool, gym, sauna and restaurants. **$$**
Ambassadeur
Elvegate 18
Tel: 73 52 70 50
One of Trondheim's best-value hotels with roof terrace. **$**
Elgeseter Bed & Breakfast
Tormodsgate 3
Tel: 73 94 25 40. Fax: 73 93 18 73
Ten minutes' walk from centre. **$**
Prinsen
Kongensgate 30
Tel: 73 53 06 50
A wealth of facilities including a fine restaurant, bistro, bar, grill room, wine tavern and beer garden. **$**

Chalets

There are abundant holiday *hytter* (cabins or chalets) available for rent. These usually house four to six people. For details contact:

Den Norske Hytteformidling,
Kierschowsgate 7, PO Box 3404
Bjølsen, N-0406 Oslo.
Tel: 22 35 67 10. Fax: 22 71 94 13

Fishermen's Cabins

In the Lofoten islands in the north, you can rent a traditional former fisherman's cabin (*rorbu*). Contact:
Destinasjon Lofoten, PO Box 210, N-8301 Svolvær.
Tel: 76 07 30 00. Fax: 76 07 30 01.

Camping

Norway has more than 1,000 camp sites, classified by one to five stars, depending on the standard and facilities available.

The Norwegian camping card (*Norsk Campingkort*) offers a faster checking-in service along with special discount. It is available from participating camp sites.

Many camp sites have cabins that may be booked in advance. Some are small and basic, but others are large and well equipped with a sitting room, one or two bedrooms, kitchen, shower and toilet.

For more information, write to:
Norwegian Camping Guide,
Essendropsgt. 6, N-0305 Oslo.

B&Bs

Bed and breakfast are catching on, and they are all of a high standard. You can book at local tourist offices or at Oslo's central railway station. Or look out for signs for *Rom* or *Husrom*. A B&B guidebook, *Rom i Norge*, is available from bookshops in Norway or from:
Norsc Holidays
Mail order, tel: 22 27 85 09.

Youth/Family Hostels

There are around 100 youth hostels of a relatively high standard, divided into three categories. You must book in advance in high season. For details, contact:
Hostelling International Norway,
Dronningens Gate 26, N-0154 Oslo.
Tel: 23 13 93 00. Fax: 23 13 93 50.
E-mail: hostels@sn.no

Where to Eat

What to Eat

Norwegians eat hearty breakfasts, but light lunches; the size of the evening meal depends on the day of the week and the occasion. With the abundant supply of seafood and what can be gleaned from forest and field, the Norwegian diet is in the main healthy and appetising.

The hunting season (early autumn) offers some irresistible temptations: pheasant, grouse, fresh elk and reindeer steaks served with peppercorns and rich wild mushroom sauces. It is also a good time of year for seafood.

Coffee breaks with pastries are popular. *Frokost* (breakfast) is more or less a variation of the lunch *Koldtbord*, a spread including breads (try *grovbrød*) and *flatbrød* (crisp cracker), sausages, cheeses (try the piquant *Gudbrandsost*, a delicious burnt goats' milk cheese with a dark golden colour), eggs, herrings, cereal, *gravlaks* (marinated salmon), cereals, and coffee and tea. The lunch version has hot dishes, such as sliced roast meats, meatballs or fish. *Øllebrød* (beef marinated in beer and served inside pitta bread with salad) makes a hearty, inexpensive lunch; an open-faced shrimp or ham sandwich is another staple.

Dinner in a city restaurant can be anything you wish. In more remote places, menus are limited by availability. *Smørbrød* is a snack (called *aftens* when eaten late at night), usually of brown bread with butter, cheese and salami or ham.

Where to Eat

There has been a significant increase in the variety of what's on offer if you eat out. Pizza has become very popular, as has Asian and oriental food.

Continental European cuisine has always played a role in Norwegian food, but pride in the native cuisine is growing.

At lunch time many restaurants offer fixed-price menus. More casual meals can be had at *stovas, kaffistovas, kros, bistros, kafés, kafeterias* and *gjæstgiveris* that may sell beer and wine as well as coffee and soft drinks.

Drinking Notes

No one talks about a trip to Norway without complaining of the high cost of alcohol. For those who can afford the prices, in Oslo you can drink spirits until midnight and wine or beer until 3am. Outside Oslo it's less predictable; the Christian Democratic Party (Kr.F) is anti-alcohol and holds sway in many west-coast areas, so they are virtually dry.

Vinmonopolet (state off-licences/liquor stores) in cities are open weekdays 9am–5pm and Saturday 9am–2pm; but closed on election days, holidays and the preceding day.

Most Norwegians drink beer. *Akevitt*, derived from potato and caraway seeds, is also a favourite; it can be sipped neat in small glasses preferably at room temperature, or cold with beer as an accompaniment to salty, spicy or pungent dishes.

Restaurants Listings

Restaurants are grouped by area starting with Oslo. They are listed alphabetically in price order, with the most expensive first.

OSLO

International
Fuji
Munkedamsveien 100, Skillebekk
Tel: 22 43 11 80
If you like Japanese sushi, this is the place for you. **$$$**

Price Guide

Price categories are based on an average cost per head of a three-course meal (excluding drinks but with tax):

$$$ More than NOK270
$$ NOK120–27
$ Less than NOK120

Dinner
Stortingsg 22. Tel: 22 42 68 90
No punches-spared Szechuan. **$$**
Quatro Amigos
Stortingsgate 16. Tel: 22 42 48 30
Hot Mexican food. Friendly. **$$**
Spaghetteria Santinos
Tordenskioldsg 8–10
Tel: 22 41 16 22
Popular downtown restaurant with tasty Italian pizza and pasta. **$$**
Zorbas
Torgg 32. Tel: 22 29 78 56
Great Greek food. **$$**
Mother India
Pilestredet 63B. Tel: 22 60 81 04
Indian atmosphere. Great food. **$**

Norwegian
Annen Etage
Hotel Continental
Grand style, setting and food. **$$$**
Bagatelle
Bygdøy Allé 3. Tel: 22 44 63 97
The best restaurant in Scandinavia with two Michelin stars. **$$$**
Blom
Karl Johansgate 37–41
Tel: 22 42 73 00
The place to impress someone. Big range of Norwegian dishes. **$$$**
Feinschmekker
Balchensgate 5. Tel: 22 44 17 77
Expensive but good value. **$$$**
Gamle Raadhus
Nedre Slottsgate 1
Tel: 22 42 01 07
Old-style restaurant serving hearty Norwegian specialities. **$$**
Grand Café
Karl Johansgate 31
Tel: 22 42 93 90
A virtual shrine to Ibsen, who spent many hours here. Wide choice from pastry and coffee to elk stew. **$$**
Kastanjen
Bygdøy Alle 18. Tel: 22 43 44 67
Bistro. Norwegian-style food. **$$**

Stortorvets Gjæstgiveri
Grensen 1. Tel: 22 42 88 63
Authentic Christiania inn with warm atmosphere. Live jazz. **$$**
Theatercafeen (Hotel Continental)
Stortingsgate 24. Tel: 22 82 40 50
Famous Viennese-style café. **$$**
Peppe's Pizza
Specialises in pan-fried pizzas. Cheaper on Monday. **$**
Vegeta Vertshus
Munkedamsveien 3B
Tel: 22 83 40 20
Vegetarian heaven; this place even got a *New York Times* write-up. **$**

BERGEN

Emily
Hotel Clarion Admiral
C Sundtsgt 9–13. Tel: 55 23 64 00
Stylish. Good Continental fare. **$$$**
Fiskekrogen
Fish Market. Tel: 55 55 96 60
The very best of Norwegian cuisine. Superb fish and shellfish. Friendly, knowledgeable waiters. **$$$**
Bryggen Tracteursted
Bryggen 6. Tel: 55 31 40 46
Your selection from the fish market will be prepared to your tastes; in the old Hanseatic district. **$$**
Fløien Folkerestaurant
Top of Fløien funicular
Tel: 55 32 18 75
Good, reasonably priced food with intoxicating view. Work up an appetite by walking there! **$$**
Holbergstuen
Torvalmenning 6. Tel: 55 31 80 15
Fresh fish from the market to your specifications; lively. **$$**
Wesselstuen
Engen 14. Tel: 55 90 08 20
Fish and stews are served here to a loyal local crowd. **$$**

TRONDHEIM

Bryggen
Øvre Bakklandet 66
Tel: 73 53 40 55
One of the best and most elegant restaurants in Trondheim right by the River Nidelva. Serves an international menu using finest ingredients. **$$$**

Big Horn Steakhouse
Munkegt. 14, Ravnkloa
Tel: 73 50 94 90
Specialises in tasty spare ribs and
juicy steaks. **$$**

Grenaderen
Kongsgårdsgt. 1e. Tel: 73 51 66 80
In a 16th-century forge with a large
terrace. Offers a traditional
Norwegian menu including fish and
reindeer. **$$**

Havfruen
Kjøpmannsgt. 7. Tel: 73 53 26 26
Finest Norwegian fish and seafood,
plus some meat. Trendy bar. **$$**

Hos Magnus
Kjøpmannsgt. 63. Tel: 73 52 41 10
Specialises in fish and seafood
dishes in the local tradition.
Excellent service in a relaxing
atmosphere. **$$**

Vertshuset Tavern
Sverresborg. Tel: 73 52 09 32
Home-made food, including
Norwegian sour cream porridge,
fish cakes and smoked ham.
Popular tavern. **$$**

Zia Teresa Pizzeria Trattoria
Vår Frue Strete. Tel: 73 52 64 22
Pizza Norwegian-style. **$$**

TROMSØ

Compagniet
Sjøgata 12. Tel: 77 65 57 21
A good reputation; serves gourmet
fare. **$$$**

Peppermøllen Mat-og Vinhus
Storgata 42. Tel: 77 68 62 60
Menu features about 160 dishes,
using Norwegian ingredients. Fish is
a speciality. **$$**

Skarvens Biffhus
Strandtorget 1. Tel: 77 61 01 01
Popular restaurant serving several
varieties of steak. **$$**

STAVANGER

Cartellet
Øvre Holmegate 8
Tel: 51 89 60 22
Fascinating architecture merits a
visit in itself. Serves international
food. **$$$**

Storyteller
Tårngalleriet. Tel: 51 89 44 11
Extensive à la carte menu,
including tasty American and Cajun
dishes. **$$**

Sørensens Dampskibsekspedisjon
Skagen 26. Tel: 51 89 12 70
Popular and friendly restaurant
serving Norwegian cuisine. **$$**

Culture

Music and Opera

Whether the performers are
Norwegian or foreign, the season
winter or summer, Norway has a
rich and varied musical and
operatic life.

In summer the arts take to the
outdoors in Norway, and classical
music and opera are no exception.
For Oslo dates, pick up the *What's
on in Oslo* guide.

At Holmenkollen in summer,
orchestral and operatic
performances are given from a
floating stage on the lake.

Each September, an opera
performance is held in Oslo at
Youngstorvet (Young's Market
Square), outside the Opera House
in the open air.

Akershus Fortress and the Henie
Onstad Art Centre (in Høvikodden)
are two other fine settings for
summer concerts.

Theatre and Dance

Theatre is booming in Norway, with
small, contemporary theatres
springing up everywhere; but
performances are in Norwegian.
The exception is September's
Gjøglerne kommer festival of
performing arts in Porsgrunn,
Telemark (two and a half hours by
car from Oslo) when international
dramatists take to the stage.

Dance is now a significant part
of the festival. Contact Grenland
Friteater, tel: 35 55 51 69, for
further information.

Classical ballet is performed at
the Oslo Opera House. Traditional
folk dances can be seen in many
towns on National Day (17 May), or
at Oslo's Konserthus every Monday
and Thursday at 9pm in July and

August, when the Bondeungdomslaget folk dance group performs.

Cinema

The Norwegians love films. Oslo has around 40 screens including the latest Panasonic IMAX Theatre at Aker Brygge.

First-run and repertory films are always shown in the original language, with Norwegian subtitles. Kiosks, newspapers, and local city guides have listings.

Booking by phone is possible and is recommended for Sundays, traditional movie night.

Nightlife

Oslo, once considered a big yawn at night, is now vying with Stockholm and Copenhagen to be Scandinavia's nightlife capital. Check locally for up-to-date venue listings, or the official Oslo Guide provided by Oslo Promotion on the website: www.oslopro.no. All the major cities have both official and unofficial nightlife guides.

In Bergen, Stavanger, Trondheim and Tromsø nightlife exists to a much lesser extent. But you can guarantee that most large hotels have nightclubs and bars. International rock, folk, and jazz groups often include Oslo on European tours.

There are only two things you need to be warned about before a night out: the high cost of drink, and age restrictions (some clubs have minimum ages as high as 26, although 21 and 23 are more common).

Bergen Festival

Bergen's International Festival in late May offers music, drama, ballet, opera, jazz and folk arts.

For further details contact the tourist office or:
Tel: 55 21 06 30
Fax: 55 21 06 40.
Website: wwwfib.no

Sport

If Norwegians can contrive a sport as an excuse to be outdoors, they'll do it. That's why there are such great facilities here. For a full listing of the range of sports and sports facilities in the Oslo region, see the Outdoor Activities pages of the *Oslo Guide*, from tourist offices.

Canoeing

Some of the best canoeing and kayaking lakes and rivers are in the Femund area, Østfold, Aust and Vest Agder, Telemark and suburban Oslo. Contact the local tourist office for details.

Cycling

For details *see Getting Around, page 376*.

Fishing

The fishing is excellent in Norway, whether you're at sea or on a fjord, lake or river. You need a local fishing permit to fish sea char, salmon or sea trout and a national fishing licence for inland fishing in Norway. You can buy a fishing permit at or near to your holiday spot. See the tourist board's *Angling in Norway* for full details.

Golf

Norwegian golf courses are by and large difficult and challenging. Most require either a Green Card or a handicap under 20. Green fees are in line with most European golf courses. Some nine-hole courses offer day fees.

In the Oslo region professional competitions are held at Bogstad, Larvik, Borre and Vestfold golf

clubs, but by far the most beautifully situated is the Tyrifjord golf links. For information, contact:
The Norwegian Golf Federation
Hauger Skolevei 1, 1351 Rud.
Tel: 67 15 46 00. Fax: 67 13 86 40.

Hiking

The country's extensive mountain ranges and high plains make ideal walking terrain. The most popular areas include the Jotunheim, Rondane and Dovrefjell mountains; the Hardangervidda plateau in the Trollheimen district; and the Finnmarksvidda plain. Mountain cabins are open from the end of June until mid-September, plus Easter.

The Norwegian Mountain Touring Association (DNT) runs about 300 guided hikes in summer, and glacier walks in winter. Membership includes hut access. For details:
Den Norske Turistforening
Storgate 3, PO Box 7 Sentrum, 0101 Oslo.
Tel: 22 82 28 00. Fax: 22 82 28 01.

Horse Riding

There are riding centres and hotels all over Norway where you can hire a horse for organised trekking or take lessons. For further details contact tourist offices, or:
Norges Rytterforbund
Serviceboks 1 Ullevål Stadion.
Tel: 21 02 96 50. Fax: 21 02 96 51.

Skiing

Along with hiking, this is the primary participant sport in Norway. Even in summer Norwegians take to the slopes (as a rule from June to September), and the sight of people swooping down the slopes in bikinis and trunks is something to behold.

The main ski resorts are at Lillehammer, Trysil, Geilo, Hemsedal, Norefjell (the nearest to Oslo) and Voss, but there are many more; all tourist offices can advise on local ski facilities for cross country and slalom. Also check the Norwegian ski guide on the website: www.skiinfo.no

Glacier Hiking

Glacier hiking is an exhilarating and exciting experience – which should be attempted only with an experienced local guide. Several Norwegian tour companies offer guided glacier walks (*breer*), particularly in the following areas:

Fjord Norway: Hardangerjøkulen, Folgefonna, Buarbre, Bondhusbre, Smørstabbre, Fannaråkbre and Nigardsbre.
Oppland: Styggebre.
Norland Reiseliv: Svartisen and Engenbreen.

For details, contact **Glacier Information Centres** in western Norway at Oppstryn (tel: 57 87 72 00), Fjærland (tel: 57 69 32 88) and Josterdalen (tel: 57 68 32 50).

Sailing

Foreign visitors are always welcome in boating circles, and there are sailing and boating clubs and associations throughout Norway. Without your own boat, sailing of any sort can be expensive, and the closest you may get is a small catamaran or even a windsurfer. In Oslo you can hire equipment from:
Seasport Oslo AS
Dronning Mauds g 1/3.
Tel: 22 83 79 28.
Fax: 22 83 92 95.
White Water AS, Cort Adelers g 27.
Tel: 22 55 11 07.
Fax: 22 55 11 48.
Norges Seilforbund
Serviceboks 1, Ullevål Stadion.
Tel: 21 02 90 00.
Fax: 21 02 90 17.

Swimming

Temperatures along the coast and inland reach 20°C (68°F) in summer, and even in the north it can be warm enough to swim. Nude beaches are to be found in Oslo, Moss, Halden, Tønsberg, Larvik, Molde, Ålesund, Bergen, Trondheim and Salten. Most larger hotels have pools and there are numerous leisure centres throughout Norway.

Water Sports

There are several possibilities for waterskiing and windsurfing along the coast, as well as on Norway's numerous lakes.

White-water rafting is available on the following rivers: Sjoaelva in Oppland, Trysilelva in Hedmark and Driva in Sør-Trøndelag.

The Norwegian coast offers very good conditions for diving. There are several diving centres along the west coast, particularly in the counties of Møre and Romsdal.
Norwegian Diving Federation
Sognsveien 75L, Serviceboks 1
Ullevål Stadion, N-0480 Oslo.
Norwegian Wildlife & Rafting AS
Randsverk, 2680 Vågå.
Tel: 61 23 87 27.
Fax: 61 23 87 60.

Winter Sports

Skiing is just one of Norway's winter attractions. There are snowmobile trips to the North Cape, reindeer safaris and dog-sled races over the plane of Finnmarksvidda. You can go on horse-drawn sleigh rides, or try your hand at ice fishing, snow boarding or ice skating. Several companies offer winter train journeys along the spectacular coast. *For details, see Tour operators on page 370.* or contact the Norwegian tourist board.

Spectator Sports

Skiing is the primary spectator sport with annual competitions, such as the Holmenkolen Ski Festival. In summer large crowds come to see athletics during the Bislet Games. There are several horse trotting and race tracks in Norway. Other popular spectator sports include marathon running, football, ice hockey and boat races. Check Oslo or local area guide or tourist office for details.

Shopping

What to Buy

Popular souvenirs from Norway include knitted jumpers, cardigans, gloves and mittens, pewter, silver jewellery and cutlery, hand-painted wooden objects (like bowls with rose designs), trolls and fjord horses carved out of wood, goat and reindeer skin, enamel jewellery, woven wall-designs, furs, handicrafts, glassware and pottery – to name just a few (*see Tax-free Shopping for how to reclaim VAT*).

The major department stores are Christiania Glasmagasin and Steen & Strøm, both of which have a good selection of most of these items.

Anyone interested in buying Norwegian art will have ample prospects – from south to north, Norway abounds in galleries. Get a local recommendation.

Tax-free Shopping

The Norwegian Tax-free Shopping scheme covers around 3,000 stores. For purchases over NOK 308, the store issues you with a tax-free slip for the amount of VAT paid. When you leave Norway, a refund of 11–18 percent (depending on the sale price) will be refunded (in your local currency) on presentation of the goods, the tax-free slip and your passport, on condition that the item has not been used while in Norway.

Norway Tax-free Shopping has its own representatives at airports, on board all international ferries and at the main border crossings. Check opening times, however, as they are not open 24 hours. Leaflets are at participating stores.

Enquiries to Norway Tax-free Shopping AS. Tel: 67 14 99 01.

Language

There are two variations of the Norwegian language: *bokmål* and *nynorsk*. Both belong to the western group of the Scandinavian branch of the Germanic languages, one of the subfamilies of the Indo-European languages.

The Sami population (Lapps) in north Norway speak Lappish. English is widely understood in the towns.

The following is a list of useful words and phrases.

General

yes ja
no nei
good morning god morgen
good afternoon god ettermiddag
good evening god kveld
today I dag
tomorrow I morgen
yesterday I går
hello hei
How do you do? God dag/Morn
goodbye adjø/ha det (bra)
thank you takk
How much is this? Hvor mye koster det?
It costs... Det koster...
What time is it? Hvor mye er klokken?
It is (The time is...) Den er... (Klokken er...)
Could I have your name please? Hva er navnet?
My name is... Mitt navn er...
Do you speak English? Snakker du engelsk?
I only speak English Jeg snakker bare engelsk
May I help you? Kan jeg hjelpe deg?
I do not understand Jeg forstår ikke
I do not know Jeg vet ikke
It has Den har
to rent leie
free ledig
room to rent rom til leie
chalet hytte
Could I have the key please? Kan jeg få nøkkelen?

Directions

How do I get to...? Hvordan kommer jeg til...?
Where is...? Hvor er...?
right høyre
to the right til høyre
left venstre
to the left til venstre
straight on rett frem

Emergencies

hospital sykehus
doctor lege
police station politistasjon

Signs

Parking Parkering
Toilet Toalett/WC
Gentlemen Herrer
Ladies Damer
Vacant Ledig
Engaged Opptatt
Entrance Inngang
Exit Utgang
No entry Ingen adgang
Open Åpent
Closed Stengt
Push Skyv
Pull Trekk
No smoking Røyking forbudt

Eating Out

breakfast frokost
lunch lunsj
dinner middag
eat spise
drink drikke
Cheers! Skål!
Can I order please? Kan jeg få bestille?
Could I have the bill please? Kan jeg få regningen?

Getting Around

aeroplane fly
bus/coach buss
car bil
train tog

Numbers

1	en
2	to
3	tre
4	fire
5	fem
6	seks
7	syv or sju
8	åtte
9	ni
10	ti
11	elleve
12	tolv
13	tretten
14	fjorten
15	femten
16	seksten
17	sytten
18	atten
19	nitten
20	tjue
21	tjue-en
22	tjue-to
30	tretti
40	førti
50	femti
60	seksti
70	sytti
80	åtti
90	nitti
100	hündre
200	to hundre
1,000	tusen

Shopping

money penger
department store hus/atormagasin
chemist apotek
grocery store (in countryside) landhandel
shop butikk
food mat/kost
to buy kjøpe
sauna badstue
off-licence/liquor store vinmonopol

Buying a Ticket

adult voksen
child barn
single énveisbillett
return tur-retur-billett

Further Reading

Tourist Publications

Some useful publications from the Norwegian Tourist Board include: **Accommodation in Norway, Norwegian Camping Guide** and **Tourist Timetables in Norway**. These booklets are issued free by the Tourist Board or the nearest Norwegian embassy or consulate.

Guides

Adventure Roads in Norway: Where is the Best Scenery? A selection of fascinating routes chosen by some of Norway's foremost travel experts. The routes and places of interest are marked on maps and the book is illustrated with beautiful colour photographs.
2,500 miles on the Coastal Steamer A description of the popular coastal voyage from Bergen to Kirkenes in Arctic Norway and back. Illustrated by attractive colour photos and explanatory maps.
Mountain Hiking in Norway Describes Norway's mountain regions and suggests itineraries. It also has details about chalets and other accommodation in the mountains.
Angling in Norway A 160-page illustrated guide covering salmon, sea trout and freshwater fishing, as well as information on fishing regulations and conservation.
Cruising in Norwegian Waters With soft cover and colour illustrations, this 120-page book gives accounts of harbours along Norway's coastline and fjords.

Orders for any of these books should be sent to: The Scandinavian Collection, 26 Woodford Square, London W14 8DP. Tel: 020 7602 0657; or Nortrabooks, PO Box 2893 Solli, N-0230 Oslo, Norway.
E-mail: nortra@online.no

Rutebok for Norge is a complete list of ferry, train, bus and plane timetables for Norway, together with details of hotels, guesthouses and other accommodation.
Order from: Norsk Reiseinformasjon AS, Tollbugt 32, 0157 Osloy.
Tel: 22 47 73 40. Fax: 22 47 73 69.
Living in Norway by Michael Brady (Palamedes Press). The A to Z source book for anyone living and working in the country, with 850 topics in 49 chapters.

History

Norway: A History from the Vikings to our own Times by Rolf Danielsen (Scandinavian University Press, Oslo). An account of the social and economical development of Norway.

Fiction

Norwegian Folk Tales by Peter Christen Asbjørnsen and Jørgen Moe (Grøndahl og Dreyers Forlag; Oslo). The ultimate collection of Norwegian folk tales, superbly illustrated.
A Taste of Norway by Arne Brimi (Norwegian University Press; Oslo). A collection of traditional Norwegian recipes by one of Norway's most renowned chefs.

Other Insight Guides

Over 200 titles in the acclaimed **Insight Guides** series cover every continent. Titles in the region include *Norway*, *Denmark*, *Sweden*, and *Finland*. Insight **Pocket Guides**, with an itinerary-based approach, include *Oslo & Bergen*. Insight **Compact Guides** to the region include *Norway*, *Denmark*, *Copenhagen* and *Finland*. Insight **Fleximaps** combine clear, detailed cartography with essential travel information. The laminated finish makes the maps durable, weatherproof and easy to fold. Scandinavian titles include *Norway*, *Copenhagen* and *Stockholm*.

SWEDEN

The Place

Area 449,790 sq km (173,620 sq miles).
Capital Stockholm.
Population 8.8 million, of whom 1.6 million people live in the Stockholm area, 778,000 in Göteborg and 510,000 in Malmö.
Languages Swedish, Finnish and Sami.
Religion 94 percent of Swedes are Evangelical Lutheran.
Time zone Central European Time Zone. One hour ahead of Greenwich Mean Time (GMT), six hours ahead of Eastern Standard Time. Clocks go forward one hour from the end of March to the end of October.
Currency Swedish krona (plural kronor, marked "kr" or "Skr" in shops, or SEK internationally, and split into 100 öre.
Weights and measures Metric.
Electricity 220 volts AC, two-pin round plugs.
International dialling code: +46, then 8 for Stockholm, 31 for Göteborg and 40 for Malmö.

Climate

In summer Sweden's weather is similar to that in Britain – and just as unpredictable – although in a good year some remarkably high temperatures can be recorded in the Arctic regions. The area round Piteå on the Gulf of Bothnia is known as the Northern Riviera because of its warmth. But in the north, autumn and winter arrive early and spring comes in late May.
Winter can be cold; even in Stockholm, maximum temperatures in the day are likely to remain below freezing in January and February.

Government

Sweden is a constitutional monarchy, with a parliamentary government and a one-chamber legislature. The prime minister is appointed by a majority of the Swedish Parliament and heads a cabinet with about 12 ministries.

The country is divided into 24 provinces, headed by a governor appointed by the cabinet. Regionally elected provincial councils are responsible for medical care and local planning, and the lowest tier of local government is exercised by the 284 municipalities, whose remit includes planning, welfare and local education.

Sweden joined the European Union in January 1995.

Economy

Sweden's rich natural resources of ore deposits, forests and hydro-electric power have made it a highly industrialised country. Companies like Volvo, Saab and Electrolux are household names worldwide.

The old mining region of Bergslagen is still the home of the iron and steel industry, and electronics is thriving in Stockholm and Västerås.

Farming is still important, above all in southern Skåne, but only some five percent of Sweden's workforce is involved in agriculture and less than 10 percent of the country is farmland.

Forestry and the pulp and paper industries are important, particularly along the Gulf of Bothnia and Lake Vänern. Telecommunications and Internet-related business is booming.

Planning the Trip

Visas and Passports

A valid passport entitles you to stay up to three months, and visas are not normally required. If you arrive from another Scandinavian country, passports aren't usually checked. If you intend to stay longer than three months you will need to obtain a resident's permit, which you can do once you are in Sweden.

Customs

Swedish Customs formalities are usually painless.

Duty free

Visitors from EU countries aged 18 or over can import duty free 300 cigarettes/150 cigarillos/75 cigars or 400 g tobacco. Visitors aged over 20 can import 1 litre of spirits or 3 litres of dessert wine, 5 litres of wine plus 15 litres of beer.

Visitors from non-EU countries aged 18 or over can import duty free 200 cigarettes/100 cigarillos/ 50 cigars or 250 g tobacco. Visitors aged over 20 can import 1 litre of spirits or 2 litres of dessert wine, 2 litres of wine plus 15 litres of beer.

Gifts

For visitors from non-EU countries presents up to a value of 1,700 Skr may be taken into the country, but the value of any food you are bringing is included in this limit.

Health

Standards of hygiene in Sweden are among the highest in the world. No inoculations are needed, and tap water is safe to drink.

Tour Operators

Arctic Experience
29 Nork Way, Banstead, Surrey SM7 1PB.
Tel: 01737 218800.
Website: www.arctic-discover.co.uk
Baltic Travel Service
Little Acres, The Causeway, Hitcham, Suffolk IP7 7NE
Tel: 01449 743121.
Fax: 01449 743122.
Bridge Travel Service
55-59 High Road, Broxbourne, Herts EN10 7DT.
Tel: 01992 456300.
Crystal Holidays
Crystal House, Arlington Road, Surbiton, Surrey KT6 6BW.
Tel: 01235 824324.
DFDS Seaways
Scandinavia House, Parkeston, Harwich, Essex CO12 4QG
Tel: 0990-333666.
Explore Worldwide
1 Frederick Street, Aldershot GU11 1LQ.
Tel: 01252 319448.
Norvista
227 Regent Street, London W1R 8PD
Tel: 020 7409 7334.
Fax: 020 7409 7733.
Scandinavian Travel Service
2 Bergem Mews, Blythe Road, London W14 0HN
Tel: 01443 822242
ScanMeridian
28b Hampstead High Street, London NW3 1QA.
Tel: 020 7431 5393.
Scantours
47 Whitcomb Street, London WC2H 7DH
Tel: 020–7839 2927
Fax: 020–7839 5891
Taber Holidays
30A Bingley Road, Saltaire, Shipley, West Yorkshire BD1 2SX.
Tel: 01274 594642.
Yes
Broadway, Peterborough, PE1 1RS.
Tel: 01733 340345.

However, in the far north of Sweden in high summer, strong precautions need to be taken

Tourist Info at Home

● **UK**
Swedish Travel & Tourism Council, 11 Montagu Place, London W1H 2AL.
Tel: 020 7870 5600.
Fax: 020 7724 5872.
E-mail: info@swetourism.org.uk
Website: www.visit-sweden.com

● **USA**
Swedish Travel & Tourism Council, PO Box 4649, Grand Central Station, New York, NY 10163-4649.
Tel: 212-885 9700.
Fax: 212-885 9710.
E-mail: info@gosweden.org

● There are no Swedish tourist offices in Canada, Australia and New Zealand, but the Swedish Consulate/Embassy supplies information and literature.

against mosquitoes. Consult your pharmacist at home, and on arrival at your destination it is also advisable to ask the local pharmacist to recommend the most effective product.

MEDICAL TREATMENT

Sweden has reciprocal agreements with the UK and other countries, under which visitors are entitled to the same medical treatment as Swedes. But it is very important for EU nationals to bring a form E111 (available in the UK at post offices) which allows visitors to pay the same fees as Swedes.

Visitors from outside the EU pay higher consultation fees, although these are modest compared with those charged in North America.

For hospital visits you have to pay the actual cost. Therefore, it is important to take out medical insurance before travelling (and to keep receipts for any treatment you have so you can reclaim the money on your return home).

Money Matters

There is no limit on the import of Swedish and foreign currency.

Traveller's cheques can be exchanged without difficulty at banks all over Sweden. A foreign exchange service is also provided by about 500 post offices with the "PK Exchange" sign. Forex and Wexex, *bureaux de change* with branches in most major towns, usually have better exchange rates than the banks and post offices and don't charge any commission.

All the leading credit cards are accepted by most hotels, restaurants and shops throughout the country, and you can also take out cash on these cards at foreign exchange offices and banks.

What to Bring

Sweden's weather is unpredictable, so plan for any eventuality. In summer, even in the Arctic north, you could have hot, sunny days that call for shorts and T-shirts, or sweaters and rainwear may be needed. Winters can be very cold, but this is dry cold. Still, you should take a heavy coat and warm headgear as well as sturdy footwear for the slushy streets.

Getting There

BY AIR

Scandinavian Airlines (SAS), Finnair, Braathens/Malmö Aviation, Ryanair and British Airways operate direct flights daily from the UK (Heathrow, Gatwick and Stansted) to Stockholm. SAS also flies direct to Stockholm from Manchester but not as frequently as from London.

SAS and British Airways fly daily to Göteborg (Gothenburg), and Braathens/Malmö Aviation runs from London City Airport direct to Malmö and Stockholm. Ryanair operates daily from Stansted to Skavsta Airport, which is about an hour's drive south of Stockholm. The travel time is around 2 hours and 30 minutes from the UK.

Ryanair offers the lowest prices

but other airlines often have special offers so do check with your travel agent before booking.

From the UK
SAS Tel: 0845 60727727.
Website: www.flysas.co.uk
Finnair Tel: 0990 997711.
Website: www.finnair.fi
British Airways Tel: 0345 222111.
Website: www.britishairways.com
Braathens/Malmö Aviation
Tel: 08705 074074.
Website: www.braathens.se
Ryanair Tel: 0541 569569.
Website: www.ryanair.co

From the US
SAS Tel: 1-800-221 2350.
Finnair Tel: 1-800-950 5000.
Icelandair Tel: 1-800-223 5500.
Website: www.icelandair.com.
American Airlines Tel: 1-800-433 7300.
Website: www.americanairlines.com

BY SEA

DFDS Seaways (tel: 0990 333111/0990 333666 in the UK) has a year-round service twice a week to Göteborg from Newcastle (about 25 hours). This is ideal for motoring holidays in Sweden as it cuts out the long drive across Europe.

You can also take the ferry from Harwich to Esbjerg in Denmark (three or four times a week) and then drive up to Grenå or Frederikshavn and catch another ferry from there to Sweden. Or you can drive through Denmark and cross the Öresund Bridge that connects Copenhagen and Malmö.

BY TRAIN

The fastest rail route from the UK to Sweden is via the Eurostar service through the Channel Tunnel from London Waterloo International or Ashford International in Kent to Brussels, with onward trains to Copenhagen and connecting services to Sweden.

For further information call:

Eurostar Tel: 0990 186186.
International Rail Centre
Tel: 0990 848848.

BY COACH

Eurolines is the leading operator of scheduled coach services to 16 destinations in Sweden. Coaches depart up to three times a week from London Victoria Coach Station. Eurolines offers competitive fares with reductions for children, young people and senior citizens.
For information call:
Eurolines Tel: 0990 143219 or 020 7730 8235.

BY CAR

With the new 16-km (10-mile) Öresund road and rail bridge connecting Copenhagen with Malmö, you can drive all the way to Sweden from Denmark. The drive from Copenhagen Airport to Malmö takes about 45 minutes.

Practical Tips

Media

NEWSPAPERS AND MAGAZINES

English-language newspapers are widely available at kiosks in larger cities, usually on the day of publication. Kulturhuset (the cultural centre) at Sergels Torg, Stockholm, has a good selection of English publications that can be read for free, as does the City Library in Göteborg on the main square, Götaplatsen.

TELEVISION

Sweden's state-run STV1, STV2 and Kanal 4 show foreign films (with subtitles) most evenings. The commercial STV3 and Kanal 5 run American chat shows, sport, movies and soap operas. Plus there are many satellite/cable channels, featuring CNN, BBC and MTV, broadcast in English with subtitles.

RADIO

Radio Sweden has programmes in English with news and information about Sweden on medium wave 1179KHz (254m), and also in the Stockholm area on FM 89.6MHz. A variety of BBC and NPR programmes is also available on Channel 89.6.

Postal Services

Post offices (*Posten*) generally open 9am–6pm on weekdays and 10am–1pm on Saturday (some may close on Saturday in July). The post office at Stockholm's Central Station is open Monday to Friday 7am–10pm and weekends 10am–7pm.

Stamps (*frimärken*) are also on sale at Pressbyrån newsstands, bookstalls and stationers' shops. You will find two different mailboxes, blue for local letters and yellow for all other destinations.

Telecommunications

Post offices do not have telephone facilities, but there are plenty of payphones, credit card phones (signposted CCC) and special telegraph offices (marked Telia or Telebutik). Most of the payphones operate only with a telephone card (*Telia telefonkort*) which are available in Pressbyrån, kiosks, bookstalls and stationers' shops.
You can send faxes from hotels, motels and youth hostels, or (in larger towns), from Telia shops.

Tourist Information

Two good starting points for national tourist information are:
The Swedish Travel & Tourism Council (Sveriges Rese-och Turistråd), Box 3030, Kungsgatan 36, SE-103 61 Stockholm.
Tel: 08 72 55 50 0.
Fax: 08 72 55 53 1.
E-mail: info@swetourism.se
Website: www.swetourism.se
The Swedish Tourist Federation (Svenska Turistföreningen).
Tel: 08 46 32 10 0.
Fax: 08 67 81 95 8.
Website: www.meravsverige.nu

LOCAL OFFICES

Sweden has a countrywide network of *Turistbyrå* (tourist information offices) that can be identified by the international "i" sign. They usually have a hotel booking service, *rumsförmedling* or *hotellcentral*, and supply information about local sightseeing and sporting activities. Some are open during the summer only. A complete list can be obtained from The Swedish Travel & Tourism Council (*see above*).
Stockholm
Sverigehuset (Sweden House),

Useful Numbers

- **Police, fire, ambulance**
  112 (calls are free)
- **Swedish directory enquiries**
  118 118
- **International directory enquiries** 118 119

Hamngatan 27, at the corner of Kungsträdgården
Tel: 08 78 92 49 0
Fax: 08 78 92 49 1
E-mail: info@stoinfo.se
Website: www.stockholmtown.com
This is the country's busiest tourist office. Run by the Stockholm Information Service (SIS), it has its own Excursion Shop (tel: 08 78 92 41 5, fax: 08 78 92 49 1) for booking sightseeing tours.

SIS also publishes a guide, *Runaway for a Day*, with details of excursions in the Stockholm area, and its brochure *Stockholm This Week* lists current cultural attractions.

Other tourist offices in Stockholm can be found at T-Centralen (the Central Station), in the Kaknästornet (Kaknäs TV Tower) and, during the summer, at Stadshuset (the City Hall) and the Värtahamnen (Värta ferry terminal).

Dalarna
Trotzvägen 10-12, SE-791 83 Falun
Tel: 023-640 04
Fax: 023-833 14
E-mail: dalarna.tourist@welcome.falun.se
Website: www.dalarna.se
Göteborg
Kungsportsplatsen 2, SE-411 10
Tel: 031 61 25 00
Fax: 031 61 25 01
E-mail: turistinfo@gbg-co.se
Website: www.gbg-co.se
Gotland
Hamngatan 4, Box 1403, SE-621 25 Visby
Tel: 0498 20 17 00
Fax: 0498 20 17 17
E-mail: info@gtf.i.se
Website: www.gotland.com
Norrbotten/Lapland
Kronan H3, SE-974 42 Luleå
Tel: 0920 43 45 10

Fax: 0920 43 45 19
E-mail: info@norrbottens-turistrad.se
Website: www.norrbottens-turiststad.se
Skåne
Skiffervägen 34, SE-224 78 Lund
Tel: 046 12 43 50
Fax: 046 12 23 72
E-mail: info@skanetur.se
Website: www.skaneturist.nu
Småland
Västra Torg 18A, Box 1027, SE-511 11 Jönköping
Tel: 036 19 95 70
Fax: 036 71 43 01
E-mail: smalands.turistrad@f.komforb.com
Website: www.smalandsturism.com

Travelling with Kids

The Swedes are good at devising excellent attractions for the whole family, like amusement parks such as **Liseberg** (www.liseberg.se) in Göteborg and **Gröna Lund Tivoli** (www.tivoli.se) in Stockholm.

Astrid Lindgren fantasies

The famous Swedish author Astrid Lindgren is a master at creating fantasy characters that appeal to children. Pippi Longstocking, Emil and Karlsson on the Roof are just some of the attractions at Junibacken.
Junibacken, Galärvarvsvägen
Tel: 08 58 72 30 00
Fax: 08 58 72 30 99
Website: www.junibacken.se

In Vimmerby in the province of Småland you can also visit Astrid Lindgren's World, another fairy-tale land with living characters from her books. Open May to August.
Astrid Lindgren's World
Tel: 0492 79 80 0
Fax: 0492 15 88 5
E-mail: info@alv.se
Website: www.alv.se

Sommarland Centres

There is an increasing number of Sommarland developments, the largest of which is at Skara (www.sommarland.se), northeast of Göteborg. It has 50 attractions, including a waterslide, a grand prix

race track, a mini-zoo, a railway and three boating lakes.
Tel: 0511 64 00 0.

Zoos

The best-known zoo/safari park is at Kolmården (www.kolmarden.com) near Norrköping. It has lions, giraffes and so on, as well as Sweden's only dolphinarium.
Tel: 011 24 90 00.

Santaworld

Not far from Mora is Santaworld, where children can explore Santa's house, workshop and animals and the Snow Queen's Palace, and place orders for Christmas.
Tel: 0250 21 20 0.

Business Travellers

The Swedes tend to be rather formal about business. There is little small talk and few lengthy business lunches. Formal business dress, punctuality and preparation are essential. If invited to a client's home for dinner, a gift like a bottle of malt whisky – very expensive in Sweden – is welcomed, and flowers or chocolates for your hostess.

Public Holidays

- **1 January** New Year's Day
- **6 January** Epiphany
- **March/April** Good Friday and Easter Monday
- **1 May** Labour Day
- **May** Ascension (usually second part of the month); Pentecost (10 days after Ascension)
- **June** Midsummer's Day (around the 24th)
- **November** All Saints' Day (usually at start of the month)
- **25 and 26 December** Christmas

Note: If the holiday is one day away from the weekend, offices tend to be closed the day between (known as *klämdag* or "squeeze day").

It is virtually impossible to transact business during July.

Business Hours

- **Shops** mainly 9.30am–6pm on weekdays and until between 1 and 4pm on Saturdays. In the larger cities a lot open on Sundays, usually noon–4pm. Shops generally close early the day before a public holiday.
- **Department stores** may remain open until 8pm or 9pm and possibly also on Sundays.
- **Post offices** generally open 9.30am–6pm on weekdays and 9.30am–1pm on Saturday.
- **Banks** Monday to Friday 9.30am–3pm (6pm in some cities). The bank at Stockholm Arlanda Airport's arrival hall is open daily 8am–10.30pm and at the departure hall Monday to Friday 6.30am–9pm, Saturday and Sunday 6.30am–8pm.

Travellers with Disabilities

In line with its enlightened social attitudes, Sweden has long been a pioneer in accommodating travellers with disabilities. Many hotel rooms and facilities are adapted for the needs both of people with mobility problems and those suffering from allergies. Toilets with the handicap symbol can be found almost everywhere. In Stockholm, most buses are designed for easy access for people with wheelchairs and pushchairs (one parent can travel for free on buses if the baby is in a pushchair). Mainline and underground trains have lifts or ramps.

The annual guide *Hotels in Sweden* (*see Choosing a Hotel, page 392*) lists facilities and chalet cabins with wheelchair access.

Gay Travellers

Sweden is renowned for its liberal attitudes to sex, and its age of consent is 15 for heterosexuals and gays. But there is nevertheless little open affection between gay couples and the gay scene is less apparent in Stockholm than in other capitals, with few places for gays only.

Medical Services

HOSPITALS

Sweden does not have a GP system, so the place to go for any type of treatment is the nearest hospital. Casualty (*Akutmottagning*) deals with serious problems, but Vårdcentral or Husläkarmottagning out-patients clinics are a better option since you will normally be seen within an hour. Take your passport with you.

PHARMACIES

Chemists (*apotek*) should be your first port of call for minor ailments. Generally, they are open from Monday to Friday 9am–6pm, although some also open on Saturdays, usually from 9.30am to 1pm. If you need medicine outside office hours, go to the nearest hospital. There is also one all-night pharmacy in Stockholm (C.W. Scheele, Klarabergsgatan 64; tel: 08 45 48 10 0).

DENTISTS

Dental surgeries are indicated by the sign *Tandläkare*. In Stockholm there is an emergency dental service at St Eriks Sjukhus, Polhemsgatan 48; tel: 08 54 55 12 20 (open daily 7.45am–8.30pm).

Security and Crime

Sweden is generally a law-abiding country. Crime figures are low, and the streets are by and large safe. Since Sweden is one of the most progressive countries in the world, with the highest percentage of women in the workforce and half its ministers women, lone female travellers rarely encounter problems.

A far less permissive attitude is, however, taken to drinking. Sweden's drink/driving laws are strict (*see Getting Around, page 391*), and it is an offence to drink alcohol or be found drunk in any public place. Drug trafficking is also a very serious offence, which carries heavy prison sentences.

For emergency assistance anywhere within Sweden (police, fire service or ambulance) dial 112. Calls are free from pay phones.

Religious Services

The Swedish State Church is in the Lutheran tradition and has churches throughout the country.

Stockholm has the widest range of places of worship, including a Greek Orthodox church, several synagogues and three Islamic mosques.

Protestant services in English are usually held once a week in major cities. Inquire at your hotel for more information.

Tipping

Restaurants A service charge is included in the bill and a further tip is not expected, although it's usual to round up the bill to the nearest 10/20 Skr.
Taxis Drivers usually get an extra 5 Skr but this is optional.
Cloakrooms at restaurants and clubs charge about 10 Skr.
Hotels Tipping for special services by staff is fine but not expected.

Embassies/Consulates

Australia
Sergels Torg 12, Stockholm
Tel: 08 61 32 90 0
Fax: 08 24 74 14
E-mail: info@austemb.se

Canada
Tegelbacken 4, Stockholm
Tel: 08 45 33 00 0
Fax: 08 24 24 91

UK
Skarpögatan 6–8, Stockholm
Tel: 08 67 19 00 0
Fax: 08 66 29 98 9

US
Strandvägen 101, Stockholm
Tel: 08 78 35 30 0
Fax: 08 66 05 87 9

Getting Around

On Arrival

All three of Sweden's major international airports – Stockholm (Arlanda), Göteborg (Landvetter) and Malmö (Sturup) – have excellent links to the city centre. From Arlanda, passengers can use the new Arlanda Express high-speed train which operates four times an hour to Stockholm Central Station and takes only 20 minutes. There are also frequent bus services, *Flygbussarna*, from Arlanda's international and domestic terminals as well as from Skavsta Airport to the city terminal at Klarabergsgatan above Central Station. In Göteborg and Malmö, coaches operate from the airport to the cities' central stations.

Taxis are always available but make sure that you get a price for your destination before getting into the taxi. At Arlanda Airport, Taxi Stockholm, Taxi Kurir, Taxi Card and some other companies have fixed fares for rides into the city centre.

By Air

All major cities and towns are linked by an efficient network of services operated mainly by SAS, Skyways and Braathens/Malmö Aviation.

Cheap flights are available on selected domestic services all year, as well as standby flights for under 25s and special fares for senior citizens. But many of the best deals are during the summer peak season in July when few business executives are travelling.

The Scandinavia/Nordic Air Pass, for eight one-way flights over three months, is available to foreigners. Details from travel agents.

Braathens/Malmö Aviation
Tel: 020 22 52 25.
Skyways Tel: 08 50 90 50 50.

By Train

Swedish State Railways, or SJ (website: www.sj.se), operate an efficient network, mostly electrified, covering the entire country. Trains are frequent, particularly on the main trunk route linking Stockholm with Göteborg, on which there is an hourly service. The high-speed train X2000 travels at up to 200 kph (125 mph) and is a good choice if you want to travel long distances; the journey from Göteborg to Stockholm takes only three hours.

Rail passes

Swedish State Railways offer a wide range of fares for both business and leisure travellers. Conditions and prices may depend on whether you buy your ticket in Sweden or abroad. A number of discount fares are available, including:
● **Sweden Rail Pass** offers unlimited rail travel within Sweden, either first or second class. Choose between a Flexi Pass with three travel days over one week or five travel days within two weeks, or a Consecutive Pass with seven or 14 days of travel. You can buy your Sweden Rail Pass from:
UK: Deutsche Bahn UK
Tel: 020 74 08 09 79
Fax: 020 74 91 46 89
Canada: DER Travel ServicesRail Europe.
US: DER Travel ServicesRail Europe.
● **ScanRail Pass** gives you unlimited rail travel within the Nordic countries. It is available for first and second class and for differing periods: there is the Flexi Pass with five travel days during a 15-day period or 10 travel days over a month, or the Consecutive Pass with 21 days of travel.
For more information, prices and bookings call: 020 75 75 75.
● **Tågplus** If you want to combine rail, bus and boat in one ticket, the best way is probably to buy a Tågplus ticket that enables you to

reach over 3,000 destinations within Sweden. For more details and to book, call: 020 75 75 75.

By Bus

Travelling by bus is usually cheap and an efficient network of express services links all major towns and cities, operated mainly by:
Svenska Buss Tel: 020 67 67 67.
Swebus Express Tel: 020 21 82 18.
Linjebuss Tel: 08 440 85 70.

In Stockholm

The bus network in Stockholm is claimed to be the world's largest and is run by the Stockholm Transit Authority, which also operates the *Tunnelbanan* (underground) and local mainline rail services.

Instead of paying cash on the bus, it is cheaper to buy a *Förköpshäfte* (from Pressbyrån and on the underground) which is a voucher for 10 rides within the centre. The driver stamps your ticket when you start your journey and you are allowed to travel freely within one zone on the bus, train and underground for an hour on the same ticket. There is no self-service system for buying tickets on the *Tunnelbanan*; use the *Förköpshäfte* or pay cash when you pass the ticket office which is always staffed. You can also buy the SL Tourist Card, which gives free public transport in the Greater Stockholm area for 24 or 72 hours. The 72-hour card also includes admission to Gröna Lund Tivoli and Kaknästornet.

By Underground

Stockholm is justifiably proud of its underground, known as T-banan (identified by the "T" sign). It is spotless, with almost 100 stations covering more than 95 km (60 miles). Commuter trains (*pendeltåg*) take you quickly to the suburbs of Stockholm and to Nynäshamn, where you can board the ferry to the island of Gotland.

In Göteborg
Göteborg has a superior tram system, as well as a good network of bus routes. The *Göteborgskortet* pass gives free public transport, admission to Liseberg Tivoli, some museums, free boat trips and free parking. Valid for 24 hours.

In Malmö
Malmökortet, available for one, three or four days, gives free public transport, discounts or free admission to museums, free parking, discounts on sightseeing tours and on boats to Copenhagen.

By Boat or Ferry

There are innumerable commuter services in the Stockholm archipelago operated by the famous white boats of the Waxholm Steamship Company. During the summer, visitors can buy a 16-day season ticket (*Båtluffarkortet*), which gives unlimited travel on the Waxholm boats. For information call: 08 67 95 83 0.

Strömma Kanalbolaget's website also has information on sightseeing and excursions in Stockholm: www.strommakanalbolaget.se.

The Baltic island of Gotland has services from Nynäshamn and Oskarshamn. For details check with a tourist office or call Destination Gotland, tel: 08 20 10 20.

By Taxi

Swedish taxis are usually efficient, but rely more on the telephone booking than being flagged down. Fares are steep. There is a minimum charge, and the meter starts as soon as the taxi arrives at your address. The bigger firms accept credit cards.

In Stockholm, some companies have a maximum fare for rides within the centre. This is good value if you want to travel, for example, from the north to the south of town or if there is a traffic jam.

To book a taxi, call:
Taxi Stockholm Tel: 08 15 00 00
Taxi Kurir Tel: 08 30 00 00
Taxi Card Tel 08 97 00 00

By Bicycle

Many of Sweden's towns are ideal for exploring by bike, with good cycle lanes. Cycling holidays are also popular. Bikes can be hired in most places; just enquire at the local tourist office.
Cykelfrämjandet, Box 6027, Torsgatan 31, SE-102 31 Stockholm (tel: 08 32 16 80), publishes cycling guides in English.

On Foot

Stockholm, Malmö and Göteborg are compact enough to explore on foot. An age-old Swedish law, *Allemansratten* (Everyman's Right) states that you can venture into the countryside anywhere you like and pick berries and flowers, fish, camp, swim in the lakes and roam at will – as long as you don't harm crops or animals.

Hitchhiking is officially discouraged, and in any case finding a lift can be hard in the holiday season.

By Car

Main routes
Sweden's roads are uncrowded, with toll-free motorways covering more than 1,100 km (700 miles), trunk roads some 80,500 km

Scenic Train Route

One very beautiful journey to take by train is the *Inlandsbanan* (Inland Railway), which runs for more than 1,300 km (800 miles) down the spine of Sweden from Gällivare, north of the Arctic Circle, to Kristinehamn in the south.

The ticket is valid for 10 days and you may stop and continue wherever you please in the direction in which you are heading. For the travel back, you must buy a return ticket. For more details contact:
Inlandsbanan AB, Köpmangatan 22B, S-831 27 Östersund. Tel: 020 53 53 53.

Speed Limits

Motorways 110 kph (70 mph)
Dual carriageways 90 kph (55 mph)
Unsigned roads 70 kph (43 mph)
Built-up areas 50 kph (31 mph), 30 kph (19 mph) in school areas

(50,000 miles). There are thousands of kilometres of often picturesque byroads.

Rules of the road
● Traffic gives way to approaching traffic from the right, unless signs indicate otherwise, and gives way to traffic already on a roundabout.
● Everyone must wear seat belts.
● Headlights are obligatory both day and night.
● Drivers are not required to call the police after accidents but must exchange names and addresses. If you do not stop at all you may be liable to a fine or imprisonment.
● In the event of a breakdown, contact the police or Larmtjänst, a 24-hour set-up run by insurance companies (telephone numbers are listed in directories). The emergency number 112 should be used only for accidents or injury.
● Sweden's drink-drive laws are strictly enforced, with spot checks and heavy fines.

CAR HIRE

Stockholm
Avis, Vasagatan 10B.
Tel: 020 78 82 00/08 20 20 60.
Arlanda Airport.
Tel: 08 79 79 97 0.
Budget, Klarabergsviadukten 92.
Tel: 020 78 77 87/08 41 11 50 0.
Arlanda Airport.
Tel: 08 79 78 47 0.
Europcar, Hotel Sheraton, Tegelbacken 6.
Tel: 08 21 06 50/020 78 11 80.
Arlanda Airport.
Tel: 08 59 36 09 40.
Hertz, Vasagatan 26.
Tel: 020 21 12 11/08 24 07 20.
Arlanda Airport.
Tel: 08 79 79 90 0.

Where to Stay

Choosing a Hotel

Swedish hotels are of a uniformly high standard, although expensive. But hotel rates do come down in high summer because the expense-account business travellers are on holiday themselves.

Scandic and Sweden Hotels are the country's leading multiples. Away from the big cities, there are plenty of privately owned hotels with the individuality lacking in chains.

DISCOUNTS

All the hotel groups run discount schemes during summer. Stockholm, Göteborg and Malmö also offer special discount packages at weekends year-round and daily in summer. These often include free public transport and free admission to visitor attractions.

Nationwide Chains

The big international hotel chains like Hilton or Sheraton have made little impact. Accommodation is dominated by Scandinavian chains such as Scandic or Sweden Hotels.

Best Western Hotels
Skyttelholmsvagen 2, SE-171 11, Solna. Tel: 08 566 293 70/ 020 79 27 52
Website: www.bestwestern.se

Choice Hotels
Asagatan 46, SE-111 20 Stockholm. Tel: 08 44 04 44 0/ 020 66 60 00

First Hotels
Linnégatan 87D
SE-104 51 Stockholm
Tel: 08 44 28 40 0/020 41 11 11
E-mail: info@firsthotels.se
Website: www.firsthotels.com

Good Morning Hotels
Tel: 020 44 48 88
Website: www.goodmorninghotels.se

Scandic Hotels
Hälsingegatan 40, Box 6197, SE-102 33 Stockholm
Tel: 08 51 75 17 00. Website: www.scandic-hotels.com

Sweden Hotels
Sveavägen 39, SE-111 34 Stockholm. Tel: 08 70 17 90 00 or 020 77 00 00

Hotel Listings

Hotels are grouped by area, starting with Stockholm. Within each city or region, they are listed alphabetically in price order, with the most expensive first.

Price Guide

$$$	1,800–2,600Skr
$$	1,000–1,800Skr
$	up to 1,000Skr

Price categories are based on the average cost (including tax) of a double room for two, usually with breakfast.

STOCKHOLM

Hotell Diplomat
Strandvägen 7C, SE 104 40
Tel: 08 45 96 80 0
Fax: 08 45 96 82 0
E-mail: info@diplomat-hotel.se
Website: www.diplomat-hotel.se
Beautiful waterside location on the city's most exclusive street. **$$$**

Lydmar Hotel
Sturegatan 10, SE-114 36
Tel: 08 56 61 13 00
Fax: 08 56 61 13 01
E-mail: info@lydmar.se
Website: www.lydmar.se
One of the best soul and jazz stages in Stockholm. Central with an excellent restaurant. **$$–$$$**

Villa Källhagen
Djurgårdsbrunnsvägen 10, SE-115 27
Tel: 08 66 50 30 0
Fax: 08 66 50 39 9
E-mail: villa@kallhagen.se
Website: www.kallhagen.se

Modern, charming hotel with good restaurant. Close to parks. **$$**

First Hotel Crystal Plaza
Birger Jarlsgatan 35, SE-111 45
Tel: 08 40 68 80 0
Fax: 08 24 15 11
E-mail: central@crystalplaza.se
Website: www.crystalplaza.se
Central. Different room rates on offer. **$–$$**

Gustav Vasa Hotel
Västmannagatan 61, SE-113 25
Tel: 08 34 38 01
Fax: 08 30 73 72
E-mail: gustav.vasa@wineasy.se
Website: www.hotell.wineasy.se/ gustav.vasa
In popular residential area near restaurants and shops. Three underground stops from centre. **$**

Hotell Tre Små Rum
Högbergsgatan 81, SE-118 54
Tel: 08 64 12 37 1
Fax: 08 64 28 80 8
E-mail: info@tresmarum.se
Website: www.tresmarum.se
Simple but very good-value B&B in the trendy suburb of Södermalm. **$**

AROUND STOCKHOLM

Grythyttan
Grythyttans Gästgivaregård
Prästgatan 2, SE-712 81
Tel: 0591 14 70 0
Fax: 0591 14 12 4
E-mail: info@grythyttan.com
Website: www.grythyttan.com
Sweden's best-known inn in a lovely setting. Expensive but exquisite restaurant and wine list. **$$**

Mariefred
Gripsholms Värdshus & Hotel
Kyrkoplan 1, SE-647 23
Tel: 0159 34 75 0
Fax: 0159 34 77 7
E-mail: info@gripsholmsvardshus.se
Website: www.gripsholmsvardshus.se
Carefully renovated. Beautiful individually furnished rooms. **$$–$$$**

Skokloster
Skokloster Wärdshus & Hotel
SE-746 96 Skokloster
Tel: 018 38 61 00
Fax: 018 38 60 55

E-mail: info@skokloster.se
Website: www.skokloster.se
Beautiful surroundings close to
the castle. **$**

Uppsala
First Hotel Linné
Skolgatan 45, SE-750 02
Tel: 018 10 20 00
Fax: 018 13 75 97
E-mail: linne@firsthotels.se
Website: www.firsthotels.com
Modern hotel with a view over
Linnaeus Garden. Situated in a
quiet area. **$$**

GÖTEBORG

Elite Plaza Hotel
Västra Hamngatan 3, SE-404 22
Tel: 031 72 04 00 0
Fax: 031 72 04 01 0
E-mail: info@gbgplaza.elite.se
Website: www.elite.se
New luxury hotel in the centre. **$$$**
Hotel Eggers
Drottningtorget, Box 323, SE-401
25
Tel: 031 80 60 70
Fax: 031 15 42 43
E-mail: hotel.eggers@mailbox.
swipnet.se
Website: www.bestwestern.se
Classic 19th-century railway hotel
with individually furnished rooms.
By the station and near the city
centre. **$$**
Novotel Göteborg
Klippan 1, SE-414 51
Tel: 031 14 90 00
Fax: 031 42 22 32
E-mail: info@novotel.se
Website: www.novotel.se
By the water overlooking harbour,
near good public transport. **$$**
Mornington Hotel
Kungsportsavenyn 6, SE-411 36
Tel: 031 17 65 40
Fax: 031 71 13 43
E-mail: goteborg@mornington.se
Website: www.mornington.se
First-class with generous breakfast,
right in the centre on Avenyn. **$$**
Hotel Excelsior
Karl Gustavsgatan 7, SE-411 25
Tel: 031 17 54 35
Fax: 031 17 54 39
E-mail: hotel.excelsio@tripnet.se

Website: www.tripnet.se/
excelsior.se/
Charming old-style hotel with
individually furnished rooms, within
easy walking distance of Avenyn. **$**
St Jörgens Hotell & Pensionat
Gamla Lillhagsvägen 127B,
SE-422 04
Tel: 031 55 39 81
Fax: 031 55 39 82
E-mail: hotellet@st-jorgen.nu
Website: www.st-jorgen.nu
Charming and small in rural setting
within easy reach of the centre. **$**

Price Guide

$$$	1,800–2,600Skr
$$	1,000–1,800Skr
$	up to 1,000Skr

Price categories are based on
the average cost (including tax)
of a double room for two, usually
with breakfast.

MALMÖ

Scandic Hotel Triangeln
Triangeln 2, SE-200 10
Tel: 040 69 34 70 0
Fax: 040 69 34 71 1
Website: www.scandic-hotels.se
Modern high-rise glass building.
Most rooms have a nice view. **$$$**
Hotel Noble House
Gustav Adolfstorg 47, SE-211 39
Tel: 040 66 43 00 0
Fax: 040 66 43 05 0
E-mail: noblehouse@hkchotels.se
Website: www.hkchotels.se
Right in the centre. **$$**
Hotell Astoria
Gråbrödersgatan 7, SE-211 21
Tel: 040 78 66 0
Fax: 040 78 87 0
E-mail: info@astoria.gs2.com
Website: www.astoria.gs2.com
In the old part of the town within
walking distance of station and
ferries. **$**
Hotell Royal
Norra Vallgatan 94, SE-211 22
Tel: 040 66 42 50
Fax: 040 12 77 12
E-mail: info.royal@swedenhotels.se
Website: www.hotelroyal.com
Small hotel in an old building close
to shops, station and ferries. **$**

SOUTHERN SWEDEN: SMÅLAND & ÖLAND

Åhus
Åhusstrand
Kolonivägen, SE-296 32
Tel: 044 28 93 00
Fax: 044 24 94 80
E-mail: info@ahusstrand.com
Website: www.ahusstrand.com
Right on the beach with a 200
metre (650 ft) landing outside.
$–$$

Helsingborg
Elite Hotel Mollberg
Stortorget 18, SE-251 10
Tel: 042 37 37 00
Fax: 042 37 37 37
E-mail: mollberg.helsingborg
@elite.se
Website: www.elite.se
Classic, well-known and beautiful
hotel right in the centre of town.
$$

Kalmar
Provobis Calmar Stadshotell
Stortorget 14, SE-392 32
Tel: 0480 49 69 00
Fax: 0480 49 69 10
E-mail: calmar.stadshotell
@provobis.se
Website: www.provobis.se
Beautiful building with individually
furnished rooms in the centre. **$$**

Lund
Grand Hotel
Bantorget 1, SE-221 04
Tel: 046 28 06 10 0
Fax: 046 28 06 15 0
E-mail: hotel@grand.lundia.se
Website: www.grand.lundia.se
Newly renovated in an attractive old
building, right in the centre. **$$–$$$**

Öland
Guntorps Herrgård
Guntorpsgatan, SE-387 36
Borgholm
Tel: 0485 13 00 0
Fax: 0485 13 31 9
E-mail: guntorp.herrgard
@swipnet.se
Website: www.guntorp.oland.com
Beautiful manor house just outside
Borgholm, with lovely restaurant,
pool and charming rooms. **$**

Youth Hostels

Sweden has about 280 youth hostels (*vandrarhem*), from mansion houses and castles to renovated ships like the 100-year-old *af Chapman* in Stockholm harbour, and modern purpose-built hostels. There are also plenty of youth hostels in the Stockholm archipelago. Most have two- and four-bedded rooms or family rooms. Hostels have self-catering facilities, but meals or snacks are provided in some. Bring your own sheets and towels. For details: Swedish Tourist Federation (STF). Tel: 08 463 21 00. Fax: 08 678 19 58 Website: www.meravsverige.nu.

Västervik
Best Western Västerviks
Stadshotell, Storgatan 3, SE-593 30
Tel: 0490 82 00 0
Fax: 0490 82 00 1
E-mail: stadshotellet@stadshotellet.nu
Website: www.bestwestern.se/vastervik
Modern hotel right in the centre of town, close to the waterfront. **$–$$**

Vimmerby
Vimmerby Stadshotell
Sevedegatan 39, SE-598 37
Tel: 0492 12 10 0
Fax: 0492 14 64 3
E-mail: info@vimmerbystadshotell.se
Website: www.vimmerbystadshotell.se
Pleasant and on town square. **$$**

Ystad
Ystads Saltsjöbad
Saltsjöbadsvägen 6, SE-271 39
Tel: 0411 13 63 00
Fax: 0411 55 58 35
E-mail: info@ystadssaltsjobad.se
Website: www.ystadssaltsjobad.se
Newly renovated with panoramic Baltic view. Relaxing. **$$**

GOTLAND

Visby
Wisby Hotell
Strandgatan 6, SE-621 24
Tel: 0498 25 75 00
Fax: 0498 25 75 50
E-mail: info@wisbyhotell.se
Website: www.wisbyhotell.se
Old hotel with modern rooms in the centre of town. **$$**

THE WEST COAST

Halmstad
Hotel Tylösand
Tylöhusvägen, SE-301 16
Tel: 035 30 50 0
Fax: 035 32 43 9
E-mail: info@tylosand.se
Website: www.tylosand.se
First-class hotel overlooking the beach with top-class golf courses nearby. **$$**

Lysekil
Hotel Lysekil
Rosvikstorg 1, SE-453 30
Tel: 0523 66 55 30
Fax: 0523 15 55 20
E-mail: info@hotel-lysekil.net
Website: www.hotel-lysekil.net
Modern hotel with all facilities. Situated near the water and a wide range of water activities. **$**

Marstrand
Grand Hotel Marstrand
Rådhusgatan 2, SE-440 30
Tel: 0303 60 32 2
Fax: 0303 60 05 3
E-mail: info@grandmarstrand.se
Website: www.grandmarstrand.se
Attractive late-19th-century hotel. Located by the water. **$$**

Varberg
Varbergs Stadshotell
Kungsgatan 24–26, SE-432 41
Tel: 0340 69 01 00
Fax: 0340 69 01 01
E-mail: info@varbergsstadshotell.com
Website: www.varbergsstadshotell.com
Carefully renovated hotel from the turn of the 20th century. Centrally located. **$$**

THE GREAT LAKES

Borås
First Hotel Grand
Hallbergsgatan 14, SE-503 05
Tel: 033 10 82 00
Fax: 033 41 07 69
E-mail: info@firsthotelgrand.se
Website: www.firsthotelgrand.se
First-class and modern. **$$**

Karlstad
First Hotel Plaza
Västra Torggatan 2, SE-652 25
Tel: 054 10 02 00
Fax: 054 10 02 24
E-mail: karlstad.plaza@firsthotels.se
Website: www.firsthotels.se
First-class hotel in the centre. **$$**

Lidköping
Best Western Stadt Lidköping
Gamla Stadens Torg 1, SE-531 02
Tel: 0510 22 08 5
Fax: 0510 21 53 2
E-mail: hotel@stadtlidkoping.se
Website: www.stadtlidkoping.se
Old waterfront hotel. **$$**

Nora
Nora Stadshotell
Rådstugugatan 21, SE-713 31
Tel: 0587 31 14 35
Fax: 0587 14 16 10
E-mail: nora.stadshotell@swipnet.se
Family-owned hotel with good restaurant in the town square. **$**

GÖTA KANAL

Karlsborg
Kanalhotellet
Storgatan 94, SE-546 32
Tel: 0505 12 13 0
Fax: 0505 12 76 1
Website: www.kanalhotellet.se
Late 19th-century hotel. **$**

Söderköping
Romantik Hotel Söderköpings Brunn
Skönbergsgatan 35, SE-614 21
Tel: 0121 10 90 0
Fax: 0121 13 94 1
E-mail: info@soderkopingsbrunn.se
Website: www.soderkopingsbrunn.se
Charming hotel in a park. **$–$$**

Camping

There are about 750 officially approved sites, many in pretty locations. Most open from early June to the end of August. Rates are claimed to be among the cheapest in Europe.

You can also rent camping chalets and cottages, caravans and motor homes. For fast check-in and check-out plus insurance while at the site, you should get the Swedish Camping Card. This is free, and you can apply for it before you leave for Sweden, but you have to pay a small validation fee at your first site. The card is available (allow one month for delivery) from:
Sveriges Camingvardars
Riksforbund, Box 2455, S-451 17 Uddevalia. Fax: 522 64 24 30.
E-mail: ck@camping.se
Or from the very useful website: www.camping.se

DALARNA

Falun
First Hotel Grand
Trotzgatan 9–11, SE-791 71
Tel: 023 79 48 80
Fax: 023 14 14 33
E-mail: grand.falun@firsthotels.se
Website: www.firsthotels.se
Dalarna's biggest hotel, in centre. **$$**

Mora
First Resort Mora
Strandgatan 12, SE-792 30
Tel: 0250 71 75 0
Fax: 0250 18 98 1
E-mail: mora@firsthotels.se
Website: www.firsthotels.se
Modern hotel in the centre close to Zorn museum and finishing line of Vasaloppet ski race. **$$**

Tällberg
Hotell Klockargården
Siljansvägen 6, SE-793 70
Tel: 0247 50 26 0
Fax: 0247 50 21 6
Charming timber houses with an exhibition of art and craftwork nearby and great views of Lake Siljan. **$–$$**

THE CENTRAL HEARTLANDS

Åre
Åregården
SE-830 13
Tel: 0647 17 90 0
Fax: 0647 17 89 8
E-mail: reservations.are@diplomat-hotel.se
Website: www.diplomat-hotel.se
First-class family-owned hotel in the centre of town with skiing facilities, shops and nightclubs close. **$–$$$**

Sundsvall
First Hotel Strand
Strandgatan 10, SE-851 06
Tel: 060 12 18 00
Fax: 060 61 92 02
E-mail: strand.sundsvall@firsthotels.se
Website: www.firsthotels.se
Marine-style hotel with a popular bar and restaurant. **$$**

Price Guide

$$$	1,800–2,600Skr
$$	1,000–1,800Skr
$	up to 1,000Skr

Price categories are based on the average cost (including tax) of a double room for two, usually with breakfast.

LAPLAND

Arvidsjaur
Laponia Hotel
Storgatan 45, SE-933 33
Tel: 0960 55 50 0
Fax: 0960 55 59 9
E-mail: laponia@laponia-gielas.se
Website: www.laponia-gielas.se
Modern. Offers winter sports. **$$**

Kiruna
Hotell Vinterpalatset
Järnvägsgatan 18, SE-981 21
Tel: 0980 67 77 0
Fax: 0980 13 05 0
E-mail: vinterp@kiruna.se
Website: www.kiruna.se/~vinterp
Small privately owned hotel built in 1904 but fully renovated. **$–$$**

Riksgränsen
Riksgränsen
SE-981 94
Tel: 0980 40 08 0
Fax: 0980 43 12 5
E-mail: reservation@riksgransen.nu
Website: www.riksgransen.nu
Rooms and self-catering, by a lake with skiing facilities and opportunities for hiking nearby. **$$**

THE NORTHEAST COAST

Haparanda
Haparanda Stadshotell
Torget 7, SE-953 31
Tel: 0922 61 49 0
Fax: 0922 10 22 3
E-mail: info@haparandastads hotell.se
Website: www.haparandastads hotell.se
Early 20th-century hotel in the town centre. The restaurant's specialities include reindeer, elk and grouse. **$$**

Piteå
Piteå Stadshotell
Olof Palmes Gata 1, SE-941 21
Tel: 0911 19 70 0
Fax: 0911 12 29 2
E-mail: info@piteastadshotell.com
Website: www.piteastadshotell.com
Restored late 19th-century hotel in the centre of town. **$$**

Umeå
First Hotel Grand
Storgatan 46, SE-903 26
Tel: 090 77 88 70
Fax: 090 13 30 55
E-mail: umea.grand@firsthotels.se
Website: www.firsthotels.se
Renovated hotel with a nightclub on Friday and Saturday. Central. **$$**

Bed and Breakfast

The bed and breakfast system is becoming more popular. Look for the *Rum* sign (it means "room" and does not include breakfast). Ask at local tourist offices if any *rum* accommodation is available. Prices are very reasonable.

Where to Eat

Choosing a Restaurant

Sweden, once known as the land of *husmanskost* (homely fare), is enjoying a culinary renaissance, thanks to the creative genius of a new generation of chefs who know how to give a sophisticated twist to classic Swedish dishes such as reindeer, elk, lingonberries, salmon or herring.

Eating out has become increasingly popular, but can seem expensive if you drink a lot of wine or beer. Stockholm has more than 700 restaurants covering at least 30 national cuisines. Göteborg is particularly good for seafood, and Malmö claims to have more restaurants per head than any other Swedish city.

For travellers on a tight budget there is no shortage of inexpensive places to eat. Look for the *dagens rätt* (dish of the day), a lunch that usually includes bread, a simple salad and soft drink for a set price. Traditional Swedish food like meatballs, *pytt i panna* (fried potatoes, onions, meat and sausage served with beetroot), and pea soup is widely available. The famous *sill* (pickled herring) is served mostly around midsummer with new potatoes. You can find all kinds of pickled herring; with onions, mustard, barbecue sauce, garlic or herbs, or *matjessill* (with sour cream and chives).

Salmon has less of a luxury connotation than in other countries. *Gravad lax* (marinated salmon) and *rökt lax* (smoked salmon) can be found on the *smörgåsbord* and on most Swedish menus.

Fast food outlets are everywhere. The ubiquitous *korvkiosk* sells grilled chicken, sausages, hamburgers and *tunnbrödsrulle* (a parcel of mashed potato, sausage and ketchup or mustard wrapped in soft bread). Some serve *strömming* (fried herring) and mashed potato.

The Swedes generally eat fairly early. Restaurants start serving lunch at about 11am and some small hotels, particularly in country areas, serve evening meals around 6pm. In country areas they often stop serving early, but at motels and in the cities you can eat later.

Restaurant Listings

Restaurants are grouped by area with Stockholm first. They are listed alphabetically in price order, with the most expensive first.

Price Guide

Price categories are based on an average cost per head of a three-course meal (excluding drinks but with tax):

$$$ more than 400Skr
$$ 200–400Skr
$ up to 200Skr

STOCKHOLM

Gondolen
Stadsgården 6
Tel: 08 64 17 09 0
Highly recommended. Offers traditional Swedish cuisine with a great view over the city. **$$$**

Operakällaren
Operan (Royal Opera House)
Tel: 08 67 65 80 0
Arguably Stockholm's best-known restaurant. Its Christmas *smörgåsbord* was nominated by Jan Morris in London's *Times* as "the best meal in the world". **$$$**

PA & Co
Riddargatan 8
Tel: 08 61 10 84 5
Well known restaurant, so reserve your table in advance. **$$**

Sturehof
Stureplan 2
Tel: 08 44 05 73 0
Stylish Swedish food. Has a popular bar and live music. **$$**

Farbror Frej
Frejgatan 79
Tel: 08 32 05 25
Intimate restaurant run by a cycling legend. Great food and a warm welcome. **$–$$**

Indian Curry House
Scheelegatan 6
Tel: 08 65 02 02 4
Small, basic restaurant with good Indian food at reasonable prices. **$**

AROUND STOCKHOLM

Grythyttan
Grythyttans Gästgivaregård
Prästgatan 2
Tel: 0591 14 70 0
Well-known romantic inn. Excellent modern Swedish food. **$$–$$$**

Södertälje
Oaxen Skärgårdskrog
Oaxen (30 km/19 miles from Södertälje)
Tel: 08 55 153 10 5
Beautifully located and friendly. Excellent Swedish cooking. **$–$$**

SOUTHERN SWEDEN & SMÅLAND

Malmö
Petri Pumpa, Hotel Savoy
Norra Vallgatan 62
Tel: 040 66 44 88 0
Rated among Sweden's top five restaurants. **$$–$$$**

Restaurang Johan P
Isak Slaktaregatan 8
Tel: 040 97 18 18
Excellent and beautifully presented fish dishes. **$$**

Tempo Bar & Kök
Södra Skolgatan 30A
Tel: 040 12 60 21
Popular bar/restaurant with a mixed international menu. Live music. **$$**

Brogatan
Brogatan 12
Tel: 040 30 77 17
Popular among the famous. Organic Swedish food and live music. **$–$$**

There is an area worth visiting in Malmö called Lilla Torg, where the market hall is located and new restaurants are opening all the time offering various cuisines.

Helsingborg
Elinor
Kullagatan 53
Tel: 042 14 32 71
Charming restaurant specialising in fish and seafood. **$$**

Kalmar
Calmar Hamnkrog
Skeppsbrogatan 30
Tel: 0480 41 10 20
Gourmet restaurant with a sea view. Classic and international food. **$$**

Simrishamn
Karlaby Kro
In the village of Tommarp, 7 km/ 4 miles from Simrishamm
Tel: 0414 20 30 0
Cosy restaurant serving fresh local produce. **$$–$$$**

Torekov
Kattegat Gastronomi & Logi
Storgatan 46
Tel: 0431 63 00 2
One of Sweden's best restaurants. Excellent food and service. **$$–$$$**

GOTLAND

Visby
Donners Brunn
Donners Plats
Tel: 0498 27 10 90
Friendly gourmet restaurant with "Best Lamb Chef" in Sweden. **$$**
Bakfickan
Stora Torget 1
Tel: 0498 27 18 07
Cosy serving excellent fish. **$–$$**

THE WEST COAST

Göteborg
Fiskekrogen
Lilla Torget 1
Tel: 031 10 10 05
Best fish restaurant in town, with exciting wines for a good price. **$$$**

Price Guide

Price categories are based on an average cost per head of a three-course meal (excluding drinks but with tax):
$$$ more than 400Skr
$$ 200–400Skr
$ up to 200Skr

Trädgår'n
Nya Allén
Tel: 031 10 20 80
Exotic award-winning international restaurant. Has live music. **$$$**
Hemma Hos
Haga Nygata 12
Tel: 031 13 40 90
Cosy local restaurant, serving great fish dishes and desserts. **$$**
Mannerström
Arkivgatan 7
Tel: 031 16 03 33
Gourmet restaurant, commendable for its fish and desserts. **$$**
Noon
Viktoriagatan 2B
Tel: 031 13 88 00
Asian bar/restaurant. Friendly and professional. Good desserts. **$$**
Smaka
Vasaplatsen 3
Tel: 031 13 22 47
Bar and restaurant serving homely Swedish fare, with live music. **$$**

Halmstad
Pio & Company
Storgatan 37
Tel: 035 21 06 69
Traditional Swedish food. **$$**

Hamburgsund
Skäret
Strandvägen 10
Tel: 0525 34 58 0
Charcoal-grilled fish. **$$**

Tanumshede
Tanums Gestgifveri
Apoteksv 7, 30 km (19 miles) from Strömstad
Tel: 0525 29 01 0
Inn/restaurant. Swedish food. **$$**

THE GREAT LAKES

Borås
Vivaldi
Plaza Hotel, Allégatan 3
Tel: 033 41 02 00
Fine place with classic Swedish food, good wine and beer. **$$**

Jönköping
Svarta Börsen
Kyrkog 4
Tel: 036 71 22 22
Traditional with excellent fish. Good-value business lunches. **$$–$$$**

Karlstad
Tiffany
Västra Torggatan 19
Tel: 054 15 33 83
Stylish restaurant specialising in local fish and game. **$$–$$$**

GÖTA KANAL

Dalarna
Borlänge
Värdshuset Dala Floda
Badvägen 6, Dala Floda (40 km/25 miles from Borlänge)
Tel: 0241 22 05 0
Excellent well-known inn/restaurant. International menu. **$–$$**

Falun
Dössbergets Värdshus
Bjursås (20 km/12 miles from Falun)
Tel: 023 50 73 7
Beautifully located with traditional Swedish and gourmet food. **$$**

Leksand
Åkerblads Hotell & Gästgiveri
Sjögattu 2, Tällberg (13 km/8 miles from Leksand)
Tel: 0247 50 80 0
Traditional Swedish. Buffet lunch and smörgåsbord at weekend. **$$**

Söderköping
Romantik Hotel Söderköpings Brunn
Skönbergsgatan 35
Tel: 0121 10 90 0
Fine Swedish and international cooking, with vegetarian dishes. **$$**

What to Drink

Alcohol is a luxury in Sweden due to the high taxes. Alternatives include low- or medium-strength beer, Ramlösa mineral water, or one of the excellent indigenous schnapps.
There is no difficulty in ordering a drink with your meal, although the stronger Class III beer (*starköl*) may not be available in restaurants and bars until noon. The Swedish authorities have a puritanical attitude towards drinking: you can buy alcohol only through branches of the State-controlled monopoly

Systembolaget, open Monday to Friday 9am–6pm but closes early the day before a public holiday (some branches are open on Saturday).
The minimum age for buying alcohol is 20; you may be asked for proof of your age if you are in your early 20s.
It's worth looking out for bars and cafés advertising a reduced-price happy hour. This may be at any time of the day, but is worth finding as it can bring the cost of half a litre of lager down to half the price charged in nightclubs.

Cafés

STOCKHOLM

Vete-Katten
Kungsgatan 55
Tel: 08 20 84 05/21 84 54
Traditional café in the shopping area of downtown Stockholm.
Rosendals Trädgård
Rosendalsterrassen 12
Tel: 08 66 22 81 4
Situated within the garden by Rosendal Palace on Djurgården. Serves delicious cakes, desserts and other foods.

GÖTEBORG

Ahlströms Konditori
Korsgatan 2
Tel: 031 13 48 36
Founded in 1905.
Junggrens Café
Kungsportsavenyn 37
Tel: 031 16 17 51
A classic café for young people.

Vadstena
Starby Kungsgård
Ödeshögsvägen
Tel: 0143 75 10 0
Excellent. Traditional Swedish and gourmet international cuisine. **$$**

THE CENTRAL HEARTLANDS

Åre
Villa Tottebo
Parkvägen 1
Tel: 0647 50 59 9/50 62 0
Pleasant restaurant serving mostly local products. **$$**

Östersund
Mikado
Grytan, Brunflo (10 km/6 miles from Östersund)
Tel: 063 20 90 8
Prettily served Japanese cuisine. **$$–$$$**

Sundsvall
Fem Rum och Kök
Östra Långgatan 23
Tel: 060 17 62 62
Cosy restaurant with Swedish food and a variety of single malts. **$$**

LAPLAND

Jukkasjärvi
Jukkasjärvi Wärdshus
Marknadsvägen 63

Tel: 0980 66 88 0
Excellent restaurant specialising in local products such as reindeer, grouse, char and cloudberries. **$$**

Tärnaby
Sånninggården Restaurang & Pensionat
Klippen, Hemavan (25 km/15 miles from Tärnaby)
Tel: 0954 33 03 8
Beautifully located restaurant that specialises in game, poultry and local produce. **$–$$**

THE NORTHEAST COAST

Luleå
Margaretas Värdshus
Lulevägen 2, Gammelstad (10 km/6 miles from Luleå)
Tel: 0920 54 29 0
Picturesque inn with a restaurant, serving mostly local specialities. **$–$$**

Umeå
Rex Bar & Grill
Rådhustorget, Umeå
Tel: 090 12 60 50
Trendy bar/restaurant. Serves local food with inspiration from the Mediterranean. **$$**
K-A Svensson Kök och Matsalar
Blå Huset, Vasaplan
Tel: 090 77 98 00
Serves Swedish dishes with an interesting twist. **$–$$**

Nightlife

There is an active nightlife in the larger cities but nothing particularly hectic in the smaller communities. Many of the hotels listed have bars, nightclubs and sometimes even live dance music. The university cities like Uppsala, Lund, Linköping and Umeå have quite a busy nightlife, at least for the students.

Skiing resorts like Åre and Sälen are also good for nightlife (mostly for younger people) during the season, from December to April. After-ski is often very lively with bands playing covers of well-known tunes to packed crowds.

Out in the countryside and in smaller towns *dansband* (Swedish country-style) music is very popular.

Given the high cost of drinking in Sweden, a night out on the town can be expensive.

Nightclubs & Discos

Nightclubs and discos usually close around 3am, but in Stockholm some places extend this to 5am.

Stockholm
Café Opera
Operahuset. Tel: 08 41 10 02 6
Expensive but ever-popular.
Spy Bar
Birger Jarlsgatan 20
Tel: 08 61 16 50 0
Trendy with recent dance music.
Biblos
Biblioteksgatan 9
Tel: 08 61 18 03 0
Popular restaurant with large bar and small dance floor downstairs.

Göteborg
Park Lane
Kungsportsavenyn 36–38
Tel: 031 20 60 58
Fancy nightclub with international

atmosphere. Three bars, casino restaurant and live performances.
Trädgår'n
Nya Allén
Tel: 031 10 20 80
Restaurant with live performances.
Valand
Vasagatan 41
Tel: 031 18 30 93
Three bars and a restaurant with live performances most nights.

Malmö
Slakthuset
Jörgen Kocksgatan 7A
Tel: 040 10 99 30
Three dance floors. House, classic old hits and Top 40 (disco).
KB
Bergsgatan 18. Tel: 040 30 20 11
A popular haunt among more tough rock lovers, but also features pop.
Privé
Malmborgsgatan 7
Tel: 040 97 46 66
Disco popular among the older generation; people dress up.

Bars and Live Music

Stockholm
Fasching
Kungsgatan 63. Tel: 08 21 62 67
Stockholm's largest and probably most popular jazz club.
Lydmar
Sturegatan 10. Tel: 08 56 61 13 00
Popular bar and jazz club.
Pelikan
Blekingegatan 40
Tel: 08 74 30 69 5
Unpretentious bar and beer hall.
WC
Skånegatan 51. Tel: 08 64 41 98 1
Very busy popular bar.

Göteborg
Brasseri Lipp
Kungsportsavenyn 8
Tel: 031 10 58 30
French bistro/bar. Older crowd.
Palace
Södra Hamngatan 2
Tel: 031 80 21 00
Classic bar, popular among business people on Friday.
Trädgår'n
Nya Allén. Tel: 031 10 20 80
Restaurant with live performances.

Malmö
La Couronne
Södra Förstadsgatan 36
Tel 040 12 37 70
Bar & restaurant, very popular among musicians and art people.
Hipp
Kalendergatan 12
Tel: 040 97 40 30
Beautiful restaurant/bar with club arrangements. Salsa evenings.
KB
Bergsgatan 18. Tel: 040 30 20 11
Popular with tough rock lovers.

Music

The musical scene is busiest in autumn, winter and spring, but there is still a lot on in summer. In Dalarna several communities organise music festivals.

Stockholm
The main concert hall is the **Konserthuset** (tel: 08 10 21 10), home of the Stockholm Philharmonic Orchestra, whose season runs from September to May or June.

Berwaldhallen (the Berwald Concert Hall, tel: 08 784 50 00) is the base for Swedish National Radio's musical activities, with regular performances by the Radio Symphony Orchestra.

Stockholm's famous **Kungliga Operan** (Royal Opera House, tel: 08 24 82 40) has top international performances mid-August to June.

Göteborg
Konserthuset (the Concert Hall, tel: 031 61 53 10) hosts the Göteborg Symphony Orchestra, which is known worldwide and performs every week, often with guest artists, from August to June.

The modern **Göteborgsoperan** (Göteborg's Opera House, tel: 031 13 13 00) offers a varied programme (including opera, ballet and musicals) from August to June.

Malmö
The 1,300-seat **Konserthuset** (Concert Hall, tel: 040 34 35 00) is permanent home for the Symphony Orchestra.

Theatre

Sweden has a lively theatrical life in the major cities, but many theatres tend to be closed during the peak summer months. Performances are usually in Swedish.

Stockholm
The most prestigious theatre is **Dramaten** (Royal Dramatic Theatre, tel: 08 66 70 68 0) on Nybroplan, with four auditoriums. The most unusual one is **Drottningholms Slottsteater** (Drottningholm Court Theatre at Drottningholm Palace, tel: 08 66 51 40 0) founded by King Gustav III in 1766. Many sets from the 18th century are still in use today. In summer there are ballet and opera performances.

Current performances are listed in the *Stockholm This Week* booklet. There is a booth on Norrmalmstorg Square where you can buy last-minute theatre seats at prices at least 25 percent below normal box-office rates.

Göteborg
The two main theatres are **Stadsteatern** (tel: 031 81 99 60) and **Folkteatern** (tel: 031 60 75 75), both open from late August to early June.

Malmö
The **Musikteatern** (tel: 040 20 85 00) stages plays in Swedish, but you can often catch an opera or musical performance.

Cinema

Virtually all foreign films are shown with their original sound tracks and Swedish subtitles. Local newspapers have full details of programmes and times. In Stockholm, cinemas showing first-run international films include Filmstaden Sergel, Filmstaden Söder, Rigoletto, Biopalatset and Astoria. The two dominating film companies, SF and Sandrews, have websites where you can book your ticket for any cinema:
SF: www.sf.se
Sandrews: www.sandrews.se

Sport

Spectator Sports

Göteborg is probably the most sport-conscious town in Sweden, and its Scandinavium (tel: 031 81 10 20) is the venue for many major events, including tennis, ice hockey and table tennis. The city's other main arena is Ullevi Stadium (tel: 031 81 10 20), where international tournaments in football, athletics and speedway are staged regularly.

Tennis is Sweden's top spectator sport. The main tournaments are the Swedish Open at Båstad on the southwest coast in mid-July and the Stockholm Open which is held in early November.

Athletics meetings are usually in early July. Stockholm also stages a large marathon, which is usually in early June.

The famous Globen arena (tel: 08 60 03 400) in Stockholm holds sporting events and concerts.

Horse racing and trotting are popular, with courses at Stockholm (Täby), Göteborg (Åby) and Malmö (Jägersro). The Swedish Derby is in July at Jägersro, which is also the venue for a major horse show in August. Another important annual international horse show is held at the Göteborg Scandinavium in April.

Canoeing

Svenska Kanotförbundet Idrottens Hus, Storforsplan 44, SE-123 87 Farsta. Tel: 08 60 56 00 0. Fax: 08 60 56 56 5.

Cycling

Svenska Cykelsällskapet Box 6006, SE-164 06 Kista. Tel: 08 75 16 20 4. Fax: 08 75 11 93 5.

Fishing

Swedish Angling Federation Box 2, SE-163 21 Spånga. Tel: 08 79 53 35 0. Fax: 08 79 59 67 3. E-mail: hk@sportfiskarna.se

Golf

Svenska Golfförbundet Kevingestrand 20, SE-182 11 Danderyd. Tel: 08 62 21 50 0. Fax: 08 75 30 52 2. E-mail: sgf@golf.se Website: www.golf.se

Hiking

Swedish Walking and Hiking Association, Idrottens Hus, Storforsplan 44, SE-123 87 Farsta. Tel: 08 60 56 44 9. Fax: 08 60 56 44 6. **National Parks** Website: www.environ.se

Horse Riding

Svenska Ridsportförbundet Sandhamnsgatan 39, SE-115 93 Stockholm. Tel: 08 56 70 56 01. Fax: 08 56 70 56 70.

Sailing

Svenska Seglarförbundet Af Pontinsvägen 6, SE-115 21 Stockholm. Tel: 08 45 90 99 0. Fax: 08 45 90 99 9. E-mail: ssf@ssf.se

Skiing

Svenska Skidförbundet Smidesvägen 8, SE-171 18 Solna. Tel: 08 58 77 20 00. Fax: 08 58 7720 88.

Tennis

Svenska Tennisförbundet Lidingövägen 75, SE-115 94 Stockholm. Tel: 08 66 79 77 0. Fax: 08 66 46 60 6. E-mail: info@tennis.se Website: www.tennis.se

Shopping

What to Buy

Sweden is famous the world over for its elegant design, and you will find plenty of good buys in glassware, stainless steel, silver, pottery, ceramics, textiles and leather goods. Department stores such as NK and Åhléns have branches all over the country and are noted for their high-quality, inexpensive kitchenware.

Glass The best bargains are to be found in "Glass Country" – Småland, in the southeast – where there are more than 15 glassworks. Major glassworks like Orrefors, Kosta-Boda, Älghult and Skruf have shops adjoining their factories where you can pick up seconds. For flawless glass products you need to shop at the major department stores like NK, Crystal Art Centre or Nordiska Kristall in Stockholm.

Porcelain Sweden is also renowned for its high-quality porcelain, and bargains can be found at the Gustavsberg factory outside Stockholm and at the Rörstrand factory in Lidköping.

Fashion Clothing at inexpensive prices can be found at Hennes & Mauritz (H&M), Lindex, JC and KappAhl. But the best place to pick up good buys in textiles is probably Borås, 60 km (37 miles) from Göteborg. Knallebygden is a large shopping centre in Borås.

Books English-language books are widely available. In Stockholm, excellent bookshops include: Sweden Bookshop, Sweden House (Sverigehuset), Hamngatan 27. Website: www.si.se
Hedengrens Bokhandel, Stureplan 4. Website: www.hedengrens.se
Akademibokhandeln, Mäster Samuelsgatan 32, on the corner of Regeringsgatan. Website: www.akademibokhandeln.com
English Book Centre, Surbrunnsgatan 51. Website: www.engbookcen.se

Markets

Stockholm has markets at Östermalmstorg and Hötorget, while Göteborg has its Fish Church fish market. Stockholm has what is claimed to be northern Europe's largest flea market at Skärholmen, 20 minutes on the underground from the city (open daily, but Saturday and Sunday are best).

Local Crafts

In the countryside, it's worth looking out for Hemslöjd handicraft centres, where you can buy attractive locally produced items. Women's and children's clothes are especially good buys, as well as furs and needlework.
Below is just a small selection of outlets in Stockholm and Göteborg:
Svensk Hemslöjd
Sveavägen 44, Stockholm.
Tel: 08 23 21 15.
Svenskt Hantverk
Kungsgatan 55, Stockholm.
Tel: 08 21 47 26.
Bohusslöjd
Kungsportsavenyn 25, Göteborg.
Tel: 031 16 00 72.
    There's also a website for *Gula Sidorna* (*Yellow Pages*) listing shops throughout Sweden: www.gulasidorna.se (search for *hantverk*).

Design

Several shops in Stockholm are worth visiting:
DesignTorget
Kulturhuset, Sergels Torg 3.
Tel: 08 50 83 15 20 and Götgatan 31.
Tel: 08 46 23 52 0.
Norrgavel
Kungsgatan 33.
Tel: 08 20 50 10.
Svenskt Tenn
Stranvägen 5.
Tel: 08 67 01 60 0.

Language

The Alphabet

The Swedish alphabet has 29 letters. The additional three are å, ä and ö and come after the letter Z. To find Mr Åkerblad in the telephone book, therefore, look at the end of the listings.

Getting By

yes ja
no nej
hello hej
goodbye adjö
please tack/var så god
good morning god morgon
good afternoon god eftermiddag
good evening god kväll
how do you do goddag
excuse me ursäkta
thank you tack
Do you speak English? Talar du engelska?
I only speak English Jag talar bara engelska
I do not understand Jag förstår inte

Getting Around

aeroplane flygplan
bus/coach buss
car bil
train tåg
How do I get to...? Hur kommer jag till...?
Where is ...? Var är ...?

In an Emergency

accident and emergency akutmottagning
clinic vårdcentral
hospital sjukhus
doctor doktor
police station oolisstation

right höger
to the right till höger
left vänster
to the left till vänster
straight on rakt fram

Eating and Drinking

breakfast frukost
lunch lunch
dinner middag
eat äta
drink dricka
Cheers! Skål!
off-licence systembolaget
Can I order, please? Pår jag beställa?
I would like jag skulle vilja
Could I have the bill please? Kan jag få notan?
hot varm
cold kall

Shopping

Can I help you? Kan jag hjälpa till?
to buy att köpa
money pengar
How much is this? Vad kostar det?
It costs Det kostar
shop affär
department store varuhus
supermarket snabbköp
grocery store (in countryside) lanthandel
bakery bageri
chemist apotek
bookshop bokhandel
food mat
big stor
small liten

Accommodation

do you have any vacancies? har ni några lediga rum?
twin room dubbelrum med två
single room enkel rum
chalet stuga
to rent att hyra
room to rent rum att hyra
Could I have the key please? Kan jag få nyckeln?

Clothes/Laundry

clothes kläder
coat/overcoat kappa/överrock
jacket jacka

suit kostym
shoes skor
skirt kjol
blouse blus
jumper tröja, jumper
wash tvätta
launderette tvättomat
dry cleaning kemtvätt
dirty/clean smutsigt/ren

Signs

Toilet Toalett
Gentlemen Herrar
Ladies Damer
Vacant Ledig
Engaged Upptagen
No smoking Rökning förbjuden
Entrance Ingång
Exit Utgång
No entry Ingen ingång
Open öppen/öppet
Closed Stängt
Push Srag
Pull Drag

Numbers

1	en/et
2	två
3	tre
4	fyra
5	fem
6	sex
7	sju
8	åtta
9	nio
10	tio
11	elva
12	tolv
13	tretton
14	fjorton
15	femton
16	sexton
17	sjutton
18	aderton
19	nitton
20	tjugo
21	tjugoen
22	tjugotvå
30	trettio
40	fyrtio
50	femtio
60	sextio
70	sjuttio
80	åttio
90	nittio
100	hundra

Time

today idag
tomorrow i morgon
yesterday i går
morning morgan
afternoon eftermiddag
evening kväll
What time is it? Hur mycket är klockan?
it is... den är...
the time is... klockan är...
Sunday söndag
Monday måndag
Tuesday tisdag
Wednesday onsdag
Thursday torsdag
Friday fredag
Saturday lördag

Further Reading

Good books on Sweden are few and far between, but the best source of information on publications in English is the Swedish Institute, which itself publishes a good range of guides. Its website has a good list and has an ordering service.

Svenska Institutet
Hamngatan 27, Kungstradgarden
Box 7434, 103 91 Stockholm.
Tel: 08 78 92 00 0.
Fax: 08 20 72 48.
Website: www.si.se./ (Search under Sweden bookshop.)

History

Sweden: A Traveller's History by Eric Elstob (Boydell Press). Swedish history from its beginnings.
Swedish History in Outline by Jörgen Welbull (Swedish Institute).
The Vikings, Lord of the Seas by Yves Cohat (Thames &Hudson). History of the Vikings, with excellent colour photography.

Architecture

A Home by Lena Rydin (Carl Larsson Gården/Dalaförlaget). Artist Carl Larsson's farm in Sundborn in the Dalarna region in photographs and paintings.
Great Royal Palaces of Sweden by Göran Alm (M.T. Train/Scala Books). A dozen castles, palaces and pavilions belonging to Swedish royalty over the past 500 years.

Art and Design

A History of Swedish Art by Mereth Lindgren, Louise Lyberg, Birgitta Sandström and Anna Greta Wahlberg (Bokförlaget Signum). A bird's-eye view of Swedish painting, sculpture and architecture.
The Swedish Room by Lars Sjöberg and Ursula Sjöberg (Frances Lincoln Limited). Some of Sweden's most classic interiors.

Food

The Swedish Kitchen: A Culinary Journey by Lennart Hagerfors (Norstedts). A cookbook by one of the best-known chefs in Sweden, with 198 modern Swedish recipes.
Smörgasbord: A Swedish Classic by Kerstin Torngre (Swedish Institute). A short guide to Sweden's traditional buffet spread.

Fiction

The Wonderful Adventures of Nils and **The Further Adventures of Nils** by Selma Lagerlöv. Captivating stories about a boy who flies around Sweden on a goose, have made Lagerlöv one of the nation's most popular children's authors. As travelogues, they're enjoyable for adults too.

Guides

Live and Work in Scandinavia by Victoria Pybus and Susan Dunne (Vacation Work Publications). Jobs and how to obtain them.
Sailing in Sweden by Bobby Andström (Legenda). A personal account.
National Parks in Sweden: Europe's Last Wilderness edited by Ingvar Bingman (The National Environment Protection Board, available through the Swedish Institute). Details of Sweden's vast forest land.
Off the Beaten Track – Scandinavia edited by Margaret Rogers and Robin Rogers (Moorland Publishing). Places of character to stay in away from the tourist trail.

Other Insight Guides

Over 200 titles in the acclaimed **Insight Guides** series cover every continent. Titles in the region include *Sweden*, *Norway*, *Denmark*, and *Finland*. Insight **Compact Guides** to the region include *Norway*, *Denmark*, *Copenhagen* and *Finland*. Insight **Fleximaps** are durable, weatherproof and easy to fold. Scandinavian titles include *Stockholm*, *Copenhagen* and *Norway*.

FINLAND

The Place

Area 338,000 sq km (130,600 sq miles).
Capital Helsinki.
Population 5.1 million, of whom about 40 percent live in rural areas and around one million in greater Helsinki.
Language Finnish and Swedish; Sami is spoken by the indigenous people of Lapland.
Religion About 87 percent are Evangelical Lutheran, with 1 percent Finnish Orthodox and 12 percent unaffiliated.
Time zone Greenwich Mean Time (GMT) + 2 hours; Eastern Standard Time (EST) + 7 hours.
Currency Markka (Finnmark/FIM).
Weights and measures Metric.
Electricity 220 AC (two-pin plug).
International dialling code: +358.

Geography

Finland is set on the Baltic Sea. Its neighbouring countries are Sweden, Norway, Russia and on the opposite shore of the Baltic, Estonia. Finland is 65 percent covered by forest, 10 percent by lakes, and 8 percent by cultivated land.

Climate

Finland has cold winters and fairly warm summers. In July, the south has similar temperatures to England, Holland and Belgium, though there is less rain and more sunshine. The hottest months are July to August, when average temperatures are 18°C (65°F); the coldest are January and February, averaging -4°C (25°F). In south and central Finland snow settles at the start of December and melts in mid to late April (or May in the forests).

In the north the snowy season comes about five weeks earlier and ends about three weeks later.

Economy

Until the end of World War II Finland received a modest income from agriculture and the textile trade. Since then the lords of Finnish industry have been pulp and paper products/machinery, forestry, a few electronics and engineering giants (such as Nokia mobile telephones) and Neste oil refining. Today only 10 percent of the population is involved in farming.

Government

Finland is a parliamentary democracy with a president, a prime minister and a 200-member, single-chamber parliament. The president is elected, while the prime minister is chosen by a conference of parties participating in the current government. Coalition governments led by Social Democrats have dominated Finland's short history as an independent republic. In 2000, Tarja Halonen, a Social Democrat, was elected president for a six-year term and has the distinction of being Finland's first woman to hold this office. With several other women in positions of power, this was not considered unusual.

Tourist Info at Home

● **UK**
Finnish Tourist Board
30 Pall Mall, London SW1Y 5LP
Tel: 020 7839 4048
No personal callers.
● **US/Canada**
Scandinavia Tourist Board, 655 3rd Avenue, New York, NY 1007
Tel: 212-885 9700
● **Australia**
The Embassy supplies tourist information.
● **Websites**
Finland: www.finland-tourism.com
Helsinki: www.hel.fi/english

The People

Finland is the sixth-largest land area in Europe, but the population is extremely sparse with only 16 inhabitants per sq km (6 per sq mile).

In general Finns are courteous, particularly to foreign guests, about whom they are quite curious. If you are going to a Finn's house for dinner, take a plant or flowers; and a bottle of wine or other spirits is always appreciated considering the high cost of alcohol.

Planning the Trip

Visas and Passports

Citizens of most western countries do not need visas to travel to Finland; a valid passport will suffice. EU citizens may enter with a valid ID card.

Customs

The following items may be brought into Finland.

Cigarettes/tobacco
Non-EU citizens over 17 years of age may bring in 200 cigarettes, 50 cigars or 250 g (1–2 lb) tobacco products duty free. Europeans aged 17 or over can bring in 300 cigarettes, 75 cigars or 400 g of tobacco products.

Alcohol
Any visitor aged 20 or over can bring in 15 litres of beer, 2 litres of other mild alcohol (drinks containing not more than 22 percent by volume of alcohol) and 1 litre of strong alcohol (spirits). For visitors of 18 years of age, the quantity limit is the same, but must not include strong alcohol.

Health

You'll have little to worry about healthwise in Finland. However, you may have an uncomfortable time with the mosquitoes in northern and central parts in July and August. Ask your GP about mosquito treatment before you go and enquire at chemists in Finland about the most effective repellant.
Finland's medical facilities have an excellent reputation worldwide. The country has reciprocal health

Tour Operators

● **Bridge Travel Service**
Bridge House, 55-59 High
Street, Broxbourne,
Herts EN10 7DT.
Tel: 01992 456300.
● **Crystal Holidays**
Crystal House, Arlington Road,
Surbiton, Surrey
KT6 6BW.
Tel: 01235 824324.
● **Norvista**
227 Regent Street, London
W1R 8PD.
Tel: 020 7409 7334.
● **Page & Moy**
136–140 London Road, Leicester
LE2 1EN.
Tel: 0116 250 7979.

● **ScanMeridian**
28b Hampstead High Street,
London NW3 1QA.
Tel: 020 7431 5393.
● **Scantours**
47 Whitcomb Street, London
WC2H 7DH.
Tel: 020 7839 2927.
● **Scandinavian Travel Service**
2 Berghem Mews, Blythe Road,
London W14 0HN.
Tel: 020 7559 6666; brochure
line tel: 01443 82222.
● **Wilderness Adventure/ Peak
International**
15 Moor Park, Wendover,
Aylesbury HP22 6AX.
Tel: 01296 624 225.

arrangements with other EU
members, so visitors are entitled to
the same treatment as Finns (UK
citizens must provide an E111
form, available from post offices).

Money Matters

Finland's unit of currency is the
markka (Finnmark or FIM), referred
to as a "mark". There are 100
pennies (p) in the markka. There
are 10p, 50p, 1 FIM, 5 FIM and
10 FIM coins. Notes are available in
20, 50, 100, 500 and 1000 FIM
denominations. Finland will adopt
Euro bank notes and coins by
2003. Shops and businesses
operate a rounding-off system; if
the cash register rings up 50
markkas and 74 pennies, for
example, you pay 50 markkas and
70 pennies.

How to pay

Credit cards MasterCard, Visa,
Diner's Club and American Express
are accepted in most
establishments in main cities.
Traveller's cheques and common
currencies can easily be exchanged
in banks.
ATMs Automatic Teller Machines
marked OTTO give local currency if
you have a card with an international pin number (Visa, Cirrus,
PLUS, MasterCard and so on).

What to Bring

The best advice on packing for
Finland is to bring layers of clothes,
no matter what the season. In
winter, gloves, long underwear,
hats, woollen tights and socks, and
several layers of cotton topped by
wool and something waterproof are
recommended. In winter, bring
heavy-duty footgear not only to keep
out damp but to avoid good shoes
being ruined by salt and gravel put
down to melt the ice on pavements.
Spring and autumn are rainy, and
summers are usually pleasantly dry
and sunny, but occasionally wet.

Getting There

BY AIR

Finnair, the national carrier of
Finland, operates internationally
and has national routes to more
than 20 cities. Both Finnair and
British Airways connect London and
Helsinki with daily flights. Finnair
(and many other airlines, especially
SAS) fly direct between Helsinki and
most European capitals, and Finnair
also links with several North
American cities including New York.

SAS Tel: 0845 60727727.
Website: www.flysas.co.uk
Finnair Tel: 0990 997711.

Website: www.finnair.fi
British Airways Tel: 0345 222111.
Website: www.britishairways.com

Value-for-money packages and
charter flights from New York or
London are available from the
Norvista Tours in London.
Tel: 020 7409 7334.
Fax: 020 409 7733.

BY SEA

The Silja Line and Viking Line
operate daily ferries between
Stockholm and Helsinki that are
reasonably priced, luxurious and
well equipped with restaurants,
saunas, swimming pools, tax-free
shops and children's playrooms.
Silja Line Tel: 9 18 04 1.
Fax: 9 18 0 4 27 6.
Website: www.Silja.com
Viking Line Tel: 9 12 35 1.
Fax: 9 64 70 75.
Website: www.vikingline.fi

BY RAIL

It's a long haul to Finland from just
about anywhere by rail, because
you inevitably finish the trip north
with a 15-hour journey by boat and
train from Stockholm to Helsinki.
From Britain, the handiest route is
Sealink from Harwich to the Hook
of Holland, overland to
Copenhagen, then connecting train
to Stockholm and boat or boat and
train to Helsinki. Total travel time is
about 45 hours. To get to north
Finland you have to end the journey
by bus as Finnish rail lines run only
as far as Rovaniemi and Kemijärvi
(or Kolari in winter).

Practical Tips

NEWSPAPERS AND BOOKS

With the exception of the *International Herald Tribune*, which arrives on the afternoon of its publication date, you'll have to wait a day and a half for English-language newspapers to get to Helsinki. Foreign papers are sold at Helsinki railway station and Akateeminen Kirjakauppa (Academic Bookstore) at Pohjoisesplanadi 39, where you can also get books in English), and at the larger hotels in other cities, as well as at main airports.

TOURIST PUBLICATIONS

Helsinki Happens, free from the tourist office at Vantaa Airport and most hotels, is an English-language guide to cultural and tourist events in the capital.

Business Hours

Shops In larger cities generally 9am–5pm, with late-night opening on Thursday. In Helsinki, many open until 9pm on weekdays and 6pm on Saturday. Larger food stores usually open 9am–8pm weekdays and 9am–4pm on Saturday. The only really late shops are in the tunnel under the Helsinki railway station: open weekdays 10am–10pm and weekend noon–10pm. **Banks** Monday to Friday 9.15am –4.15pm, *bureaux de change* open a bit later. The one at the airport opens daily 6am–11pm.

City, a weekly newspaper with a calendar of cultural events and restaurant listings in Helsinki, publishes a quarterly edition in English available at most hotels. *Helsinki This Week* is published by the Finnish Tourist office and available at most hotels.

RADIO AND TELEVISION

For news in English, you can tune in to 103.7 FM in Helsinki or to channel 1 at around 9am on weekdays. Transmission time changes with the season, so ask the tourist board for an updated schedule; they will also supply information on broadcasts in other parts of Finland. Many hotels subscribe to British or US cable news networks.

Emergency Numbers

Ambulance, rescue services, fire department and police 112
24-hour medical advice hotline (Helsinki only) 10 023

Postal Services

Post offices are open 9am–5pm. Services include stamps, registered mail and *poste restante*. The *poste restante* address is Elielinaukio, 00100 Helsinki. It's on the railway square side of the main post office (Mannerheiminaukio 1) and is open Monday to Friday 7am–9pm, Saturday 9am–6pm and Sunday 11am–9pm.

Telecommunications

Public telephones take either coins or phonecards (on sale at most kiosks and in the City Tourist office at Pohjoisesplanadi 9, Helsinki). The best way to call overseas cheaply is at post and telegraph offices in main cities. Look for the *Lennätin* (telecommunications) section. To make a standard direct call, use any booth with a green light and pay the cashier afterwards. You must dial 00, 999, 994 or 990 to get a line

Public Holidays

● **1 January** New Year's Day
● **6 January** Epiphany
● **March/April** Good Friday, Easter Sunday
● **1 May** May Day
● **May/June** Ascension Day
● **May/June** Whitsun
● **end of June** Midsummer's Eve and Day
● **early November** All Saints' Day
● **6 December** Independence Day
● **24–26 December** Christmas Eve and Day, Boxing Day

outside. Don't forget that hotels usually add surcharges for calls made from your room.

MOBILE PHONES

One in five Finns owns a mobile. The two Finnish operators are Radiolinja (numbers starting with 050) and Sonera (040). A GSM1800 system is currently expanding, and may soon be available in major towns.

Business Travellers

Doing business in Finland does not differ greatly from elsewhere in Europe, with a few exceptions. **Business hours:** Lunch can be as early as 11am. Offices operate from 8am to 4pm, and in summer until 3pm. **Business style:** Finns tend to present things as they are, warts and all. They do not go in for exaggeration, so their way of selling things might seem a bit subdued. **Business entertaining:** You are as likely to be invited on a ski outing or sailing trip as on a night out on the town. These days, Finns tend not to drink at lunch, but after-hours drinking is still *de rigueur*. **Etiquette:** Finns are punctual and courteous, though formal. Handshakes are good for all occasions **Holidays:** Try to avoid business in July and early August. Other blackout periods for business are the spring skiing break in late

February (southern Finland) or early March (northern Finland), plus two weeks over Christmas and a week at Easter.

Medical Services

HOSPITALS

If you need medical treatment, almost any *Terveysasema* (health clinic) or *Sairaala* (hospital) will treat you for a nominal fee or will bill your insurance firm. All doctors speak English. Casualty is generally called *Ensiapu*. Visitors needing hospital care in Helsinki should contact the following:
For surgery and medicine:
Meilahti Hospital, Haartmaninkatu 4, Helsinki. Tel: 9 47 11, or the 24-medical advice hotline (*see Emergency Numbers, page 406*).
For serious accidents:
Helsinki University Hospitals' Töölö Hospital, Topeliuksenkatu 5, Helsinki. Tel: 9 47 11.
For medicine and surgery:
Meilahti Hospital, Haartmaninkatu 4, Helsinki. Tel: 9 47 11.
For 24-hour private medical care:
Mehiläinen, Runeberginkatu 47a, Helsinki. Tel: 9 43 14 44 4.

PHARMACIES

A pharmacy is called *apteekki*. There is usually at least one open late night in larger towns. In Helsinki, the Yliopiston Apteekki at Mannerheimintie 96 is open 24 hours a day.

DENTISTS

In emergencies: Ympyrätalo Dental Clinic, Siltasaarenkatu 18A, Helsinki. Tel: 9 70 96 61 1.

Tourist Information

Finland has over 50 main tourist information offices, marked with an "i", as well as many summer tourist offices. The following are the main tourist offices, but a full list can be obtained at most offices:

Finnish Tourist Board
Eteläesplanadi 4, 00130 Helsinki. Tel: 9 4176 9300. Fax: 4176 9301. Postal address: PO Box 249, 00131 Helsinki.
Helsinki City Tourist Office
Pohjoisesplanadi 19, 00100. Helsinki. Tel: 9 16 93 75 7. Fax: 9 16 93 83 9.
Rovaniemi Tourist Information
Koskikatu 7, 96200 Rovaniemi. Tel: 16 34 62 70. Fax: 16 34 24 65 0.
Tampere City Tourist Office
Verkatehtaankatu 2, FIN-33101 Tampere. Tel: 3 31 46 68 00. Fax: 3 31 46 64 63.
Turku City Tourist Office
Aurakatu 4, 20100 Turku. Tel: 2 26 27 44 4. Fax: 2 23 36 48 8.

Security and Crime

Until recently vandalism was the only noticeable sign of crime. But now lone pedestrians may encounter groups of inebriated young men looking for a challenge late at night. Try to walk on busy streets and keep out of their way.

There is also occasional pickpocketing on the Helsinki metro and at main railway stations. Be on your guard and avoid using these forms of transport after 11pm.

Religious Services

In Helsinki, services in English are held at the Temppeliaukio Church, and the Church in the Rock on Lutherinkatu. There is one mosque and one synagogue in Helsinki.

Disabled Travellers

Travelling should not pose big problems. The Finnish Tourist Board has a list of travel agencies that specialise in tours for the disabled traveller. Most newer buildings have access for disabled people, and the Tourist Board's *Finland Hotel Guide* indicates which hotels have access and facilities for disabled people. When ordering a taxi, specify your needs (wheelchair is *pyörätuoli*). Some city buses "kneel", making it

easier to board. For more information, contact: Rullatenry, Pajutie 7C 02770 Espoo. Tel: 9 80 57 39 3. Fax: 9 85 52 47 0. E-mail: hile.meckelborg@pp.kolumbus.fi

Travelling with Kids

In Helsinki, the Tourist Board can provide a list of babysitters.

ATTRACTIONS

Heureka, the Finnish Science Centre (in Tikkurila 15 minutes by train from downtown Helsinki), has permanent and temporary "hands-on" exhibitions, a planetarium and an IMAX theatre. Tel: 9 85 799.

There are several good spots in the Lakeland region:
The Messilä Vacation Centre, in Hollola near Lahti, features many supervised activities, including pony riding and (in winter) skiing.
The Musta and Valkea Ratsu Dollshouse and Puppet Theatre is north of Hollola, towards Hartola, on road 52 (signposted), 19230 Onkiniemi. Tel: 3 71 86 95 9.
The Land of the Mountain Troll, in Outokumpu, north of Savonlinna, is an amusement park and mineral and mining exhibition.
The Visulahti Tourist Centre in Mikkeli has a dinosaur theme park and waxworks. Not far away is an arboretum. Tel: 15 15 14 44.
Santa Claus's Village Rovaniemi, near the Arctic Circle. Rumour has it Santa stops off here when travelling from his secret hideaway. Open daily year round.
Åland Islands Check out the amusement park by the west harbour, Pommern ship museum at the west harbour, and Lilla Holmen bird park on the east harbour.

Embassies/Consulates

UK
Itäinen Puistotie 17
Tel: 9 22 86 51 00
US
Itäinen Puistotie 14, Helsinki
Tel: 9 17 19 31

Getting Around

On Arrival

Finland's main international airport, Helsinki-Vantaa, is connected by Finnair bus to central spots in Helsinki. Yellow taxis are slightly cheaper than regular ones because they take a minimum of four passengers and take longer to reach destinations.

By Air

Finnair and Air Botnia both operate domestic flights. Fares are relatively inexpensive all year round, but particularly cheap in July. For more information, contact:
Finnair www.finnair.com
Air Botnia Tel: 9 22 80 22 22 in Finland.

Passes

The Finnair Holiday Pass offers up to 10 flights over a period of 30 days (but is not valid on Blue Flights, which are usually the most popular business travel times). The pass is available to any foreign resident who flies to Finland, and can be obtained from Finnair and the Norvista travel agency in London (tel: 020 7409 7334). as well as other agencies in the UK and some in the US.

By Rail

The Finnish train network offers good services to major places such as Turku and Helsinki.

Passes

Finnrail passes are available for three, five or 10 days. In summer, you can get a Loma-Lippu (Holiday Ticket) for three or seven days in a

month. For information, contact:
Finnish State Railways
Vilhonkatu 13, PB 488, 00101 Helsinki.
Tel: 9 70 71. Fax: 9 70 74 29 0.
Website: www.vr.fi

By Water

The Silverline and Poet's Way begins in Tampere and covers much of the western Lakelands, with tours in the Päijänne region and over the country's largest lake, Saimaa, in eastern Finland. Many other operators run trips on the lakes. For details, contact local tourist offices, or the following:
Silverline and Poet's Way
Tel: 3 21 24 80 3
Lake Päijänne Cruises
Tel: 14 61 88 85
Roll Cruises of Kuopio
Tel: 17 26 26 74 4
   Helsinki's only real commuter island is Suomenlinna, with ferries travelling roughly every half hour.

By Bus/Coach

There are coach services on 90 percent of public roads (with 40,000 long-distance departures a day) that cover the areas that trains don't, particularly in the north.
   For details about buses, contact:
Matkahuolto, Lauttasaarentie 8, 00200 Helsinki. Tel: 9 68 27 01. Fax: 9 69 22 86 4.

By Car

Finland's roads are not too plagued by traffic, although they do get very busy between the capital and the countryside on Friday and Sunday during summer.
   Foreign cars entering Finland should carry a nationality sticker. In most cases, your own insurance with a green card will suffice to drive in Finland, but check ahead to be sure. If you are driving a foreign car and are involved in an accident, contact the Finnish Motor Insurers' Bureau. Tel: 9 68 04 01.
   Pay attention to road signs showing elk and reindeer zones, as collisions with these animals are

usually serious. Be especially careful at dusk when the animals are most active.

Rules of the road

● Drive on the right and overtake on the left. Exceptions are on roads marked by a triangle sign; if this is facing you, you must give right of way; if you are on a major road it is likely that the feed-in streets will have triangles, giving you the right of way. The first vehicle to reach the roundabout has right of way.
● Headlights are obligatory outside built-up areas, at dusk, at night or in bad weather (UK cars must have stickers over their lights to divert the beam).
● Seat belts are compulsory for both drivers and passengers.
● Speed limits are signposted, and range from 30 kmph (18 mph) in school zones to 100 kmph (62 mph) on motorways.
● Studded tyres are compulsory from 1 December to 28 February or when weather conditions require.
● Do not drink drive. Fines are steep and imprisonment possible.

By Taxi

Taxis run throughout the country. City centres, as well as most major airports, bus and railway stations, have stands. Otherwise, local telephone books list the number of the nearest firms (under *Taksi* in the *White Pages*). It is worth finding the closest one as taxis charge from their point of departure (and add an order fee). In a few places you can also hail a cab in the street.

By Bicycle

Finland is a good cycling country. Some hotels, holiday villages, camp sites, tourist information offices and most youth hostels hire out bicycles. The Finnish Youth Hostel Association offers planned routes (including accommodation).
Finnish Youth Hostel Association
Yrjänkatu 38B, 00100 Helsinki.
Tel: 9 69 40 37 7. Fax: 9 69 31 34 9. E-mail: info@srm.inet.fi

Where to Stay

Choosing a Hotel

Hotels throughout Finland are clean and well equipped, though expensive. A good breakfast buffet is usually included and one can find bargains at the chain hotels (generally up to 60 per cent of standard prices) at weekends, and in summer when they lose their business and conference trade.

Budget accommodation includes youth and family hostels, farmhouses, guesthouses, family villages, camping and various forms of self-catering. During the summer holidays, some student residences become Summer Hotels, opening on 1 June. Details of youth hostels are available from:
The Finnish Youth Hostel Association, Yrjsnkatu 38B, 00100 Helsinki. Tel: 9 69 40 37 7. Fax: 9 69 31 34 9. E-mail: info@srm.inet.fi

Local tourist offices and booking centres will provide up-to-date prices, including details of weekend and summer discounts. General information on accommodation is available from the Finnish Tourist Board in your home country, or from the head office in Helsinki (see Tourist Information, page 405). Or Helsinki has its own booking centre at the railway station:
Hotel Booking Centre, Asema-aukio 3. Tel: 9 22 88 14 00. Fax: 9 17 55 24. E-mail: hklapj@hel.fi

Hotel Chains

Finland has many large hotel chains of its own, as well as foreign ones. Scandic, Sokos and Cumulus offer fairly comfortable standard services in most big towns; Radisson SAS and others have even more comfortable facilities. Most are reliable, with clean rooms and restaurants with identical menus. Some of the best known are:
Best Western Finland
Annankatu 29A, 00100 Helsinki
Tel: 9 64 55 00
Cumulus
Restel Hotel Group
Tel: 800 1 28 68
Fax: 9 73 35 39 9
E-mail: webmaster@restel.fi
Scandic
Tel: 800 0 69 69
Fax: 9 61 64 39 58
E-mail: info@scandic-hotels.com
Sokos Hotels
Tel: 9 13 10 01
Fax: 9 13 10 02 90
E-mail: sokos.hotel@sok.fi
Summer Hotels
YrjSnkatu 38, 00100 Helsinki
Tel: 9 69 31 34 7

Discounts

A systematic way to get discounts is to enrol in the Finncheque scheme, in which some 250 hotels participate. By spending around 200 markka on a Finncheque, you get a night's free accommodation in these hotels.

Further details can be obtained from the Finnish Tourist Office in Helsinki (see page 408).

Price Guide

Price categories are based on the average cost (including tax) of a double room with breakfast.
$$$ £150–200
$$ £100–150
$ £50–100

HELSINKI

SAS Scandic Hotel Continental
Mannerheimintie 46, 00260
Tel: 9 40 55 1
Fax: 9 40 55 32 55
E-mail: continentalhelsinki@scandic-hotels.com
One of Helsinki's oldest upmarket hotels. Well-furnished rooms with all amenities, many with park views. Sauna, massage and pool. $$$

Scandic Hotel Simonkenttä
Simonkatu 9
Tel: 9 68 380
Fax: 9 68 38 11
E-mail: simonkentta@scandic-hotels.com
New hotel (opened 2000) in the city centre. Comfortably furnished; some rooms have their own sauna and terrace with magnificent views. $$$
Klaus Kurki
Bulevardi 2–4, 00120
Tel: 9 61 89 11
Fax: 9 60 85 38
Website: www.sokoshotels.fi
On a pretty street with a popular bar, restaurant and deli. Attracts a modern urban crowd. $$$
Hotel Anna
Annankatu 1, 00120
Tel: 9 61 66 21
Fax: 9 60 26 64
E-mail: info@hotelanna.com
Quiet, comfortable and centrally located with 64 rooms with all amenities. Excellent breakfast buffet. $$
Radisson SAS Plaza
Mikonkatu 23, 00100
Tel: 9 77 59 0
Fax: 9 77 59 71 00
Website: www.radissonsas.com
All modern amenities. $$
Torni
Yrjsnkatu 26, 00100
Tel: 9 131 13 1
Fax: 9 13 11 36 1
Website: sokoshotels.fi
Gracious 13-storey hotel with an older Art Deco-style section. $$
Academica
Hietaniemenkatu 14, 00100
Tel: 9 13 11 43 34
Fax: 9 44 12 01
E-mail: hostel.academica@hyy.fi
Basic summer hotel providing small, modern rooms with their own kitchen. Family rooms available. $
Eurohostel
Linnankatu 9, 00160
Tel: 9 62 20 47 0
Fax: 9 65 50 44
E-mail: eurohostel@eurohostel.fi
Located on Katajanokka Island by the ferry terminals, this no-frills hostel has shared facilities including kitchen, laundrettes, sauna and café. $

THE SOUTH

Hanko
Pensionat Garbo
Raatimiehenkatu 8, 10900
Tel: 19 24 87 89 7
Like a Hollywood museum – each themed room features a star from the silver screen. **$$**
Villa Maija
Appelgrenintie 7, 10900 Hanko
Tel: 19 24 84 91 7
This fine 19th-century villa is one of many on this attractive street. **$$**

Kotka
Sokos Hotel Seurahuone
Keskuskatu 21, 48100
Tel: 5 18 60 90
Fax: 5 18 68 81
Website: www.sokoshotels.fi
This very central hotel has superb rooms and a fine restaurant. **$$$**

Naantali
Naantali Spa & Congress Hotel
21100 Naantali
Tel: 2 44 55 0
Fax: 2 44 55 62 1
Website: www.naantalispa.fi
In a charming seaside town near Turku, this unique hostelry offers luxury in a yacht next to the spa. **$$**

Turku
Scandic Marina Palace
Linnankatu 32, 20100
Tel: 2 33 63 00
Fax: 2 25 16 75 0
E-mail: marinapalace@scandichotels.com
Picturesque riverside spot, with all amenities and attractive rooms. Bar, restaurants, meeting rooms. **$$$**
Good Morning Hotels Ateljee
Humalistonkatu 7, 20100
Tel: 2 33 61 11
Fax: 2 33 66 99
Designed by Alvar Aalto. Two of the 230 well-equipped rooms contain furniture by the master. Many artists display their works here. **$$**
Scandic Hotel Plaza Turku
Yliopistonkatu 29
Tel: 2 33 200
Fax: 2 332 01 11
E-mail: plazaturku@scandic-hotels.com
Designed in 1929 by Erik

Bryggman, a friend of Alvar Aalto, this hotel has 107 comfortable and simply styled rooms. Good restaurant and popular bar. **$$$**
Park Hotel
Rauhankatu 1, 20100
Tel: 2 27 325 55
Fax: 2 25 196 96
E-mail: spaavola@netti.fi
This elegant Jugenstil building (1902) was once a private mansion. Each of the well-furnished rooms is different, some with a park view. **$$**
Turku City Hostel
Linnankatu 39
Tel: 2 26 27 68 0
Fax: 2 26 27 67 5
E-mail: hoteltk@saunalahti.fi
A reasonably priced alternative within walking distance of sights. **$**
Best Western Hotel Seaport
Matkustajasatama (Passenger Harbour), 20100
Tel: 2 28 33 00 0
Fax: 2 28 33 100
Website: www.bestwestern.fi/seaport
By the castle, a 19th-century warehouse with red-brick facade in original neo-Gothic style with beautiful wooden beams inside. **$**

LAKELAND

Imatra
Scandic Hotel Imatran Valtionhotelli
Torkkelinkatu 2, 55100
Tel: 5 68 88 1
Fax: 5 68 88 88 88
E-mail: imatra@scandic-hotels.com
Art Nouveau castle, next to the Imatra rapids. **$$$**

Jyvsskyla
Hotel Yspuu
Yliopistonkatu 23, 40100
Tel: 14 33 39 00
Fax: 14 62 05 88
E-mail: hotelli.yopuu@co.inet.fi
Best of this chain. **$$$**

Kuopio
Scandic Hotel Kuopio
Satamakatu 1
Tel: 17 19 511 1
Fax: 17 19 517 0
E-mail: kuopio@scandic-hotels.com

This large hotel on the waterfront is one of the finest in town. **$$$**
Sokos Hotel Puijonsarvi
Minna Canthinkatu 16, 70100
Tel: 17 17 01 11
Fax: 17 17 01 17
E-mail: sales.puijonsarvi.sok.fi
Modern, pleasant ambience. **$$$**
Hotel-Spa Rauhalahti
Katiskaniementie 8, 70700
Tel: 17 47 34 73
Fax: 17 47 34 70
Website: www.travel.fi/int/Rauhalahti
This fine spa hotel includes a wing with budget apartments. **$–$$**

Lappeenranta
Scandic Hotel Patria
Kauppakatu 21, 53100
Tel: 5 67 75 11
Fax: 5 45 12 44 1
E-mail: patria@scandic-hotels.com
Modern hotel close to the harbour and fortress area; 130 rooms, restaurants and saunas. **$$$**

Punkaharju
Punkaharjun Valtionhotelli
58450 Punkaharju 2
Tel: 15 73 96 11
Fax: 15 44 17 84
Wooden Russian-style villa with lots of ambience and 24 rooms. **££**

Savonlinna
Spa Hotel Casino
Kasinosaari, 57130
Tel: 15 73 95 0
Fax: 15 27 25 24
E-mail: casino.myynti@svlkylpylaitos.fi.
Large complex, on an island. Cheap hostel beds in summer. **$$$**
Perhehotelli Hospitz
Linnankatu 20, 57130
Tel: 15 51 56 61
Fax: 15 51 51 20
Cosy, family-run hotel. Often fully booked in summer. **$$**

Tampere
Cumulus Koskikatu
Koskikatu 5, 33100
Tel: 3 24 24 11 1
Fax: 3 24 24 39 9
E-mail: koskikatu.cumulus@restel.fi
Vibrantly modern with excellent bar and dining facilities. **$$**

Sokos Hotel Tammer
Satakunnankatu 13, 33100
Tel: 3 22 281 11
Fax: 3 23 30 75 7
Website: www.sokoshotels.fi
Dramatic hotel, part Art Deco. Set
in a green, hilly district. **$$**

Victoria
Itsenäisyydenkatu 1, 33100
Tel: 3 24 251 11
Fax: 3 24 25 10 0
Website: www.finntrip.fi
Simple hostel with a lively bar and
restaurant. **$** (group discounts)

WEST COAST

Oulu

Spa Hotel Eden
Nallikari, 90500
Tel: 8 55 04 10 0
Fax: 8 55 04 10 0
Spa facilities in a beach area. **$$$**

KARELIA

Joensuu

Sokos Hotel Kimmel
Itäranta 1, 80100
Tel: 13 27 71 11
Fax: 13 27 72 11 2
E-mail: minna.taponen@sok.fi
The town's liveliest evening spot.
Request a quiet room. **$$$**

LAPLAND

Rovaniemi

Rantasipi Pohjanhovi
Pohjanpuistikko 2, 96200
Tel: 16 33 71 1
Fax: 16 31 39 97
E-mail: hotel@pohjanhovi.fi.
Legendary luxury riverside hotel
with pool, nightclub and casino.
$$$

Price Guide

Price categories are based on
the average cost (including tax)
of a double room with breakfast.
$$$ £150–200
$$ £100–150
$ £50–100

Where to Eat

What to Eat

Finnish cuisine has broadened and
improved enormously in recent
years. The wild game dishes are a
real treat and are usually served
with exquisite mushroom and berry
sauces. In summer, you are strongly
recommended to try *ravut* (crayfish).
Crayfish feasts are often held in
hotel restaurants and include lots
of *schnapps* and songs!

Finns tend to eat a large hot
lunch, then a smaller cold meal in
the evening. Dining out has become
more popular, with Italian, Chinese
and French restaurants in almost all
major towns. The best Russian
cuisine outside of Russia is found
in Helsinki.

Where to Eat

In the past, it was difficult to get a
really cheap meal in Finland, but
you can find places where you will
definitely get value for money. Fixed-
price lunches are often very good
deals and are usually advertised on
boards outside restaurants. The
Sokos and Stockmann department
stores have excellent food halls;
otherwise, for snacks there are
more and more cafés sprouting up
that supply sandwiches, quiche,
soups and salads at reasonable
prices.

Many hotels (particularly Sokos
and Scandic) in Helsinki, Turku,
Tampere and elsewhere have good
restaurants, ranging from gourmet
to wine bars and cafés.

Restaurant Listings

Restaurants are listed in
alphabetical order by region, with
the most expensive first.

HELSINKI

Bellevue
Rahapajankatu 3. Tel: 9 17 95 60
Superb cuisine in Helsinki's oldest
and most refined Russian
restaurant. **$$$**

George
Kalevankatu 17. Tel: 9 64 76 62
Excellent, with Finnish ingredients
served elegantly and originally. **$$$**

Pääkonttori (Radisson SAS)
Mikonkatu 23. Tel: 9 77 59 60 01
Seasonal Finnish ingredients
prepared in a refined manner. The
Bistro offers more casual fare. **$$$**

Price Guide

Price categories are based on an
average cost per head of a three-
course meal (excluding drinks but
with tax):
$$$ more than £25
$$ £10–25
$ under £10

Walhalla
Suomenlinna. Tel: 9 66 85 52
Open in summer, this restaurant is
set in the old fortress. Seafood and
game are specialities. **$$$**

Babushka Ira
Uudenmaankatu 28
Tel: 9 680 14 05
Charming restaurant with adjoining
café serving an extensive buffet of
Russian delicacies. **$$**

Kynsilaukka Garlic Restaurant
Fredrikinkatu 22. Tel: 9 65 19 39
Specialises in garlicky food. **$$**

Lappi
Annankatu 22. Tel: 9 64 55 50
Authentic Lapland food. **$$**

Maxill
Korkeavuorenkatu 4
Tel: 9 63 88 73
Has a loyal clientele who come for
the consistently good menu. **$$**

Pulp
Mannerheiminaukio 3
Tel: 9 68 44 29 0
A chic watering hole with simple yet
very refined cooking. **$$**

Bar Tapasta
Uudenmaankatu 13. Tel: 9 64 07 24
Where the young and hip come for
tapas, pasta and good wine. **$**

KarlJohan
Yrjönkatu 21. Tel: 9 61 21 12 1
Traditional Finnish dishes at fair
prices. Homey atmosphere. **$**

Kasvis
Korkeavuorenkatu 3. Tel: 9 63 68 92
Delicious vegetarian with an ethnic
flair til 6pm daily except Sunday. **$**

THE SOUTH

Turku
Summer in Turku is not complete
without a session in one of the
dozen boat restaurants on the River
Aurajoki.

Enkeliravintola
Kauppiaskatu 16. Tel 2 23 19 08 8
Fine restaurant serving delicious
food. Desserts are excellent. **$$$**

Pinella
Porthaninpuisto. Tel: 2 25 17 55 7
Popular place serving delicious
crêpes and seafood. Just below is
Ribs, serving steaks and grilled ribs
in a cave-like ambience. **$$**

Samppalinna
Itäinen Rantakatu. Tel: 2 31 11 65
Continental cuisine. **$$**

Panimoravintola Herman
Läntinen Rantakatu 37
Tel: 2 23 03 33 3
This brewery-restaurant serves a
popular inexpensive lunch buffet on
its ground level, while upstairs more
gourmet food is offered. **$–$$**

Sergio's Pasta House
Linnankatu 3. Tel: 2 23 30 06 8
A good selection of pastas,
sandwiches and *antipasti*. **$**

LAKELAND

Kuopio
The small *muikku* (whitefish) is a
speciality in Kuopio, although more
famous is the *kalakukko* (loaf of rye
bread crust filled with fish and pork)
that can be found at the market.

Musta Lammas
Satamakatu 4. Tel: 17 26 23 49 4
A pleasant restaurant, considered
Kuopio's best. **$$$**

Vapaasatama Sampo
Kauppakatu 13. Tel: 17 26 14 67 7
Informal serving excellent fish. **$$**

Wanha Satama

Rustic and lively by the passenger
harbour. Serves tasty *muikku*. **$$**

SAVONLINNA

The market is busy and popular.
Prices are steep during the opera
festival, but the market is also at
its liveliest then.

Majakka
Satamakatu 1. Tel: 15 53 14 56
A popular place near the market
serving good fish and meat. **$$**

Sillansuu
Verkkosaarenkatu 1
Tel: 15 47 60 251
Popular pub near Market Bridge. **$$**

Tampere
Astor
Aleksis Kivenkatu 26
Tel: 3 21 33 52 2
Live piano music every night. **$$$**

Merirosvo
Näsinneula, Särkänniemi
Tel: 3 24 88 23 4
Revolving restaurant high in the
Näsinnuela Observation Tower
serving fine Finnish cuisine. **$$$**

Silakka
Koskikeskus. Tel: 3 21 49 74 0
Typical Finnish cooking with a Baltic
herring buffet served daily. **$$**

Eetvartti
Sumeliuksenkatu 16
Tel: 3 31 55 53 00
Run by the Pirkanmaa Hotel and
Restaurant School. High-quality food
cooked by the students. **$**

Plevna
Itäinenkatu 8. Tel: 3 23 30 11 1
Lively pub/café specialising in
steaks, sausages and beers. **$**

Salud
Tuomiokirkonkatu 19
Tel: 3 36 64 46 0
Popular tapas restaurant with a fine
wine selection. **$**

WEST COAST

Vaasa
Gustav Wasa
Raastuvankatu 24. Tel: 6 32 69 20 0
Cellar restaurant serves excellent
meat portions, and some fish. **$$$**

Kanttarellis
Kauppapuistikko 15
Tel: 6 31 70 11 0
Worth visiting for the decor. **$$**

Karelia
Parppei Pirtti
Parppei Hill, Ilomantsi. Tel: 13 88
14 21
Buffet/à la carte menu of authentic
Karelian food. Open 11am–4/5pm
daily, and until 8pm in July.

LAPLAND

Rovaniemi
Restaurant Puolukka
Valtakatu 20. Tel: 16 31 02 22
Popular and central, specialising
in fish with some international
fare. **$$**

Drinking Notes

Alcohol is expensive in Finland due
to high taxes.
Beer The Finnish *tuoppi* is about
30 percent larger than the British
pint; and a *pieni tuoppi* is about
two-thirds of that quantity. If you
don't specify, you will be served a
large, strong (number 4, which is
4.5 percent alcohol) beer. You
must say if you want the 3.5
percent beer, known as *keski-olut*
(medium). Number 1 beer (*ykkss-
olut*) is the weakest, just over 1
percent proof.
Wine in Finland is imported and
very costly in restaurants, but there
is more choice in Alko outlets (the
state alcohol monopoly).

Where to buy
Spirits and wine can be bought only
from Alko shops (Stockmann
department store in Helsinki has a
unit on the ground floor). Medium-
and lower-alcohol beer can be
bought in supermarkets.

Licensing laws
A restaurant marked *B-oikeudet*
is licensed only to serve beer
and wine. Most bars are open
until at least midnight in Helsinki,
and some stay open until
3am or 4am.

Culture

Turku is a lively musical city, and the Turku Musical Festival in August is one of the oldest in Finland, attracting visiting composers and international musicians. Further Information from the Foundation for the Turku Music Festivals, Uudenmaankatu 1, 20500 Turku. Tel: 2 25 11 16 2.

Nightlife

Museums

Finland is a country of small museums, the grandest of which is the Ateneum in Helsinki. The Helsinki Card includes free entrance to many museums as well as free public transport. Turku recently introduced a similar card. Opening hours are reduced in winter, and most museums close on Monday.

Classical Music/Opera

Most larger cities have a steady round of concerts throughout the year, but music festivals abound in summer. The most famous, in July, are: Savonlinna Opera Festival at Olavinlinna Castle, in eastern Finland; Kuhmo Chamber Music Festival, also in eastern Finland; and Kaustinen Folk Festival, in western Finland. The festivals have Finnish and international stars.

Opera has a great following, and much of it features Finnish composers and performers.

HELSINKI

In late summer Helsinki has its Juhlaviikot (Festival Weeks) featuring broad-ranging programmes with artists from Finland and abroad. Information from: Helsinki Festival Office, Rauhankatu 7E, 00170 Helsinki. Tel: 9 13 54 52 2.

Also, try the weekday evening concerts at the Temppeliaukio (Church in the Rock) in Töölö, Helsinki.

During the rest of the year, the Finlandia Concert Hall features major performances. The national opera (and ballet) company perform at the Opera House.

TAMPERE

Since 1975 the city has held an international choir festival each year and the Tampere Biennale is a festival of new Finnish music. The Tampere Hall is a prestigious venue. For information contact: Tampere Biennale, Tullikamarina-ukio 2, 33100 Tampere. Tel: 3 21 96 13 6.

Theatre

Tampere rivals Helsinki and Turku for year-round theatrical events but most performances are in Finnish. One exception is the Pyynikki Outdoor Summer Theatre where you can see plays from mid-June to mid-August, with synopses in English. Booking is necessary. Tel: 3 21 60 30 0.

The Tampere Theatre Festival in August includes many international companies. Tel: 3 22 28 53 6.

Cinema

Finns do not dub foreign films, and you can enjoy as good a selection of movies here as in any other European city of moderate size.

In Helsinki, there are large complexes like the Tennispalatsi and Forum as well as intimate art houses like the Orion Film Archive, Eerikinkatu 15–17 (tel: 9 69 46 55 8) and the Andorra, Eerikinkatu 11 (tel: 960 48 73).

In Turku and Tampere, there are several multiscreen cinemas in the city centres.

Pubs, Bars and Clubs

Pub crawling remains popular and there are several clubs that attract the best pop bands. Occasionally a good jazz or rock act will make it to Helsinki's Hartwall Arena, but the city is certainly not on the itinerary of most major performers.

The minimum age for drinking alcohol is 18 but some clubs have an age limit of 21. Entrance fees varie. It is normal to pay the doorman/bouncer a fee (around 6 markkas) to hang up your coat.

Nightclubs and discos have become more popular in recent years. The popular Copacabana salsa club, the Helsinki Club and Tenth Floor dance bar at the Hotel Vaakuna in Helsinki are good examples. For good nightlife try:

HELSINKI

Highlight Café
Frederikinkatu 42. A sports-theme pub with American-style food.
Corona Bar
Eerikinkatu 11. Tel: 9 64 20 02
Attracts a young hip crowd who come to talk, drink beer, eat toasted sandwiches and play pool.
Kuu
Töölönkatu 27. Tel: 9 27 09 09 73
An intimate, older, small bar serving excellent Finnish cuisine. The adjacent Kuu Kuu bar is a hangout of Finnish writers and artists.
O'Malleys
Yrjönkatu 28. Tel: 9 61 13 31
Irish, mellow, small and usually crowded tavern. Some live music.
Storyville
Museokatu 8. Tel: 9 40 80 07
A cosy jazz club to have a late drink. There is a over charge.

Tavastia
Urho Kekkosenkatu 4.
Tel: 9 40 80 07. This university-owned club attracts some of Helsinki's best live music.
Torni
Yrjönkatu 26. Tel: 9 13 11 31
Try the Ateljee Bar on the 13th floor of this hotel for light meals and drinks (outdoor seating in summer) offering the best view in Helsinki.
Vanhan Kellari
Vanha Yliopisto, Mannerheimintie 3. Tel: 9 17 43 57
The students' union-owned Vanha is set in a Neo-Classical building and flows with the traffic of devoted beer-drinkers year round. Occasional live music.
Zetor
Kaivopiha. Tel: 9 66 69 66
This "tractor-style" rock 'n' roll disco has to be seen to be believed. Experience the surrealism of the Finnish countryside.

TAMPERE

Nightlife is very evident on the main street, Hämeenkatu. Bar hopping is easy, although more "traditional" pubs are elsewhere, such as Salhojankadun Pub on Salhojankatu, and Ohranjyvä at Näsilinnankatu 15. Locally brewed beer is available at Plevna (Itäinenkatu 8) and Vanha Posti (Hämeenkatu 13A).

TURKU

Panimoravintola Koulu
Eerikinkatu 18. Tel: 2 27 45 75 7
This former school has a brewery and the classrooms are now pubs or restaurants.
Old Bank
Aurakatu 3. Tel: 2 27 45 70 0
Once a very fine bank, this pub serves more varieties of beer than any other pub in town.
Uusi Apteekki
Kaskenkatu 1. Tel: 2 25 02 59 5
Literally "new pharmacy", this pub is set in an old chemist.

Sport

Participant Sports

Orienteering, golf, hunting, fishing, tennis, badminton and squash are a few of the popular sports. For details on any sport, contact:
Suomen Valtakunnan Urheiluliitto (The National Sports Association), Radiokatu 20, 00240 Helsinki . Tel: 9 15 81. Fax: 9 14 73 04.

Cycling
The countryside is ideal for cyclists, flat on the west coast leading to gently rolling hill areas. For suggested cycle routes, contact:
The Finnish Youth Hostel Association (*see page 410*).

Sailing
Most harbours have guest marinas where one can dock for reasonable overnight fees. Canoeing is also popular in the Lakelands region.

Spectator Sports

The most popular spectator sports include ski jumping, sailing and hockey.
 In early July the Hanko sailing regatta takes place off Finland's south coast. Kotka also sponsors a yearly Tall Ships event. The biggest inland sailing regatta is on Lake Päijänne, in July. Details from the **Finnish Yachting Association** Radiokatu 20, 00093 Helsinki. Tel: 9 348 12 1. Fax: 9 34 81 23 69.
 In mid-June the Finlandia Canoeing Relay is held in the Lakelands (the venue changes annually).
 In mid-February, the 75-km (47-mile) Finlandia Ski Race is one of the top events. For details contact:
Finlandia Ski Race Office
Urheilukeskus, 15110 Lahti. Tel: 3 73 49 81 1. Fax: 3 75 10 07 9.

Shopping

What to Buy

FINNISH DESIGN

Choose from jewellery, woodwork, clothing, glass or kitchenware. Lapponia Aarikka and Kaleva Koru jewellery are particularly Finnish, the first being a mainly contemporary collection and the second a collection based on designs from the Finnish epic poem *Kalevala*, rendered in silver, gold, and brass. Aarikka also supplies some fine woodwork products, including chopping boards, Christmas decorations, toys and wooden jewellery.
 The most impressive ceramic work is commissioned by Arabia, one of the older Finnish firms. Its factory (about 20 minutes' tram ride from Helsinki centre) has a small museum upstairs, and first- and second-quality goods on sale downstairs. Pentik is known for its ceramics as well as beautifully crafted leather clothing.
 Iittala makes beautiful glassware at its factory. Marimekko is the quintessential Finnish clothing designer, with its typical brightly coloured fabrics for men, women and children, as well as more elegant clothing for women and textiles for home use. These companies can be found both in their own stores and department stores in most Finnish towns of any size, including three shops on the Pohjoisesplanadi in Helsinki.

Shopping Areas

HELSINKI

Apart from mainstream department stores, shopping centres (Aleksi

13, Forum and Kamp Galleria) and boutique shopping in Helsinki, there are several market squares that sell both fresh food and a range of other consumer goods of greatly varying quality, from second-hand clothes and records to designer jewellery, Sami mittens and fur hats.

Kauppatori is the main market, followed by Hietalahdentori and Hakaniementori, all near the centre. Note that markets have extended hours in summer and are open until about 8pm, but close briefly from about 2pm. Otherwise, the Esplanade is the hub of shopping delights in Helsinki.

TURKU

Turku has its own Stockmann store at Yliopistonkatu 22. Also on Yliopistonkatu are Pentik (No. 25), famous for ceramics, and (No. 27B) Aarikka, for handmade wooden crafts and decorations.

For crafts, look into Sylvi Salonen, specialising in linens and decorative crafts at Yliopistonkatu 29, or Neoviska, Juhana Herttuan Puisto 10 for handmade *ryijy* (rya) rugs and other textiles. The markets are generally open daily except Sunday. Turku's open-air market features flowers, fish, fruit, vegetables and some crafts. The indoor market hall offers all that and more, including bread, cheese, coffee, tea, spices, snacks and many handicrafts.

TAMPERE

Tampere has most of the medium-sized department stores found in Helsinki and Turku, as well as a host of smaller boutiques. A good collection is at Kehräsaari Boutique Centre, Laukontori 1, Keräsaari, in a converted textile mill.

Visit the Verkaranta Arts and Crafts Centre at Verkatehtaankatu 2 for a good selection of handicrafts and toys. The main Tampere Market Hall, at Hämeenkatu 19, is open Monday to Saturday.

Language

Getting By

good morning hyvää huomenta
good day hyvää päivää
good evening hyvää iltaa
today tänään
tomorrow huomenna
yesterday eilen
hello päivää or terve
How do you do? Kuinka voit
goodbye näkemiin or hei hei
yes kyllä or joo
no ei
thank you kiitos
What time is it? Paljonko kello on?
It is... (the time is...) Kello on...
Could I have your name? Saisinko nimesi?
My name is... Nimeni on...
Do you speak English? Puhutko englantia?
I only speak English Puhun vain englantia
Can I help you? Voinko auttaa sinua?
I do not understand En ymmärrä
I do not know En tiedä
Could I have the key? Saisko avaimen?

Directions

How do I get to..? Miten pääsen..?
Where is...? Missä on...?
right oikealla
to the right oikealle
left vasemmalla
to the left vasemmalle
straight on suoraan

Eating Out

breakfast aamiainen
lunch lounas
dinner illallinen
to eat syödä

to drink juoda
I would like to order... Haluaisin tilata...
Could I have the bill? Saisko laskun?

Signs

Toilet Vessa
Gentleman Miehet (Swedish: Herrar)
Ladies Naiset (Swedish: Damer)
Vacant Vapaa
Engaged Varattu
Entrance Sisäänkäynti
Exit Uloskäynti
No entry Pääsy kielletty
Open Avoinna, Auki
Closed Suljettu, Kiinni
Push Työnnä
Pull Vedä

Days of the Week

Monday Maanantai
Tuesday Tiistai
Wednesday Keskiviikko
Thursday Torstai
Friday Perjantai
Saturday Launantai
Sunday Sunnuntai

Shopping

money raha
How much does this cost? Paljonko tämä maksaa?

Useful Words

chemist apteekki
hospital sairaala
doctor lääkäri
police station poliisilaitos
parking paikoitus
phrase book turistien sanakirja
dictionary sanakirja
car auto
bus bussi
coach linja-auto
train juna
aeroplane lentokone
Cheers! Kippis! (Swedish: Skål!)
to rent vuokrata
for sale myytävänä
free, no charge ilmainen
room to rent vuokrattavana huone

Numbers

1	yksi
2	kaksi
3	kolme
4	neljä
5	viisi
6	kuusi
7	*seitsemän*
8	kahdeksan
9	yhdeksän
10	kymmenen
11	yksitoista
12	kaksitoista
13	kolmetoista
14	neljätoista
15	viisitoista
16	kuusitoista
17	seitsemäntoista
18	kahdeksantoista
19	yhdeksäntoista
20	kaksikymmentä
30	kolmekymmentä
40	neljäkymmentä
50	viisikymmentä
60	kuusikymmentä
70	seitsemän-kymmentä
80	kahdeksan-kymment
90	kahdeksan-kymmentä
100	sata
200	kaksisataa
1,000	tuhat

It costs... Se maksaa...
handicraft käsityö
grocers ruoka kauppa
shop kauppa
food ruoka
to buy ostaa
off-licence alko

Clothes/Laundry

clothes vaatteet
overcoat päällystakki
jacket takki
suit puku
shoes kengät
skirt hame
blouse pusero
jersey puuvilla or villapusero
launderette pesula
dry cleaning kemiallinen pesu
dirty likainen
clean puhdas
stain tahra

Further Reading

General Interest

A Guide to Finnish Architecture by Kaipia & Putkonen (Otava). A fascinating town-by-town guide to buildings, with plenty of photographs and illustrations.
Finland: A Cultural Encyclopedia (Finnish Literature Society, 1997).
Facts about Finland (Otava). The most comprehensive coverage of Finland's history and culture, by a range of Finnish authors.
Food from Finland by Anna-Maija and Juha Tanttu (Otava). An excellent guide to Finnish food, including recipes and colourful features on raw ingredients, such as berries and fungi.
Helsinki Culture Guide (Aquarian Publications, 1996). This alphabetical guide is like a mini-encyclopedia of Helsinki culture, including practical and pertinent information on entertainment, cuisine, history and architecture.
A Brief History of Finland by Matti

Klinge (Otava, 1999). This revised edition offers a concise account of the nation's history.
Sauna, Sisu and Sibelius (A Survival Guide to Finnish for Business People) (Yrityskirjat, 1998). Offers humourous insight into Finnish culture.

Other Insight Guides

More than 500 Insight Guides, Insight Pocket Guides, Insight Pocket Guides and Insight Maps cover every continent.
Insight Guide titles in the region covered by this book include *Finland, Norway, Denmark* and *Sweden*. **Insight Pocket Guides**, with an itinerary-based approach, include *Oslo & Bergen*. **Insight Compact Guides** to the region include *Finland, Norway, Denmark* and *Copenhagen*. **Insight Maps** are specially laminated, making them durable, weatherproof and easy to fold. Scandinavian titles include *Norway, Copenhagen* and *Stockholm*.

Feedback

We do our best to ensure the information in our books is as accurate and up-to-date as possible. The books are updated on a regular basis, using local contacts, who painstakingly add, amend and correct as required. However, some mistakes and omissions are inevitable and we are ultimately reliant on our readers to put us in the picture.

We would welcome your feedback on any details related to your experiences using the book "on the road". Maybe we recommended a hotel that you liked (or another that you didn't), as well as interesting new attractions, or facts and figures you have found out about the country itself. The more details you can give us (particularly with regard to addresses, e-mails and telephone numbers), the better.

We will acknowledge all contributions, and we'll offer an Insight Guide to the best letters received. Please write to us at:

Insight Guides
PO Box 7910
London SE1 1XF
United Kingdom
Or send e-mail to: **insight@apaguide.demon.co.uk**

ART & PHOTO CREDITS

Peter Adams 144/145
AKG London 18, 22, 27, 31, 32, 34, 36, 40, 41, 46/47, 48/49, 50, 51, 55, 56, 115, 127BL
B & C Alexander front flap top, spine centre,back flap top, back cover top right & centre left, 2/3, 5B, 23, 70, 74/75, 137, 138, 138T, 140, 141, 143, 148/149, 173, 181T, 187, 188, 189, 191, 194, 201, 209BL, 210, 214, 215, 218/219, 271, 279, 280, 280T, 292, 302, 306TR, 306BR, 307T, 308
Mark Azavedo 107, 146/147, 197T, 199
Gonzalo M. Azumendi 2B, 10/11, 14, 61, 63, 227, 248, 273, 279T, 282, 286/287, 288/289, 295, 305, 347, 347T
Jan Dago 6/7, 65, 69, 80/81, 84/85, 88, 89, 90, 91, 122, 127BR, 128, 129
Fritz Dressler 335TL
Drottingholm Theatre Museum 52
Christian Erichsen 45, 99, 102, 104L/R, 108, 112, 113, 116T, 117, 252, 259T, 306TL, 308T, 321BL
Richard K. Evans 67, 169, 177T, 179, 179T, 182, 192, 192T, 205, 209TR, 209BR
Macduff Everton/Corbis 265TL, 265BL
Johan Fjellström 277
Robert Fried 1, 25, 33, 321TL, 321BR, 322, 334, 335BL
Glyn Genin 131T
Olivier Grunewald/OSF 352
Marlene Hamstrom/IBL Bildbyra 257T
Blaine Harrington front flap bottom, 26, 62L, 66, 98, 106TL/TR/BL/BR, 108T, 115, 131, 132, 153, 155, 160, 161, 162T, 163, 164, 165L/R, 165T, 167, 168, 170, 171, 177, 190, 200T, 207, 224, 225, 241, 261, 263, 266, 268, 269
D & J Heaton 96
Esa Hiltula 68, 293, 335TR, 335BR, 336, 339
Jim Holmes/Apa 314, 315, 317, 317T, 318, 318T, 320, 320T, 321TR, 326, 327, 328, 329, 329T, 330T, 331, 333, 333T, 334T, 337, 340, 341, 343, 343T, 349, 350, 351

Dave G. Houser 4/5, 4B, 12/13, 152, 188T, 200, 214T, 242T, 244T, 250T, 264, 302T, 306BL, 310, 319, 325, 348, 349T
Jack Jackson 105T
Michael Jenner 101T, 193, 234, 237, 238, 239, 244, 245BL, 245BR, 251, 252T, 253TL, 253TR, 294, 300, 301, 304T, 309L, 330
Layne Kennedy 290
Kenneth Johansson/Hasselblad 260
M. Kapanen/Alvar Aalto Museum 57
Hans Klüche back flap bottom, back cover centre, 24, 54, 71, 76, 119, 120, 142, 142T, 172, 185, 198, 208, 212T
Kobal Collection 154
Bob Krist back cover centre right, 8/9, 21, 60, 82/83, 86, 109, 116, 125, 133, 135, 150, 220/221, 222, 232, 233, 235, 235T, 236, 236T, 238T, 240, 240T, 243, 245TR, 269T
Lyle Lawson 284/285
Lebrecht Collection 58, 127TL
Leslie Garland Picture Library 209TL, 257
Mary Evans Picture Library 20
Buddy Mays 323, 345
Ingrid B Morejohn/Pictureworks 253BR
National Board of Antiquities 16/17
National Museum of Finland 39, 43, 304
Nordiska Museet 37, 44
Richard Nowitz back cover bottom, 162, 166, 168T, 184, 187T, 194T, 196
Ny Carlsberg Glyptotek 100

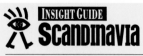

INSIGHT GUIDE

ScanDinavia

Cartographic Editor **Zoë Goodwin**
Production **Linton Donaldson**
Design Consultants
Carlotta Junger, Graham Mitchener
Picture Research
Hilary Genin, Britta Jaschinski

Panos Pictures 195, 276
Erhard Pansegrau 118, 121, 121T
Barry Pringle/Billed huset 97, 98T, 101, 103, 105, 123, 125T, 126, 127TR
Alain Proust/Cephas 62R
Rex Features 42, 339T
Robert Harding Picture Library 64, 72, 216/217, 245TL, 254, 255, 259, 270, 274, 275, 309R
The Ronald Grant Archive 59
Jeroen Snijders/Apa 133T, 134, 134T
Statens Konstmuseer (SKM) 53
Erik Cornelius/SKM 30
Bodil Karlsson/SKM 35
Swedish Tourist Board 249, 267, 272
Sylvia Cordaiy Library 73, 103T, 136, 139, 167T, 183, 197, 204, 211, 253BL, 281, 282T, 283, 311
Nigel Tisdall 207T, 226, 273T
Topham Picturepoint 19, 38, 176
Patrick Ward/Corbis 265TR, 265BR
Odd Inge Worsoe/Fjord Norway 178
Gregory Wrona/Panos 303, 307

Picture Spreads

Pages 28/29: *Top row, L–R;* Mary Evans, Hans Klüche, Sylvia Cordaiy, Hans Klüche, Statens Historiska Museum(SHM), Jeroen Snijders. *Centre row:* SHM (2), Blaine Harrington. *Bottom row:* Michael Jenner, SHM, Michael Jenner.
Pages 110/111: *All photography;* Danish Design Center.
Pages 202/203: *Top row, L–R;* Blaine Harrington, To-Foto A.S, Blaine Harrington, B&C Alexander. *Centre row:* B&C Alexander, Nancy Bundt. *Bottom row:* Blaine Harrington, Per Eide, B&C Alexander.
Pages 246/247: *All photography;* Gonzalo M. Azumendi except *top and bottom centre right:* Blaine Harrington.
Pages 312/313: *All photography;* Layne Kennedy except *top left:* Esa Hiltula, *top centre right:* Robert Harding Picture Library.

Map Production Gar Bowes Design
© 2001 Apa Publications GmbH & Co.
Verlag KG (Singapore branch)

Denmark

Numbers in italics refer to photographs

Norway

*Numbers in italics refer
to photographs*

B
C
D
E
F
G
H
I
J
a
b
c
d
e
f
g
h
i
j
k

Helsinki Metro

Copenhagen S-tog (S-train)